The
Education of the Negro
in the
American Social Order

The
Education of the Negro
in the
American Social Order

by

Horace Mann Bond

*(With a new preface
and an additional chapter by the author)*

1966

OCTAGON BOOKS, INC.

New York

Copyright 1934 by Prentice-Hall, Inc.

New material copyright © 1966
by Horace M. Bond

Reprinted *1966*
by special arrangement with Horace M. Bond

OCTAGON BOOKS, INC.
175 FIFTH AVENUE
NEW YORK, N. Y. 10010

LC
2801
.B65
1966

LIBRARY OF CONGRESS CATALOG CARD NUMBER: 66-18055

Printed in U.S.A. by
NOBLE OFFSET PRINTERS, INC.
NEW YORK 3, N. Y.

TO

MY MOTHER

525-18

Preface To The Octagon Edition

WHEN this book was first written more than three decades ago, I thought the most apt quotation in it was one taken from Horace Mann's speech on slavery and the slave trade in the District of Columbia, delivered in the United States Congress on February 23, 1849: "Sir, he who denies to children the acquisition of knowledge works devilish miracles!" This, to Horace Mann, was the quintessential sin, the institution of chattel slavery, compounded. It is a conviction I share with him; and my book recorded the only slightly lesser wickedness we had observed in the seventy years that had then passed since the Emancipation Proclamation, in the form of public school systems that were a travesty of the name.

We are now a full century beyond that partial emancipation. The great-grandchildren, the grandchildren, and the children of the institution of slavery, even to the tenth and eleventh generations, are with us today; they have dragged their heavy burden of generations of enforced ignorance, and of wretched schools "after freedom," into the slum ghettoes of cities—South, North, and West; and great, indeed, are the devilish miracles wrought by those who denied, systematically and without conscience, the acquisition of knowledge to children.

There have been vast changes in the world since this book was first published, and many of them go deep to the roots of the future education of Negro children.

Perhaps the most important change has been in the initially scholarly, later public, psychology of race. When Carl C. Brigham published his *A Study of American Intelligence* in 1922, his interpretations of the Army "intelligence test" scores in terms of national and racial origins had the explicit approval of almost every leading psychologist in the United States—Terman, Woodworth, Thurstone, Thorndike, to list a few. Now scarcely a voice—other than that of Henry E. Garrett—is to be heard championing the racist cause in the ranks of acknowledged scholars in the field.

What has happened is that the world has witnessed, since this book was published, the rise and fall of Hitler's racism that took the lives of twenty million human beings, six million of them the Jewish victims of the racist cult; and it has recoiled in horror from what it saw. The world, likewise, has shrunk beyond former imagination; and the result in the United States has been salutary in terms of the regard directed toward persons of other racial stocks.

A second considerable influence has come from the great strides made toward developing a true "science of society," and the dissemination of its objective findings through the entire population. Beneath the old platitudes that accepted without question assertions of perfection for the American system, the fact that color caste has existed in this democracy has been acknowledged and faced by the American public. A similar discovery of the profoundest importance for educational policy has been that social class does exist in our presumed land of absolutely equal opportunity, and that the educational achievement of a child is likely to correspond with his location in the social class structure. The application of the methods of social anthropology to the structure of our own society, and to the learning of children, has greatly affected educational perspectives and planning.

A third great change influencing the education of the

great majority of American children within the last three
decades has been the acceleration of technological change,
combined with urbanization. We have become, indisputably,
an urban nation. For no portion of the American population has this change been so critical as for the Negro child.
The vast majority of those who, within two generations, were
obliged to make the wrenching transition from rural to urban
life, were the Americans who had the poorest opportunity
to acquire the accommodating techniques and skills and
habits of the culture that might have made for a smooth and
easy transition to urban living. The most notable accounts
of the slum-dweller who rose out of the slum to great achievements in commerce or literature or industry or scholarship
are in fact accounts of persons from families with long
histories of membership in stable and literate European
cultures. The child or adult whose grandparents or great-
grandparents had a family tradition founded on the quick-
sand of the slave family relationships, an educational
tradition of total illiteracy and no effective educational
system whereby it might have been reduced, is scarcely the
stuff of whom such fabled escapes from the ghetto are made.

Out of these worldwide effects and internal reactions has
come the Movement. Awareness by the Negro of his mis-
treatment in the American body politic and social, and a
willingness to articulate his dissatisfaction, have appeared;
that is in itself an ironic tribute to the even limited education
Negroes have received. It calls to mind a story told by the
civil rights leader the Reverend Ralph D. Abernathy of the
little Negro boy who, when asked to explain why his price
of fifty cents for day-old puppies had, a week later, gone up
to five dollars, laconically replied: "They's eyes is opened."
Large-scale civil rights activity by Negroes, in alliance with
sympathetic friends among the elders of the white community, and with white youth with an astonishing devotion

to a cause that is reminiscent of the post-Civil-War Yankee
missionary activity in the South, has been decisive in litigation and in "direct action" demonstrations.

When this book was written more than thirty years ago,
the institution of racial segregation appeared to be an im-
mutable feature of the American social order. In the con-
cluding chapter, this author did not even include the
abolition of separate schools as the obvious "ideal" answer
to the problem posed by universally inferior formal educational facilities for Negroes. His "ideal" projection envisioned equality of educational expenditures, to be financed
by federal funds; his "plan," projected to meet the facts of
life, was a form of gradualism by which "separate but equal"
expenditures were to be attained by a year-by-year lessening
of the gap between expenditures for white and Negro children, over a period of twenty years (see pages 436-463).
Such "planning" would, the author estimated, assure the
equalization of teachers' salaries in a city such as Nashville,
Tennessee, by 1952-1953.

As it happened, the salaries of Negro teachers in Nashville
were in fact equalized by 1942, ten years ahead of the
schedule of the author's "planned," gradualistic program,
that no one ever took seriously. Salary equalization in
Nashville resulted from litigation by Negro teachers supported by the National Association for the Advancement of
Colored People. The strategy of resort to the courts to
correct inequalities in the provision of public education was
only in the planning stage in 1934, when this book was
originally published; a long series of cases involving principally admission to segregated higher educational institutions preceded the first frontal attack on segregation in
education as discriminatory *per se*. That attack was a case
from Clarendon County, South Carolina, tried before a
special three-judge court at Charlestown, South Carolina,

May 29, 1951. Decided against the Negro plaintiffs, by a 2-1 vote, the Clarendon County case became one of the five similar cases heard on appeal by the United States Supreme Court in 1953–1954, and decided on May 17, 1954, in the historic *Brown v. Board of Education of Topeka, Kansas,* in which the Court ruled unanimously that school segregation provided an education that was inherently unequal and, therefore, unconstitutional.

Accompanying the rising strength of successive court decisions on the side of equalitarianism, has been a rising tide of local and national legislation, building a structure of law by which minority rights could be assured.

Three decades ago I wrote: "Along with educational improvements, there should go far-reaching coordinations between other agencies of social betterment in the extension of these services to the masses of Negroes and whites. Housing, health, wages and working conditions need to be synchronized with educational reforms as objectives of attack." This was a modest foreshadowing of the ideals and means of "the Great Society."

The first extensive programs of the New Deal were being projected when this book was first published in 1934. The Great Depression has given way to the feverish activity of World War II, and to a sustained postwar industrial activity that has sent individual and family incomes for Americans generally soaring to unimagined heights. The basic civil and social legislation initiated by the Kennedy Administration, and greatly strengthened through Lyndon B. Johnson's first two years in office, hold the promise of a wide and deep attack upon problems rooted in centuries of slavery followed by the extremely limited participation of the Negro caste in the benefits of the American society.

The *Report* of the McCone Commission on the August, 1965 Watts riots in Los Angeles has just been released as this Preface is written. The recommendations of the Commission as to what needs to be done are as obvious now as they were in 1934:

> ... Cooperative programs for employment and training ....
> A new and costly approach to educating the Negro child.
> An emergency program, including verbal and language
> classes for 3- and 4-year olds. The Commission said the
> average fifth-grade student in Watts and other disadvantaged
> areas scored a reading vocabulary ranking of 20—compared
> with an average of 81 in advantaged areas—and apparently
> can't "make use of reading and writing for ordinary purposes
> in his daily life."[1]

It is the same story in Chicago, New York, Philadelphia, Boston, Pittsburgh, Cleveland, Detroit. The twelfth-generation end product of the system Horace Mann said perpetrated "devilish miracles" is with us. It remains to be seen if the social order will deal more decisively and more gently with the generations yet to come.

HORACE MANN BOND, *Atlanta University*
December 7, 1965

---

[1] Quoted from *The Atlanta Constitution*, December 7, 1965.

Introduction

TOO little importance has been attached to the status and contribution of the minority cultural groups to American life and civilization. Particularly is this neglect evident in the case of the Negro, in spite of the fact that perhaps the most outstanding achievement in educational progress of any single group in the United States, or elsewhere, has been the advancement of Negro education since the Civil War. Negro formal education began with his freedom.

Previous to the Civil War, education for the Negro was provided only in scattered schools in the North where 1.7 per cent of the Negro population of school age attended schools. Thus we may say that sixty odd years ago Negro education in the United States, as a whole, was near the zero point. Therefore, the development of Negro education to its present state has taken place during the past seventy years. In order to visualize this development the following table is presented:

THE DEVELOPMENT OF NEGRO EDUCATION

	Total Pop. 5–20 years	No. Attending School	Per cent
1920	3,796,957	2,049,741	54.0
1910	3,677,860	1,670,650	45.4
1900	3,499,187	1,096,734	31.3
1890	3,126,497	999,324	32.0
1880	2,633,683	856,014	32.5
1870	1,958,237	180,372	9.2
1860	1,859,370	32,629	1.8
1850	1,524,829	26,461	1.7

Introduction

The advancement of the Negro is indicated by increased attendance not only at schools but at institutions of higher learning, and he has made distinct contributions to every phase of our civic, social, and literary life.   Mr. Bond, in the pages of this book, has given us a vivid picture of the Negro in the American Social Order.

E. GEORGE PAYNE

Contents

PART I

HISTORY

Contents

xviii

Contents

Part III

CURRENT PROBLEMS

Contents

Figures and Maps

Tables

Tables

HISTORY OF THE EDUCATION OF NEGROES IN THE SOUTH—1860–1933

CHAPTER I

The Education of the Negro
in the American Social Order

WHEN Justice Taney of the United States Supreme Court gave his celebrated decision in the Dred Scott case, he argued that the foundation of the American State had not included the Negro as a participating element, or as a beneficiary of its privileges. The judgment of the distinguished jurist was overruled by the Civil War, and the recognition of Negroes as an integral portion of the citizenry of this country is now, under the law, no longer a matter of question.

The delayed appearance of political recognition should not, however, obscure the fact that the Negro has been a member of the body social since the beginning of civilization on the American Continent. Legal enactments or political pronouncements merely accentuate and define the shifting relations of social forces. The definitive pattern is not always consistent: in 1855, Lincoln wrote to his friend Speed,

> . . . How can anyone who abhors the oppression of Negroes be in favor of degrading classes of white people? Our progress in degeneracy appears to me pretty rapid. As a nation we began by declaring that "All men are created equal." We now practically read it, "All men are created equal, except Negroes." When the Know-Nothings get control, it will read, "All men are created equal except Negroes, and foreigners and Catholics." When it comes to this, I shall prefer to migrate to some country where they make no pretense of loving liberty—to Russia, for instance, where

3

despotism can be taken pure and without the base alloy of hypocrisy.[1]

The theory of the democratic State, as expressed by its noblest exponents, depends upon the equalization of opportunity for all of its citizens, irrespective of creed or color. In the realization of this ideal, contemporary public opinion sets the only limits to the extent to which government may go. In other times it was not seriously believed by any considerable portion of our population that women should be allowed to vote or to hold office.

Fifty years ago, in the United States Senate, Senator Morgan argued against Federal aid to education in the States on the ground that it was unthinkable that such "interference" should be attempted; and he added that no sane man would think of asking the Federal authorities to regulate telephone or telegraph companies, railroad corporations, or businesses engaged in the manufacture of food and drugs. Yet all of these "unthinkable" things were actually brought to pass within less than thirty years from the time when Senator Morgan made this unchallenged assertion in the Senate.[2]

It is true that neither constitutional amendments nor public opinion has made the Negro a full participant in the American social order. It is even highly possible that this day will never come. We are only justified in believing that the full realization of the American ideal must of necessity include the Negro. Conversely, the ideal cannot be realized so long as the Negro is not reckoned with by the American social order.

----

[1] Quoted in Kimball Young, *Social Psychology*, Alfred Knopf, New York, 1930, p. 483.

[2] Speech in Congress, reported in *Congressional Record*, February 11, 1886, Washington, United States Government Printing Office, 1886, p. 1341.

The Social Order and the Second Industrial Revolution

At this historic moment, the fortunes of Negroes are bound up with an adequate solution of the great revolutionary process which men have dubbed the Second Industrial Revolution.   Much of the misery of the world, past and present, has come from the exploitation of many workers who toiled for a pittance in order that a few should live in plenty. Human slavery represented the most primitive type of such economy.   The first Industrial Revolution gave men the first fruits of a release from what may justly be called the necessity of exploitation.   With that first revolution came tumults, slums, and unheard-of misery; but fast upon these iniquities there came greater wealth and a lengthened life for the masses of the population.   The new system was not as ruthless as the old, which had built upon a pyramid of human clods a narrow apex of autocracy; for, while the pyramid still retained its characteristic form, the base had been lifted up and the summit broadened to include those middle layers of society upon which democracies have so far rested.

The nineteenth century, we now know, witnessed only the beginning of the utilization of machinery for producing goods and for distributing them.   The twentieth century is an era in which a change is proceeding in our system of life no less profound than the revolution which, a century ago, began to transform agrarian into industrial civilizations. Our great contemporary problem appears to be that of distributing the "blessings of the machine" to all men.   The intense shock of the change which is taking place has dislocated the entire structure of our life, because invention in labor-saving devices has outrun the capacity or willingness of men to make changes of corresponding importance in the mechanism of government and social organization.

Man has learned how to produce the goods he needs.   He

must learn how to organize this immense productive capacity and how to distribute the tremendous potential output. Unless the machine is a Frankenstein that will crush both the inventor and the system which has grown up around it, the lesson will at some time in the future be learned. In the process, we may expect no less of the human wretchedness and of the bitter and relentless struggle between man and man, nation and nation, which has been the price of every former human advance. The citizens of tomorrow must be equipped as best we know how to equip them, with the techniques which will soften, if not entirely alleviate, the shock of our continuous transition.

The Negro in the New Social Order

If no one knows precisely in what manner the new order of our social system is to differ from the old, it is impossible to foresee what will be the specific rôle of any particular ethnic group. The belief has been expressed here that the new social order, if there is to be one, will consist largely in a redefinition of basic economic functions. It will certainly rationalize our present jumble of overproduction and underconsumption.

In the old order, the Negro found a place primarily as a producer of raw materials. It is not altogether untrue that he was valued in the degree to which his labor could be exploited as a producer of tobacco, indigo, cotton, sugar, coal, and iron. It was his greatest misfortune that, so far as his future place in society was concerned, he was thrown into direct competition with white labor. If there is hatred for the Negro among that class of the population in the South known as "poor whites," the only unreason in that bitterness is that one victim should despise the other victim of a system, and not that system itself. The ante-bellum "poor white" did despise the institution of chattel slavery, but he also nourished spite against his fellow-victim, the black slave—and this feeling of antipathy was mutual.

The old difficulties are renewed in any period, as in the present, when the stress of economic depression accentuates the struggle for a place in the machinery of production. Meanwhile, the mere producer comes to have an increasingly smaller rôle in the system.   Within the last three decades, we have seen industries develop in which the producers of essential goods are a minority in the total employed force. A multitudinous class has grown up to assist in fabricating goods and in distributing them to consumers.   Clerks, designers, engineers, salesmen—middlemen of all degrees of training and intelligence—represent a class which had no place in the economic theorizing of the last century and which yet holds a position of great importance both numerically and politically.

Compared to the mushroom growth of these new members of the distributive class, Negroes have entered in considerable numbers only as fabricators or as performing the lower levels of the service classifications.   The present economic plight of the Negro may be imagined if we reflect upon the scarcity of Negro clerks, filling station operators, and radio and telegraphic operators.   To these and a thousand other like fields, Negroes find no entry except in rendering services to their own people.

If, however, the new world actually does rationalize the fundamental processes of economic life, we need not disturb ourselves too greatly over the future of the Negro in the system.   In every previous generation, there have been woeful prophecies as to the fate of the Negro, and rose-colored solutions have been offered for improving his perilous position in the scheme of life.   Neither the prophecies nor the solutions have been realized.   It is important to recall that the emancipation of the chattel Negro slave also set free the poor white of the South; and, without the latter transformation, the Negro as a producer cannot hope to be permanently secure. When, as above stated, it was suggested that the future of the Negro was bound up with a solution of our whole series of problems, the implication was that no "freedom" can be achieved by any one group without being shared in by the whole of our citizenry. If the American social order does solve these great problems successfully, the position of the Negro cannot help but be improved. If the effort to go forward fails, the Negro can scarcely be in any worse condition than he has been in the past, or the entire country in any worse than it finds itself at present.

The Education of the Negro

Our consideration of the environing social order, past, present, and prospective, leads to a crucial issue: Shall the school in which Negro children are enrolled have objectives, curricula, and methods which are distinct from those obtaining in schools enrolling American white children?   Here is a race which lives in a psychical, often a physical, ghetto. Here is a group most of the members of which belong to the lower economic classes, and which yet is separated from other persons on the same level of life by barriers of custom and law.   A fine shade of popular discrimination conceives of them, not as Americans, but as American Negroes.

Various definitions of the educated man and the ideal of educational institutions in the American system have been proposed in the past.   However open to criticism for their failure to detail educational activities, the famous "Seven Cardinal Principles" offer a conception of educational aims which, with its broad scope, merits consideration here. American schools, it was proposed, were to seek to develop better health, give a command of the fundamental processes, develop vocational efficiency, create worthy home members, build better citizens, teach worthy uses of leisure time, and refine ethical character.

These foundation stones need no reorientation for Negro children, for it is impossible to conceive of any future status of the Negro, or any social configuration of the American State, in which it will not be desirable to cultivate these qualities where Negro children are concerned. The difficulty comes here as in other descriptions of the subject matter of the schools: as Charters has said,[3]

> The impossibility of deriving subject matter from the aims of Plato and Comenius is due to the fact that their aims are statements of *ideals isolated from activities*. For the curriculum is properly concerned not only with the ideals which govern life, but also with the things which a person does and thinks about. . . . Some ideals, such as virtue, or swift-footedness, piety, or social efficiency, must be set up in the system of education: but in order to determine the curriculum, it is absolutely essential for a teacher to know the activities, problems, thoughts, or needs which these ideals are to influence and control.

It is the opinion of the writer that there is not a great difference between the activities which are best suited to translating our common ideals into teachable form, where Negro and white children are concerned. Most of the different "needs" are those of economic dissimilarities, and not of race. The activity curriculum for the attainment of health, the fundamental processes, occupational efficiency, worthy home membership, and other objectives would hardly be different for the children of white and Negro tenants on Southern cotton farms.

If there is to be a differentiated series of activities for

---

[3] W. W. Charters, *Curriculum Construction*, The Macmillan Company, New York, 1933, p. 9.

Negro children, it should probably come in those phases devoted to instruction in social relationships and where the selection of materials allows introduction of subject matter dealing particularly with the Negro. One of the best examples of the "activity curriculum" ever known was inaugurated at Tuskegee Institute by Booker T. Washington several decades before the name became current in educational literature. At rhetorical exercises, students at Tuskegee did not give the expected orations about efficiency or cleanliness; Washington aimed at these ideals, but his students spoke about the efficient way of milking a cow, or the cleanly way to make butter. Under Washington's tutelage, they went much further. A cow was introduced upon the platform, and the student went through the activity of milking while delivering his "oration." A girl giving an essay on butter-making had on the platform beside her a churn, milk, and moulds. It is hardly necessary to remember that there is no "Negro way" of milking a cow: there is a right way and a wrong way. In cultivating these ideals, however, Booker T. Washington took every opportunity to make his students familiar with Negroes who were good citizens, who were vocationally efficient, who had created good homes, and who otherwise objectified the best.

The materials presented in this volume deal principally with past and present institutionalized effort to educate Negro children. America has definitely accepted the theoretical responsibility for providing education for all of the people on both the elementary- and secondary-school levels. These two lower levels, it is agreed, should provide for what has been called "General Education." The ideals and objectives of this education should not vary from race to race, from group to group, within the American social order. Activities intended to realize a teachable program may vary, but only within the limits of the fundamental ideals already established.

Social Planning and Control

From all of the present confusion concerning the future has arisen one dominant conviction which is characteristic of world thought today. It is that society need not be at the mercy of every changing wind of circumstance, but may find within itself the possibility for its own salvation. If men have so bungled affairs that all of the world is at a ragged edge, it is possible that they may overcome much of the mischief which has been of their own making and go beyond mere recovery from stagnation to unlimited levels of human comfort and well-being. The idea of setting up definite and tangible goals of endeavor promises to be as decisive in its influence upon the future as the effect of the machine itself. Certainly, men can avoid much stumbling by charting the path of their social organizations. Cooley cautions that

> . . . Until man himself is a mechanism, the lines of his higher destiny can never be precisely foreseen. It is our part to form new ideals and try to realize them, and these ideals give us a working test of progress; but there can be nothing certain or final about them. . . . So the collective intelligence must wait upon the motions of humanity, striving to anticipate and further their higher working, but not pressing to impose a formal programme upon them.[4]

The panaceas which have been publicized from time to time regarding a "solution" of the problem of the Negro in the American social order are numberless. They have ranged from annihilation to complete absorption, and no generation has been without advocates of each plan. Elaborate "blueprints" have actually been worked out to accompany these solutions; in the last century, one disturbed person calculated that the Negro problem could be solved by exporting annually fifty thousand Negro women of child-

---

[4] C. H. Cooley, *The Social Process*, Scribner's, New York, pp. 406–407.

bearing age for a period of twenty years, and went so far as to estimate the number of ships required for this enforced emigration and the per capita cost of transportation to the Federal government. We cannot, therefore, say that the problem of Negroes in America has been without definite quantitative planning. But the plans that have been made either ignored certain fundamental realities of a material sort, or have preferred to disregard the spiritual reality that Negroes are human personalities. Without these two conceptions, the attempt to make plans for the future is bound to be fruitless of any real achievement.

Educators have not hesitated in the past to regard the school as the most important factor in elevating the life of a people. So firmly has this belief been held, not only by teachers, but by the American populace as well, that extravagant claims have been made as to the effectiveness of the school as a social leaven of prime importance. It has been thought by many to transcend the family, the church, and the entire social organization generally as the most powerful of all influences in moulding personality and conveying ideas. A vast amount of national wealth was accumulated during a period when the schools were enjoying unprecedented growth and development, and nothing could have been more natural than that the pedagogical mind should attach a cause-and-effect relationship to these two incidents. We have no sure means of knowing how far the schools are responsible for a higher level of national intelligence and material well-being, as we have no definite measure to show how much of the growth of free educational institutions has been secondary to the economic upswing.

Of one thing, at least, we can be sure: that is the unsoundness of relying upon the school as a cure-all for our ills. Far more than in the past, we need to correlate, in our thinking and in our practice, the massed agencies and factors working upon individuals and groups, with a proper recognition of the limitations and possibilities of the school. In the restricted sense of pupil-teacher relationships within the classroom, no "school" can be expected to solve the problems of Negro health, economic dependence, or family disorganization.

We must think of the school, then, as a single institution which has a wide reach, and which may help transform the life of a people over a long sweep of time. To understand the place of the school and the function of the educational process, we must explore as many facets of community life as are visible. Social planning must include great improvement in educational facilities, but this improvement will fall short of its mark if each social process is not coördinated with the school in a planned order laying even emphasis upon all aspects of the forces which work upon individuals. Better schools cannot of themselves save a population which is condemned by economic pressure to remain in a half-starved, poverty-stricken environment. No amount of health education in the classroom can overcome the effect of poor housing and lack of space in congested cities. Character education, no matter how skillfully conducted, cannot be depended upon to reduce greatly the high rates of juvenile delinquency found in Negro communities so long as Negro children in cities suffer from the economic disabilities of their parents and are exposed to the full gamut of a variety of severe family disorganizations. Strictly speaking, the school has never built a new social order; it has been the product and interpreter of the existing system, sustaining and being sustained by the social complex. Schools for Negro children can perform the older function of the school; but even more they can adventure beyond the frontier and plan for a new order in those aspects which affect the race. To do this, however, they must function as coördinate elements of a unified system, and not in utter isolation from the world of action and social change.

CHAPTER II

Social Classes and the Beginning
of Reconstruction

THE Civil War was one of those catastrophes without which social change tends to remain slow and uncertain. Whatever its origin, its consequences were those of a great earthquake, so far as the social system was concerned. In the South, the outbreak of the War found a civilization almost exclusively agrarian, based on the plantation system of agricultural production. In this Southern world, there were at least three sharply differentiated social classes. Dominant in the picture were the five per cent of white landowners who owned more than seventy-five per cent of the slaves. Foreshadowing the rise of another economic class of white people to control was the book *The Impending Crisis*, written by Hinton Rowland Helper, of North Carolina. In this book, Helper voiced the cry of the great numbers of white persons in the South who owned no slaves and found the pressure of a slave system bearing heavily upon them. Writing in 1857, Helper concluded by saying:

> Our work is done. It is the voice of the nonslaveholding whites of the South, through one identified with them by interest, by feeling, by position. That voice, by whomsoever spoken, must yet be heard and heeded. The time hastens—the doom of slavery is written—the redemption of the South draws nigh.[1]

---

[1] Hinton Rowland Helper, *The Impending Crisis of the South: How to Meet It*, A. B. Burdick, New York, 1860, p. 413.

The final class to be reckoned with was also a distinct racial group—the Negro population, slave for the most part with here and there a considerable proportion of free Negroes.

The effect of the War was to shatter this social pyramid to its very foundations. Soldiers of the South returning to their homes at the conclusion of the struggle found that a new order had to be built up. Properly speaking, the term "reconstruction" is not a mere historical appellation to represent a period of years; it is also a highly appropriate description of what actually went on below the surface of heated political disputation. If there is any fundamental desire of human beings, it is that for security. In the old social order, even the Negro slave had a place that was reasonably secure. No class or race knew its place in the new system, or, indeed, knew what was to be the final system. Gradually there arose from the confusion certain tendencies which must be understood if we are to appreciate the history of educational or any other institutions in the section transformed by the Civil War.

The conservatives. Early in 1865 it became apparent that three sharply differentiated theories were held among white southerners as to the future of the system which had fallen in ruins about them. These diverse opinions are easily recognizable as the persistence after the War, with relation to the new developments, of theories of political adjustment which had their origin in the ante-bellum South. In the first place, one may identify a group of white persons who wished to build society as nearly as possible on the old foundations.[2] In every Southern state, this element showed

---

[2] In Henry C. Warmoth, *War, Politics and Reconstruction*, The Macmillan Company, New York, 1930, there are several legislative documents (in the Appendix) reflecting the wish of certain Louisiana governing bodies to rebuild the new order much as the old had been. *Vide* also: J. W. Burgess, *Reconstruction and the Constitution, 1866–1876*, Charles Scribner's Sons, New York, 1902.

its dominance of public opinion. One needs but to note the restrictive laws passed with reference to the Negro population. The "Black Codes" of 1865–1868 in South Carolina, Georgia, Mississippi, and other states were reflected in similar enactments of county and municipal bodies. These acts, preliminary to a final adjustment, were invalidated by the passage of the thirteenth, fourteenth, and fifteenth amendments, but their transient popularity at this time helps us to understand the prevailing opinion of the men who dictated the course of the newly reconstituted political bodies.

Alabama "declared 'stubborn or refractory servants' or those 'who loiter away their time' to be vagrants, who could be hired out at compulsory service by law, while all Negro minors, far from being sent to school, were to be apprenticed, preferably to their father's former master or mistress." [3] In Louisiana, rigid apprentice laws were drawn up in municipalities, and the police juries of several delta and Red River parishes kept in vogue the old restrictions against the education of Negroes.[4] In the latter state, the Pro-Union Constitutional Convention of 1864 witnessed a bitter debate with regard to the education of Negroes, one delegate (Mr. Abell) saying:

> The question is upon the education of the black children, and, sir, here is one who will never vote for it. Never will I vote for a measure that will imbrue the hands of the people in blood. The question is upon Mr. Sullivan's substitute, if I am not mistaken, and if I am, I call upon the chair to correct me. . . . To those who have acquired a little property and have invested it in Negroes, he says it is a shame that your property shall be torn from you and then that you shall be taxed to educate negro children. I say the proposition is an honor to the state and not a disgrace. I say that

---

[3] W. E. B. DuBois, *The Negro Common School,* Atlanta University Publications No. 6, Atlanta University Press, Atlanta, 1901, p. 36.

[4] Warmoth, *War, Politics and Reconstruction,* pp. 271–285.

the levying of taxes upon us to pay for the education
of a race that we expect to be torn from us is an indignity.
Why are we called upon to educate these negroes? They
have been acquired and held heretofore under the laws of
the land, acquired by purchase, earned by the sweat of honest industry. Is this Convention (to) . . . tear away
millions of that property, and then levy a tax upon them
to educate it? Shall we tear the slave away from his master
and then force the master to educate him? [5]

The moderates. The proscriptive legislation outlined
in the "Black Codes" was speedily outlawed by the activities
of Federal agents working under the authority of the Reconstruction acts, as well as by the growing realization on
the part of a large group of Southern white moderates that
a persistence in this attempt to recreate a system analogous
to slavery was impossible. A second group found a voice,
accordingly, in those men who accepted the facts of emancipation and enfranchisement of Negroes and determined to
make the best of the situation.[6] These men set out to create
a new social order that would recognize the accession to
citizenship on the part of the Negro and that would take
care to prepare the race gradually for the duties and responsibilities that arose from its elevation to a new political
status. The sentiments of such figures as Dr. J. L. M.
Curry, Bishop Galloway, Atticus M. Haygood, General
John B. Gordon, and Wade Hampton were much in accordance with the presidential plan of reconstruction that was
dimly suggested by Lincoln in his last writings and forwarded in some degree by his successor, Andrew Johnson.

This second class numbered many of the more substantial
figures of the ante-bellum era. Owners of large planta-

---

[5] *Debates in the Louisiana Constitutional Convention of 1864* (printed
for the Convention, New Orleans, 1864), proceedings of May 2nd, 1864.

[6] See testimony of James H. Clanton before *The Joint Select Committee
on Affairs in the late Insurrectionary States*, 42nd Congress, 2nd Session,
Report No. 22, Pt. 8, Alabama. Government Printing Office, Washington,
1872, pp. 226–227 and 246.

tions, they realized that some concession would have to be made to the suddenly awakened desire of Negroes for education as one of the devices by which they could secure for their enterprises a reliable labor supply. They visualized on the one hand the plight of the South with estates deserted by Negroes going elsewhere in search of schools, and on the other hand, a less selfish vision of the necessity for educating Negroes to the duties of citizenship. These men were not inimical to Negroes. They had employed them, lived with them, worked with them all of their lives, and so had come to recognize the essential humanity of these persons who were, though slaves, yet in a very rare sense personally dear to them. They represented the best traditions of the old Southern "slavocracy": "large-hearted gentlemen," in some degree more at home with their Negro slaves than with the unlettered and unpropertied whites of their own race.

The unpropertied whites and small farmers. A third class may be recognized in a group whose leaders at first actively coöperated with Negroes, but who were soon alienated from this alliance by the vagaries of the political storms which arose. We are often led to neglect the considerable proportion of Southern whites of little or no wealth who were active allies of Negroes during the early years of Reconstruction. A tradition has grown up which regards these people as isolated renegades and "scalawags," but their proportion was large in the earliest attempts at reconstituting society in the South.[7] It is a well-known fact that in every Southern state the "white" counties were at first almost as strongly Republican or "radical" in political sympathies as the "Black Belt" areas where Negroes dominated.

---

[7] Walter Lynwood Fleming, *Civil War and Reconstruction in Alabama*, Columbia University Press, New York, 1905.

An individual case of ironic, if not historical, interest lies in the fact that Judge Robert Heflin, of Alabama, the deceased uncle of former Senator J. Thomas Heflin, was a prominent "scalawag" in Alabama during the Reconstruction Period.

"White counties" contributed in no small degree to the ranks of the Union armies.

These white Republicans—and Hinton Helper expresses their stand when he says that his purpose was neither to "cast unmerited opprobrium upon slaveholders, or to display any special friendliness or sympathy for the blacks"—had not that spirit of recognizing slaves as human personalities which was a matter of common acceptance with the master class and the post-war conservatives. They found themselves allied with the Union cause, and with Republican politics immediately after the War, not from any love for the Negro but rather because of their traditional rôle as competitors of the slave system. In the first few years after the great struggle, they found themselves fighting alongside of Negroes because they and the Negroes had both been unprivileged classes. If the Negroes had been deprived of political power, so had they in large measure. If the Negroes had been deprived of education, the dominant plantation oligarchy had likewise retarded the rise of free schools for the poorer sections where white people were a majority of the population. In the course of a few years, the settling of the social order into a new pattern would realign the poor whites and Negroes into something approaching their old and more familiar rôles of competitors. Until that time, however, the years immediately following 1868 were to witness the coöperation of these two classes in the establishment of a free school system, the extension of the franchise, and the achievement of other social reforms which had waited upon the final emancipation of the poorer whites as much as upon the enfranchisement of the enslaved Negroes.

Northern whites. To that of these white southerners, we must add the influential share in rebuilding the new social order which fell to the lot of Northern men and women. There can be no doubt that many of the "carpetbaggers," as they were called, were vicious spoilsmen bent on rapine and graft. On the other hand, all were not adventurers. Many of the white men from the North who entered politics were of unquestioned ability and great honesty, and the white men and women who came in large numbers to teach schools opened for Negroes were representative of the finest ideals of America. The latter class was fired with the missionary spirit, and they have endured in death as in life the contumely usually bestowed upon that evangel of the gospel and of learning in all times and in all lands. The greatest fault of the missionaries, if fault it was, consisted in the intolerance for the existing social order which has ever been the brand of their craft. They had no sympathy for the entrenched slave order, for its prejudices, or for the persistence of its attitudes in the white southerners with whom they not infrequently came in violent contact.

The New England "schoolmarms" who came to the South immediately after the War found themselves in violent opposition to public opinion. Preposterous stories have been given credence with reference to the easy virtue of many of these early missionaries, their corrupt political intrigues among Negroes, and their total failure in general to adapt themselves to the situation which they found. We should remember that these stories arose from a public opinion which regarded the education of Negroes itself as an unnatural phenomenon, and that the odium attached to engaging in this task, if not sponsored directly by Southern opinion, was sufficient in those times to brand an individual as an infamous character advocating perverted ideas.

The social mechanism of the South at the beginning of Reconstruction, we have seen, was totally without any order. To the perplexed confusion of the circumstances attending the birth of a new order were brought a number of handmaidens with diverse ideals as to the way in which the delivery should be accomplished. The white

South itself contributed rascals, as well as many honest men, and both of these groups found their fit associates in all other groupings. The white North contributed also a considerable number of men and women who brought to the task of social reconstruction a distinctly new ideal. The greatest problem faced by the rebuilders of the social structure was, of course, to determine the place that the Negro should occupy in the new system.

The Negro. At the time of the Emancipation Proclamation, for three decades laws which prohibited the instruction of slaves had existed in every Southern state; and in several states, notably Mississippi, it was forbidden even to instruct free persons of color.[8] Because of these restrictive measures, the generation which was emancipated in 1863 was almost entirely without instruction. Such education as the slaves possessed was surreptitiously gained in most cases, or the result of the ministrations of a kindly master or mistress here and there who defied existing law to impart a reading knowledge of the Bible to their slaves. One-eighth of the Negroes in America were free at the time of the census of 1860, and it is probable that a much larger proportion of these were literate than could be found among their slave fellows.[9] Nevertheless, in the slave states, hardly more than 5 per cent of the Negro population possessed the simplest tools of learning.

Stripped though they were of the very essentials of civilization, devoid even of any experience in the difficult art of independent living, the Negro slaves, once emancipated, brought to their new official status an immense urge for progress. In their desire for advancement, they followed the patterns with which they were most familiar. The first efforts of Negroes for education were so artificial that they

---

[8] Ulrich Bonnell Phillips, *American Negro Slavery.* D. Appleton and Company, New York, 1918, Chap. XXIII.

[9] *Cf. United States Census,* 1850, 1860, 1870.

immediately became the target for ridicule and scorn.   The
search after "their little French and less Latin" has become
the accustomed butt of jokers in want of a ready focus of
easy humor.[10]   Yet, we must remember that there was no
college for whites in the ante-bellum South that did not
worship at the feet of the same curricular gods.   Higher
education in the South was the classical, "gentleman's education" of the scholastic tradition.   The Negroes are not
to be greatly censured because in their groping way they
reached out after those tools of learning which had received
the highest veneration of their masters.   They had no model
to suggest an education for them more suited to their needs;
in all America there was at that time no such institution.
They identified wealth, leisure, and culture with Latin and
Greek.   Here was the same spirit that speaks through the
mouth of Bill Fletcher, the shrewd "poor white man" of
Ellen Glasgow's novel *The Deliverance*.

> "Lord, man, you ought to be able to do it—don't you know
> Greek?"
> Carraway nodded.   "Not that it ever availed me much
> in an argument," he confessed frankly.
> "It's a good thing to stop a mouth with, anyway.   Thar's
> many and many a time, I tell you, I've lost a bargain for
> the lack of a few rags of Latin or Greek.   Drag it in; stuff
> it down 'em; gag thar mouths—it's better than all the swear-
> ing under heaven.   It's been done at me, suh, and I know
> how it works—that's why I've put the boy upstairs on 'em
> from the start.   'Tain't much matter whether he goes far
> in his own tongue or not, that's what I said, but dose him
> well with something his neighbours haven't learnt." [11]

As the master believed, so did the man of color.   The
missionary teachers from New England, fresh from the

---

[10] Twelve Southerners, "I'll Take My Stand, The South and the Agrarian Tradition," *The Briar Patch*, by Robert Penn Warren, Harper &
Bros., New York, 1930, p. 248.
[11] From *The Deliverance*, by Ellen Glasgow, copyright 1904, by Doubleday, Doran & Company, Inc.

then-recent victories of Horace Mann and Henry Barnard
in the battle for a free public school, encouraged the freedmen in their conviction.   At no time or place in America
has there been exemplified so pathetic a faith in education
as the lever of racial progress.   Grown men studied their
alphabets in the fields, holding the "blue-back speller" with
one hand while they guided the plow with the other.
Mothers tramped scores of miles to towns where they could
place their children in school.   Pine torches illumined the
dirt-floored cabins where men, women, and children studied
until far into the night.   No mass movement has been more
in the American tradition than the urge which drove
Negroes toward education soon after the Civil War.

The Birth of a New Social Order Characteristic of the Period

We intend to trace the development of a public school
system for Negro children in the period marked at its beginning by the termination of the Civil War and at its other
limit by the year 1875.   It will be necessary to keep in
mind at every point the presence of different social and
economic forces which added immensely to the complications
of race and section.   In the disturbing years to come, the
dominant characteristic will be seen to be the reaching out
by men, white and black, after a new social order; and much
of the turmoil and failure of that period will appear as the
inevitable conflicts of human personalities burdened with
the inertia of a powerful tradition.

The Church and the Army

The Federal Army was the first enemy which sought the
destruction of the old Southern social order.   In its track
came missionaries.   If the military forces brought fire and

sword, the teachers brought instruments of intellectual culture, which, the Old South had clearly seen, could be equally as destructive to the slave system. Speaking on the question of educating Negroes, Mr. Jefferson Davis, at that time a Member of the Senate from the State of Mississippi, was asked by Senator Durkee:

> "Are you opposed to leaving the colored population to educate themselves?"
> Mr. Davis: "Oh, no. I have no objection to their having any education to which they are susceptible. . . . It is when Northern radicals come to our slaves spreading pernicious doctrines that we object. . . ." [12]

The first foothold gained by Union forces on Southern soil was at Fortress Monroe, Virginia. Here was established in September of 1861, a bare six months after the beginning of hostilities, the first day school for Negroes under the new dispensation.[13] The school was promoted by the American Missionary Association for those miserable refugees from neighboring plantations whom General Butler had picturesquely called "contraband of war." The first teacher was Miss Mary L. Peake, a "free woman of colour," who had been educated in England. On the foundation supplied by this humble beginning arose the great institution, Hampton Institute, which today can lay claim not only to the distinction of having trained Booker T. Washington, but also to an unbroken record of almost seventy years of leadership in the field of Negro education.

In the following year, 1862, schools were established by the American Missionary Association and other agencies at Portsmouth, Norfolk, and Newport News, Virginia; at New-

---

[12] "Remarks of the Honorable Jefferson Davis, Senator from Mississippi, on the Bill for the benefit of the schools in the District of Columbia, April 12, 1860," *Congressional Globe.*

[13] Francis G. Peabody, *Education for Life, the Story of Hampton Institute*, Doubleday, Page and Co., New York, 1918, p. 38.

bern and Roanoke Island, North Carolina; and at Port
Royal, South Carolina.[14]   In each case, the military occupation was followed by the establishment of a school by some
missionary agency.   More significant in the provision of
widespread educational opportunity was the appointment
of Colonel John Eaton on November 11, 1862, by General
U. S. Grant to be Commissioner for Freedmen in Arkansas.
The conciliatory tactics of President Lincoln had at first
discouraged the entry of slaves into the Federal lines, but
with the issuance of the Emancipation Proclamation, to take
effect in the areas still within the Confederate lines as of
January 1, 1863, the way was opened for the fullest activity
on the part of the educational propagandists.

The educational uplift of Negroes appealed widely to
benevolently minded northerners in the light of a new cru-
sade.   By pouring funds into the South for this purpose
they partook vicariously of the obligations which warfare
imposed more directly upon the soldiers in the fields.   The
economic issues between the two sections were obscured in
the belief that the Northern cause was primarily one of
unselfish humanitarianism.   The logical end of this humanitarian participation in the struggle was, of course, the
elevation of the Negro to a fuller life as an American citizen.   The passionate New England faith in the common
school as the creator of all civic virtues transferred itself
to the Southern scene with redoubled enthusiasm.   "The
brother in black" needed, it was thought, but the touch of
education to prepare him for his new duties.   It was, perhaps, a naïve faith, but simple only in the pathetic assumption by Negroes and whites that this transformation could
be achieved in the course of a few years.   It was certainly
the flowering of the American ideal in a time when idealism
was most needed, and the tragedy is more in the fact that

---

[14] DuBois, *The Negro Common School*, p. 22.

the ideal was not maintained than in the enthusiasm with which it was initiated.

It was not yet time, however, for a diminishing of interest. Missionary societies and individual churches poured funds and teachers into the South as the lines of the Union Army gradually extended farther into that region where lived the greatest number of Negroes. In the Department of the West, Colonel Eaton consolidated the various enterprises already established into something approaching a system. In Louisiana, General Banks must be credited with the first systematic effort to establish a regular system of free public schools for Negro children that was supported by taxes levied upon the property of citizens.

On August 5, 1863, Lincoln had written Banks on the subject of reconstruction, and in this letter he had stated that "some provision should be made for the education of the young blacks." [15]

General Order No. 38. In an official rescript from the "Headquarters, Department of the Gulf, New Orleans, March 22, 1864," General Banks laid down a system for adoption in the area controlled by the soldiers under his command which is worth repeating in full.

> In pursuance of the provisions of General Orders No. 23, in order to furnish rudimental instruction of the freedmen of this department, placing within their reach the elements of knowledge which give intelligence and greater value to labor, and reducing the provisions necessary therefor to an economical and efficient school system;
>
> It is ordered that a Board of Education, consisting of three persons, be hereby constituted, with the following duties and powers:
>
> 1st. To establish one or more common schools in each and every school district that has been or may be defined by the parish provost marshals under orders of the provost marshal general.

---

[15] John G. Nicolay and John Hay, *Abraham Lincoln, A History,* The Century Co., New York, 1904, Vol. 8, p. 421.

2nd. To acquire by purchase or otherwise, tracts of land, which shall be judged by the Board necessary and suitable for school sites, in plantation districts, to be not less than one-half acre in extent.

3rd. To erect upon said plots of land such school-houses as they may judge necessary and proportioned to the wants of the population of the district, where there are no buildings available and proper for school purposes.

4th. To select and employ proper teachers for said schools, as far as practicable, from the loyal inhabitants of Louisiana, with power to require their attendance for the purpose of instruction in their duties, one week at least at a normal school, to be conducted by the Board.

5th. To furnish and provide the necessary books, stationery and apparatus for the use of such schools, and in addition thereto to purchase and furnish an outfit of a well-selected library, etc., for each freed person in the several school districts who is above the age of attending school duty, at a cost to each, including a case to contain the same, not exceeding two and a half dollars, which sum shall be included in the general tax hereinafter provided, but shall be deducted from the laborer's wages by his employers, when such books are provided.

6th. To regulate the course of study, discipline and hours of instruction for children on week days, and adults on Sundays; to require such conformity to their regulations and such returns and reports from their teachers as they may deem necessary to secure uniformity, thoroughness, and efficiency in said schools.

7th. To have generally the same authority and perform the same duties that assessors, supervisors and trustees have in the Northern States, in the matter of establishing and conducting Common schools.

And for the full accomplishment of these purposes and the performance of the duties enjoined upon them, the Board shall have full power and authority to assess, and levy a School Tax upon real and personal property, including crops of plantations, in each and every before mentioned School District. The said taxes so levied shall be sufficient in amount to defray the cost and expense of establishing, furnishing, and conducting for the period of one year the school or schools so established in each and every of the said districts; and said taxes shall be collected from the person or persons in the occupation of the property assessed.[16]

---

[16] *Constitutional Convention, Proceedings and Debates,* Louisiana, 1864.

The system envisioned by General Banks was thoroughly paternalistic, of course; but it is interesting to note the far-reaching provisions, not only for the education of children, but for adult education as well. That there was violent opposition to this system even among "Loyalists," that class of Southern whites who upheld the cause of the Federal Government, is evidenced by the debate, a portion of which has already been cited.[17]

The Church and the Freedmen's Bureau

Experience soon taught that the church societies of various denominations working within the Union lines were likely to do their work without any unity in direction, or even in the distribution of desired services. Frequently, zealous efforts of army chaplains added to the confusion. The result was the creation of the "Bureau for Freedmen, Refugees and Abandoned Lands" by an act of Congress on March 3, 1865. This powerful governmental agency was to reflect during its five years of life the will of its creator. In its final assumption of duties granted by legislation passed in 1866,

> . . . the Freedmen's Bureau became a full-fledged government of men. It made laws, executed them and interpreted them; it laid and collected taxes, defined and punished crime, maintained and used military force, and dictated such measures as it thought necessary and proper for the accomplishment of its varied ends.[18]

In the number of its far-flung interests, the education of the freedmen was generally considered a paramount obligation of the Bureau. J. W. Alvord was appointed the first Superintendent of Schools, extending the work of Colonel

---

[17] *Op. cit.,* p. 13.

[18] W. E. B. DuBois, *The Souls of Black Folk,* A. C. McClurg and Co., Chicago, 1904, p. 27.

Eaton. During his administration he followed the practice of adding substantial appropriations of the Bureau to the educational funds of the different missionary societies. In general, the funds of the Freedmen's Bureau were devoted to the construction of buildings, while the benevolent societies were encouraged to support the teachers for the schools thus established.[19]

In order to "facilitate and systematize" the education of the freedmen, as Alvord stated in his first report, superintendents were appointed in each state. These officials were in most instances recruited from the ranks of the Federal Army, men who in their active capacity as members of an army of occupation early incurred the opposition of Southern whites to their educational, as well as military, functions.

Whatever its faults, the Freedmen's Bureau may justly be credited with the establishment of a widespread and fairly well organized system of free schools for Negroes in the South. In the five years of its operation, it was instrumental in the initiation of 4,239 separate schools. The extent of its work can further be gauged by the fact that it employed 9,307 teachers and instructed 247,333 pupils.[20] The total expenditures for the schools operated under the protection of the Bureau amounted to more than three and one-half million dollars. To this sum the benevolent societies added more than a million and a half, and a conservative estimate of the contribution of Negroes in tuition fees and gifts to these schools is not less than a million dollars.

The Bureau has been accused, in the past as well as today, of graft and actual theft. Considering the lush times

---

[19] J. W. Alvord, *Semi-annual Reports on Schools and Finances of Freedmen, 1866–1870: Ten Reports,* Washington, Government Printing Office, 1866–1870.

[20] J. W. Alvord, *Semi-annual Reports on Schools for Freedmen,* No. 10.

of local and national corruption in which these vast sums
were expended, these charges certainly have a reasonable
foundation.   It was the age of "Boss Tweed" in New York,
of organized rapine in the Reconstruction governments of
the South, of a general let-down in the honesty of governmental administration that finds no parallel unless in events
of the last decade of our own times in states and municipalities, North and South.

In the sphere of advancing the higher educational interests of the freedmen, and so providing a corps of excellent
teachers in the rank and file of the race, the Bureau made
efforts the results of which were invaluable.   Its officials
early realized that the vast number of Negro children in
the South necessitated a "native" teaching force, and that
the schools could not depend permanently either on Northern missionaries or on Southern whites.   The list of colleges and "universities" established by the Bureau in
coöperation with religious societies includes almost every
well-known Negro institution of this caliber in the present
day.

Berea College, in Kentucky, which admitted Negro students along with whites until the passage of a state separation law in 1904, received almost $200,000 from the Bureau
for buildings and salaries.   The Bureau aided the Atlanta
Baptist College, known now as Morehouse College, and
Atlanta University. Biddle University at Charlotte, North
Carolina, now under the name of Johnson C. Smith University; Fisk University, of Nashville, Tennessee, the institution which has done so much in the past in preserving and
popularizing the wealth of Negro spirituals; and Howard
University, of Washington, D. C., now the largest of all
Negro colleges, with support guaranteed by the National
Government, were all Bureau schools.[21]

[21] Alvord, *op. cit.*

Opposition had already developed to Negro schools in the early days. Much of this opposition resulted from the fact that the system was dominated by the Bureau. In the confused reports of what actually happened during this period of adjustment, it is difficult to disentangle from various prejudices an impartial account of the degree to which opposition was engendered by the ideal itself or by its sponsorship. There is no doubt but that opposition of both sorts developed. In many sections, Negro schoolhouses were burned and white and Negro teachers beaten and expelled from communities where no other reason can be cited save an intense hatred for the very idea of educating Negroes.[22]

Indeed, it would be contrary to all knowledge of human nature to assume that the once dominant social caste would accept such a transformation of the rôle of the Negro as was implied by his education within less than a decade after emancipation without harboring and exhibiting a violent feeling of outrage. It has been pointed out that the education of Negroes did do just this kind of violent outrage to the susceptibilities of persons steeped in a tradition that was founded upon the Negro as a chattel slave.

There are also extant many instances of opposition to Negro schools which originated in antagonism toward the political affiliations of these schools rather than their social implications. The schoolhouses became a natural meeting ground for the Negro electors and their white associates and leaders. The Negro school-teacher was held in such veneration by his patrons that it was inevitable that he should become, with the local pastor, the voice of political leader-

22 *Vide: Report of Joint Committee on Affairs in the Late Insurrectionary States, op. cit.*, Alabama, pp. 236, 52, 140, 754, 932, 1025, 1026, 1043, *et al.*; Georgia, pp. 10, 298, 594, 1100, 1137, 1167, 1188, 1189; Mississippi, pp. 76, 82, 83, 86, 87, 261, 282, 283, 302, 326, *et al.*

ship. The doctrine of political expression was no less a part of the American ideal newly acquired by the freedmen than that of education; they were two inseparable hand-maidens which have accompanied each other in all parts of the country and with reference to all racial and social groups.

It was no less certain, however, that both of these activities should prove distasteful to the palate of the Old South as they were presented in a mixed portion of Negro ex-slaves and Yankee ex-enemies. Negro schoolhouses were burned because they were meeting places of the Union League, and the excesses of that organization became a boomerang that rebounded against the acceptance of the theory of Negro education. All in all, the times were full of mutual suspicion, and the conjoint activities of educational leaders who at the same time were political leaders did not work in the direction of allaying the suspicion in which the Negro schools were held by the Southern whites.

Opposition to education of Negroes not universal. It should not be supposed that the acts of violence mentioned here reveal a universal antagonism toward the cause of educating Negroes. In every Southern state, prominent white people came forward to advocate the education of Negroes. Alvord's first reports concerning the activities of the Freedmen's Bureau give many evidences of this attitude. "At Ocala, Florida, E. J. Harris, one of the oldest and most respected citizens of the town, donated the lot on which was erected a church and school for the Freedmen." At Meridian, Mississippi, sites for Baptist and Methodist churches and a schoolhouse for Negroes were donated by L. A. Ragsdale, a wealthy and influential citizen. Numerous requests were received from large planters, seeking teachers for the children of their Negro tenants. "At Canton, Mississippi, the Rev. T. J.

Drane, a Baptist minister of fine reputation, organized a school for Freedmen." [23]

The far-sighted liberality of this class of people cannot but be spoken of in terms of the highest admiration. It is, perhaps, to cavil with a generous Providence to suggest that here and there ulterior motives can be discerned in this generosity. Many of the Southern leaders, as we have said, had come to the conviction that the verdict of the War could not be reversed. There then remained the necessity of making the best of a bad situation and recovering from the ruin of the old social order what fragments might remain. In an editorial of 1867, the powerful *Montgomery Advertiser* denied that it was opposed to the education of freedmen:

> The Negroes must be taught, and if not taught by your own people, will be placed under the control of men and women imported from the Northern States, almost invariably of a class of people destitute either of money, character, or virtue, merely adventurers in search of the means of sustaining life, with little or no regard to the mode or manner in which it is obtained.[24]

Accordingly, the *Advertiser* wished to place white teachers from the South in the Negro schools, and thought this would be a peculiarly fitting employment for the widows of Confederate veterans, or for ex-soldiers of the Confederate Army who had been disabled in the War. A more direct self-interest is found in an example quoted by a Republican paper of that time, the *Alabama State Journal*:

> Mr. Saunders, of Marion, Perry County, Alabama, has employed a gentleman to teach a colored school on his plantation. Mr. Saunders bears all of the expenses of boarding and paying the teacher, and yet expects to be the gainer from having plenty of good, steady laborers well satisfied with their situation. That is to say, the mere

---

[23] J. W. Alvord, *Report on Schools for Freedmen*, 1866.
[24] *Montgomery Advertiser*, January 27, 1869.

prospect of being able to learn something is regarded as a temptation likely to be more powerful than any other on the minds of the freedmen.[25]

In speeches made soon after the close of the Civil War, General Clanton, of Alabama, General Gordon, of Georgia, and other equally prominent leaders advocated the education of Negroes and urged white southerners to enter the classroom.[26] The policy, indeed, went farther than mere speechmaking or editorializing. The Parish Superintendent of East Baton Rouge Parish in Louisiana reported to the State Superintendent, R. M. Lusher, in 1877, that

> . . . I am very happy to be able to say that many of our best teachers have laid aside an objection that was very natural to teaching in colored schools; and now, for the most part, the colored schools are as ably presided over as the white schools.[27]

However, in Caddo Parish, of the same state, W. A. Seay, Parish Superintendent, reported that the colored patrons were not yet educated up to the point of taking white teachers, nor were white teachers educated down to the point of taking colored schools.[28] But in every Southern state, large numbers of Southern white people were actively engaged in teaching Negro schools. It has, indeed, been but recently that the Negro schools of Charleston, South Carolina, replaced their white teachers with Negroes; and even at the present time all of the principals

---

[25] *Alabama State Journal* (Montgomery), May 1, 1869.

[26] Said General Clanton, "A great many Confederate soldiers are teaching these schools. An orderly sergeant of mine is teaching, a schoolmate of mine also, and a cousin of my stepmother. The widow of a soldier who fell as a color-bearer came to me to know what to do; she was weakly, and had children to bring up. I advised her to take a negro school. She consented and I got a school for her to teach." See *Report of Joint Committee, op. cit.*, Alabama, p. 236.

[27] *State Superintendent's Report, Louisiana*, 1877, p. 18.

[28] *Ibid.*, p. 17.

of the Negro schools in Richmond, Virginia, are white persons.[29]

Summary

Merely to say that the interest in Negro education exhibited by Southern whites was to some degree conditioned by reasons of policy rather than a consuming desire to see Negroes educated, however, does not do credit to the men and women of the Old South who were bold enough to advocate Negro schools.   They were, perhaps, of all the participants in the educational drama being enacted, those most attuned to the reality of the situation.   Neither Northern white missionaries, Southern Negroes, nor conservative white southerners realized quite as clearly the part that education would have to play in the new social order; nor, in fact, did any other class of the interested individuals see with such clarity the fact that the new social order would have to be built with great care and some adherence to the old foundations.   On the one hand, the Northern missionaries foresaw an entirely new social order and wished to use the schools for Negroes as the instrument for levelling all vestiges of the past.   On the other hand, the conservatives of the South looked upon the Civil War as an incident that might be overcome by appropriate legislation that would restore the Negro to practically the same status he had occupied before that struggle.   In the middle of the road were the southerners like Generals Clanton and Gordon, whose vision foresaw a long and arduous period during which Negroes might be inducted into a new order, and who looked upon education by southerners as a means by which the process could be carried out with least friction.   It was a tragic fact that circumstances were to al-

---

[29] Note: Negro principals are to be substituted for white principals in the school year 1933–1934, *on a lower salary scale.*

low no compromise. The future was to take its course without plan and without large vision as to the social order of the morrow.

CHAPTER III

The Origin of Tax-Supported Schools for Negroes

State Systems of Education

SEVERAL Southern states had made definite provision for the education of white children at public expense before the Civil War. Only in South Carolina did the constitution fail to mention education up to 1868.[1] School funds were set up in these states. North Carolina enjoyed, perhaps, the greatest progress in this direction, and under the leadership of Calvin H. Wiley, its first Superintendent of Education, the system achieved a degree of efficiency not duplicated until many years after the War. Knight[2] has shown that creditable beginnings had been made and a firm foundation laid for a tax-supported system of public instruction in the entire section before 1865.

If the advance gained, however, did not equal that made in Northern states during the same period, the reason is not difficult to find. The Southern states were governed primarily by men of an aristocratic tradition. This class offered great resistance to the expenditure of public monies for the property-owning classes, and dominated so entirely the legislative system that they blocked all efforts to divorce state from private contributions to education. Further-

---

[1] E. W. Knight, *Public Education in the South,* Ginn & Co., Boston, 1922, pp. 215 *ff*.

[2] *Ibid.,* pp. 306 *f*.

37

more, they insisted on that feature of public-school support that proved everywhere in the country so obnoxious to the poorer classes, the "pauper school" clause by which free tuition was to be granted only to those whose parents were unable to pay it. These two limitations reduced to a great degree the possibilities of the system. On the one hand, school funds were dissipated in the support of private academies and colleges; on the other, proud but poor parents refused to allow their children to attend school under the stigma of pauperism.

The same process had been witnessed in the period from 1820 to 1850 in Northern states. It was not until late in the eighteen forties that Thaddeus Stevens, as a member of the Pennsylvania Legislature, succeeded in removing the schools there from the dual evils of private participation in public funds and the "pauper rule." [3] The rise of the common man in the North and West had brought about an extension, not only of the privilege of the franchise, but of free schools in those sections. There are numerous conjectures as to the course of social evolution between the two principal economic classes of whites in the South. Certainly the period just prior to the Civil War was rife with signs that the suppressed element of poorer whites was about to challenge the plantocracy for domination of the political scene. As to whether this challenge could have been successfully carried out in the South as it was in other portions of the country must of course remain a matter of historical conjecture. As Hinton Helper pointed out, the middle- and lower-class whites in the South had a fearful incubus to overcome in the dead hand of a slave system and Negro slave-labor competition which was not the fate of the submerged economic classes among whites in the North.

[3] J. P. Wickersham, *History of Education in Pennsylvania*, published by the author, Lancaster, 1886.

Yet it can hardly be gainsaid that the offering of any state aid at all for the public schools of Southern states was a concession won but shortly before the outbreak of the Civil War by the poor white populations of the "piedmont" and mountain sections of the states affected. When it had finally been attained, the rulers managed to hedge public-school legislation about with limitations which in many cases defeated the purpose of such legislation as was intended to create a free system. The rich planters from the "bottom" and "delta" lands, the tidewater aristocrats in sea-bordered states, found no particular advantage accruing to their economic class in the establishment of public schools. The white families in these rich alluvial lands were too far distant from one another to permit of the establishment of schools of large enrollment. The meager appropriation of the state fund was a mere bagatelle in the instruction of two or three pupils who might be assembled together for the formation of such a school. Accordingly, the planters found it much more to their liking to hire private tutors or send their children to boarding schools in neighboring towns and cities. Considering the definite spirit of class cleavage then in existence, it is even doubtful that they would have tolerated the attendance of their children at public schools open as well to the children of white overseers or white independent farmers.

However the men from the piedmont might stretch forth their hand for political power, they never actually seized enough of it to enforce their demands in effective school legislation. In Virginia the struggle was as old as the political activity of Patrick Henry, Thomas Jefferson, and John Randolph. In Virginia, a compromise was struck by which a state fund was established, but the plantocracy obtained the restriction that state appropriations might be made to private schools. Since the private schools operated almost entirely without supervision, a state system of pub-

lic school education was more nominal than real. It is not
entirely without significance that the poorer classes of
whites in the piedmont area were becoming articulate to a
large degree only in those states where the slave economy
was definitely receding at the beginning of the Civil War—
Virginia, Tennessee, North Carolina, South Carolina, and,
in general, those states of the lower Atlantic seaboard where
soil exhaustion and impoverished estates already forecast the
eventual disappearance of Negro slavery or its transfer in
large part to the more fertile and virgin lands of the Southwest.

The war between the states came to divert all energies
to the paramount task of prosecuting the conflict and to
bring to a sudden conclusion what might have been a repetition of the evolution by which Northern states had already won the battle for free schools. In addition, the
conflict further dissipated educational efforts in the South
by dissolving many of the accumulated school funds that
had been built up laboriously in the course of several decades. Many historians have erroneously laid all of the
blame for the evaporation of Southern state school funds
upon Reconstruction legislatures and, particularly, upon
the wastage of Negro politicians in that period.[4] Such was
not the case in all instances. In several of the states involved, the public-school fund was invested in state and Confederate bonds which became worthless with the final defeat
of the Confederacy.[5] The result was that 1865 found public education in the South resting upon little more than
statutory provisions which were in themselves largely incap-

---

[4] School history textbooks in use in Southern states are particularly
given to similar overstatements. *Vide*: L. D. Reddick, *Attitudes Toward
the Negro in Southern History Textbooks*, Fisk University, Nashville,
unpublished master's thesis, 1933.

[5] F. H. Swift, *Federal Aid to Public Schools*. Bulletin 47, U. S. Office of Education, Department of the Interior, Washington, Government
Printing Office, 1923. P. 38.

able of execution. So far as Negroes were concerned, the codes actually provided heavy penalties for instruction. These states and localities within the states had enacted proscriptive legislation which left the education of Negroes in the province of felonies and misdemeanors.

In those states where a tentative effort to reconstruct the social order was made in the period known as "Presidential Reconstruction," or under the policies advocated by President Andrew Johnson, no effort was made to provide a system that should include the education of Negroes. The legislatures generally reënacted the laws which dealt with education in force in their states prior to secession, but these statutes did not include Negroes.

The first state to provide for a separate system of public schools for Negroes in the South was West Virginia. In 1863, at the time when this western portion of Virginia was constituted as a separate political unit, a constitution was adopted in which provision was made not only for public schools, but also for the education of Negroes in schools which, though separate, were to be equal in efficiency.[6] The distinct anti-slavery sentiment of this section of the Old Dominion enabled the Lincoln plan of reconstruction to be carried out there. The next state system to be effected was that of Louisiana, established by General Banks in 1864. Effective only within the limits of the Federal jurisdiction and motivated by a military rather than a strictly representative regime, the Louisiana experiment indicates nothing as to the true sentiment of the majority of the native white population. In 1865, Missouri included Negroes in her public school system.[7] Here, again, the percentage of Negroes was small, and the reins of political control were still in the hands of a faction definitely dominated by Unionists. The Florida Legislature of 1866 passed an act pro-

---

[6] *Report of the United States Commissioner of Education,* 1870.
[7] *Ibid.*

viding for the appointment of a superintendent of education for freedmen. The Florida body was under the
domination of a Union army, as was the legislature which
had in Louisiana approved of General Banks' "General
Order No. 38."

In Kentucky, Negroes made up a small proportion of the
population, but the sentiment that had kept the state from
active coöperation with the Confederacy was due more to
a desire to see the Union perpetuated than to a liberal attitude toward the emancipation of Negroes. After the
War, their small number prevented any great influence in
molding legislation. The first law affecting the training of
Negro children was an apprentice law framed in 1865.
While the masters of white apprentices were required to
teach their wards "reading, writing and arithmetic up to
the rule of three," Negro apprentices did not have this
clause in their indenture papers. In 1867, a tentative effort was made to establish schools for Negroes, "providing
that the capitation and other taxes collected from Negroes
and mulattoes should be set apart and constitute a separate fund for the support of their paupers and the education of their children." Representative Davis, of Kentucky, in 1871 argued against the Hoar Bill in Congress
on the ground that it would force Kentucky to establish
schools for Negroes and levy $1,000,000 in additional tax-
ation. This, he said, Kentucky would not do.[8]

As an indication of the probable disposition of the problem of Negro education in those states that went through
the period of "Congressional Reconstruction," the action
of the border states is significant. Wherever the slavery
interest had been powerful, as in Maryland, Kentucky, and
Delaware, the actual establishment of schools for Negroes
was deferred until several years after the end of the War.

[8] Reported in *Congressional Globe.*

When legislation was passed making provision for the establishment of Negro schools under public control, the support for these schools was limited to monies collected from Negroes in poll or property taxes. Considering the poverty of the newly emancipated Negroes and their sparsity in the population of these states, such a restrictive measure was bound to enfeeble whatever system was established almost to the point of nullifying its provisions. The hesitation of the legislators to make provision for Negro public schools in those states where the problems of prejudice and expense were not aggravated indicates the sentiment in the "Lower South" generally.

One argument that has always been powerfully effective in winning support to schools in America has been the need for an intelligent electorate. In 1875, the State Superintendent of Kentucky said in his annual report, with reference to illiterates,

> The elevation of this class is a matter of prime importance, since a ballot in the hands of a black citizen is quite as potent as in the hands of a white one. To the 49,000 white voters unable to read their ballots, add more than 50,000 Negroes, making an aggregate of more than 90,000 illiterate electors, or more than one-third of the entire voting population of the commonwealth.[9]

However, there was no reason for thus educating the Negro prior to the acceptance of the fourteenth and fifteenth Amendments; and in 1866 and 1867, every non-reconstructed legislature in the South rejected the fourteenth Amendment. While the historian Rhodes believed that the states involved rejected the Amendment principally because "of the penal section which disfranchised from holding office the political leaders of the Old South," [10] there can be no

---

[9] DuBois, *The Negro Common School*, p. 38.
[10] J. F. Rhodes, *History of the United States,* The Macmillan Company, New York, 1920, 8 vols. See Vols. VI and VII (1850–1896).

doubt that Negro suffrage was unpalatable to the legislatures of this period, whether they were composed of conservative, old-line leaders, or Southern white loyalists. If
left to themselves, these bodies would probably have granted
electoral rights to Negroes, but grudgingly, if at all. The
preparation of Negroes for voting, accordingly, had but
small weight as an argument for the education of Negroes
with the immediate post-war legislatures.

The United States Congress first set the precedent for
segregating Negro taxes for the support of Negro public
schools by its enactments establishing a public school system in the District of Columbia. In 1862, a partial ac-
knowledgment of the theory of education at public expense
for Negroes was made when the Congress passed a measure
setting aside ten per cent of taxes collected from Negroes
as a fund for Negro public schools. Successive acts in
1864 and 1866 set up a board of three trustees for Negro
schools, "and ordered the white school board to pay over
to them the Negro *pro rata* of the school monies according
to population. The first public school was organized in
March of 1864." [11]

The action of the Federal Congress in the early eighteen
sixties with reference to Negro schools in the District of
Columbia—a Congress in which, of course, there was no
representation from the seceded states—is perhaps even a
clearer indication of the tenor of the times in regard to
public schools for Negroes. If the national body hesitated
to give Negro children a full claim upon public taxation
and restricted public-school funds to monies contributed by
the Negroes themselves, it stands to reason that the general
sentiment in more Southerly states was hardly more favorable.

---

[11] Henry Wilson, *Anti-Slavery Measures in Congress, 1861–1864,* Boston,
Walker, Wise and Co., 1864, Chap. VIII, "Education of Colored Youth
in the District of Columbia."

Summary—Public Schools for Negroes at the Beginning of Reconstruction

From our survey of legislation affecting schools for Negroes in the brief period between the outbreak of the Civil War and the beginning of reconstruction, it appears that the sentiment of the conservative legislatures of the deeper South was not favorable to the establishment of systems of public, tax-supported schools for Negroes. Even more, the Border States, and indeed the National Government as well, were inclined to limit the claims of Negro children upon public funds to the amounts paid in taxes by Negroes themselves. Reasons for this unfavorable attitude have been suggested, and may well be recapitulated here: (1) The dominant tradition of the South was opposed to the education of any considerable number of children at the entire expense of the State. The concession of partially free schools had been granted to a militant white unpropertied class but shortly before the outbreak of the Civil War. (2) The aristocratic tradition found a peculiar strength where it was a question of the education of the children of Negroes, a class with even less economic resource than the poor whites and, in addition, lacking the weapon of the ballot, with which these poor whites had forced a grudging assent to the principle of free schools from the aristocracy. (3) An argument for free education for whites was their possession of the ballot and the theoretical consideration that in a democracy the social order demanded enlightened and literate voters. This argument had no meaning in connection with the Negro. (4) The education of Negroes symbolized their elevation to a status inconsistent with prior conceptions of the rôle they played in the social system. The bare fact of the Emancipation Proclamation had not sufficed to change age-old attitudes in the light of which Negroes were regarded as chattels, common property, beings "something less than human." Public schools for Negroes would not only increase the tax rate and give the race tools of citizenship it was not to employ, but would also fly in the face of all existing conceptions regarding the race and its capacities. Many looked upon the literary education of a mule as an absurdity no greater than that of teaching Negroes to read and write. Muleteers may love their beasts but they do not try to teach them the alphabet.

Schools for Negroes during Reconstruction. By the "Reconstruction Period" we mean the years from 1867 to 1875, during which the Southern States were readmitted to the Union under certain provisions laid down by the United States Congress and governed in accordance with these provisions. The latter period of "Congressional Reconstruction" is to be distinguished from the two years immediately following the assassination of Lincoln; this earlier period was that of "Presidential Reconstruction," dictated by the policies of Lincoln and President Andrew Johnson. We have to do here with the later era. It was ushered in by the passage of laws by the United States Congress on March 2 and 23 and July 17, 1867. These laws were allegedly provoked by the refusal of Southern legislatures to accept the Fourteenth Amendment to the Federal Constitution, which guaranteed the privileges of citizenship to the Negro. Congress sought to enforce "peace and good order" through the division of the section comprising the greater part of the Old South into five military districts.[12] Most important of the provisions of this legislation was the attempt of Congress through control of the military forces of the Federal Government to enforce the statutes relating to Negro suffrage.

---

[12] William Archibald Dunning, *Reconstruction, Political and Economic*, Vol. 22 of *The American Nation* (ed. by A. B. Hart), Harper & Bros., New York and London, 1907.

The date usually given for the end of the period is the selection of Hayes as President-elect in the bitterly contested election in which Tilden was defeated in 1876. In some states, however, the end of "Reconstruction" was signalized two or three years prior to this event by the return to power of the conservative white southerners. In Louisiana and South Carolina, it was not until the inauguration of Hayes in the following March of 1877 that final control was assured to the Democratic Party in those states with the withdrawal of the last Federal troops from the South.

During the period, state governments were established by the coöperation of "carpetbaggers," or northerners newly come to the South, "scalawags," or native white southerners allied with the Republican Party, and the newly enfranchised Negroes. The governments set up by this combination in the various states of the South set up constitutions and enacted laws which placed the education of Negroes on an equable basis with that provided for whites.

The Border States. Kentucky gave an example of the kind of legislation affecting Negro schools during the period. The system for white children was supported, first, by the income from a state tax which amounted to a levy of two mills on the dollar of assessed property. In addition, a poll tax of fifty cents was levied on male patrons with educable children. Local districts were also in some cases permitted to have an option of levying local taxes varying from two and one-half to three and one-half mills on the dollar, according to the classification of the district.

Negro schools were not provided for in law until 1871. Further legislation enacted in 1873 and 1879 changed the original system but slightly. Property taxes on Negro-owned property were diverted to the support of Negro schools; and this fund, with a poll tax of one dollar for each Negro adult male, constituted the sole apportionment available for the support of these schools. Fees on deeds and licenses appertaining especially to Negroes were also allocated to the schools for the race.

The division of school funds on the basis of taxes paid by the race to benefit therefrom is significant, for Kentucky became a test situation which was frequently alluded to by legislators of states in the Lower South who contemplated the adoption of such a system. In the case of *Claybrooks* vs. *the City of Owensboro,* the allocation of such taxes to Negroes or to whites was declared unconstitutional. This case established the claim of Negroes to public-school funds beyond those contributed by their own taxes, but left unaffected the system of control by which Negroes were selected to guide the policies of schools within what are known as "colored districts." Both Delaware and Maryland used the same method for finding support of the schools for Negro children.

Tennessee. Tennessee began the reconstruction of her public school system in 1867. In this state, the Reconstruction Government, under the leadership of the redoubtable "Parson" Brownlow, was a government by the mountain whites of east Tennessee, and not of enfranchised Negro freedmen. An attempt to include Negro schools in the legislation of 1867 was abortive, owing chiefly to "a bitter opposition from quarters not desirous of educating Negro children." [13] This opposition came from the ranks of the mountain Republicans as well as the Democrats from the Black Belt counties of west Tennessee. Tennessee was the original home of the Ku-Klux Klan, and the various missionary societies operating in the state reported the burning of numerous schoolhouses by marauders allegedly connected with this order. Laws passed in 1870 and 1873 designed to establish schools for Negroes were usually ineffective, largely because of the financial prostration of the

---

[13] DuBois, *The Negro Common School,* p. 38.

state. The regime that succeeded Brownlow's faction in power in 1873–1874 effected a system of state and county supervision that strengthened the claim of Negroes to a fair share of public funds.

The Lower South. Between 1868 and 1870, the education of Negro children was placed on a basis of equality before the law in those states where Negroes were an important factor in the electorate. In five states—Arkansas, Louisiana, Mississippi, Florida, and South Carolina—Negroes were elected to the state superintendency of education. Two of these men were alleged to be notoriously corrupt. The other men were never accused of either inefficiency or dishonesty, even by their bitterest political opponents. In Louisiana, the Negro superintendent James Brown "was a quiet, inoffensive man," who did not "obtrude himself" into white schools where he was unwelcome, according to the testimony of one of the Democratic legislators of the day.[14] In Florida, Johnathan C. Gibbs became Superintendent of Education in 1872. He was a graduate of Dartmouth College and of the Theological Seminary at Princeton, New Jersey. His administration was marked by ability and character.[15]

In Arkansas, J. C. Corbin was Superintendent of Schools for two years during the Reconstruction regime.[16] Corbin was a graduate of Ohio University in the class of 1853 and had conducted a private school for free Negroes in the city of Louisville before the Civil War. He was a man of distinguished honesty, and after the overthrow of the Republican Party in Arkansas was appointed to the principalship of the state school for Negroes at Pine Bluff. This

---

[14] Thomas H. Harris, *The Story of Education in Louisiana*, published at Baton Rouge for the author, 1924.

[15] *Report of the United States Commissioner of Education for 1876*, Washington, Government Printing Office, 1878, p. 64.

[16] For biographies of Gibbs and Corbin, see W. J. Simmons, *Men of Mark*, Geo. M. Rewell and Co., Cleveland, 1887.

appointment was made by a Democratic administration.

The school laws enacted by the radical Reconstructionists differed in three important aspects from the school systems existing before their advent to power. In the first place, they opened the schools to Negro children. In the second place, they attempted a greater centralization of authority and a closer supervision by state officials. Finally, they made possible a large increase in the funds available for schools by levying larger taxes and creating additional sources of income. Each of these reforms aroused violent opposition from the conservatives, and at the conclusion of the period, the only one retained was the provision of educational opportunity for Negro children. The conservatives stated that the centralization of state school affairs was an unwise device intended to strengthen the political machinery of the radicals. The extension of the financial basis of support, they said, was a dishonest trick intended to provide more funds to be squandered by the Reconstruction grafters.

Mixed schools. A major issue that affected the cause of Negro education was whether the two races should be obliged to attend school together. The issue has been made much of by those wishing to show that all of the educational works of the Reconstruction legislatures were totally without merit. In addition, it was undoubtedly a source of great antipathy toward the education of Negroes when the conservatives regained power in the South. The deep passions which the issue involved made it one of the most effective political rallying cries that campaigners could invoke. Furthermore, it has had wide ramifications in affecting the course of national legislation with reference to education. The Hoar Bill, designed to appropriate money to the Southern States for the education of the illiterate population, was defeated in the early eighteen seventies largely because of

this issue.[17]   The Blair Bill of the next decade owed much
of its failure to reach a vote in the House, after being passed
by successive affirmative votes three times in the upper
chamber, to the lingering bitterness of the mixed-school issue in the South.[18]   It is therefore of some importance to
understand just what were the basic facts in this controversy.

In Louisiana, South Carolina, and Mississippi, the question was of prime importance because of the heavy Negro
populations in those states.   Here and there in other states,
such as Alabama, Virginia, and North Carolina, an occasional radical leader advocated the establishment of a single
system.   In South Carolina the legislature decreed the establishment of a mixed system.   In 1873, one of the oldest
colleges in the South for the aristocratic white youth—the
South Carolina College at Orangeburg—opened its doors to
Negroes, not merely as students, but also as members of the
faculty.[19]   For a year or two, a few white students continued to attend the institution; but increasing numbers of
Negro applicants soon found the school totally deserted by
whites.   In certain cities of the state, notably Columbus and
Charleston, there were established mixed schools in which
white children attended classes in one room while a class of
Negro children might be found across the hall in another
room.

In Louisiana, the free Negroes of New Orleans furnished
a militant leadership for the Negroes of that state.   The
result of the activities of this group of free Negroes was
the adoption by the radical convention of 1868 of a clause
to the effect that the system should be one to which "all

---

[17] H. C. Roberts, *The Attitude of Congress Toward the Education of
Negroes, 1860–1890,* Fisk University, Nashville, typed thesis, 1933.
[18] *Ibid.*
[19] F. B. Simkins and R. H. Woody, *South Carolina during Reconstruction,* University of North Carolina Press, Chapel Hill, 1932, p. 441.

children should be admitted without distinction of race, color, or previous condition." The strange fact is that in this state there was but one recorded instance of insistence by Negroes upon the "rights" given them by the constitution. In one school in New Orleans—a secondary school, the sole one in the city at that time—Negroes did seek admittance. P. B. S. Pinchbeck, a Negro, at that time Lieutenant-Governor of the state, sent several of his children to the Boys High School. The white students soon organized a mob that drove the Negro children from the school. One of the leaders said afterwards, "They were good enough Niggers, but still they were Niggers." [20] In an attempt to reduce to absurdity the arguments put forward by advocates of mixed schools, some historians of the Reconstruction Period have quoted uncritically from contemporary newspaper reports of the speeches made by Negro proponents of the issue. The period was the heyday of Petroleum V. Nasby and Bill Arp, and conservative reporters delighted in reducing the speeches of Negro legislators to the dialect popularized by these humorists. A Virginia Negro, a member of the State Constitutional Convention, is quoted as saying that he

> . . . didn't want to see no such claw in the Constitution, and the fust thing we know, dere would be similar claws regards waship. Ez fer dis, dere was worser company of white children dan he wished his children to be wid; and dese was secesh children.[21]

One would hardly expect a truly illiterate Negro to use such fairly straightforward grammar with such marked adherence to the pronunciations suggested by the spelling of his words, nor to spell (in a speech) "clause" as "claws" while spelling "similar" (again in a speech) as correctly as represented in the newspaper report.

---

[20] Harris, *op. cit.*, p. 45.
[21] Knight, E. W., *Public Education in the South*, p. 321.

Senator Revels, of Mississippi, a Negro, argued in the Senate that he wanted no separation of the races because it was uneconomical to support two systems where one would suffice, and further, that it was the first step toward inequality.[22]   Charles Sumner supported his argument by saying that it was impossible for the South to maintain two equally efficient systems, and that separation would tend inevitably to give Negro children inferior opportunities.[23]

There are other reasons to believe that those Negroes and whites who insisted on the adoption of mixed schools believed that only in this way could equal facilities for the two races be maintained.   In the North Carolina Constitutional Convention of 1868, an amendment was proffered to the educational section by a conservative, Graham.[24]   The amendment was "That there shall be separate and distinct schools and colleges for the white and colored races."   Albion W. Tourgee offered a substitute, which said: "That separate and distinct schools may be provided for any class of citizen in the state; provided, that in all cases where distinct schools shall be established, there shall be ample and complete facilities afforded for the one class as for the other, and entirely adequate for all, and in all districts where schools are divided, the apportionment to each shall be equal."[25]

An enlightening discussion of the attitude of Negroes toward the question of mixed schools is given by a contemporary observer of this scene, the Reverend Barnas Sears, General Agent of the Peabody Fund:

> The most remarkable feature in the agitation of this question of "mixed schools" is the total difference of prin-

---

[22] *Congressional Globe.* See debates on Civil Rights Bill, introduced by Sumner in May, 1870.

[23] *Ibid.*

[24] Edgar W. Knight, *Public School Education in North Carolina,* Houghton Mifflin Company, Boston, 1916.

[25] *Ibid.*

ciple between many of the white and the colored advocates
of the measure. With the one, the coeducation of the two
races is fundamental; with the other, equal means of education is the only important point. If the right to the
former is necessary to secure the latter, it is desired by
the colored people as a means but has no particular value
as an end. It was precisely on this ground that a large
petition was got up in a Southern city and sent to Congress.
The writer of this article attended a meeting of colored
citizens at that place, on the occasion of the dedication of
a magnificent school-house erected for their use.

In a free conversation with their leaders, he asked them
what was the precise object of the petition. "Do you wish
to send your children to the schools of the white people?"
They replied, "No." "What, then," he continued, "is your
object?" "To have the right to send to those schools, and
to use that right as the means for exacting as good schools
for ourselves," was the reply. "But what if the public
schools should, by such a procedure, be broken up: what
then would be the value of this right?" They answered
the question by saying they had not thought of that. "It
was probably a mistake; but we followed the advice of our
Member of Congress, who said to us, 'That is the way to
get equal schools.'" This same Member of Congress afterwards admitted his mistake, and said that he would vote
against mixed schools and would induce his many friends
to do the same. A colored Member from South Carolina
said to the writer about the same time: "All we desire is to
have equality in the schools. We do not wish to enter the
white schools. We have now by our State laws the right
to do so, but do not choose to exercise it." Other colored
Members made statements to the same effect.[26]

At another time, Reverend Sears advised a group of
South Carolina Negroes that they had nothing to fear as to
an inequable proportion of the state funds if they did not
press the issue of mixed schools. "They came around to
my point of view and agreed that so long as they received
an equal share of the public-school funds, they would not
desire mixed schools." [27] It is an ironic commentary on the

---

[26] *Proceedings of the Trustees of the Peabody Education Fund,* Oct.,
1874, John Wilson and Co., Boston, 1875, p. 403.
[27] *Ibid.,* p. 411.

assurances given by the Reverend Sears to his Negro audience that in 1932 the county of Bamberg in that state expended $178 on each white child enrolled in the public schools, and $8 on each Negro child.

The trustees of the Peabody Fund issued a statement in which they urged Congress not to pass the Civil Rights Bill, stating that it was now assured that the Southern States would maintain equal systems of education for both races. They also urged Negroes to work against the bill, giving them the same assurance and stating with emphasis that the South was now irrevocably committed to the provision of equal educational advantages for both races. The resolutions of the special sub-committee of the Fund read in part:

> . . . Step by step, the *natural* tendency in their (Southern) communities towards free and equal education for *both classes,* by the method of equal but separate schools, has manifested itself to the observation of the Board, by every form of concurrent evidence. They feel, therefore, that what the wide and varied and now continued observation of the Board has shown them in reference to their own practical participation in the commencement and growth of the systems of public education at the South may safely be accepted as true for the entire field of public education which would be affected by the proposed legislation. . . . They . . . emphatically pronounce as the result of their responsible consideration of the whole subject the decided opinion that compulsory legislation by Congress in favor of "mixed schools," as the system of public education, will be most pernicious to the interests of education in the communities to be affected by it, and that the colored population will suffer the greater share of this disastrous influence.[28]

It is interesting to note the caliber of the men who passed this resolution unanimously, for their belief may serve as an illustration of the inability of even the wisest of men to essay correct social prophecy: the Hon. J. H. Clifford, of Massachusetts; William Aiken, of South Carolina; William

---

[28] *Peabody Proceedings, op. cit.,* p. 439.

Evarts, of New York; William A. Graham, of North Carolina; Samuel Wetmore, of New York; A. H. H. Stuart, of Virginia; Samuel Watson, of Tennessee; George W. Riggs, of Washington; Richard Taylor, of Louisiana; and Dr. Barnas Sears, the General Agent of the Board. The gentlemen from the South were undoubtedly sincere in their belief that the provision of equal opportunities for Negro children was a "natural tendency" in the South. They could not well foresee the end of Reconstruction and its consequence, the overthrow of the social class to which they belonged and the substitution in control of a social class that would upset all "natural tendencies" toward an "equal education" for both races.

Summary

Prior to the Civil War, the South had been slow in developing systems of public education for white children. The delay was due largely to the control over legislation exercised by the dominant planter class. The "unreconstructed" legislators either made no provision for the education of Negroes or placed the responsibility for support upon taxes levied upon Negroes and not upon general tax funds. The Reconstruction legislatures under Congressional domination, with carpetbaggers, scalawags, and Negroes coöperating, instituted systems of universal free education for all children.

The mixed-school issue was put forward by white idealists who believed that the separate school was undemocratic, and that only in this manner could equal opportunity be afforded all children. Negroes who supported the movement cared less for the higher principles involved, but were practical enough to see that separate schools meant inferior schools. They wished to use mixed schools as a lever to obtain equality in efficiency.

Those who argued against mixed schools were right in believing that such a system was impossible in the South, but they were wrong in believing that the South could, or would, maintain equal schools for both races. Those who argued for mixed schools were right in believing that separate schools meant discrimination against Negroes, but they were opposed to the logic of history and the reality of human nature and racial prejudices.

CHAPTER IV

Profit and Loss
at the End of Legal Reconstruction

FOUR years of war left the South almost entirely exhausted. Accumulations of capital had been destroyed by a change in the basis of currency and by its subsequent collapse. The diversion of all energies to the prosecution of the War deprived the section of any possibility of progress and left it impoverished and wasted. Invading armies had devastated wide areas, among them the most fertile of the South. In addition, a crowning source of despair was the destruction of the labor system upon which the plantation, the heart of the prosperity of the Old South, depended.

These factors were quite sufficient to explain the hesitation of southerners to embark upon any extensive legislative program which might call upon their meager resources for heavy taxes. Of all the objections to the educational legislation of the Reconstruction bodies, that with regard to increased taxation provoked the strongest opposition. The people from the "white counties" had no particular bias in the matter because of the exemptions which were given to small property owners. The taxes fell most heavily upon the wealthier "Black Belt" counties where plantation owners saw their taxes inordinately increased for the support of a system designed to educate the children of their former slaves and present tenants. Because of the sparsity of the white population and their age-old preference for private schools, this class felt a double sense of injustice. Under a public school system, a dozen owners might be obliged to pay, in their taxes, the expenses for the schools of an entire county in which Negro children were an overwhelming majority of the school population.   It must also be said that the taxes were an intolerable burden, whatever their ultimate purpose.   They amounted to crushing imposts at a time when the entire economic system of the South was in fragments, and, together with other taxes, amounted to demands which were little short of confiscatory.   In many counties, 75 per cent or more of the land was advertised for sale because of the inability of owners to meet tax payments.

Land taxes the heaviest burden in a depressed system. The taxes levied were imposed directly upon the land.   No system of indirect taxation had been devised at that time, and the ever-present token of governmental and educational expense borne by the landed proprietors was a constant reminder of the expense of educating Negro children.

Graft.   Another objection was that increased taxes were not only intolerable when devoted to their designated purposes, but that they became absolutely unbearable when they were the mere instruments of wholesale graft.   Increased taxes meant more plunder.   The complex machinery borrowed by the Northern carpetbaggers from their home states provided numerous opportunities for the useless expenditure of school money.   Mississippi has had an unhappy record of the embezzlement of school funds by her public officials, black and white, that has persisted until today.[1]   In that state, the

---

[1] In December of 1932, Bura Hilbun, State Supervisor of Negro Education (white), was convicted in Mississippi of embezzling a sum of Julius Rosenwald Fund money.   Mr. Hilbun, it was said, had given fictitious locations for Negro schools and collected the appropriation from the Rosenwald Fund, but had never actually constructed the buildings.   It is interesting to recall that in 1874, Cardozo (Negro), at that time Superintendent of Education in the State of Mississippi, resigned while under impeachment for embezzlement.   The case was never prosecuted after his resignation, along with other cases pending against the entire Republican administration headed by General Adelbert Ames.

machinery of administration alone cost the state $100,000 in 1872.   Superintendent Pease himself said that "$50,000 was absolutely thrown away." Noble says [2] that in the same state,

> Mr. James Sykes, of Lowndes County, testified . . . that a tax of $3,800 had been levied upon the sub-district in which he lived, to support two schools.   Upon investigation, he found that the county had been charged with $300 for rent, fuel and repairs on an old church which he had built for his Negroes before the War, and for which no rent had been charged, and no repairs made. [3]

---

[2] Stuart Grayson Noble, *Forty Years of the Public Schools in Mississippi*, Teachers College, Columbia University, New York, 1918, p. 36.

[3] The difficulty of obtaining a truthful picture of the alleged fraud of Reconstruction governments is shown in the treatment of this incident by Noble, one of the most competent and impartial students of education in the South. Noble states that "charges of fraud and corruption" were brought in Mississippi against the Reconstructionists, and "In many cases these charges were well founded. James Sykes, a prominent citizen of Lowndes County, testified before the 'ku-klux' investigating committee that a tax of $3,800 was levied upon the sub-district in which he lived, to support two schools. Upon investigation, he found that the county had been charged with $300 for rent, fuel, and repairs on an old church which he had built for his Negroes before the war, and for which no rent had been charged, and no repairs made." (P. 36.)

A reading of the full testimony (in *Joint Select Committee on the Condition of Affairs in the Southern States*, Sub-committee for Mississippi, Vol. II, pp. 728–770) indicates that Noble has used only that portion of Sykes' testimony elicited by questioning during a session of November 10, 1871. On November 11, 1871, the witness was recalled. It then developed that the first total assessment for the entire county was set at $45,000, of which $21,000 was to be obtained from the city of Jackson. This money, added to the income from the Chickasaw Fund, was to operate schools and to purchase and build schoolhouses for 1,902 white and 6,108 Negro children. The Superintendent's record also showed an expenditure for buildings of $9,237, of which only $1,266 was for Negroes. The expenditure of $2,784 for furniture and materials included only $300 for Negroes. Mr. Sykes also testified that he thought a salary of $25 per month for white teachers was ample during the five-months period, and that it was extravagant to pay Negro women $50 per month when they could be hired as domestics at $8 per month.

Furthermore, the tax of $3,800 was actually never collected in full, and such parts as were collected were refunded!

Regarding the fraudulent $3,800 referred to above, the testimony reads, on p. 761:

"Witness. Well, sir, that assessment and that report in record in the court was there long before they knew about—it was there long before the

In another county, a Negro by the name of J. P. Ball was chairman of the Board of Supervisors and his son was clerk of the School Board.   For these modest services, the young man was voted $1,700 in 1871 for stationery alone.   In Alabama, the State Report of 1871 lists numerous cases of the embezzling of school funds by local officials.

Despite the numerous defects and handicaps under which the new systems began to operate, the period was one of solid progress for the public schools for Negro children.   In general, progress was more notable in cities than in rural districts, both because the urban areas revived more quickly from the effects of the War and because they were the centers where philanthropy was first directed to the stimulation of public schools.

Virginia.   The city of Norfolk established public schools for Negro children in 1868.   Schools for the freedmen had previously been maintained here by various benevolent societies.   In 1869, Richmond maintained a public high and normal school for Negro children which was supported partially by philanthropic donations, as was the similar institution for white persons.   In the same year, the City Council of Winchester voted to establish one white and one Negro

---

tax commenced to be paid, and not until the people commenced to pay their taxes did they know that estimate *(Note: $3,800)* had been reduced; but the complaint of the people caused them to reduce it about one-half. That estimate was reduced—for instance, that $150 house, that $50 repairs, $75 wood-bill, and the $75 stove, and various other items, making $3,800— was reduced about one-half.

"Q. *By Mr. Rice:* Before the collection commenced?

"A.   Yes sir: before the collection commenced—just about one-half; and the people were going on paying that estimate of one-half.   Many had paid it, and it was still what we thought very burdensome.   We thought they had received too much money.   We did not know what they would do with it unless they spent it foolishly—the way they were doing."

Mr. Sykes had already testified that before the war each pupil was required to buy his own school desk and other furniture, and that he had paid about five dollars a year in tuition, once as high as ten dollars.   He thought that the purchase of school furniture by the school commissioners was "foolishly extravagant."

public school.   By 1870, Richmond was supporting 39
schools for white and 33 schools for Negro children.   There
were 2,661 children enrolled in city schools in Petersburg
in 1870, and three-fifths of them were Negroes.   The system here was instituted in 1868, a four-room building
being constructed for Negro children two years later.
Alexandria in 1870 had eight schools for 400 white children, with eight teachers, and two schools for 328 colored
children, with six teachers.

The Negro school in Norfolk was first managed by a
separate board of commissioners.   In 1871, an ordinance
was passed establishing a colored school in each ward of the
city and placing the administration under the single city
system.   Portsmouth had in 1872 a white public school
with an enrollment of 200 and a Negro public school enrolling 155 pupils.   By 1873, the enrollment of the white children had grown to 2,751 and that of Negroes, to 1,912.
In 1873, the Chairman of the School Board of Petersburg
reported,

> . . . the city has agreed to erect for us two new school
> buildings—one for the white, and one for the colored chil-
> dren.   They are intended as intermediate schools, between
> the ward schools and the high school, and they will be
> graded.   The building for white scholars has just been com-
> menced, being let by contract at $21,600.   When completed
> and furnished, it will cost $24,500.   The one for colored
> children will be built and completed this fall.   For these two
> new buildings, the city of Petersburg has agreed to issue and
> sell its bonds, for $40,000, at 8 per cent interest, payable in
> twenty-five years.[4]

Aside from the cities, little progress was made in reaching
the rural Negroes of Virginia by public schools during the
Reconstruction Period.   The total enrollment of Negro
children in the public schools of Virginia amounted to 57,-

---

[4] *Peabody Proceedings, op. cit.*, February, 1870, February, 1871, June,
1872, July, 1873.

000, or less than 40 per cent of the total number of educables. During this period, however, a number of county
associations were organized by the Negroes, supplementing
the meager donations of the public-school funds and bringing no little light to the children living in remote rural
areas. Of the total enrollment, a fair estimate is that approximately 60 per cent of the city Negro children and but
25 per cent of the rural Negro children were in public
schools during the Reconstruction Period.

North Carolina. The public school system for both
white and colored had great difficulty in beginning actual
operation, despite the enactment of legislation designed to
authorize its establishment. In the cities, "free" schools
were begun by grants from municipal governments in some
cases, and by public subscription in others. In 1870, the
tide of Northern philanthropy was beginning to wane, but
the Negroes themselves were supporting many elementary
schools. The aid of benevolent societies provided even a
better educational opportunity for the freedmen than for
the white children, in some cases. Wilmington, Newbern,
Fayetteville, Washington, and Charlotte had Negro schools
initiated by the Freedmen's Bureau and taken over by the
city governments in this period. Wilmington began making a grant for the support of the public schools in 1871.
At Washington, a white school was attended by 132 pupils
in 1872, and a Negro school, by 451 pupils.

However, the General Agent of the Peabody Fund was
obliged to say in 1873, "It is to be feared that in many, if
not in most, of the districts, there will be no schools at all,
on account of the aversion of the people to paying school-
taxes." [5]

South Carolina. "Free schools," in the sense that no
tuition was charged, although supported principally by

---

[5] *Peabody Proceedings*, Vol. 1, p. 361.

philanthropy, appeared under the control of certain South
Carolina cities in 1868. At Pendleton, a school was conducted by the daughter of Jasper Adams, a renowned ante-
bellum white educator, and her husband.[6] One member of
the family taught 100 white children; another taught 100
colored children. Illustrating the early provision of quasi-
free schools: "In Abbeville, a School Association, which is
a corporate body, proposes to systematize their schools and
make them free; all the eminent men of the town manifested
the liveliest interest in the subject. There are 125 white
children in the place. A new colored school of 200 pupils
has just been opened (1868)."[7] In Charleston, by 1871,
1,742 colored children were attending public schools, as compared to 2,101 white children. However, "the schools are
in great distress, the teachers having received no salaries
in six months. The treasury is empty, and no money can
be obtained till after the passage of a bill by the legislature
empowering the city to levy a special tax."[8] As an indication of the somewhat peculiar nature of these "public"
schools, Greeneville reported that her "free schools" were
supported by an expenditure of the Board of Education
amounting to $5,261; the "white amount is covered by the
donation of Mr. Peabody's agent, the subscriptions of our
citizens, and the proceeds of a concert."[9]

In 1871, the condition of the public schools in South
Carolina was deplorable. In the State Superintendent's
Report, ". . . complaints are made and reiterated of the
unfaithfulness of State officials in the use of the school
funds, and of the incompetency and indifference of many
of the school officers."[10] In 1874, the general wastefulness

6 *Ibid.*, p. 101.
7 *Ibid.*, p. 103.
8 *Ibid.*, p. 247.
9 *Ibid.*, p. 247.
10 *Ibid.*, p. 302.

of the State Republican Administration had completely bankrupted the school funds. "Except in the city of Charleston, scarcely any schools in the State are kept throughout the year. They are, moreover, so poorly supported and badly managed that no aid we can give will make them attractive to intelligent families." [11]

Georgia. The extension of public-school facilities to Negro children was much slower in Georgia than elsewhere in the South. Only 14,412 Negro children, little more than 5 per cent of the educables, were reported as attending public schools in the state in 1871. In 1872, the city of Atlanta reported 800 Negro children attending schools supported by a tax upon the city property as compared to 2,200 white children. At this time, the mission schools for Negroes were flourishing in the city. Augusta reported 683 Negro children attending ten schools in 1872. Five teachers had charge of 210 Negro children in Brunswick.

In 1872, however, "there were no public schools in operation, under the general school laws of the State. The unlawful diversion of the school fund to other than school purposes, and the grave error of administration by which, in the absence of resources, a debt of near three hundred thousand dollars was run up against the State, by prematurely putting schools in operation," [12] was responsible for this condition. Negro legislators played a very insignificant part in the Georgia Reconstruction bodies, and had no place in the state administration at all.

Schools were still, however, conducted by specific grants from cities, or by public subscription and benevolent aid. In 1873, the City Superintendent of Atlanta reported, "We have considerably extended our accommodations for colored children, and we are now providing a new school for

[11] *Ibid.*, pp. 416–417.
[12] *Ibid.*, p. 365.

them." [13]   In Augusta, in 1873, there were nine schools for white children, enrolling 420, and seven schools for Negro children, enrolling 325 pupils. "The colored schools have school houses erected by the Freedman's Bureau, and are supplied with everything needful, and are in a flourishing condition.   The white schools are using rented rooms, which are not well furnished." [14]

In Savannah, public appropriations to Negro schools were not made prior to 1873, although 2,513 white children were attending free schools in the city in 1872.   The reason for the delay in setting up schools for the Negro children is given by the President of the Board of Education in this report for 1872:   "The subject of schools for colored children in the city has long excited the interest and attention of the Board.   As the State has as yet contributed no funds to the county for educational purposes, it has been entirely out of the power of the Board to take any steps in the premises heretofore." [15]   In 1873, however, it could be said of Savannah that:

> The Board is making an earnest and honest effort to educate the colored children of the city. They have rented and fitted up a building, at an expense of $800, capable of seating 200 pupils, and requiring four teachers. The Board expects to make no difference in the salaries of the teachers of the white and the colored schools.[16]

Columbus, likewise, reported progress in 1873.   The City Superintendent said in that year:

> These schools are upon the same basis as the white schools, controlled by the same rules, same officers, taught same length of time during the year, etc. The only difference is that the buildings and furniture are not so well adapted to their purpose. The teachers (colored) are or-

[13] *Ibid.,* p. 367.
[14] *Ibid.,* p. 368.
[15] *Ibid.,* p. 368.
[16] *Ibid.,* p. 369.

ganized into a normal class, meeting twice a week. We expect a daily attendance of 300, and a total enrollment for the year of 450.[17]

Only 17,658 Negro children, out of a total school population of more than 200,000, were attending school in 1874. Describing the problem in his annual report, the State Commissioner of Education said:

> With regard to those who favor the return to the poor school system, the weighty fact that we have tried the policy which they advocate for many long years, with the most unsatisfactory results, is against them. . . . I beg leave further to call attention to what is comprehended in the return to the poor school policy in the altered condition of society. Under the Constitution of this State and that of the United States, we cannot make any distinction between the races, even if we thought it wise to do so. We are compelled to make such provision as we may be able for all the destitute, or to leave all in hopeless ignorance. Under the poor school system, therefore, the property holders would be compelled, after paying out of their own private purses for the education of their own children, to respond in the way of taxation in amount sufficient to provide education for the children of the indigent of both races.

The Superintendent reported further in 1874 that "but for the pendency of the Civil Rights Bill before Congress, I have had hopes of obtaining the needed legislation next winter. This agitation had had the effect of checking the growth of a favorable public opinion. The Public School system has been gaining friends rapidly. The passage and attempted enforcement of the Civil Rights Bill will be the death of the system." [18]

Florida. The Reverend Sears, of the Peabody Fund, found this state "very backward in education, with no schools in the rural districts" in 1868. In 1870, the state was found to have ". . . a very good system of public

---

[17] *Ibid.*, p. 370.
[18] *Ibid.*, p. 421.

schools established by law, but its funds are, at present, inadequate to supply the wants of the people." [19] In 1869, the City Council of Appalachicola "afforded free instruction to all the children of the city." A colored school enrolling 100 pupils was under the superintendence of the public-school authorities. Quincy raised $4,000 by a tax in 1869, and maintained separate schools for white and colored children under different boards of trustees. . . . In the entire state, there were less than 3,000 Negro children enrolled in the public schools in 1870. Key West operated in that year two "public free schools," one for white children, with 216 pupils, and another for Negro children, with 172 pupils. Ocala had "an excellent colored school of over 100 pupils, kept ten months under the supervision of the County Superintendent. It occupies a spacious building, erected by the Freedmen's Bureau, and is designed to be a school of high character." [20]

The number of Negro children enrolled in the public schools had grown to more than 6,000, out of a school population of 35,000, in 1872, exceeding the white children in the percentage of educables attending. There were "flourishing" Negro public schools in St. Augustine, Greeneville, Key West, Monticello, Pensacola, Ocala, Appalachicola, and Tallahassee. In the last-named city, "the schools for white children are graded, from the primary to the classical department. Those for colored children have four grades. The total number of pupils is 445, of whom three-fifths are colored." [21]

Jacksonville had a large public school for Negro children in 1873 enrolling 360 pupils. Madison reported a school with 140 pupils in average attendance taught by "three most excellent lady teachers." In 1874, however, for the

---

[19] *Ibid.*, p. 206.
[20] *Ibid.*, p. 207.
[21] *Ibid.*, p. 423.

entire state, only 8,000 out of 40,000 Negro educables were enrolled in school.

Alabama. There were few free public schools for Negroes in Alabama in 1868. In 1867, the Board of School Commissioners of Mobile appointed a committee "to inquire whether our system of public instruction can be extended to colored children in Mobile, and if so to report in what manner and by what means such instruction can be effectually accomplished.[22] In 1868, the School Commissioners reported, "All the scholars of the primary grade, which includes the entire number of colored children, were taught free of tuition." [23]

In 1870, the schools were involved in litigation with regard to the control of the city system, the state authorities finally removing the Board of School Commissioners on the basis of alleged noncoöperation. The Board of Commissioners retorted that the State Superintendent was actively engaged in aiding wholesale thievery from the county and city funds. The American Missionary Association had established in Mobile the Emerson College for Freedmen. In the first years of its operation, public funds were given to this school on behalf of the Negro school children of the city. In 1870, the Board of Commissioners accused the principal of this institution, known by the Negroes as the "Blue College," of having made fictitious reports by which he had collected funds from the Association and from the city far in excess of his actual expenditures. For example, he had allegedly reported each teacher of a grade as the principal of a separate department or school, and had pocketed the money paid him in excess of the regular salaries for ordinary teachers. The result of this incident was to alienate the activities of the benevolent societies and the pub-

---

[22] Booker T. Washington, *Manuscript History of Education for Negroes in Alabama*, 1891. (In possession of author.)
[23] *Ibid,*

lic school officials of the state in the period in which the conservatives succeeded the radicals in power.[24]

Selma had several public schools for Negroes in 1869. In Huntsville and its environs, 1250 Negro children were enrolled in public schools in 1869. Hale County had thirteen Negro schools in the same year. More than 50,000 Negro children were enrolled in the public schools of the state, and the salary scale for white and Negro children was the same, based, as it was, on a strict per capita apportionment of school funds according to the number of educables.

In 1870, the Negro children in the public schools of the city of Huntsville outnumbered the white children by 447 to 226. The term for both schools was eight months. Lafayette had over 200 Negro children, "all of whom are as poor as when they were made free." The white children were housed in a "good college building," the Negro children awaiting a house "in process of building, to serve as a church and schoolhouse for the colored people." The term here was ten months.

One great difficulty of the system of education in Alabama during the Reconstruction Period was a constant conflict between the state legislature and the state board of education, the latter being endued with the legislative powers usually reserved to the elective body. A Negro, Peyton Finley, was a member of the Board of Education for three years. During this time, he insisted on the policy of equal appropriations for the two races, and obtained the passage of a bill setting up a "Lincoln Normal University" under state auspices at Marion, Alabama.[25]

In 1873, the State Superintendent lamented in a spirit prophetically appropriate to Alabama's more recent educational difficulty,

---

[24] Fleming, *Civil War and Reconstruction in Alabama*, p. 322.
[25] *Proceedings of the Alabama State Board of Education for 1872*, J. W. Screws, State Printer, Montgomery, 1873.

From the unofficial reports of County Superintendents, I am informed that large amounts of warrants remain in their hands unpaid. It has been impossible, therefore, for County Superintendents to balance their accounts with this office. In this connection I would say that the affairs of this department cannot be satisfactorily administered until the General Assembly provides money to meet the annual educational apportionments. The failure of the Treasury to cash school warrants had a depressing effect upon all the township schools.[26]

An eight-months school term in Selma was provided for white and black children by aid supplied by "the Peabody Fund, the State, and the City," in 1873. The continued impoverishment of the state led to such difficulties in 1874 that few, if any, schools were continued by state funds.

Mississippi. The state system of education in Mississippi resulted from the constitution of 1868. The greatest difficulty with the system was found in the expensive nature of its administrative machinery and the ease with which this machinery might break down under the weight of excessive taxation or corruption, neither of which was lacking. In 1873, the State Superintendent, Cardozo, said:

Again it is objected that a general tax compels white men of the State to educate the children of the Negro. But as the Negro forms a majority of the entire population of the State, and in an eminent degree a majority of the producing classes, as such classes of every population—the laborer, tenant, and consumer—indirectly bear the burdens of taxation, it follows that an assessment upon the property of the State would be principally paid by the Negro and, therefore, the ground of complaint, if any, against a general tax is with the colored people and not with the white.[27]

In the early years of Reconstruction, the work of benevolent societies among Negroes was widespread. There were 1130 colored children enrolled in private schools in Vicks-

---

[26] *Peabody Proceedings*, p. 376.
[27] *Ibid.*, p. 378.

burg in 1867.   Natchez was reported as having the "best system" of schools, but none for Negroes.   Jackson employed 8 Negro teachers in 1869.   At Hillsboro, the County Superintendent reported in 1872 that "for the ensuing year, arrangements have been made for colored schools at Hazlehurst, Crystal Springs, and Wesson.   We have 3 colored schools in this county kept in operation 5 months by the free school system, and 5 by private subscription.   They have an enrollment of from 140 to 150 each, and a daily average attendance of over 100.   One of the schools, the one at Hazlehurst, has a large school-house built up by the colored people themselves, without the aid of the county or State Board of education." [28]

Toward the end of the Reconstruction Period, the diversion of educational funds to other expenses of the state left the public schools with almost no resource.   In many instances, these schools were continued by private subscription.   Numerous associations were formed among the Negroes for the purpose of continuing these schools or those which had been established by Northern philanthropy.   In 1873, Jackson had two Negro schools, with four teachers employed at public expense, a decrease of four from 1869.   However, "the Society of Friends in Ohio are carrying on a large colored school, and employing three teachers, thus making a saving to the city of three teachers' salaries." [29]

Louisiana.   In Louisiana, the scarcity of funds for operating the schools resulted in an almost complete absence of public schools outside of the large cities.   In 1874, it was said that "the white population take little part in them beyond paying their taxes." [30]

Arkansas.   The conservative legislature of 1866 excluded Negro children from the privileges of the public school sys-

---

[28] *Ibid.*, p. 318.
[29] *Ibid.*, p. 380.
[30] *Ibid.*, p. 425.

tem set up in that year by specifying "white" children. A radical constitutional convention in 1868 provided for the education of Negro children. Public-school activity, however, was very limited in extent. The condition of culture in the confused political struggles of the day is reflected in the impression made upon a visitor in 1868. "I scarcely need remark that Arkansas is in a state of complete anarchy. . . . Shooting men appears to be a mere pastime, and is constantly spoken of with little apparent horror." [31]

The work of the Freedmen's Bureau, together with the missionary societies, extended into this state and laid a foundation that was later to be taken over by the state.

> At Pine Bluff, on the Arkansas River, there is a population of three thousand, of whom two thousand are white and one thousand colored. There is a fine school building in process of erection, for the colored children, by government aid and the contribution of benevolent societies, but there is no house for the white children. . . . Little Rock has a population of ten thousand, with fifteen hundred white children and one thousand colored. The latter have the best school house and the best school in town.[32]

By the school law of 1869, the state was divided into circuits, for each of which a superintendent was appointed. The general depression of 1872 sadly affected the rural schools. The cities, however, reported some progress. Little Rock had more than 700 Negro children enrolled in schools supported by the city. Helena had an enrollment of 200 white and 182 Negro children. The schools were supported by a district tax that yielded over $10,000.

In 1873, the circuit superintendent's offices were abolished by law. They had been made the basis of political manipulation, as they were an exceptionally tempting political plum, with a salary of $3,000 a year attached to the duties of the office.

[31] *Ibid.*, p. 124.
[32] *Ibid.*, p. 128.

Tennessee. While Tennessee made no provision for Negro public schools in the early years of the Reconstruction government, various cities anticipated the activity of the legislature on the subject. In October of 1868, Civil District No. 12, Montgomery County (including the city of Clarksville), "organized a system of graded schools both for white and colored children, with an attendance of about five hundred, instructed by ten teachers. A tax of $5,700 was levied upon the district." [33] By 1873, practically every city and town in the state was supporting a public school for Negroes.

Texas. The constitution of 1868 provided for the education of "all children" in separate schools. Legislation was enacted in 1870 to set up a school system. The law was contested in several localities by individuals wishing to throw down the constitutionality of the measure because it applied to the collection of taxes from white people for the support of Negro schools, but these attempts failed. The law proved unpopular and a new one was instituted in 1873. However, this instrument proved as unsatisfactory as its predecessors and was again amended in 1874. One notable feature of the Texas educational system has been the constitutional guarantee of the equal distribution of the state school fund, which yields the largest income of any in the entire country. This fund has been constantly augmented, and the total today amounts to much more than Negro children receive in almost any other state in the South from all sources combined.

The end of Reconstruction. The years between 1874 and 1876 marked the resumption of power by the conservative whites of the South in the control of state and local government. The period had begun with the control of state politics in the hands of white southerners under the Presi-

---

[33] *Ibid.*, p. 133.

dential plan of reconstruction. Only in Missouri, West Virginia, and Texas were Negro schools given the sanction of law as the fit subjects of public, tax-derived funds. Under the Congressional plan of reconstruction, Negroes were given the franchise and a system of tax-supported schools for Negro children was established in every Southern state. Of all of the legislation of this second period of Reconstruction, only the provision for free schools for Negro children survived.

The "scalawag." It must not be forgotten that the educational systems framed by Reconstruction constitutional conventions and legislatures were more the work of white men than of Negroes in these bodies, although the Negro electorate behind many of the white representatives was considerable. Only in South Carolina did Negroes predominate in the constitutional convention. Here were 76 Negroes and 48 whites. Of the white delegates, 23 were native South Carolinians. Of 133 members of the North Carolina convention, only 15 were Negroes. One hundred and ten were native white North Carolinians. In Texas, only 9 Negroes were members of the constitutional convention. In Georgia, there were almost three times as many native white Georgians in the constitutional convention as Negroes, and only 9 white men from the North. In Mississippi, 121 out of 126 members were whites; and of the whites, 92 were native.

To neglect the part played by the "scalawag" is to fail to understand much of what came before and what was to occur later in Southern history. In no small degree, this despised creature was none other than the political leadership of the "poor white" South which had long struggled for expression in Southern politics before the War and found itself emancipated by that struggle. The class contributed numerously to the Union Army during the War, and after that conflict found itself for the first time in a

position to become effective as well as articulate in affairs of
State. They have been vilified by historians as "homeless,
houseless knaves." Yet no final judgment of them can be
complete that does not consider the fierce passions which
gave rise to their present disfavor.

They were largely unpropertied persons, although such
men as Holden, in North Carolina, Brownlow, in Tennessee,
Alcorn, in Mississippi, and Brown, in Georgia, were men of
substance in their communities and prominent in state politics in the South for a decade prior to the Civil War. In
Alabama, the representatives of the Northern tier of "poor
white" counties combined with the Negroes to receive constitutional exemption from taxation for all farms with a valuation less than $500.[34] They voted with Negroes to extend
the suffrage and to remove literacy and property qualifications. They voted, with the Negroes, to allow local taxation for the support of schools. As late as 1901, there were
in Alabama from twelve to fifteen "white" counties in which
no Democrat had a chance to be elected to office. These
men were represented in the constitutional conventions and
in the legislatures of the Southern states during the Reconstruction Period.

The "scalawags" brought to the constitutional conventions a desire for a free franchise, as did the Negroes and
the Northern "carpetbaggers." They brought with them a
desire for a system of free schools for their children, supported by state and local taxation. The Northern whites
brought a tradition of free, tax-supported schools and local
taxation, and certain ideas with regard to centralized administration, which they contributed to the new constitutions.
The Negroes brought a clamorous desire for education, for
they believed religiously that learning pointed the way to

---

[34] Pat McGauley, *Stenographic Transcript of the Proceedings of the
Alabama Constitutional Convention of 1901*, Brown Bros., Montgomery,
1901, 39th Legislative Day.

full emancipation. The white men from poor counties, entirely dominated by native whites, brought as insistent a demand for the extension of the school system to every school child. Out of this combination came the new school systems.

We have said that the "scalawags" incurred a peculiar onus from white conservatives as traitors to their race and state. For a time, they submerged their traditional hatred of Negroes, who were their erstwhile competitors, in a common desire to extend the franchise and to acquire a system of free schools. The Negroes were aligned against their former masters, and the poor whites, against a social class which had before the War regarded them as but little better than their black slaves. Their end was achieved, and the rising tide of antipathy toward the Reconstruction governments finally turned enough political support from the "white" counties to overthrow the strangle hold which Negroes and carpetbaggers had upon the "Black Belts" of the Southern states.

Without the aid of the inhabitants of the "white" counties, it would have been difficult for a Republican regime to sustain itself in Virginia, North Carolina, Georgia, Alabama, Tennessee, Arkansas, and Florida; and it was not until this portion of the population was weaned away from the radicals that the conservative whites were successful. To do this, the conservative white Democrats adopted in several states a new strategy to end Republican rule. Their party platforms, at first innocent of any extensive provision for public schools, adopted planks pledging maintenance of the system. On the one hand, they appealed to the white voters to close their ranks, to boycott "carpetbaggers" and "scalawags," to fight against "Negro Domination," "Social Equality," and "Mixed Schools." On the other hand, they appealed to Negro voters to return to the support of their best friend, the Southern white man; to support at the polls those whom they had known of old, whom they could trust, and with whom they shared the common destiny of their section. The conservatives strained every nerve to obtain Negro votes. Newspapers gave much space to the meetings of Negro Democrats, and every major candidate on the conservative ticket in every state pledged Negroes that equality in sharing school funds should be regarded as a solemn mandate if elected. Where persuasion proved ineffective, resort was had to intimidation and fraud.

The persuasiveness of campaign orators was effective enough, however, to turn the tide of Negroes to the Democratic Party. In South Carolina, Wade Hampton, in his campaign for the governorship, pleaded for Negro votes. He referred to the fact, universally recognized among Negroes, that he had been a kind and patient master before the War, and that the more than two thousand slaves who had lived upon his baronial plantations in South Carolina and Mississippi had not attempted to desert his plantations, though freedom had come to them. He promised to keep Negroes in possession of their political rights, and to insure their continued enjoyment of equal educational privileges. Speaking of this election in the Senate in 1885, Wade Hampton made the simple declaration: "The Negroes elected me."

In Louisiana, General Nicholls, Democratic candidate for the governor's chair, was as emphatic in pledging continued enjoyment of all the privileges with which Negroes had been dowered by the Republican Party. He received strong support from the Negro electorate in the disputed election of 1876, in which the state government was allowed to become Democratic while the vote of the state in the electoral college went to the Republican candidate, Hayes. As a token of his intention of seeing that Negroes received a fair share of educational opportunity, Governor Nicholls appointed

P. B. S. Pinchbeck, the somewhat notorious Negro Republican politician of the Reconstruction era, as a member of the State School Board.[35]

During the electoral campaigns of 1874–1876, which restored the Southern States to the undisputed control of the Democratic Party, the candidates, while making no attempt to hide their firm intention to restore the rule of white people in the disputed states, had yet nicely balanced the weight of their appeal to white as opposed to Negro voters. The division of the white voters in the "White" Belt gave an opportunity for the wealthier sections to seize the reins of party power. The successful fight against the Republican Party was won by substantial men of property. Their election meant that political leadership in the South had again devolved upon the old Whig class, which had dominated the situation in ante-bellum times. It meant further that the challenge to that leadership furnished by the white men from the hill country was to be deferred for almost two decades, while the conservatives maintained their power through the prestige of their victory as well as through their continued manipulation of the Negro vote to favor their own interests.

For the Negro continued to vote—or, at least, to be counted as voting—under the new Democratic regime. Moreover, the conservative leaders honorably fulfilled their pledges to Negro voters by maintaining their schools on an equality with those for white children. Superintendent R. M. Lusher reported for Louisiana in 1879—three years after the accession to power of the conservatives—the statistics for white and colored for typical counties shown in Table I following.

---

[35] *Annual Report of R. M. Lusher, State Superintendent of Education for the State of Louisiana*, 1877. (Printed at Baton Rouge for the State of Louisiana, 1878.)

TABLE I [36]

STATISTICS OF TYPICAL LOUISIANA PARISHES, PUBLIC SCHOOLS,
1879

Counties	Ascension		Assumption		Avoyelles		E. Baton Rouge		W. Baton Rouge	
Data	White	Col.	White	Col.	White	Col.	White	Col.	White	Col.
No. Schools ..	8	11	15	8	19	12	15	11	5	6
Enrollment	321	747	384	383	923	1035	476	471	62	83
No. Teachers..	9	11	15	8	18	13	21	15	5	3
Av. Mo. Sal...	$30	$30	$40	$40	$38	$34	$42	$42	$30	$30
Length Sch. Term (mos.)	4	4	2	2	3½	3½	....	....	....	....

It will be seen from Table I that expenditures for the public schools of the two races were on a fairly even level of equality in this year. The equality of salaries may have been due to the fact that many white teachers were employed in teaching Negro schools and demanded the same salary obtained by teachers of schools for white children. In Alabama, however, where the number of white teachers employed in the Negro schools was far less than in Louisiana, the same condition of equality may be noticed in a report for the year 1880, when few if any white teachers were employed in the latter state. Three "black" and three "white" counties have been selected for comparison.

TABLE II [37]

STATISTICS OF ALABAMA COUNTY SCHOOL SYSTEMS, BY RACE, 1880

		Black Belt Counties			"White" Counties		
		Au-tauga	Wil-cox	Bul-lock	Dale	Dekalb	Jackson
No. of Children	W.	1642	2057	2346	3924	4087	6395
	C.	2355	6457	6023	721	225	1053
Length of School (days)	W.	62	63	76	60	62	62
	C.	83	77	79	56	90	60
No. of Teachers	W.	22	53	42	21	76	73
	C.	19	70	21	4	2	3
Teacher's Salary	W.	$22	$17	$20	$24	$14	$19
	C.	$25	$26	$34	$19	$9	$12

---

[36] *Report of R. M. Lusher, State Superintendent, for the year 1879.*
[37] *Annual Report of the Superintendent of Education in Alabama, 1880.*

Now these figures for monthly salaries include supplements paid by patrons, and it is obvious that the amount of money paid as supplements by white people would be greater than those paid by Negro patrons. Nevertheless, it is a remarkable fact that in each of the "black" counties, the length of the school term for Negroes exceeded that for whites, as did the salaries paid teachers. The salaries of Negro teachers in "white" counties stand comparison with those paid white teachers. This condition existed in Alabama five years after the passage of control from radical to conservative hands.

Summary

The Reconstruction constitutional conventions and legislatures extended the provisions of educational statutes to include Negroes. They placed expenditures for the education of Negro children on a parity with expenditures for white children. The voting power of Negroes exacted promises of continued fairness from Democratic leaders who overthrew the "carpetbag" regime in the years 1874–1877.

The largest development of schools for Negroes during this period took place in the cities, where public funds came to the aid of schools established by the Freedmen's Bureau, and by benevolent societies when that Federal institution began to languish in the early eighteen seventies. In the rural areas, Negroes generally received a fair proportion of the public-school fund during the Reconstruction Period and for several years thereafter. The turmoil, poverty, and graft of the period, however, reduced available state funds to a minimum.

It is doubtful if the Reconstruction legislatures could have achieved their educational or electoral reforms without the coöperation of the white representatives, frequently called "scalawags," many of whom were from "white" counties in the states. The latter part of Reconstruction found political lines drawn largely on race lines, but during the first years, the representatives from the "white" counties voted together with "carpetbaggers" and Negroes for their common objectives.

Finally, the pledges made to Negro voters by Democratic candidates in their successful fight to overthrow the radical administrations were not the sole guarantee of their continued enjoyment of educational privilege in the immediate future. A sort of tacit agreement existed between the North and the South at the end of the period. Tired of the fruitless turmoil and the unedifying spectacle of Reconstruction politics, the citizens of the North were more and more inclined to leave the South to whatever disposition of its Negro problem it wished to make. In this agreement, there were certain qualifications well understood by both sides. The North gave up its effort to place the Negro unreservedly in the front rank of citizenship, but it exacted a tacit compromise from the South which could hardly be denied. If the South pleaded that Negroes were unfit for citizenship, if Henry Grady, as its representative, asked for tolerance on the part of the North for its treatment of Negroes, the North was willing to acquiesce if assured that conditions would not be allowed totally to revert to ante-bellum strictures upon the mobility or education of the Negro. If the Negro was not yet ready for citizenship, it was implied that the South should prepare him for his gradual assumption of the rôle. If the Southern States, immediately upon the end of Reconstruction, had deprived the Negro not only of citizenship rights but also of educational privileges, it is doubtful whether the North would have shown the same complaisance which it did exhibit. In the same way, then, that Southern candidates advised their supporters to avoid riots, brawls, and other disturbances which might give some Northern Republican a chance to "wave the bloody shirt," the leaders of the conservative regime pledged themselves and their parties to a continued participation of the Negro in educational privileges, while they quietly but firmly stripped him of his political power.

CHAPTER V

The Middle Period:
The Social Structure Solidified

THE end of Reconstruction found the conservatives again in control of the powers responsible for legislation referring to public schools. We may forecast here their fate. They exercised almost complete sway during the Civil War. During the brief period of "Presidential Reconstruction," they largely dominated the constitutional conventions and legislatures of the years 1865–1868. Disfranchised by the demands of the radicals during the period of "Congressional Reconstruction," they found themselves with fortunes almost entirely dissipated by the War, but with an immense prestige among their white fellow-citizens. This prestige enabled them to rally most of the white people of the Southern States to their standards in the successful battle against the "carpetbagger," the "scalawag," and the Negro. They ruled thereafter for a brief decade. Their final decay was exhibited when the older men of the group were fast dying out and younger men of different economic circumstances arose from the ranks to challenge their leadership.

In Georgia,

It was during the interval between the restoration of home rule in the seventies and the rise of dissent in the nineties that the "Bourbons" established their system; it was also during that time that cleavages appeared in the Southern

Democracy which largely conditioned the alignments of the latter decade.[1]

And, generally, throughout the South this was true.

> Nor did the common man at once become articulate. Reconstruction imposed a severe repression. He had been accustomed to listen with respect to his old commanders, and not until the late eighties and the early nineties did he find his voice and rise in rebellion. Now he rules from Virginia to Texas.[2]

The conservatives restrict educational expenditures. In explaining the decline in educational interest following the Reconstruction Period, Knight says that it was a "natural result" of the corruption of that period, which caused a ". . . serious crippling of schools and a deadening of public interest in education, for during the regime of riot and rascality the schools fell victim to the vengeance and cupidity of adventurers and malefactors . . . in some of the Southern States public educational conditions were less wholesome and reassuring in the nineties than 1860." [3]   We shall miss the point, however, if we do not keep in mind the fact that what was happening was the natural consequence of the clash of economic classes and the conflict between the conservative theory of education and the expansion of school needs.   In 1860, the conservatives had to deal with a school system for only 65 per cent of the population.   In 1876 they had to provide schools for 100 per cent of the population, as well as to retrench along all lines, in accordance with party platforms and class sympathies.   Obviously, the two pledges were impossible of fulfillment, and they could not maintain efficient schools for both Negro and white chil-

---

[1] Reprinted from A. M. Arnett, *The Populist Movement in Georgia,* with the permission of the Columbia University Press.

[2] Thompson, Holland, *Industrial Changes in the South and Society,* Annals of the American Academy of Political and Social Science, Philadelphia, 1931, p. 20.

[3] Knight, *Public Education in the South,* p. 379.

dren while limiting the tax rate.   They had three alterna-
tives: (1) To maintain efficient schools for both races, to do
which would necessitate a continuation of, or an increase
upon, Reconstruction rates of taxation.   This procedure
would have been in violation of their pre-election pledges to
white property owners.   (2) To maintain a shell of a school
system for the Negro children while concentrating most of
the available school funds upon white children.   This course
was opposed, as we have shown, to their pre-election promises to Negroes and to the North.   (3) To retrench with
reference to all schools, for both races, and maintain an
equality of expenditures between the two.

It was the last alternative that was adopted by the conservatives.   They put what was actually a strait-jacket
upon educational expenditures.   They refused to allow local
taxation for the schools.   Limitations were also placed upon
the legislatures with regard to the rate of taxation which
they could levy for school purposes and the amount of
money they could appropriate for the support of public
schools.   The conservatives were determined to make the
state constitutions "change-proof" in the event that Negroes
or "carpetbaggers" should ever regain a temporary power
in the legislatures; but in doing so they also made it almost
impossible for the lower economic classes among whites to
change the constitutions and to extend the provision for free
schools.

The rise of the agrarian white South.   The conservatives were agrarians in the grand tradition.   In a plantation system, they were industrialists on a small scale as much
as they were agriculturists.   The typical white farmer in
the South and North belonged to an entirely different economic order.   The plantation was a large, self-sustaining
unit, owned by the planter, directed by the overseer, and
worked by Negro slaves, before the War, and by Negro or
white tenants after the War.   Slave-owning was not widely

distributed among white people in the ante-bellum period.
After Reconstruction, the planters found their estates dis-
integrating under the pressure of the new economic system.
The numerous small farmers constituted the vast majority
of the white population, and these men were truly emancipated by the abolition of Negro slavery as much as were the
Negroes. This was the "common man" of the South, and
he must be reckoned with as the most important factor in
the development of education in the section.

The leaders of the movement, which soon took organized
political form, were such men as Hoke Smith, in Georgia,
Vardaman, in Mississippi, Reuben Kolb, in Alabama,
Marion Butler, in North Carolina, and Benjamin R. Tillman, in South Carolina. The movement began with the
comparatively innocuous Grange and Alliance organizations, which at first were composed not only of small farmers
but also of considerable numbers of the wealthier land
barons. In North Carolina, the work of such educational
idealists as McIver and Alderman gained much force from
". . . the emphasis which the ninety-thousand Alliancemen
were putting on education." This assistance ". . . made
possible the great progress which had its small beginnings in
this state about this time." [4]

In general, the states of the South followed the same pattern of action. The small farmers stood first of all for the
extension of the public school system to all white people.
They clamored for a reform in the system of distributing
state funds, which, in accordance with long-established ideas
of fairness, had been distributed according to per capita
school population. Speaking in the Virginia Constitutional
Convention of 1901, Mr. Pollard, a delegate from Richmond
(now Governor of the State of Virginia), said:

   . . . The county the gentleman from Appomattox repre-

---

[4] Smith, *Populism in North Carolina* (typed Ph.D. thesis, Chicago, 1928),
p. 68.

sents receives on account of the negro children in that county something over $2,000 of the State money, while it uses only about $900 of the State money for negro education. Thereby the white children of his county not only get the portion that is allotted to them of the State fund, but they get a portion of that which is allotted to negroes, while the white children in the white counties cannot make any such discrimination, but can get only each one of them their share.[5]

In addition to this reform, the small farmers wanted an increase in the state fund. They also desired local taxation. In all of these aims, they found themselves violently opposed by the planters of the lowlands, men who possessed, in addition to a diverted school fund from Negroes, enough wealth to educate their children at private expense.

Through the nature of their complaints, the agrarian whites were placed in a position of bitter hostility to Negro education. As suggested above, much of this opposition arose from the fact that they were opposed, not so much to the granting of funds to Negroes, as to the use made of state funds in "black" counties. The "white" counties soon arrived at the conviction that if there was not enough educational money available for distribution to all of the children, white and black, such funds as were available should be distributed among the white children with equity.

The Negro. After Reconstruction, the Negro was possessed only of the smallest degree of political influence in the South. The conservative constitutions of 1874–1876, however, had left his legal status unaffected, and he remained a potential reservoir of voting strength. In addition, Negroes participated in the elections as Democrats and exercised no inconsiderable power in this way. Their particular function, however, was that of a tool to be manipulated by local politicians.

------

[5] *Debates in the Constitutional Convention of 1901 for the State of Virginia, Held in the City of Richmond, June 12, 1901, to June 26, 1902,* The Hermitage Press, Richmond, 1906, p. 1007.

The Negro was not only a separate racial entity during the period following Reconstruction, but also a separate economic class. As such, he exerted an enormous, though passive, influence upon the development of education in the South. With the growth of a manufacturing and urban working class among whites of the new generation, the competition with Negroes for the same jobs resulted in violent repercussions in the educational field. Education was conceived of, everywhere, as a means by which individuals could receive a better preparation for a livelihood; and there was no disposition, accordingly, to forward the educational activities which might result in making Negroes better competitors in the industrial field.

The Expansion of Educational Needs

The most striking fact concerning this general period was the expansion of educational need due to the rapid crush of the population, white and black, into the public schools. Table III indicates the growth of school enrollment between the end of Reconstruction and 1895 for ten typical Southern states in which there were separate systems. The states included in this table are Alabama, Arkansas, Florida, Georgia, Louisiana, Mississippi, North and South Carolina, Tennessee, and Texas.

TABLE III [6]

TOTAL ENROLLMENT FOR TEN SOUTHERN STATES OVER THE PERIOD 1875–1895

Year	Total Enrollment	% Increase over 1875
1875	1,323,605	
1876	1,337,003	1.0
1880	1,767,909	33.5
1885	2,213,979	67.2
1890	2,891,161	118.4
1895	3,318,964	150.7

[6] From *Reports of the United States Commissioner of Education.*

The year 1876 has been included to indicate the effect of the conservative reaction upon the public schools. With a total increase of only 1 per cent in the enrollment between 1875 and 1876, several states showed a violent decline in the enrollment registered during the last year of Reconstruction as compared to the enrollment during the first year of the system under conservative management. In Arkansas, there was an enrollment of 73,878 in 1875, which dwindled to 15,890 in 1876. In 1880, there were fewer children enrolled in the Arkansas system than were enrolled in 1875. In Florida, the enrollment fell from 32,371 in 1875 to 26,052 in 1876. It was not until 1888 that the white enrollment exceeded the Negro enrollment in Florida, although Negroes were but thirty per cent of the total population.

In Georgia, the enrollment rose steadily from 156,394 in 1875 to 436,582 in 1895. In this state, it is notable that the Reconstruction regime came to a close early in 1872, and there was, therefore, no disruption of control after 1875. In Louisiana, the enrollment of 1880 was 68,440, more than 6,000 less than in 1876, the last year of radical control. In Mississippi, the enrollment decreased from 168,217 in 1875 to 166,204 in 1876. In South Carolina, the enrollment dropped from 140,416 in 1875 to 123,085 in 1876, and did not regain the Reconstruction level until the early eighteen eighties. In Tennessee, the enrollment dropped from 199,058 in 1875 to 194,085 in 1876. In Texas, the enrollment remained practically stationary from 1875 to 1880, but thereafter had a rapid growth. In Virginia, the enrollment for both races doubled from 1879 to 1880.

Growth in white enrollment exceeds Negro. As added evidence that the resources of the school system were being flooded by a sudden growth of interest in public education which came principally from white children, enrollment figures for the period from 1880 to 1895 are significant. In the ten Southern states already mentioned, the comparative increase of the Negro and white enrollment over that of 1880 was as shown in Table IV.   In the fifteen-year period 1880–1895, the white school enrollment in these ten Southern states more than doubled, while the Negro school enrollment grew but one-half as fast.   There can be no doubt, of course, that the limitation of opportunities for Negro children was already beginning to affect the number of children enrolled; but the most significant fact to be derived from a study of these percentages is that an unprecedented number of white children were clamoring for the opportunity of a public-school education, and, as a result, were overwhelming the facilities provided.   It will be well, also, to remember that this host of white children were seeking educational opportunity in a system where the funds were, at the beginning of the period, apportioned equally between the races; and that those funds were severely restricted by the limitations upon expenditures imposed by the first conservative legislatures after the Reconstruction Period.

TABLE IV

INCREASE IN SCHOOL ENROLLMENT IN TEN SOUTHERN STATES, 1880–1895'

Year	White Enrollment	Negro Enrollment	Over 1880 Percentage Increase— Whites	Percentage Increase— Negroes
1880	1,053,025	714,884		
1885	1,378,926	835,053	13.0	11.5
1890	1,864,214	1,026,947	77.0	43.0
1895	2,176,464	1,142,500	106.0	59.0

Curtailment of educational funds by conservative legislatures. Despite the rapid increase in enrollment, the educational funds available were strictly limited by constitutional reservations of power enacted by the conservative legislatures immediately after Reconstruction which rigidly prescribed the amount of money that could be appropriated by the legislatures for the support of public schools. In addition, the school funds were restricted either to state funds or to legislative appropriation, no local taxation being allowed in many states. The first result was an actual decrease in educational revenue. In Alabama, $523,779 was spent for education in 1875, but only $375,645 in 1880. In Louisiana, educational expenditures decreased from $699,655 in 1875 to $480,320. In South Carolina, the decrease was as marked: from $426,640 in 1875 to $324,679 in 1880. In nine Southern states, Alabama, Arkansas, Florida, Louisiana, Mississippi, North Carolina, South Carolina, Tennessee, and Texas, educational expenditures were $5,181,945 in 1875, but in 1880 were a million dollars less: $4,195,389. In the five years, the educational expenditures accordingly had decreased 21 per cent, while the educational load as represented by the enrollment had increased 33 per cent. Here was an educational problem of great seriousness. With a decreased educational fund and an increasing educational responsibility, how could the states solve the dilemma?

The first solution—diversion of school funds from Negro to white children. Despite the pledges of conservative chiefs to Negroes that their educational rights should not be violated by the restored regime, it was inevitable that the divestiture of the Negro of any real political power should soon be followed by a diversion of school funds from Negro to white children. There were more children to be educated but less money available for their education; and if a choice had to be made between providing a wretched system for both races and providing a fairly good system for the white children as compared to a wretched system for Negro children, the student of human nature can understand what was actually done. A survey of legislation affecting school appropriations in representative states will show the pattern that was adopted.

The Social Structure Solidified 93

Mississippi. The first laws passed by the conservative
Democrats in 1876 in Mississippi, with reference to the
public school system, "badly crippled the school system,
yet they did much to place it on a cash basis." [7] The opposition to the school system had become outspoken during
Reconstruction, and Thomas S. Gathright, later Superintendent of the State under the restored Democracy, gave
this reason for the opposition:

> I will cite Noxubee county, for example. The tax to build
> school houses will be $40,000, and not twenty-five white chil-
> dren in the county can be benefited, while the colored popu-
> lation pay almost no part of this tax. I exhort the friends
> of our Southern children to pay the tax, and then to send
> their children to their own private schools. [8]

Now, the only dependence of the white children in the
poor counties for an education was upon the public school
system. The white planters of Noxubee County could afford
to send their children to private schools; but the poor white
population of other Mississippi counties would receive their
education in public schools or not at all. The public schools
were supported principally by a state fund, in addition to
the local tax allowed for school buildings, and this fund
was apportioned on an equal, per capita basis. The conservative legislation allowed the proviso regarding equal
appropriations to remain in the law, and we have seen that
educational need continued to grow in the state while educational revenues were cut down sharply.

Faced with this situation, the legislators made a change
in the educational laws in 1886 which facilitated the diversion of funds to white children from Negroes, which practice had already appeared with the tacit agreement of school
boards throughout the state. By 1886, the white public

---

[7] Noble, *Forty Years of the Public Schools in Mississippi*, Teachers College, Columbia University Press, New York, 1918, p. 48.

[8] *Ibid.*, p. 14.

schools had grown in popularity, the enrollment having increased from 65,000 in 1875 to 129,000 in 1885. The law of 1886 was sponsored by representatives from the Black Belt counties and set up a system of uniform examinations for teachers, with a salary scale based upon the certificates granted in this examination. The first-grade teachers were to receive from $25 to $55, second-grade teachers from $18 to $30, and third-grade teachers from $15 to $20. There are two obvious means by which school funds could be diverted from Negro to white children on this basis. Examining officers could grant Negroes lower certificates, or the local boards could grant different salaries within the limits of the scale set for the same certificate to teachers of the two races; *i.e.*, a district board could give a first-grade Negro teacher $25, and a first-grade white teacher, $55; or, it could give a second-grade white teacher $30, while it continued to pay the first-grade Negro teacher only $25.

By 1885, seventy per cent of the white school population in Mississippi was enrolled in public schools. The pressure of this growing attendance must be considered as the inevitable predecessor of the law of 1886, sponsored, as we have noted, principally by representatives from the "black" counties. Their counties, by this device, were able to support their white schools quite handsomely from the state fund alone. The constitutional provision to the effect that schools for the two races be maintained for equal lengths of time could also be met by using this device of separate salary scales for the two races. For a district in which, for example, there were 100 white and 100 Negro children, the district board could hire a Negro teacher with a third-grade certificate for the entire district, to whom they could pay $18 monthly for the constitutional term of four months. The Negro school, therefore, would be supported at a total expense for teacher's salaries of $72.

Now, imagining in this hypothetical case that the district received $1 per capita for the education of the children in the district from the state fund, that district would have received a total of $200 from the state, $100 on account of the Negro and $100 on account of the white children. The maintenance of a Negro school at a cost of $72 would leave $128 for the support of the school for white children. If the proportion (as in many Mississippi counties) was 900 Negro children to 100 white children, the same principle worked to even better advantage for the schools for white children. With the same per capita apportionment, there would be available $1,000 for all educational purposes. To spend $648 of this amount on the Negro children, assuming only a slight diversion of funds, would allow to remain $352 for the support of a school or schools for the 100 white children. The per capita expenditure for the Negro children would then be $0.72 per annum, and for the white children of this county, $3.52 per annum.

On the other hand, if we consider a county in which the majority of the population was white, there would be no great advantage in discriminating against the Negro children in the distribution of school funds. Let us take a county where, out of a thousand children, 900 are white and 100 are Negro. To divert funds from Negroes to whites in the same proportion as in the first county would add but $0.03 to the per capita for each white child in the county. Ranked according to expenditure, we should then have the following result:

Expenditures for white children in County A (black county) $3.52 per cap.
Expenditures for Negro children in County A (black county) $0.72 per cap.
Expenditures for white children in County B (white county) $1.03 per cap.
Expenditures for Negro children in County B (white county) $0.72 per cap.

A per capita apportionment unfair to white children in "white" counties as well as to black children in "black" counties. In a situation of this kind—which, in a highly

exaggerated form, soon became typical of the entire South—
one can see readily the reasons for opposition to Negro
education on the part of both white people in "white"
counties and those in "black" counties.   Citizens of "black"
counties saw that if there was an equal appropriation of
funds to Negro children, their taxes would in actuality
be devoted to the education of Negro children in much
greater proportion than for the education of white children.
In the same way, so long as these "black" counties could
divert funds from Negro to white children in their counties,
they did not need any additional funds to support the white
schools.   They therefore fought those changes in the state
constitution which would have permitted communities to levy
local taxes as being against their policy and their interests.

On the other hand, the white citizens of the "white" counties saw their schools in a condition but little better than
that of the Negro schools of their own and other localities.
They saw the diversion of funds from Negro to white children used as a means by which the white children of "black"
counties had educational opportunities immensely superior
to those of their own counties.   They were advocates of
local taxation, but found their efforts for this reform in
the state legislatures blocked by the men from the "black"
counties, who did not need and therefore did not want local
taxation.   It is apparent that the education of Negro children could not help but become the butt of invective and
recrimination where it was so easily made the point of
contact between the upper and nether millstones of the
existing educational problem.

The turning point in Mississippi.   It has been suggested
that the first solution of the educational problem was to
divert school funds from Negro to white children, and thus
furnish adequate schools for the white children in the counties where there was a large Negro population.   The law
of 1886 furnishes the decisive turning point for Negro

public schools in Mississippi.   Table V, showing the average monthly salaries of teachers in Mississippi by race, is significant in indicating the sharp break in equality of salaries which occurred immediately following the enactment of the certificate law of that year.

TABLE V [9]

AVERAGE MONTHLY SALARIES OF TEACHERS IN MISSISSIPPI, BY RACE, 1875–1895

Year	White	Negro	
1875	$57.50	$53.45	
1876	41.08	38.54	
1877	29.19	29.19	
1878	27.00	27.00	
1879	30.26	30.26	
1880	30.05	30.05	
1881	30.07	30.07	
1882	30.03	30.03	
1883	32.68	32.68	
1884	28.73	28.73	
1885	28.74	28.74	
1886	31.37	27.40	(Passage of certificate
1887	34.44	25.24	law; Negro salaries
1888	34.52	24.05	fall, white salaries
1889	33.97	24.16	rise.)
1890	33.37	23.20	
1891	32.41	22.54	
1892	32.53	24.52	
1893	30.45	22.31	
1894	33.04	21.53	
1895	33.04	21.46	

Prior to the passage of the certificate law of 1886, local boards in Mississippi could meet the constitutional requirement to maintain schools with an equal term by establishing a school for Negro children in which there was, let us say, one teacher for 100 pupils, and another school for white children in which there were two or three teachers for 100 white children.   The effect of the law of 1886, as we have seen, was to depress still further the funds available for the education of Negro children. The general result was a con-

---

[9] Table from Noble, *op. cit.*, Appendix.

tinued diversion of school funds, state and local, to the support of schools for white children, resulting in an ever-widening breach between the expenditures for children in the two separate systems which exists in even more exaggerated form today.

The Mississippi Constitutional Convention of 1890. By 1890, there were allowed in the law two methods by which Negro children in Mississippi could be discriminated against in the distribution of school funds. The first was the provision of schools with the same length of term for both races but with no provisions for equal instructional services from the viewpoint of the number of teachers or schools provided for the same number of children. The second was the permission to grant a differentiated salary scale on the basis of certificates held by teachers.

The constitutional convention of 1890 was more than a body intent upon disfranchising Negroes. The members were charged as well with the responsibility of providing more funds for the public schools, since, as we have seen, the school population of the state was growing more rapidly than available funds. The convention achieved its ends so far as the schools were concerned by liberalizing the method by which the state school fund was distributed. A great amount of discretionary power was left in the hands of local boards, in order that discriminations which hitherto had been made in evasion of the spirit of the constitutional requirement for equal school opportunities for the two races might from thence forward be done with the full acquiescence of the letter and the spirit of the law.

An even more radical proposal was made by some members of the convention to the effect that the school fund should be divided on the basis of the tax paid by the two races. This, as we have seen, was the original method by which the support of schools for Negro children in the District of Columbia was insured as early as 1863. It was a proposition that had already been enacted into law in Kentucky, Maryland, and Delaware immediately following the Civil War.   In the period from 1885 to 1900, the proposal was violently agitated in every Southern state, and the fact that it was never actually accepted by these states in the period under discussion has led many to believe that there was a majority element which consistently refused to sanction discrimination against Negro children in the distribution of school funds in the states concerned.

Certainly the voices raised against this attempt to segregate the taxes paid for the support of schools according to race—by men of the type of Bishop Galloway, in Mississippi, Ex-Governor Jones, in Alabama, and the present Governor Pollard and Senator Glass, in Virginia—were actuated by the noblest of motives.   Yet it should be remembered that there was a practical consideration working against the plan to segregate taxes by race that was of no small importance.   This consideration, which led many representatives to vote against the provision, was that if taxes were segregated, the "black" counties would no longer be in a position to support their white schools so generously at the expense of a state fund available on the basis of many Negro educables.   Wherever agitation for this proposal arose, it was typically advocated by representatives of the "poor whites" and defeated by the coöperation of the idealists and the "Black Belt" representatives.

In Mississippi, the proposition with reference to dividing the state fund on the basis of taxes paid by each race was defeated in the convention by a vote of 81 to 31.   An amendment which proposed to divide the local fund on the same basis was defeated by a much narrower margin, 57 to 53, indicating that the sentiment of the representatives from the "black" counties as to dividing the state fund, which was collected by a general state tax, was much more unanimous than was that toward the division of the local fund,

which was paid within the community affected.[10]   So long
as the "black" counties in Mississippi could divert school
funds from Negro to white children under existing legislation, the issue of the division of tax moneys from the state
fund by race hardly concerned them.

The rise of the small farmer to a place in Mississippi
politics came relatively late. This was principally because
that state had no extensive piedmont area and because the
control of the great planters was perpetuated longer in
party councils than in most of the other Southern states.
"Major Vardaman, candidate for the governorship, in 1903
made a campaign issue of the division of the school fund.
His position, to state it briefly, was that the money formerly
spent on the education of the Negro had been wasted, inas-
much as no improvements could be noted in the moral nature
of the Negro." [11]   Vardaman represented not only an expressed antipathy toward the education of Negroes, but
was also the direct voice of the "poor white" constituency
of the "white" counties, which felt aggrieved at the existing
distribution of the state school fund.

Vardaman on the education of Negroes. It is possible
to understand the intense opposition to the education of
Negro children only by remembering the fact that Negroes
stood between two economic classes of white people and were
innocent victims of the system by which school funds were
expended. The education of Negroes at public expense
was seized upon by demagogues who went before their white
constituents with the blame for a poor school system for
whites laid at the doors of Negro children. We have seen
that public funds were actually being distributed on the
basis of Negro school population to the "black" counties,
but, owing to the certificate law of 1886 and other devices,

10 *Journal of the Proceedings of the Constitutional Convention of the
State of Mississippi,* E. L. Martin, Jackson, 1890, pp. 329 *ff.*
11 Noble, *op. cit.,* p. 96.

the Negro children were not getting this state appropriation: that fund was being spent for the benefit of the few white children in those areas where Negroes were in a vast majority.

As an example of the demagogic appeals made on this issue, the speeches of Governor Vardaman of Mississippi are classic.   On one occasion, Governor Vardaman is reported to have said:

> Yes, my fellow citizens, the first duty of the State is to provide schools, improved facilities for the instruction of the masses in the rudiments of culture, especially those of her citizens who live in the country districts. The city schools are good enough.   Until this can be done, until the children living away from the towns and cities, in the backwoods, are given the same opportunity to acquire a common school education that is enjoyed by the children resident in the city, our public school system will be far from perfect and fall short of the great purpose of its creation.
>
> Thus far, what I have said on the subject of education has been with reference solely to the white children.   What shall we do with the negro?   Certainly the system of education suited to the white child does not suit the negro. This has been demonstrated by forty years of experience and the expenditures of more than three hundred millions of dollars [12] in the southern states.   It was natural and quite reasonable, immediately after the civil war, especially by those who had made but a superficial study of the negro, to expect that freedom, equal educational facilities and the example and precept of the white man would have the effect of improving his morals and make a better man of him generally.   But it has not, I am sorry to say.   As a race, he is deteriorating morally every day.

---

[12] If Governor Vardaman was referring to the public funds spent on educating Negro children, he was guilty of a gross exaggeration.   In 1909 (the date of this speech), the ten Southern states with the largest percentage of Negro school children had spent altogether not much more than $400,000,000 since the Civil War for all educational purposes. Knight states, "$110,000,000 was spent to educate Negroes by southern states between 1870 and 1900."   As late as 1910, no Southern state, with the exception of Texas, had expended as much as $500,000 in any year for the education of Negro children. While difficult to determine, the correct figure would be from a minimum of $80,000,000 to a maximum of $140,-000,000 for 1865–1908.

. . . The white people of Mississippi cannot sit idly by without at least making an effort to arrest this destructive tendency. The State, for many years, at great expense to the tax-payers, has maintained a system of negro education, which has produced disappointing results, and I am opposed to the perpetuation of that system. My own idea is that the character of negro education ought to be changed. If, after forty years of earnest effort and the expenditure of fabulous sums of money to educate his head, we have succeeded only in making a criminal of him and impairing his usefulness and efficiency as a laborer, wisdom would suggest that we make another experiment, and see if we cannot improve him by educating his hand and heart. There must be a moral substratum upon which to build, or you cannot make a desirable citizen. The negro, as a race, is devoid of that element. He has never felt the guilt of sin, and the restraining influences of moral scruples or the goading of an outraged conscience are unknown to the negro. Slavery is the only process by which he has ever been partially civilized. God Almighty created the negro for a menial—he is essentially a servant. . . . When left to himself he has universally gone back to the barbarism of his native jungles. While a few mixed breeds and freaks of the race may possess qualities which justify them to aspire above that station, the fact still remains that the race is fit for that and nothing more. At any rate, that is all that he will ever accomplish in Mississippi, and as it is in Mississippi, so will it be in all the states ultimately.

. . . It is inexplicable to me how an observant white man, informed of all the facts in the case, and who really understands the negro, can hold to any other view. The evidence is overwhelming and the conclusion inevitable. *Why the Legislature should hesitate to submit to the people an amendment to the Constitution, so as to change the absurd and expensive system now in vogue, is an inscrutable mystery to me. Until the Fourteenth and Fifteenth Amendments to the Federal Constitution shall be repealed, in dealing with the race question in educational, as in other matters, we must "sweep the horizon of expedients"* to find a way around them, and the way around them in this instance is so to change the Constitution of Mississippi that the whole matter shall be left to the wise discretion of the Legislature, who will, in turn, enact laws giving to a Board of Commissioners the power to disburse the public school fund as the interests of the public may dictate. Either that or some other expedient will be devised. Remove the Constitutional hindrance and the remedy will be discovered. Money spent today for the maintenance of public schools for Negroes is robbery of the white man, and a waste upon the negro. You take it from the toiling white men and women, you rob the white child of the advantages it would afford him, and you spend it upon the Negro in an effort to make of the negro what God Almighty never intended should be made, and which men cannot accomplish. . . .[13]

The diversion of the entire fund to white children would not have solved the problem. It has been estimated [14] that $1,515,685 was spent in Mississippi in 1907 for teachers' salaries for the education of the white children in the state. The white school population in that year was 301,548. This expenditure for teachers' salaries, therefore, represented a per capita expenditure of $5.02 for each child. In the same year, there were 410,099 Negro children of school age in the state. The salaries of the teachers employed for these children amounted to a per capita expenditure of $1.10 for each Negro child. If all of the money devoted to the salaries of teachers for Negro children had been diverted to the salaries of teachers for white children, the per capita expenditure for these white children would have been raised by $1.59, or 31 per cent, giving a per capita of $6.61 as compared to the per capita expenditure actually made in 1907 of $5.02.

Now, such a moderate increase as was represented by the entire transference of the Negro school expenditures to the white school children would not have solved Mississippi's

[13] "Message of James K. Vardaman, Governor of Mississippi, to the House and Senate of Mississippi, Thursday, January 9, 1909," *Journal of the House,* Brandon Printing Co., Nashville, 1910.
before the twelfth annual conference for education in the South, Atlanta, April, 1909 (Committee of Twelve for the Advancement of the Colored Race, Cheyney, Pa., 1909), quoted in W. E. B. DuBois, *The Common*
[14] By Charles Lee Coon, "Public Taxation and Schools," a paper read *School and The Negro American,* Atlanta University Press, Atlanta, 1911, p. 121.

104   The Education of the Negro

educational problem.   However, the elimination of Negro
children from consideration would have placed all of the
white children on the same basis.   Under the existing arrangement, the inequalities between the education of white
children in "white" and "black" counties were as striking
as between the white and Negro children in these counties.
Table VI indicates the type of advantage enjoyed under
the existing basis of distribution of funds in Mississippi in
1907, and may also indicate why representatives from the
"black" counties vigorously protested against the attempt
to eliminate Negro children from consideration in the distribution of the state school fund.

TABLE VI [15]

EDUCATIONAL EXPENDITURES IN TYPICAL MISSISSIPPI COUNTIES IN 1908–09,
BY RACE

		Enrollment		Per Capita Expenditures	
County	Description	White	Negro	White	Negro
Attala	"Black" County	3,693	3,491	$ 3.42	$1.02
Bolivar	"Black" County	1,217	10,627	7.26	1.18
Claiborne	"Black" County	947	3,761	38.00	0.27
Copiah	"Black" County	3,356	5,147	7.43	2.51
Greene	"White" County	1,787	479	9.22	4.59
Issaquena	"Black" County	185	2,202	30.00	1.00
Itawamba	"White" County	3,792	406	5.65	3.50
Madison	"Black" County	974	4,016	25.00	0.18
Noxubee	"Black" County	1,022	6,330	20.00	1.69*
Washington	"Black" County	555	6,387	80.00	2.50
Yazoo	"Black" County	2,800	7,633	15.00	1.83

* These per capita figures as based on enrollment give a more favorable
picture of the Negro educational system than facts really warrant.   For
example, in Noxubee County in 1908–1909 there were 13,048 Negro children
of school age in the county, of whom only 6,330 were enrolled in school;
while of the 1,528 white children of school age in the county, 1,022 were
enrolled in school.   If figured by per capita school population, the comparative deficiencies of the Negro system are even more obvious.

In Table VI, one can note the startling difference under
the distribution of school funds on a per capita basis be-

[15] Taken in part from pp. 72–77, *The Common School and the Negro
American.*

tween two such counties as Itawamba, a "white" county,
and Washington, a "black" county, where the white children in the former, because of the necessity for spreading
the available school fund over a large number of white
children, show a per capita of only $5.65; whereas in Wash-
ington County, local officials would receive a large amount
of state funds on the basis of the Negro school population
and, by diverting this amount in large part to the very
small white school population, maintain schools at a cost
of $80 per capita for the white school population.   It will
also be noted that the expenditures for Negro children were
much higher in the "white" counties than in the "black"
counties.   Obviously these "white" counties found little advantage in diverting the small amount of money they received on account of their Negro school population, itself
relatively insignificant, over the vast needs of the large white
school population.

Alabama.   Alabama traced the same pattern established
in Mississippi following the Reconstruction Period.   Educational expenditures were violently curtailed in the state
following the return of the conservative Democrats to power
in 1875.   Negro schools were maintained on a basis of
equality both by the constitution of 1875 and by the legislative enactments which put that instrument into effect.
The schools under the new system were to be supported by
a state fund, derived from the sale of lands and licenses and
general appropriations.   Commenting on the reactionary
legislation enacted by the conservative constitutional convention of 1875, the *Report of the State Superintendent of
Alabama* in 1919 said:

> In addition to these generous provisions (i.e., of the Re-
> construction Constitution regarding education), there was no
> restriction upon the statutory power of the legislature in the
> matter of local taxation. Perhaps no State in the Union at
> that time made more generous constitutional provision for
> this essential cause. But as in so many other matters in this

unhappy period of our history, this "but held the word of promise to the ear, and broke it to the hope." Generous as were these provisions, explicit as were the mandates of the Constitution, the period during 1868–1875 represented in educational matters as in every other the darkest days through which our State has had to travel. The moneys which the people paid into the treasury for schools were either diverted to less important purposes, or, stolen outright.

To avoid this exploitation, the Constitution of 1875 unfortunately repealed these provisions for the local support of schools. It specifically denied the right of local taxation, and limited the cities to the collection of a tax of five mills for the purpose of municipal government, a small portion of which was usually diverted to education. Since less than ten per cent of our people, at that time, lived in cities, and since the other demands of municipal life, if sufficiently performed, required much more attention than was authorized to be collected for municipal purposes, it can be stated with substantial accuracy that there was no provision or local taxation for educational purposes in the State of Alabama from 1875 to 1901.[16]

After the first few years following Reconstruction, the enrollment of the public schools was greatly increased. The white enrollment grew from 107,000 in 1880 to 186,000 in 1890. Educational revenues, however, did not grow along with the new demands upon the schools. White patrons attempted at first to meet the situation by supplementing public funds, but found the strain too great to be continued.

Becoming restive under the glaring deficiencies of the system, the white citizens of the "black" counties began to agitate for a restriction on the amount of money received by Negro children. One county superintendent demanded a change in the method of disseminating funds because "the white people object to being taxed to educate ten Negroes and one white child." [17] Another said, "Negroes pay very

---

[16] P. 24.
[17] *Biennial Report, State Superintendent of Alabama*, 1891.

little of the tax, but get all of the money." [18]   The cities attempted to levy local taxes for the support of their schools, but all ordinances of this character were declared unconstitutional by the state supreme court.[19]   From 1885 to 1890, there was a steadily rising wave of discontent toward the method of apportioning the school fund which was turned into a deep-seated opposition to the education of Negro children.

In January, 1886, the state legislature exhibited its first tendency to meet the situation by segregating the poll taxes, which were devoted to school purposes, according to race. In 1891, a means was found to circumvent the constitutional provision regarding the maintenance of equal opportunities for both races.   The device adopted was a law which empowered the county boards of education (who hitherto had been directed to divide the school funds on a strictly per capita basis) to allot funds within counties "as they should deem desirable in maintaining a system of schools equal for all children *as nearly as practicable.*"   In his report of that year, the Superintendent, the Honorable Solomon B. Palmer, stated that it was not the intention of the law to work any hardship on Negro children.   He further stated that he did not contemplate that any injustice would arise from the passage of the law.

The bill passed the house on March 17, 1890, by a vote of 65 to 0.   The assurances of the Superintendent had, apparently, facilitated its ready passage in that body.   The *Montgomery Advertiser* for the following day, however, reported that "Booker T. Washington, the Negro principal of Tuskegee Institute, was seen at the State Capitol today, buttonholing Senators with reference to the School Apportionment Bill, which he hopes won't pass." [20]   However, the

---

[18] *Ibid.*, p. 28.
[19] *Biennial Report, State Superintendent of Alabama,* 1886.
[20] March 18, 1890.

108   The Education of the Negro

efforts of the Tuskegee educator were unavailing, and the
bill passed the senate by a vote of 18 to 7.[21]

The State Superintendent's report for the following year
shows a spectacular drop in Negro teachers' salaries
throughout the state, as well as a decrease in the length of
the school term for Negro children. Table VII gives a picture of relative per capita expenditures for white and Negro
children in Alabama from 1875 to 1891, the first school

TABLE VII [22]

PERCENTAGE THAT WHITE EXPENDITURES EXCEEDED NEGRO
EXPENDITURES, PER CAPITA, 1875–1891

Year	Per Capita Expenditures for Teachers' Salaries		Percentage White Expenditures Exceeded Negro Expenditures	
	White	Negro		
1875	$1.30	$1.46	−11.0	
1876	0.83	0.82	2.2	(Note post-Reconstruction de-
1877	0.95	0.93	2.1	cline.)
1878	0.91	0.97	−6.2	
1879	0.98	0.97	1.0	
1880	0.99	0.95	4.2	
1881	1.01	0.95	6.3	
1882	0.93	0.87	6.8	
1883	1.07	0.94	13.8	(Cities begin local taxation:
1884	1.22	1.08	12.9	note Negro % decline.)
1885	1.28	1.09	17.4	
1886	1.30	1.06	22.6	
1887	1.25	0.83	50.6	(Date of segregation of poll-
1888	1.26	0.98	28.5	taxes by race.)
1889	1.04	0.89	16.8	(Local taxation declared un-
1890	1.09	0.92	18.4	constitutional in cities.)
1891	1.07	0.87	22.9	

(Law giving discretionary power to county
boards passed; state reports stop publication of expenditures by race.)

[21] *Senate Journal, Session of 1890–1891 of the General Assembly of Alabama,* Smith, Allred and Co., Montgomery, 1891. See also *Acts of the
General Assembly, Session of 1890–1891,* pp. 553–555.

[22] Table constructed from successive state educational reports for Alabama.

year in which the law took effect. It is significant that
after this year the state report stopped printing the expenditures by race, and that this separation was not again
adopted until 1909.

From a study of separate county reports, however, it is
possible to determine that Negro schools were definitely affected by the law of 1890, despite the assurances of State
Superintendent Palmer to the contrary.

TABLE VIII

COMPARISON OF SEVERAL COUNTIES IN ALABAMA BEFORE AND AFTER THE
CHANGE IN METHODS OF DISTRIBUTING THE SCHOOL FUND,
BY SCHOOL TERM AND MONTHLY SALARY, FOR
WHITE AND NEGRO SCHOOLS

		Length of School Term				Monthly Pay of Teachers			
		White		Negro		White		Negro	
County	Description	1890	1895	1890	1895	1890	1895	1890	1895
Autauga	"Black" County	58	62	95	65	$25	$28	$26	$16
Clarke*	"Black" County	72	65	82	63	21	22	22	17
Jefferson	"White" County	97	85	101	90	22	24	23	22
Lowndes	"Black" County	63	79	75	78	21	44	32	21
Mobile	"White" County	162	151	146	146	45	46	36	35
Walker	"White" County	59	59	66	70	19	22	19	22

* From *Alabama Educational Reports* for 1890–1895.

Although the period involved was one of great agricultural and industrial depression, it will be noted that in
each of the three "black" counties listed in Table VIII, the
salaries of Negro teachers were severely reduced, while those
of white teachers were substantially increased.   In Lowndes
County, the salaries of Negro teachers were reduced 33 per
cent, while the salaries of white teachers were more than
doubled.   At the beginning of the period, it will be seen that
Negro schools in the "black" counties had longer terms and
paid their teachers higher salaries than did white schools in
the same counties. This was because the concentration of

the Negro population allowed larger schools to be established for Negroes than for whites, and, owing to the strict per capita apportionment in Alabama, the salaries of Negro teachers were correspondingly higher. In the counties in which the white school population was in the majority, there was no such corresponding fluctuation in the relations between expenditures for the schools for the two races after the passage of the law of 1890. This was, obviously, because there were so few Negro children that discrimination did not pay in the same degree that it did in the "black" counties. In only one county—Walker, a "white" county —did the salaries and terms of the Negro schools increase together while the length of term for the white school remained the same, and the salaries of white teachers advance in the same manner as did the salaries of the Negro teachers.

It is clear, then, that the bill of 1890 solved the problem of education for the "black" counties but did not give any appreciable aid to the "white" counties. For these latter counties, local taxation was a necessity if the schools were to make any adequate provision for the children, who came in ever increasing throngs. Senator Hundley, a representative from Randolph County, a "white" county, introduced in every subsequent session of the legislature resolutions calling for the submission of a constitutional amendment to the people which would permit local option in the levying of local school taxes. In each instance, the resolutions were defeated by the representatives of the "black" counties. Finally, Hundley hit upon the device of segregating the taxes on the basis of race, in order to satisfy the wealthy "Black Belt" planters who feared that a local tax would go principally to Negro schools if Negroes ever regained political power. House Joint Resolution 175, without this provision, passed in the house but failed to pass in the conservative senate; but after the introduction of the segregation proviso, Senate Resolution 33, a compromise measure, was passed in both bodies in 1894.[23]

The state at the time was rent by dissension between Populists and conservatives. The agrarian movement was led by Reuben Kolb, of Barbour County, a "semi-black" county in the southeastern part of the state. Kolb declared particularly for agricultural schools, and, in the course of his campaign, enlisted a large measure of support from Negro voters. The amendment with reference to the public schools was lost in the excitement of the general election, as enough votes to make it binding were not cast on this particular measure.[24]

Following the bitterly contested strife between Populists and conservatives, the constitutional convention of 1901 witnessed the next educational development in the state. The representative of local taxation in this body was Senator Ashcraft, from a "white" county in north Alabama. The Committee on Education brought in on the 38th legislative day of the convention two reports: a majority report which permitted a county tax of one mill, after local electors had sanctioned the levy; and a minority report which permitted a much larger tax. From the experience of the past, Ashcraft realized that no bill would be acceptable to the "Black Belt" which threw open the doors of local tax funds to Negro schools. He therefore placed in his minority report a proposition to segregate the funds received from the proposed taxation on the basis of the taxes paid by each race, hoping thereby to win the support of the "Black Belt" counties. Among the strong proponents of the measure was J. Thomas Heflin, then a rising young politician from Chambers County, who then, as later in his life, drew his support from the "poor white" voters of the hill country. Senator Hundley, whose constitutional amendment to per-

---

[23] *Senate and House Journals of Alabama* for 1894–1895.
[24] John B. Clark, *Populism in Alabama.*

mit local taxation had been defeated in 1894, was another
leader for the minority report; and another prominent figure in the debate was Senator Long, of Walker County, a
"white" county.[25]

Despite the best efforts of these men, the Ashcraft
minority report was defeated by a vote of 58 to 54 on the
73rd legislative day of the convention. While the arguments against this ordinance were directed mainly at its
constitutionality, it is difficult to escape the conviction that
here again was a case where the "Black Belt," possessed
of ample funds as a result of their diversion of the state
school fund from Negro to white children, defeated the idea
of local taxation for the entire state. It is significant that
of twenty "black" counties, not a single representative voted
against the majority report or for the Ashcraft resolution.[26]

The friends of education were obliged to be content with
the one-mill levy, provided for in the majority report and
accepted by the convention as a part of the new constitution.
It is significant that while this tax was voted upon favorably
in the next twelve years by 41 counties out of the 67 in the
state, only three "Black Belt" counties were included in
this number.[27]

The convention also took the words governing the distribution of funds which had been enacted as law in 1890 to
enable county boards to discriminate against Negro schools
and placed them in the constitution, directing these bodies
to maintain school systems, not "equal" as provided
for in the constitution of 1875, but "equal as nearly as
practicable."

We have seen that per capita expenditures for white children slightly exceeded those for Negro children prior to
the passage of the law of 1890. Separate statistics en-

[25] *Proceedings, Alabama Constitutional Convention of 1901.*
[26] *Ibid.*
[27] *Biennial Report of the Department of Education, 1903–1904.*

abling us to determine comparative expenditures were not again made available until 1909.   Resuming the interrupted thread, these percentages of per capita expenditures in excess of Negro expenditures are not without a definite meaning as to the fate of the Negro schools in the period involved:

Percentage Excess, White Expenditures over Negro Expenditures, Per Capita

1890	18.4%
1891	22.4%
1909	514.8%
1910	483.9%
1911	459.0%

In other words, for every dollar received in public-school funds by the Negro child in 1890, $1.18 was received by the white child.   In 1910, however, for every dollar received in public-school funds by the Negro child, the white child received $5.83.[28]

South Carolina. In South Carolina, the rural white Democracy, under the leadership of Benjamin Tillman, did not develop into the radical populism characteristic of other sections.   In the state, emphasis was laid rather upon the principles of the more moderate alliances and granges of the earlier period.   Actuated by the growing educational need of the white children and the inability of the state to find any other means of increasing the educational revenue, various devices were used in South Carolina to discriminate against Negro schools.   In the constitutional convention of 1895, dominated by Tillman, the white schools were strengthened in accordance with the program of the alliance. In this state, there appeared in the constitution of 1895 the same provisions instituted in Mississippi by the legislature of 1886 and in Alabama by similar legislative enactment of 1890.

---

[28] *Annual Report, State Superintendent of Alabama.*

. . . (The) local school boards were given power to apportion school funds. This provision made possible a steady decline in the proportion of funds given the Negro schools —from two-sevenths in 1899 to slightly over one-tenth in 1920.[29]

Summary

The period following the political reconstruction of the South was followed by one during which the social structure gradually solidified where the status of the Negro was concerned. In the white race, brought together by the "call of blood" during the struggle to regain power led by conservatives, there appeared a split which was fraught with grave consequences to the education of the Negro. The lower economic and social classes challenged the older leadership and emerged victorious, placing the white small farmer in control of political affairs for the first time in Southern history.

At the end of the first period of Reconstruction, conservative legislatures throughout the South pledged themselves to maintain Negro schools on an equality with those for white children. They had, however, also pledged themselves to reduce expenditures. No one had bargained with the educational impulse that soon drew hosts of white children into the public schools of the Southern States, creating an educational need for more school revenue than could easily be discovered.

The leadership furnished by the conservatives of the Old South was soon overwhelmed by the rising power of the white small farmers. This class was devoted to the public school system, in which they expected their children to be educated, in contrast to the wealthy conservatives, whose tradition made them at best but lukewarm toward the prin-

[29] F. B. Simkins, *The Tillman Movement in South Carolina*, Duke University Press, Durham, 1926, p. 145.

ciple of public education at the expense of the taxpayers.

After a short period in which the Southern States struggled with the inevitable, recourse was had to a diversion of school funds from Negro to white children. As a by-product of this attempted solution, an immense amount of opposition to the theory of educating Negroes was generated by demagogues who cultivated the impression that Negro children were responsible for the poor school facilities enjoyed by white children. The "Black Belt" counties led in the adoption of "expedients" by which they could appropriate to the education of white children the money furnished by the state for the equal education of all children. Finding these devices highly satisfactory, to the point where the state fund alone would support schools for white children in "Black Belt" counties, representatives from the "Black Belt" generally blocked the efforts of the representatives from "white" counties to allow local communities the privilege of local taxation for schools. The effort to work out a compromise by which taxes should be segregated according to the race of the taxpayer was not successful.

At the beginning of the twentieth century, the condition of the schools for Negro children in the South was but slightly improved over their condition in 1875. Per capita expenditures for the race advanced slowly, if at all. Meanwhile, a general improvement was taking place in the white schools, and the process of industrialization, accompanied by urbanization, was to point a new day for schools for both races.

CHAPTER VI

The Rôle of Booker T. Washington

THE life of Booker T. Washington "had its beginnings in the midst of the most miserable, desolate, and discouraging surroundings." [1]   He was born in a slave-cabin, in surroundings similar to those in which three and one-half million Negroes lived.   Emancipation came to him, and to his fellow slaves, when he was a little child.   He graduated from Hampton Institute in 1875, at the time when the hope of political equality for Negroes was being destroyed by the furious end of Reconstruction.   He became principal of Tuskegee Institute in 1881, when 70 per cent of all Negroes above the age of ten in America were illiterate.   He delivered his famous *Atlanta Exposition Speech* in 1895, when the dictum of

> In all things that are purely social we can be as separate as the fingers, yet one as the hand in all things essential to mutual progress.[2]

caused Clark Howell, of the *Atlanta Constitution*, to say,

> The whole speech is a platform on which the whites and the blacks can stand with full justice to each race.[3]

When Washington died in 1915, the school which he had begun in an abandoned church and an old chicken-house had

---

[1] Booker T. Washington, *Up From Slavery, An Autobiography*, Doubleday, Page and Company, Garden City, New York, 1924, p. 1.
[2] *Ibid.*, pp. 221–222.
[3] *Ibid.*, p. 226.

grown to an institution whose property and endowment had increased to almost four million dollars. The life that had begun in "the most miserable surroundings" ended with the memory of acquaintances with royal families and not less powerful financial magnates who controlled the destinies of nations.

This life—colorful, powerful, dramatic—had more to do with the education of Negroes than that of any other personality in the history of the race. But Washington was not the kind of man whose impress can be measured within the confines of an academic tradition. Walter Hines Page quoted Booker T. Washington as giving the following estimate of his work:

> I do not know which to put first, the effect of Tuskegee's work on the Negro, or the effect on the attitude of the white man to the Negro.[4]

With the simple substitution of the name of the man for the name of the institution which mirrored his lengthened shadow, the dual rôle of Washington becomes more apparent. By a nice division of fortune, the first half of his life was devoted to creating an institution. The second portion of his career was spent in elucidating the educational and social theories upon which that institution rested, but even more in projecting his personality as a symbol of his race before the eye of world opinion.

Booker T. Washington as Educator

The man who taught Washington at Hampton, and who he said later "had something superhuman about him," was General Samuel Chapman Armstrong, founder of the school. Armstrong, born in Hawaii of missionary parents in 1839, completed his education at Williams College under Dr. Mark

---

[4] *Ibid.*, Preface, p. 21.

Hopkins. In tracing the intellectual ancestry of Booker T. Washington, it is important to repeat here the words of Armstrong:

> . . . Whatever good teaching I may have done has been Mark Hopkins teaching through me.[5]

Even in his busiest days at Hampton, Armstrong insisted on teaching at least one class. The subject was "moral philosophy," and the textbook was by Mark Hopkins.

In Hawaii, said Armstrong:

> . . . (There) were two institutions: the Lahaina-luna (government) Seminary for young men, where, with manual labor, mathematics and other higher branches were taught; and the Hilo Boarding and Manual Labor (missionary) School for boys, on a simpler basis, under the devoted David B. Lyman and his wife. As a rule, the former turned out more brilliant, the latter, less advanced but more solid, men. In making the plan of the Hampton Institute, that of the Hilo School seemed the best to follow.
>
> Mr. Lyman's boys had become among the best teachers and workers for their people; while graduates of the higher school, though many had done nobly at home and in foreign fields, had frequently been disappointing. Hence came our policy of only English and generally elementary and industrial teaching at Hampton, and its system of training the hand, head, and heart. Its graduates are to be not only good teachers, but skilled workers, able to build homes and earn a living for themselves and encourage others to do the same.[6]

The young Negro who left Hampton in 1881 to become principal of Tuskegee Institute translated this ideal into the words which he made the objective of his institution: an institution to develop in young men and women

> . . . the feeling and knowledge that labor is dignified and beautiful.[7]

---

[5] Samuel Chapman Armstrong, *Twenty-two Years' Work of Hampton Institute,* Normal School Press, Hampton, 1893, p. 1.

[6] *Ibid.,* p. 2.

[7] Washington, *Up From Slavery,* p. 131.

To those today who are overly enthusiastic as to the possibilities of "industrial" education, it should be instructive to remember that Washington at Hampton did study "moral philosophy" under the student of Mark Hopkins, and that he took no regular course in vocational education. He described his training in this field as an assignment "to take care of the chickens." His first duty at Tuskegee was not to erect a formidable catalogue of technical "courses"; on his first school day, he noted every missing student, every dirty collar, every filthy shirt or uncreased trouser. His first assignment was to request that these defects be repaired by the next day. Another story, perhaps apocryphal, is that he asked each student to obtain a toothbrush, and instructed them then and there in its use. The toothbrush, he liked to say, was one of the world's greatest agencies of civilization.

The objectives which Washington envisioned for Tuskegee Institute as an educational institution may be summarized as follows: (1) the development of attitudes and habits of industry and honesty in and the disciplining of raw, country youth through institutionalized activities; (2) the development of specific skills in definite crafts and occupations; and (3) the preparation of teachers for the public and private schools of the South who might, through spreading the gospel of thrift, industry, and racial conciliation, aid in constructing a firm economic foundation upon which the future aspiration of the race might stand.

The method was that of the currently popular "activity" program. As Dr. Paul Monroe described it more than two decades ago,

> . . . here I find illustrated the two most marked tendencies which are being formulated in the most advanced educational thought, but are being worked out slowly and with great difficulty. These tendencies are: first, the endeavor to draw the subject matter of education, or the "stuff" of school room work, directly from the life of the pupils; and,

second, to relate the outcome of education to life's activities, occupations, and duties of the pupil in such a way that the connection is made directly and immediately between school-room work and the other activities of the person being educated.[8]

All of the objectives mentioned above were served in the early days of the institution by such devices as a brick-kiln in which students learned how to manufacture bricks, which were afterward used in building construction on the campus, in the course of which the building industries had an opportunity to teach the trade on the job. Meanwhile, a correlation was sought between academic subjects and practice. Students were given problems in arithmetic arising from farm accounting or from simple or complex construction projects.

The educational service of Tuskegee also included extension work for Alabama communities, an innovation preceding in time the work of the Federal Government Agricultural Service by more than a decade. Washington was, himself, the best single advertisement of the virtues of educating Negroes, and his students, like him, were the apostles of education for Negroes wherever they went. Most of the graduates of Tuskegee and of the mother school, Hampton, entered the field of teaching rather than specific trades and crafts; and numerous smaller institutions on the Tuskegee plan were developed throughout the South.

The popularity of the "Tuskegee Idea" made it the model for theoretical planning for the education of Negro boys and girls. The opposition of white persons to a high-school education for Negroes was mollified by giving to such establishments the name "Industrial High School," although, to be sure, very little money was ever spent either for equip-

---

[8] From *Booker T. Washington, Builder of Civilization,* by Emmett J. Scott and Lyman B. Stowe, copyright 1926 by Doubleday, Doran & Company, Inc.

ment or for staff to make these public foundations either "industrial" or "high."

Booker T. Washington as a Leader

The formula which Booker T. Washington carried to his people was as simple as their own lives and understanding. They were to buy homes, farms; to establish themselves in even the humblest of occupations; and to exercise the virtues of thrift and honesty. They were to win the respect of their white neighbors in the South through good works. Above all, they should educate their children and prepare for the future.

Whenever the statements of Washington were challenged by Southern white malcontents, he could say simply that he never said anything before a Northern white audience, or before a Negro audience, that he would not be willing to repeat before any Southern white audience. The truth of this statement rested on two foundations. In the first place, Washington dealt with the eternal verities of human aspiration. No amount of prejudice could deny the wisdom of developing a sober, thrifty, and progressive Negro population, if, at the same time, this development went hand in hand with conciliatory tendencies toward the dominant white population. His objectives were those of the best men of all races and ages, and to take exception to them was to array oneself with the powers of darkness.

In the second place, the theory of Booker T. Washington eschewed issues which were debatable. It was couched in such an eloquent, persuasive, and far-reaching vein that his sentiments could mean all things to all men. When Washington suggested to Negroes that their immediate problem was to buy homes and farms in order to prepare for eventual political equality, the Negro could look forward to the future, while the white man could conveniently forget it.

It is significant that both Vardaman, the rabid Negro-baiter of Mississippi, and Booker T. Washington used oftenest in their speeches the phrase "education of the heart and hand" when suggesting the course which Negro education should take.   Washington frequently added "and the head" to his shibboleth, but undeniably this did not prevent many adherents of Vardaman from recognizing in Washington a man of kindred sentiments.   In many respects, Washington, the educator, was hardly superior to Washington, the realistic student of applied social psychology.

The result was that Washington, partly through his own marvellous personality, partly through the broad educational and political theories which he appeared to advocate, became the symbol of the Negro race where that symbol had been an unintelligent slave, a ludicrous minstrel, a discontented scholar, or, at least, a discontented misfit with the pretensions of scholarship.   In this rôle, he played a tremendous part in directing the destinies of organized efforts to educate Negroes.   His unfailing optimism was infectious.   All in all, Booker T. Washington was not only the greatest of Negro leaders; he was without doubt the most important individuality that came out of the South following the Civil War, and deserves a place in the ranks of the most distinguished of American citizens of his generation.

The Effect of the Tuskegee Idea

Booker T. Washington arose to prominence in 1895, the date of his *Atlanta Exposition Speech*.   Two years previously, in 1893, the high-water mark of lynchings was set when 155 occurred within a single year.   The pages of newspapers for a decade before and after his appearance on the national stage were studded with accounts of lynchings, race riots, and occasions of violence.   The eighteen nineties marked also the passage of "Jim Crow" laws and the convocation in Southern states of state constitutional conventions designed to disfranchise Negroes forever.

These incidents of racial conflict record the tumult of social change. The poor whites of the South, emancipated by Civil War and Negro freedom, were stretching out their hands for political recognition. The old master class had disappeared or had dissolved into combinations with Northern capitalists bent on the exploitation of textile factories, natural resources, and the necessary transportation facilities needed for the new growth. Whenever the poor whites threatened to get out of hand, it was always possible to bring them back into line by raising the Negro problem. Capital needed labor—not the too-intelligent labor of Northern cities, which, even then, it was beginning to desert, not the Negro plantation hands of bovine ignorance, which were too stupid for its use, but the slightly intelligent Negro or poor-white population, which could grapple with the elementary principles of the machine. In recommending Tennessee to investors as a place for locating industries, a Tennessee Chamber of Commerce in 1929 listed as a prime attraction a bountiful supply of "tractable, white labor." This labor, however, was not so "docile" that it did not seek every opportunity to replace Negro labor.

The first objective of the Tuskegee and Hampton schools—the development of attitudes and habits of industry and honesty and the disciplining of youth through institutionalized activities—has always been realized with great success. It is unfortunate that the great services of these schools in this direction have been subordinated to a popular conviction that their distinction rests on other bases. Likewise, in the preparation of teachers, these institutions and those which were built by their adherents have staffed thousands of schools in the South and North with intelligent, efficient, and coöperative workers. In a rapidly shifting world in which Negroes could ask of Fate but little more than time in which to perfect certain bulwarks of character and intelligence to resist opposing forces, the Tuskegee idea gained time, and contributed workers to add stamina and resourcefulness to the race which they represented.

The development of specific skills in definite crafts and occupations as a solution for the problem of the Negro has enjoyed less definitive success, and principally for reasons which have been without the possible purview of the initiators of the theory. The spirit has triumphed while the material element has largely been estopped, if not entirely overcome, by circumstances which no one could well foresee. Thirty years ago, Superintendent Joyner, of North Carolina, answered those who said that the education of Negroes was a failure by saying that it had never been tried. Similarly, the Tuskegee and Hampton idea was probably never tried except in the institutions which first began it. Elsewhere, the process of "industrial education" was ritualized, for there was neither the money available to purchase equipment necessary for the realization of the scheme, nor the spirit and intelligence which in Booker T. Washington's first, abandoned chicken-house made that financial support dispensable. Pretentious programs with no substance gave prominence to fakirs while it satisfied the lip-servers content to make a grand gesture in the direction both of their prejudices and their good will.

The dawning of the age of mass production, in which the individual craftsman is of increasingly smaller importance as a producer, and in which the constant expansion of the distributive factors in consumption is at the expense of production, appears to have set a definite end to the older methods of vocational training in which the training of the specialized craftsman was the ideal objective of the school. This new age has had yet another effect upon the Tuskegee idea besides that of casting doubt upon the wisdom of continuing to train workers for outmoded occupations. It threatens to throw into the labor market a great surplus of workers in case no provision is made for sharing work or curtailing the productivity of machines. Now, the political revolution by which the poor whites ousted the old land barons as the great power of the Southern demos makes it all too certain that the Negro producer, skilled or unskilled, has extra odds to overcome if he is to be placed in competition with white workmen.

A criticism of the Tuskegee system has been that no effort was made to teach Negroes the advantages of collective bargaining. Rather, they were persons whose education was financed by the great industrialists of America, who were staunchly set against trades-unionism. Adding this educational bent toward "rugged individualism" to a warranted suspicion of the white labor movement which had but infrequently shown itself able to rise above racial prejudice in the solution of labor problems, a reason is found why it has been said that Negro trades-school graduates have not even the habit of coöperation with fellow workers which might have stood them in good stead in the days of their tribulation.

Whatever the merits or demerits of the age of "industrial education" for Negroes, of racial conflict and social turmoil, the heritage of the personality of Booker T. Washington was left to the South. It was a tradition, grown soon into something almost legendary, of a great man, witty, intelligent, generous, understanding, sympathetic, tireless in championing the cause of his people, able to show the world that a Negro could be both educated and sensible, famous, yet modest, and hopeful, however realistic. No beginning could have been more lowly; and no life covered as wide a span of genuine contribution to the Amercian culture.

Summary

Booker T. Washington applied at Tuskegee Institute the educational theory he had learned from Samuel Chapman Armstrong at Hampton. The world-famed "industrial" basis of his institution had objectives no less valuable which found their fulfillment in character building and in the preparation of teachers for the Negro schools of the South.

Cast into national prominence by a speech made at a crucial period in the shifting relations between blacks and whites which were complicated by underlying changes in the economic life of the South and its people, Washington added the prestige of his powerful personality to the cause of educating Negro boys and girls everywhere in the South. Not all of his dreams were realized: shortly before his death in 1915, even his incurable optimism was obliged to confess that it would take a century or more to bring Negro schools to the level of white schools in the South. His economic program after the turn of the century met with difficulties which left the Negro farmer and worker largely helpless in the face of technology and agricultural overproduction. The virtues of his educational efforts remain undimmed: cleanliness, honesty, industry, patience, humor. The American democracy has had no greater triumph for its theory of equalitarianism than the rise of the little Virginia slave boy to a lasting place in the history of the Nation.

CHAPTER VII

The Awakening of Private Conscience

IN THE year 1862, in the town of Hampton, Virginia, a young Negro woman by the name of Mary L. Peake began a school for the refugees who had been lured into the Federal lines by the "contraband of war" policy of the Unionists. Forty miles distant was Jamestown, where in 1619 a Dutch man-of-war had landed "20 nagurs" in the first initiation of the institution of American Negro slavery.

In hundreds of other concentration camps and Federal outposts, devoted women and men, many of the latter recruited from among the ranks of army chaplains, were making similar efforts in which the alphabet was conceived of as an instrument no less potent in the destruction of the old social order than the fire and sword which it followed. Edward L. Pierce, of Massachusetts, organized a complete social service for ten thousand Sea Island refugees off the coast of South Carolina. The Penn School on St. Helena Island was established in April, 1862, by Laura M. Towne and Ellen Murray, and these devoted women created an institution for Negroes which they left only to die. Similarly, in 1862, General Grant in the West appointed General John Eaton to superintend the work for refugees in the territories swept by contending armies.

These early schools attracted the ablest and most idealistic persons in the North. The teachers were the spiritual descendants of Emerson, Whittier, Thoreau, and Horace Mann. They nourished an intense faith in the efficacy of education—a New England education—as the builder of character and racial stamina.   Their enterprises were supported by church associations and individuals who must have felt that in giving money they were partaking vicariously both in the prosecution of the struggle against the institution of slavery and in the salvation of a benighted race. The Freedmen's Bureau, inaugurated after the Civil War, had a working agreement with church associations by which the private philanthropy provided the salaries of teachers while the governmental agency contributed to the purchase of buildings and grounds.   Negroes themselves were all too eager to supplement these other funds by their own funds, raised in many cases through widespread educational associations.   It is estimated that a total of almost $6,000,000 was raised for the education of Negroes during this period, of which sum the freedmen themselves contributed at least one-sixth.[1]

By 1871, however, a reaction had set in which slowly but surely dried up the springs of philanthropy in the North. The Freedmen's Bureau was discontinued in 1870.   The country was weary from four years of war and the tumultuous aftermath.   The disposition to let the South look out for its own future grew.   Disquieting stories were heard in the North as to the political corruption and low standards of moral life in the ranks of the freedmen.   They had been educated, largely at the expense of Northern philanthropy, for all of a decade, and yet they appeared no better for it. Meanwhile, states in the South had written into their statutes laws guaranteeing the equal education of Negroes, and it appeared that the work of philanthropy was largely done. In addition, the entire enterprise had been discredited by fakirs who lost no opportunity to fleece the gullible public with pretentious claims.

---

[1] DuBois, *The Negro Common School*, p. 32.

In spite of the general apathy which greeted new demands upon Northern philanthropy for the education of Negroes, there were numerous cases where dramatic ventures earned a generous response.   In 1871, Fisk University at Nashville organized a group of singers, who called themselves the "Fisk Jubilee Singers" but who were referred to by one newspaper reporter as "General Fisk's Nigger Minstrels." Beginning with money barely sufficient to pay their train fares, this band of ex-slaves sang themselves into the hearts and conscience of America and Europe.   In Switzerland, Mark Twain heard them sing, and wrote that the music of the plantation melodies was the loveliest memory of his European travels.   Financially, the tour of the first and successive bands of singers was immediately profitable. They received for the school more than a hundred thousand dollars, enough to buy a new site and build Jubilee Hall, to replace the dilapidated army barracks in which the school had been housed up to that time.[2]

At Hampton, General Samuel C. Armstrong followed in the footsteps of the Fisk singers by organizing a tour for a group of Hampton singers.   The type of education which he proposed for Negroes appealed more permanently to the tough-minded financiers of the North than the "university" ideal was at that time able to do.   The result was that Hampton received large contributions to its endowment and physical plant that have continued until today, making it the best equipped, most heavily endowed institution for the education of Negroes in existence.   Booker T. Washington at Tuskegee earned the enthusiastic support of the wealthiest men of his time, a support that has been maintained in the years after his death.   Seth Low, Collis P. Huntington, Andrew Carnegie, John D. Rockefeller, and, in a later day,

---

[2] Gustavus D. Pike, *The Singing Campaign for Ten Thousand Pounds, or The Jubilee Singers in Great Britain*, American Missionary Association, New York, 1875.

Julius Rosenwald and George Eastman are among the great
names of American business magnates who contributed generously of their time and money to the Hampton and
Tuskegee Institutes.

The Great Foundations

The support of schools for Negro children in the South
immediately after the Civil War represented the philanthropy of the average citizen of the North, who contributed
his tithe to a missionary enterprise through his missionary
society or through individual churches. A Sunday school
would engage itself to furnish a room in a dormitory; a
devout family in moderate circumstances would pledge support for a school year to a worthy student. The reader
will probably not recall the name of "S. Griffiths Morgan,"
but this name stands after the biographical record of Booker
T. Washington in Hampton Institute records—"Educated
by S. Griffiths Morgan." [3]

With an increasing number of substantial donations to
the cause of education, self-perpetuating foundations came
to dominate the field of education among Negroes by reason
of their superior resources and more generous field of activity. In 1867, George Peabody set aside $1,000,000 for
"the promotion and encouragement of intellectual, moral, or
industrial education among the youth of the more destitute
portions of the Southern and Southwestern states of our
Union; my purpose being that the benefits intended shall
be distributed among the entire population, without other
distinction than their needs and the opportunities of usefulness to them." [4]   Substantial additions were made to the

---

[3] Samuel Chapman Armstrong, *Twenty-two Years' Work of Hampton*,
Normal School Press, Hampton, 1893, p. 58.
[4] *Peabody Proceedings*, Vol. I, p. 3.

initial gift by Mr. Peabody. Reference has been made above (Chapter IV) to the work of the Peabody Fund in establishing common schools for Negro children.

The Peabody Fund gave considerable aid to schools for the training of Negro teachers. The General Agent, the Reverend Barnas Sears, reported in 1869 that he found Fisk University of Nashville, Tennessee, "the best normal school he had seen in the South," and recommended that an appropriation of $800 be given to this school in preference to Berea College, which at that time enrolled both Negro and white students.

In the determination of policies, the Peabody Fund trustees do not appear always to have followed with wisdom the injunction of the giver, that the fund should be operated "without other distinction than" the "needs of the entire population." In 1871, at a time when teachers of schools for the two races were receiving identical salaries in the public schools, the Peabody Fund adopted a scale of payments to be made which included the proviso that colored schools would be paid for in a ratio two-thirds as great as that allotted to white schools of the same size. The reason given by the trustees was the same one cited today to justify differential salary scales, ". . . it costs less to maintain schools for the colored than for the white children." [5]

It is probable that a much smaller proportion of the Fund was devoted to the education of Negro children than to that of white children, one reason being that the general secretary felt that Negro children were being provided for by other philanthropic bodies much more adequately than the white school children. An interim report made to the trustees of the Fund by the daughter of Doctor Sears, soon after his death, carries this meaningful note:

---

[5] Ullin W. Leavell, *Philanthropy in Negro Education,* George Peabody College for Teachers, Nashville, 1930, p. 86.

The city superintendent of Montgomery writes that school affairs are in a very low state in that place. . . . The people appear too poor to build a proper schoolhouse, and during the past year over one hundred children have been refused admission to the over-crowded building. The New York Missionary Society has erected a handsome brick building exclusively for the colored race, *and the white citizens of the city have to endure this painful contrast.*[6]

As previously noted, the Peabody Fund trustees used the weight of their influence to defeat the Civil Rights Bill pending in Congress in 1873, arguing that equal facilities for the education of Negroes would come as a natural result of the separate systems already established in the South. In 1880, they petitioned Congress again, this time in support of special Federal appropriations for the education of Negroes. They argued that such grants should be made because, "although free systems of schools have been established in the Southern states, in their impoverished condition they are unable adequately to meet the emergency."[7]

In 1880, the Peabody Fund turned its attention principally to the training of teachers. The Peabody Normal College for white teachers was established in Nashville, and subsidies were made to Negro and white normal schools and teachers' institutes.

The General Agent of the Peabody Fund for many years was the Honorable Jabez L. M. Curry. This remarkable man was one of the first Southern white people of prominence to advocate the training of Negroes at public expense. Curry was born in Talladega County, Alabama, and was a member of the Alabama Legislature before the Civil War. He served with distinction in that struggle and afterward took a prominent part in political and educational affairs. Frequently he addressed state legislatures and sectional and

---

[6] *Peabody Proceedings,* Vol. II, p. 353. Italics mine.
[7] *Ibid.,* p. 284.

local conventions on the subject of education, never failing
to include a word for the Negro in his argument.

In 1914, the Peabody Fund was dissolved, and $350,000
was given over into the hands of the John F. Slater Fund
for the specific purpose of educating Negroes.   Since that
time, the funds have been distributed in accordance with the
policies of the Slater Fund.

The John F. Slater Fund.   This fund was the result of
a contribution of $1,000,000 made in 1882 by Mr. John
F. Slater of Norwich, Connecticut.   For the first few years,
the income of the Fund was devoted principally to private
schools offering higher education and to public schools for
vocational work.   The influence of Booker T. Washington
was responsible for a greater emphasis upon industrial training in the schools assisted by the Slater Fund.   Dr. J. L.
M. Curry, previously mentioned in connection with the Peabody Fund, served as General Agent for the Slater Fund
for many years, and he saw eye to eye with Booker T.
Washington.

The most significant work of the Slater Fund, however,
was done under the direction of Dr. James H. Dillard, aside
from Booker T. Washington without doubt the greatest
single figure in the history of the education of Negroes since
the Civil War.   Doctor Dillard was born in 1856 in the
tidewater section of Virginia.   We have described the educational beginnings of Booker T. Washington.   The first
school attended by James H. Dillard may serve as another
illustration of the dominant relation of the teacher in the
formation of character, a rôle that no specific sort of curriculum or material surroundings can displace.

It may be that our school was unique.   I am inclined to
think that it was, for in our school one man was the whole
school, except that a rabbi came three times a week to instruct a class in German.   The one teacher taught geography, arithmetic, algebra, geometry, Latin, Greek, French,
and Anglo-Saxon.   Yes, Anglo-Saxon! . . . And this brings

before me the man himself. I think we came as near the realization of the saying about Mark Hopkins and the log as it has ever been the fortune of a set of young fellows to experience. The man explained it. He was a remarkable combination of a scholar, a teacher, and an independent thinker.

There was never any direct appeal to the useful side of learning and knowing. So far as we were concerned, Greek was a good in itself. The utilitarian spirit did not exist. Nothing, as I recall, was ever said about getting on in the world. He had not himself got on far in the world, by the measurement of honors and wealth.[8]

The character of educational service sponsored by the Slater Fund was given a new direction under James Hardy Dillard, who became its General Agent in 1910. The rural schools in the South in most counties had no intermediate institution through which the elementary-school student of promise could bridge the gap between his first course and a teacher-training course. Indeed, it was common practice for students just graduated from the poor rural graded schools to enter immediately upon teaching.

To call Negro higher rural schools "high schools" would have brought instant opposition from many people who looked with disfavor upon any education for Negroes above a smattering of the fundamental "three r's." In addition, the term would have been a misnomer; it is a striking commentary upon the state of rural schools for Negroes in 1910 that the Slater Board required that the teaching should extend through a minimum of eight years, "with the intention of adding at least two years as soon as it shall be possible to make such extension."[9] The first such school was established in Tangipahoa Parish in Louisiana in 1911. Mr. A. C. Lewis, at that time Parish Superintendent of Schools,

---

[8] From *Sewanee Review*, October, 1921, quoted in Benjamin Brawley, *Dr. Dillard of the Jeanes Fund*, Fleming H. Revell, New York, 1930, pp. 25–33.

[9] *Ibid.*, p. 75.

now (1933) State Director of Negro Education for the State of Louisiana, in this way became a pioneer in one of the most significant developments in the education of Negroes.

By 1914, eight schools had been established, receiving $4000 for salaries from the Slater Fund and $10,696 from public tax funds. The development of the idea since has witnessed the engrafting of a system of secondary education for Negro children in the rural areas into the public school system. It is one of the most satisfying examples of the manner in which philanthropy, unable to carry by itself the entire weight of a new educational expansion, can successfully initiate an expanded program and stimulate the tax-supported system to include it in its framework.

The county training schools had increased to 368 in 1929. In that year, the Slater Fund, aided by the General Education Board, contributed $135,866 towards the support of these schools.[10]   Public tax funds, however, were responsible for the expenditure of $1,888,852 on these schools for salaries and equipment. The schools have in almost all cases outgrown their minimum of eight years of graded work and represent in every Southern state the backbone of high-school work among rural Negroes. They are schools for the open country, furnishing these communities teachers who are native to the soil, and, as standards in the Southern States are pushed upward, forming part of the educational ladder which extends now into the growing number of teachers' colleges in the South for men and women of the Negro race.

The Anna T. Jeanes Fund

If Doctor Dillard gave new spirit to the program of the Slater Fund, he created in the Jeanes Fund an agency as

---

[10] Work, *Negro Year Book, 1931–1932,* pp. 32–33.

effective.   Miss Anna T. Jeanes was a quiet Quaker woman
of Philadelphia.   At the solicitation of George Foster Peabody, of the General Education Board, she gave that foundation $200,000 in 1905 for the specific purpose of helping
Negro rural schools in the South.   She made the stipulation that Hollis B. Frissell, then principal of Hampton Institute, and Booker T. Washington, of Tuskegee Institute,
be consulted in making plans for the disposition of this
money.   The fund named for her was left at her death.
"Others," she said, "have given to the large schools; if I
could, I should like to help the little country schools." [11]

The need was too great in every section to think of dis-
sipating the funds available over every "little country
school."   It was decided to begin some measure of supervision in those counties which were receptive to the idea.
Under the original plan of the Fund, the "Jeanes" teacher
was to be stationed in one school, which would serve as a
demonstration center for the entire county, with efforts being concentrated upon the schools within easy reach of the
headquarters school.   The first teacher employed with this
idea in mind was Mrs. M. L. Sorrell, of Iberville Parish,
Louisiana.

The first plan was modified on the suggestion of Jackson
Davis, then Superintendent of Schools in Henrico County,
Virginia.   Mr. Davis had employed a capable Negro
woman, Miss Virginia E. Randolph, to inaugurate the experiment in his county.

The new plan called for the demonstration teacher to become an actual supervisor on a county-wide basis.   It was
enthusiastically accepted by Doctor Dillard, and by 1908–
1909, sixty-five "Jeanes" teachers, or county supervisors
for the Negro schools, were actively engaged in the work.
In the beginning, the Jeanes Fund paid the entire salaries

---

[11] Brawley, *Dr. Dillard of the Jeanes Fund*, p. 57.

of the workers. By 1910, 129 Jeanes teachers were employed, and it became evident that the income from the
Fund alone could not sustain this rapid expansion. Accordingly, the counties were asked to contribute to the work
from public tax funds. The impression created by the
early workers was so favorable to a continuation of the work
that there was an immediate response to this plea. In 1929,
313 Jeanes supervisors were operating in 311 Southern
counties. In support of the work, the Jeanes Fund paid
$104,095, while the amount realized from public expendi-
tures was $188,089. Since 1919, other foundations en-
gaged in the education of Negroes have contributed to the
Jeanes work, enabling the dream of the little Quaker woman
who wished to aid "the little country schools" to be more
than realized twenty years after her death.[12]

The General Education Board

Incorporated in 1903, the General Education Board was
established by John D. Rockefeller. The Rockefeller family had already made notable contributions to the education
of the Negro, principally through the American Baptist
Home Missionary Association. Morehouse College and
Spellman Seminary in Atlanta had been, and have continued, the favored objects of this philanthropy.

At the time when the General Education Board began its
work, the states were even more remiss in the support of
education upon higher levels than they were in the support
of elementary schools. They argued that the Negro was
incapable of a higher education, and that all effort should
be concentrated upon giving a bare training in those few
fundamental processes which they believed the children of
the race could actually master. This reasoning neglected

---

[12] Leavell, *Philanthropy in Negro Education*, p. 135 *f.*

that vital factor in any educational program, the provision
of trained teachers whose knowledge of the subjects taught
is far above that of their pupils.   In 1896, Charles W.
Eliot, President of Harvard, spoke to the point of the question:

> If any expect that the Negro teachers of the South can be
> adequately educated in primary schools or grammar schools
> or industrial schools pure and simple, I can only say in reply
> that that is more than we can do at the North with the white
> race.   The only way to have good primary schools and
> grammar schools in Massachusetts is to have high and normal schools and colleges, in which the higher teachers are
> trained.   It must be so throughout the South: the Negro
> needs absolutely these higher facilities of education.[13]

In 1929, the General Education Board had expended in
various services dealing with the education of Negroes $20,-
986,576.   Of this sum, $5,375,000 represented conditional
grants to the endowment campaigns of eleven Negro colleges and normal schools: Fisk University, Hampton Institute, Knoxville College, Lincoln University, Morehouse College, Shaw University, Spellman College, Talladega College,
Tuskegee Institute, Virginia Union University, and Wiley
University.[14]

Attention has been called to the manner in which the
General Education Board has synthesized the work of other
foundations with its own and contributed liberally to beginnings made elsewhere by these funds which have suffered
from lack of money necessary to take full advantage of the
innovations introduced.   One of the most important devices
by which this mutual coöperation has been forwarded has
come through the subsidies granted to Southern states for
the support of state agents specifically entrusted with the
supervision of Negro rural schools.   Initiated in 1910 in

---

[13] In a speech at Trinity Church, Boston, February 22, 1896, quoted in
DuBois, *The Negro Common School,* back cover.

[14] Work, *Negro Year Book, 1931–1932,* p. 227.

Virginia by the Peabody Fund and the Southern Education
Board, this development was taken over as one of its principal activities by the General Education Board in 1911.
Since that time, state agents for Negro schools have been
appointed in fourteen Southern states, nine states employing one such state supervisor and five states employing two
agents.[15]   The work of N. C. Newbold in North Carolina is
illustrative of the best work of this kind that has been done
in the South.

Prior to 1916, the General Education Board also supported agricultural and home economics work among Negroes in the South.   Responsibility for the agricultural
work was assumed by the Federal Government in 1916, but
the home economics division was continued until 1919 under
the name of "Home Makers' Clubs."   At that time, the Federal Government took over this type of service as well.

In 1929, the Rockefeller philanthropies were reorganized,
and a general plan was accepted with reference to the functions which should be sponsored by the General Education
Board in the future in its relations with schools for Negroes.
The plan follows:

> In elementary and secondary education, coöperation (a)
> in aiding state departments of education to develop efficient
> divisions of Negro education; (b) in helping to carry out
> state programs initiated and administered by state depart
> ments; and (c) in assisting, under special conditions, public
> schools and private schools of secondary grade; in higher
> education, coöperation (a) in developing university centers,
> including professional schools; (b) in promoting medical
> education and nurse training at a few centers; (c) in aiding
> a selected group of denominational colleges and also certain
> state-supported institutions; (d) in developing teacher-train
> ing facilities, especially in state normal schools, and state
> agricultural and mechanical colleges; (e) in providing addi
> tional training for those engaged in the field of Negro edu
> cation; and (f) in improving accounting systems in schools.[16]

---

[15] Leavell, *Philanthropy in Negro Education*, p. 102.
[16] Work, *Negro Year Book, 1931–1932*, p. 226.

The Julius Rosenwald Fund

In 1910, the year in which James Hardy Dillard became the General Agent of the Slater Fund, a canvass was being made of the wealthy men of the Hyde Park area in Chicago for the purpose of raising funds for a new building for the Young Men's Christian Association in that section of the city.   Among the prominent financiers who were visited was Julius Rosenwald, a Jew, the head of the great Sears, Roebuck mail-order merchandising house.   Mr. Rosenwald declined to make a contribution for the building, but suggested to the visitor that whenever the Chicago Y.M.C.A. got around to making some provision for Negro men, he would be glad to contribute to such a movement.   If any irony was intended by this remark, it was lost upon the canvasser; and shortly afterward, Mr. Rosenwald was approached with reference to making a contribution to a Negro Y.M.C.A., with the result that he donated $25,000 toward that purpose.[17]

In the fall of 1911, Rosenwald visited Tuskegee at the invitation of its founder.   At this time, he pledged $5,000 to the Institute for five years, conditioned, as all of his gifts were, upon additional gifts to match his donation.   But Rosenwald did more while on this visit to Alabama.   In company with Washington, he went out into the surrounding countryside to view the life of the Negroes living on the cotton plantations in the country districts.   In reply to a question from Rosenwald asking his opinion as to the most needed and immediately practicable improvement that could be effected in the manner of living which he observed among Negro tenants, Washington answered that in his opinion the rural schools offered the greatest single opportunity.[18]

---

[17] James Weldon Johnson, *The Shining Life*, a pamphlet, Fisk University Press, Nashville, 1932.

[18] Leavell, *Philanthropy in Negro Education*, pp. 77–78.

It was wisely stipulated by Rosenwald from the beginning that his philanthropic aid should be more in the nature of stimulating the people and the public officials to a broader interest in these schools, than a free gift which might entail no effort and receive no response from an apathetic community.   That policy has been persisted in until the present.   The general method was outlined by Washington. He stressed the necessity for coöperating with local county officials, believing that the interest generated by a community effort for a better building would also work toward the lengthening of the school term and an increase in the salaries paid the teachers of such schools.   The agent for the philanthropy was urged to gain the coöperation of white and black, and to create as far as possible a more favorable atmosphere for the education of the Negro children.[19]

The administration of the Rosenwald Fund, first at Tuskegee Institute, under C. J. Calloway, and later at Nashville, under the direction of S. L. Smith, established the first definite machinery for state-wide encouragement of schools for Negro children that was effective over the entire South.   The headquarters office furnished modern school-building plans, and local state agents furnished adequate leadership.   Offer of financial aid was on a fixed basis, frequently scaled downward as the idea became more and more popular, for communities and local boards which should engage to build a school for the Negro children.[20]

By July 1, 1932, 5,357 buildings had been erected, with a pupil capacity of 663,615.   Between 25 and 40 per cent of all Negro children enrolled in school in 1932 were in Rosenwald schools.   The cost of the erection of these buildings was in excess of twenty-eight millions of dollars, to which Negroes had contributed 16.64 per cent, white people 4.27 per cent, the Julius Rosenwald Fund 15.36 per

---

[19] *Ibid.*, pp. 109–117.
[20] *Ibid.*

cent, and public-school units 63.73 per cent. The success of the Rosenwald Fund in stimulating public tax bodies to assume the responsibility of building schools for Negro children is found in the fact that in the first year of the plan, only 17 per cent of the money expended came from public sources, while in 1931, public funds amounted to 72 per cent of the total expenditures.[21]

In 1930–1931, the Rosenwald Fund paid on appropriations $553,913 for "aid in building 256 public schools, in consolidation projects in five counties, in the purchase of 312 school libraries, in studies and demonstrations of organization and administration of Negro schools," all a part of the "Southern School Program" of the Fund. The sum of $90,320 was spent in aiding high schools and for "aid in buildings with modern equipment and shops at Little Rock, Arkansas, Winston-Salem, North Carolina, Maysville, Kentucky, and Columbus, Georgia." There was expended $505,005 in developing private colleges and professional schools, twenty institutions being helped in "buildings, endowment, and current expenses." The largest contributions were to Howard University, Washington, D. C.; Fisk University and Meharry Medical College, in Nashville, Tennessee; Atlanta University and Spellman College, in Atlanta, Georgia; and Dillard University, in New Orleans. The large amount of $136,692 was spent "to make possible advanced study by 165 individuals, chiefly teachers." [22]

The expanded program of the Rosenwald Fund implied by the above reference was made possible by a donation from Mr. Rosenwald four years before his death, which occurred in 1932. The gift to the trustees, consisting of 200,000 shares of Sears, Roebuck stock, was at one time valued at

---

[21] *The Julius Rosenwald Construction Map, July 1, 1932*, published by the Fund at Nashville, Tennessee, 1932.

[22] Edwin R. Embree, *Julius Rosenwald Fund, Report for the Year, 1931*, the Julius Rosenwald Fund, Chicago, 1932, p. 36.

more than $30,000,000; but this stock, in common with the entire list of securities, has shrunk considerably in value since that time.   The conditions imposed upon the trustees by the donor were of exceeding liberality, the purpose of the foundation being expressed simply as for "the well-being of mankind."   One stipulation reflecting Mr. Rosenwald's desire to prevent the frequent abuses which creep into the administration of funds held in perpetuity, was that the fund, principal as well as interest, should be expended within twenty-five years of the death of the donor.

Other Philanthropic Foundations

The Phelps-Stokes Fund.   Miss Caroline Phelps-Stokes in 1909 gave by her will the sum of $900,000, specifying that the income should be used, among other purposes, "for the education of Negroes both in Africa and the United States."   The Fund has financed fellowships at the Universities of Georgia and Virginia for students engaged in sociological study of the Negro, and has published the studies resulting from this series of fellowships.   One of its most important contributions was a survey of Negro education made in coöperation with the United States Bureau of Education and published in 1917.[23]   This exhaustive investigation covered practically all of the private and public schools purporting to offer secondary and higher education for Negroes.   The recommendations made by the author, Dr. Thomas Jesse Jones, had a wide influence at the time in determining the policies of other philanthropic boards and foundations.   The Phelps-Stokes Fund has also supported educational commissions sent from this country to Africa, and the investigations made by these commissions have laid

---

[23] Thomas Jesse Jones, *Negro Education: A Study of the Private and Higher Schools for Colored People in the United States*, in two volumes, Government Printing Office, Washington, 1917.

the foundation for a more systematic approach to the problem of the education of the native in the former home of the American Negro.[24]

The Carnegie Corporation. During his life, Mr. Andrew Carnegie was a firm friend to Booker T. Washington, and made frequent and generous contributions to Tuskegee and Hampton Institutes. The Carnegie Corporation has carried on the work thus begun by the great steel magnate. Among the sums given by Carnegie during his life or by the corporation from which educational interests of Negroes have benefited are $720,000 to Tuskegee Institute; $989,245 to Hampton Institute; for special research work, $82,500; and more than $200,000 for the building of libraries in Negro colleges.[25]

The Daniel Hand Fund. The Daniel Hand Fund, now amounting to $1,550,642, has been expended through the American Missionary Association. The fund was set up in 1888. It has been of inestimable service in supporting the schools and colleges maintained by this association throughout the South.[26]

The Dupont gifts. In the little State of Delaware, which has but three counties and a Negro school population less than twenty per cent of the total, the Dupont family has given liberally for the education of Negro children in the state. In 1928, the gift was announced of money sufficient to build and equip a schoolhouse for every school district in the state in which Negro children were enrolled.[27]

---

[24] Thomas Jesse Jones: (a) *Education in Africa: a study of West, South, and Equatorial Africa by the African Education Commission*, Phelps-Stokes Fund, New York, 1922; (b) *Education in East Africa: a study of East, Central, and South Africa by the second African Education Commission*, Phelps-Stokes Fund, New York, 1925.

[25] Work, *The Negro Year Book, 1931–1932*, p. 219.

[26] *Ibid.*, p. 216.

[27] N. C. Newbold, "Common Schools for Negroes in the South," *The Annals of the American Academy of Political and Social Science*, Vol. CXXX, November, 1928; *The American Negro*, The American Academy of Political and Social Science, Philadelphia, 1928, p. 221.

Self-Help: The Growth of Negro Philanthropy

Throughout the entire history of the Negro in this country, he has aided greatly in his own education. The State Agent for Negro Jeanes Agents in Alabama recently estimated (1931) that the teachers under her direction in thirty-three counties of the state raised annually more than $300,000 from Negro citizens.[28]   This money was generally used in extending terms, increasing teachers' salaries, and for general school improvement.   During the period when the Freedmen's Bureau was operating in the South, Negroes contributed more than one million dollars in fees and donations.   Before state systems were well established, the entire burden of hiring a teacher was frequently met by Negro communities eager to give an education to the people of the community.

In addition to these contributions, which are being made even today to subsidize the public school system for Negroes in Southern states, there have been individual instances of philanthropy on the part of Negroes that reveal a spirit more generous even than that of some of the larger foundations, considering the sacrifices involved in the effort.

The Saint Francis Academy.   In 1829, the Saint Francis Academy was established in Baltimore by a number of Negro sisters of the Catholic Church who had formerly lived in the West Indies.   A free woman, Nancy Allison, gave $15,000 to the school, and Louis Bode, a Haitian Negro, gave $30,000.[29]

Thomy Lafon.   Born in 1810 in New Orleans, a free Negro, Thomy Lafon, accumulated a large fortune, first as a grocer, next as a money-lender, and finally as a dealer in real estate.   His will, at his death in 1893, disposed of

---

[28] Record files of Mrs. Mary Foster McDavid, State Jeanes Agent for Alabama, Montgomery, Alabama.

[29] Work, *Negro Year Book, 1931–1932*, p. 203.

an estate appraised at $413,000. He stipulated that this money should be used for the support of schools and orphanages for both races in the city of New Orleans.[30] The largest elementary school for Negroes in the South, located in the city of New Orleans, bears the name of this singular man.

Mary E. Shaw. This woman, of New York City, left $38,000 to Tuskegee Institute.[31]

William V. Chambliss. A student of Tuskegee Institute in the early period under Booker T. Washington, William V. Chambliss, gave, during his life and by his will, more than $105,000 to the Tuskegee institution.[32]

The Burrus Estate. Soon after the Civil War, two brothers, James and John Burrus, entered Fisk University, in Nashville, Tennessee. It is said that they wished to refute by their own achievements the statement of John C. Calhoun, made thirty years before, to the effect that "if a Negro could be found who could parse Greek or explain Euclid, I should be constrained to think that he had human possibilities." One brother, John, made the ancient languages his specialty, while the other brother, James, gave special attention to mathematics. James Burrus was graduated from Fisk in 1875, in the first graduating class at that institution. From Fisk, he went to Dartmouth, where he graduated with honors. He returned to the South to teach at Fisk, as the first Negro member of the faculty. For years, he was a professor in Greek at Mississippi A. and M. College for Negroes, at Alcorn, and served as President of the same institution for some years. Believing that the great need of Negroes was economic security, the two brothers left the schoolroom to engage in business in Nashville. As they prospered, all of the profits were religiously

---

[30] *Ibid.*
[31] *Ibid.*
[32] *Ibid.*

saved, or reinvested in their business.   Following the death of John Burrus, the business was carried on by James Burrus.

When this man died in 1929, it was discovered that by the terms of his will, Fisk University had been left his entire fortune, amounting to more than $125,000.   Other philanthropies have been larger, but none in the history of Negro schools has been more sacrificial.[33]

The Place of Philanthropy

There are critics of philanthropic bequests who insist that a well-ordered world should properly have no place for private gratuities to the public weal.   Most of the larger foundations have come to regard their function, where Negro education is concerned, as the stimulation of public effort. There is certainly no social or educational objective which, if it justifies the support of a private citizen, does not justify the participation of the state in its realization.   In addition, the records of philanthropic endeavor are full of futile gestures by well-meaning men of wealth which linger on as ridiculous landmarks of the past, or even as positive deterrents to progress.   Julius Rosenwald attempted to keep his last philanthropy from "the dead hand of the past" when he stipulated that the fund bearing his name should be entirely expended within twenty-five years following his death.

The states generally have been reluctant to assume responsibilities for Negroes which are universally regarded elsewhere as proper public demands upon public resources. In many cases, it has not been a matter of waiting for the growth of a favorable public opinion; for if philanthropy had not done certain things, the state would neither have sought their accomplishment then nor seek it now.

---

[33] Embree, *Brown America*, pp. 253–256.

The determination of policies ushers in another perplexing problem. The large foundations have been in a position to control the thought and opinion of Negroes to an immense degree, as compared with corresponding relationships among white givers and recipients. Some have found in this fact an opportunity to remind the race to "fear the Greeks, bearing gifts," believing that modern philanthropy gives aid to Negroes for the selfish interests of a selfish class. Others have recalled the no less sage observation, "Don't look a gift-horse in the mouth," and have gone their ways rejoicing in new philanthropies in the knowledge that only the widest stretch of the imagination could connect the gift with the "class struggle."

It is an interesting fact that Negro college graduates and students are probably the most conservative representatives of their types in America, where economic, political, and religious issues are concerned. Occasional heretics have appeared, but they are notable more for their rarity than for their views. There have been frequent complaints that the collegiate education of Negroes takes them away from their natural orientation with the masses of their race, not in the manner the enemies of higher education for Negroes feared so much that it would take them, in "wanting to get out of their place," but in the modern manner of having no sympathy for the poor and weak of their own people, and concentrating all energies on the satisfaction of middle-class ambitions and desires. It is unfortunately true that there has been an immense amount of exploitation of the ignorant of their own people by college-trained, Negro professionals.

In the opinion of the writer, the fault has not been altogether in the fact that philanthropy extended to Negroes has set up artificial patterns of belief, or that it has consciously or unconsciously sought to alienate educated Negroes from the interests of their poorly paid, leaderless fellows. Rather, Negro students reflect, for better or worse, the great American tradition of the class from which most of them come.   In the older schools, when the atmosphere of these colleges was deeply religious and service and sacrifice were the keynotes, students were largely drawn from poorly circumstanced homes.   The second generation of Negro students represents, typically, the tastes, ambitions, and viewpoint of the American middle class.

The management of the foundations has involved the usual amount of failures which may be expected in disbursing such large sums of money.   One of the great functions of the Julius Rosenwald Fund has been the creation of a more favorable public opinion, a contribution perhaps as valuable as the buildings themselves.   The record of the Rosenwald Fund, however, includes defalcations by Bura Hilbun, white administrator of Rosenwald and General Education Board funds in Mississippi.   The writer knows of three instances in two other states where old white schools have been transferred to Negroes, the Rosenwald payments being applied by the local school officials to a white school consolidation program.

The Slater, Peabody, and Jeanes Funds and the General Education Board may be justly accused of minimizing the need for higher education among Negroes at the time when the theory of industrial education made all educational experts frown upon the idea of a Negro college.   In more recent years, the policy of the foundations has changed, and the Negro college again receives philanthropic assistance. Like the error of the Peabody Fund trustees who believed that Southern states would give Negroes an equal distribution of public funds and for this reason advised Negroes to vote against the Civil Rights Bill in 1873, while confessing in 1885 that the National Government alone could give separate Negro systems equal expenditures, the faults of the foundations appear to have been caused more by an inability to understand the historical process than by a malign desire to corrupt Negroes for the sake of perpetuating a particu-

lar variety of social or economic ideas. Of the former failing, few have been guiltless. It cannot be denied that much
of the character, and almost all of the intelligence, of the
present-day Negro can be traced back to the friendly inter-
mediation of philanthropic persons of both races.

Summary

The consciences of private citizens in the North were
touched by the plight of the freedmen of the South. The
first education of the Negro was at the hands of the "New
England schoolmarms" whom this generous spirit sent to
and supported in the South.

Great foundations succeeded to the work of many individuals after a period in which the cause languished. These
foundations have synthesized work among Negroes, developed leadership within the race, and provided physically
and spiritually for the growth of opportunities for Negro
children. These opportunities would not have come from
any other source.

Where philanthropic societies have attempted to formu-
late definitive policies based on historic trends, their success
has been as varied as the direction of those trends. From
the first, however, philanthropic aid has enabled the genius
of Negro boys and girls to find fulfillment where the state
could not or would not assume responsibility.

CHAPTER VIII

The Perpetuation of Inequality

WE intend here to examine the nature of trends in educational finance for the two races in the last two decades. In this discussion, it will be necessary to remind ourselves constantly that statistics can be interpreted both absolutely and relatively. We can keep one eye on the rapidly mounting expenditures for Negro children and close the other eye to the relationship between the growth in expenditures for Negro and white children. But this attitude is both harmful and deceptive. Democratic equalization of opportunity in a changing world must mean the provision of equal facilities for all children at all times. If three times as much money is spent on the Negro child as was spent on his grandfather, all well and good; but we must ask, in no jealous or begrudging spirit, is this "progress" if five times as much money is spent on each white child as was spent on *his* grandfather? It would be small comfort for a modern worker to give him the tools of Abraham Lincoln's time if we justified ourselves by telling him how superior those tools were to the instruments used by workers in the times of William Penn or Benjamin Franklin. The modern worker is not obliged to compete with journeymen of the vintage of 1850, but with men and machines of 1933. The analogy with the education of Negroes is obvious. No matter how superior schools for Negro children are to those of a half-century ago in an absolute sense, if they have maintained their same relative inferiority over the period, the prospect is far from encouraging.

Long-Time Trends in Finance

It is difficult to follow records of expenditure in the Southern States by race, because of the many changes in record-keeping which have taken place, as well as the refusal of some states to publish strict accounts of expenditures by race.   It is possible to follow expenditures for single items in most of the states and for a larger number of items in the last decade, within which there has been a standardization of forms for reports on expenditures.   The States of North Carolina and Alabama, and the city of Nashville, Tennessee, have been depended upon here as a basis for determining basic trends.

Trends by states—expenditures for teachers' salaries. It has been shown above (in Chapter V) that there were only slight differences between expenditures per capita for white and black children in Alabama for teachers' salaries in the period before 1891.   State reports fail to yield any more information by race until 1907–1908.   Table IX shows the per capita expenditures on the basis of educables aged 6–20 for this one item from 1875 down to 1931–1932. The ratio between the two expenditures has been reduced to a comparable basis by holding the Negro expenditures constant at one dollar: for example, for every dollar spent on the Negro child for teachers' salaries in 1909–1910, $6.12 was spent on each white child.[1]

The historical factors held responsible for the changes in relationships have been discussed before.   We can recall here the fact that in 1891, in Alabama, the ratio of expenditures for teachers' salaries was $1.23 for every white child compared to $1 spent on every Negro child.   By 1907, this had changed to the vast difference represented by a ratio of $5.67 to $1.   This radical difference has been

---

[1] Files of state educational reports, giving in detail accounts of expenditures with school population, have been utilized in obtaining these data.

TABLE IX [2]

TRENDS IN PER CAPITA EXPENDITURES, SCHOOL POPULATION AGED 6–20,
FOR TEACHERS' SALARIES, BY RACE, IN ALABAMA

Year	Expenditures Per Capita		Ratio Between Expenditures	
	White	Negro	White	Negro
1875–1876	$1.30	$1.46	$0.89	$1.00
1876–1877	0.83	0.82	1.01	1.00
1877–1878	0.95	0.93	1.02	1.00
1878–1879	0.91	0.97	0.94	1.00
1879–1880	0.98	0.97	1.01	1.00
1880–1881	0.99	0.95	1.04	1.00
1881–1882	1.01	0.95	1.06	1.00
1882–1883	0.93	0.87	1.07	1.00
1883–1884	1.07	0.94	1.14	1.00
1884–1885	1.22	1.08	1.13	1.00
1885–1886	1.28	1.09	1.17	1.00
1886–1887	1.30	1.06	1.23	1.00
1887–1888	1.25	0.83	1.51	1.00
1888–1889	1.26	0.98	1.28	1.00
1889–1890	1.04	0.89	1.17	1.00
1890–1891	1.09	0.92	1.18	1.00
1891–1892	1.07	0.87	1.23	1.00

(Publication of expenditures by race discontinued; resumed, 1907.)

Year	White	Negro	White	Negro
1907–1908	5.05	0.89	5.67	1.00
1908–1909	5.61	0.93	6.03	1.00
1909–1910	6.19	1.01	6.12	1.00
1910–1911	6.42	1.10	5.83	1.00
1911–1912	6.39	1.14	5.60	1.00
1912–1913	6.77	1.20	5.64	1.00
1913–1914	6.84	1.17	5.84	1.00
1914–1915	7.04	1.17	6.01	1.00
1915–1916	7.06	1.24	5.69	1.00
1916–1917	7.08	1.18	6.00	1.00
1917–1918	8.10	1.50	5.40	1.00
1918–1919	8.97	1.50	6.10	1.00
1919–1920	9.83	1.52	6.46	1.00
1920–1921	14.10	2.48	5.35	1.00
1921–1922	14.74	2.84	5.19	1.00
1922–1923	16.07	3.13	5.13	1.00
1923–1924	15.76	3.04	5.18	1.00
1924–1925	15.91	3.22	4.94	1.00
1925–1926	16.27	3.35	4.85	1.00
1926–1927	17.64	3.46	5.09	1.00
1927–1928	18.80	4.07	4.61	1.00
1928–1929	19.78	4.50	4.39	1.00
1929–1930	19.93	4.77	4.17	1.00
1930–1931	19.66	4.80	4.09	1.00
1931–1932	17.93	4.43	4.04	1.00

[2] From Alabama *Biennial and Annual Reports of the Superintendent of Education.*

slightly reduced with the substantial reductions coming since
1920.   Compared with 1875, there was no marked advance
made in the education of Negroes until 1920.   By 1929–
1930, the ratio had been reduced to $4.17 from the peak of
$6.46 reached in 1919.   Relatively, Negro schools, as seen
in these figures, are more inferior today than they were at
any time between 1875 and 1891.   Absolutely, the expenditures for both races have increased tremendously, with the
greatest advance for Negroes coming in the period since
1920.

Similar data for North Carolina by yearly periods from
1871–1872 to 1932–1933 establish a marked similarity of
pattern.   In Alabama, the divergence in expenditures since
1891 has been far more marked than in North Carolina,
and, while the peak difference in the latter state was reached
in 1917–1918, the greatest excess of white expenditures
over Negro expenditures came in Alabama in 1919–1920.
There has been in both states since 1920 a tendency to equalize expenditures for the two races.   The year 1932–1933
showed the smallest difference for both states in twenty
years.   The "natural process" is plainly uncertain.   If we
go back to 1890 in Alabama, or to 1899 in North Carolina,
we see that there was a greater degree of relative equality
between the two races at those dates than there is now.   If
we project our curve into the future, we shall see that proceeding at the same rate of increase for both races, the expenditures for this one item will be equalized in Alabama
in from eighty to one hundred years, and in North Carolina
in from forty to sixty years.   This is, however, only if we
assume that the peak years represent the greatest difference
in expenditures, and that the ratio will steadily decline in
the future as it has declined in the last decade.   There is
no reason for making this assumption, however, aside from
believing that the processes which have brought about the
slight tendency to equalize—greater wealth, and a growing

TABLE X [3]

TRENDS IN PER CAPITA EXPENDITURES, SCHOOL POPULATION AGED 6–20,
FOR TEACHERS' SALARIES, BY RACE, IN NORTH CAROLINA,
1871–1872 TO 1932–1933

Year	Expenditures Per Capita		Ratio Between Expenditures	
	White	Negro	White	Negro
1871–1872	$0.41	$0.26	$1.57	$1.00
1872–1873	0.48	0.40	1.20	1.00
1873–1874	......	......	......	......
1874–1875	......	......	......	......
1875–1876	0.80	0.77	1.03	1.00
1876–1877	0.63	0.66	0.95	1.00
1877–1878	0.68	0.70	0.97	1.00
1878–1879	0.65	0.71	0.91	1.00
1879–1880	0.68	0.70	0.97	1.00
1880–1881	0.71	0.75	0.94	1.00
1881–1882	0.89	0.66	1.34	1.00
1882–1883	0.90	0.67	1.34	1.00
1883–1884	0.84	0.80	1.05	1.00
1884–1885	0.95	0.98	0.96	1.00
1885–1886	0.99	0.91	1.08	1.00
1886–1887	0.93	0.87	1.06	1.00
1887–1888	0.98	0.86	1.13	1.00
1888–1889	......	......	......	......
1889–1890	0.99	0.87	1.13	1.00
1890–1891	0.93	0.81	1.14	1.00
1891–1892	1.00	0.91	1.09	1.00
1892–1893	......	......	......	......
1893–1894	......	......	......	......
1894–1895	1.09	0.97	1.12	1.00
1895–1896	1.07	1.01	1.05	1.00
1896–1897	1.09	1.07	1.01	1.00
1897–1898	0.99	1.07	0.92	1.00
1898–1899	0.78	0.91	0.85	1.00
1899–1900	0.82	1.02	0.80	1.00
1900–1901	1.38	1.00	1.38	1.00
1901–1902	1.55	1.06	1.46	1.00
1902–1903	1.61	1.08	1.49	1.00
1903–1904	1.64	1.10	1.49	1.00
1904–1905	2.21	1.24	1.78	1.00
1905–1906	2.37	1.24	1.91	1.00
1906–1907	2.59	1.34	1.93	1.00
1907–1908	2.84	1.35	2.10	1.00
1908–1909	3.03	1.35	2.24	1.00

[3] From biennial and annual *Reports, North Carolina Superintendent of Public Instruction.*

TABLE X (Cont.)

Year	Expenditures Per Capita White	Negro	Ratio Between Expenditures White	Negro
1909–1910	$3.26	$1.38	$2.36	$1.00
1910–1911	3.40	1.39	2.44	1.00
1911–1912	3.84	1.40	2.74	1.00
1912–1913	4.53	1.55	2.92	1.00
1913–1914	5.15	1.91	2.69	1.00
1914–1915	5.54	1.88	2.94	1.00
1915–1916	5.81	2.01	2.89	1.00
1916–1917	6.12	2.04	3.00	1.00
1917–1918	6.53	2.12	3.08	1.00
1918–1919	7.27	2.51	2.89	1.00
1919–1920	11.67	4.33	2.69	1.00
1920–1921	16.00	5.60	2.85	1.00
1921–1922	18.15	6.70	2.70	1.00
1922–1923	19.55	7.10	2.74	1.00
1923–1924	20.85	7.61	2.73	1.00
1924–1925	22.04	8.18	2.69	1.00
1925–1926	22.94	8.56	2.67	1.00
1926–1927	23.25	8.88	2.61	1.00
1927–1928	23.37	9.23	2.53	1.00
1928–1929	24.91	10.40	2.39	1.00
1929–1930	23.28	10.06	2.31	1.00
1930–1931	24.06	10.45	2.30	1.00
1931–1932	20.24	9.40	2.15	1.00
1932–1933	19.40	9.24	2.09	1.00

spirit of fairness—will continue in full and even force.   But can we wait upon the "natural process"?

The city of Nashville, Tennessee, is presented as an exhibit of a typical Southern city system.   In this case, the figures available are for per capita expenditures for teachers' salaries on the basis of enrollment, school population figures not being available for each of the years traced, 1870 to 1932.   This population will tend to obscure differences of greater magnitude toward the first few years of the series, as a smaller percentage of Negro children than whites were enrolled in school during the first three decades.   Since 1890, however, the percentage of educables attending school has been similar for the two races, at least in the case of children in the lower age-brackets.

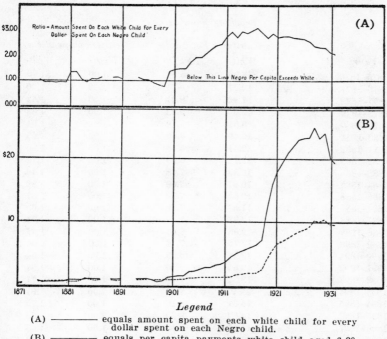

Legend

(A) ——————— equals amount spent on each white child for every
                    dollar spent on each Negro child.
(B) ——————— equals per capita payments white child aged 6–20.
       .... equals per capita payments Negro child aged 6–20.

Fig. 1.—Trends in per capita expenditures, school population aged
6–20, for teachers' salaries, by race, in North Carolina, 1871–1932.
(A) Ratio between white and Negro payments. (B) Actual per capita
payments for white and Negro children.

TABLE XI [4]

TRENDS IN PER CAPITA EXPENDITURES, ENROLLMENT, FOR TEACHERS'
SALARIES, BY RACE, NASHVILLE, TENNESSEE, 1870–1871 TO 1931–1932

Year	*Teachers' Salaries Expenditures Per Capita*		*Ratio Between Expenditures*	
	White	Negro	Negro	White
1870–1871	$11.83	$7.48	$1.00	$1.56
1871–1872	12.47	9.16	1.00	1.36
1872–1873	13.28	8.02	1.00	1.65
1873–1874	14.24	9.56	1.00	1.48
1874–1875	13.87	8.42	1.00	1.66

[4] *Annual Reports of the Schools of Nashville, Tennessee.*

TABLE XI (Cont.)

Teachers' Salaries

Year	Expenditures Per Capita		Ratio Between Expenditures	
	White	*Negro*	*Negro*	*White*
1875–1876	$13.93	$8.66	$1.00	$1.60
1876–1877	12.77	8.71	1.00	1.40
1877–1878	11.92	8.24	1.00	1.44
1878–1879	12.50	9.23	1.00	1.35
1879–1880	9.51	5.79	1.00	1.64
1880–1881	10.49	6.45	1.00	1.63
1881–1882	10.51	6.56	1.00	1.60
1882–1883	11.12	6.53	1.00	1.70
1883–1884	10.38	7.08	1.00	1.46
1884–1885	10.81	5.69	1.00	1.89
1885–1886	10.65	7.72	1.00	1.37
1886–1887	11.83	7.36	1.00	1.60
1887–1888	12.72	7.40	1.00	1.71
1888–1889	12.83	7.67	1.00	1.67
1889–1890	12.76	7.76	1.00	1.64
1890–1891	12.13	6.59	1.00	1.64
1891–1892	12.65	6.40	1.00	1.97
1892–1893	13.37	7.78	1.00	1.71
1893–1894	14.40	7.54	1.00	1.91
1894–1895	14.37	8.16	1.00	1.76
1895–1896	14.82	8.89	1.00	1.66
1896–1897	14.45	9.45	1.00	1.53
1897–1898	13.75	7.65	1.00	1.79
1898–1899	14.71	7.56	1.00	1.94
1899–1900	14.35	7.33	1.00	1.95
1900–1901	14.07	8.08	1.00	1.74
1901–1902	14.00	8.53	1.00	1.64
1902–1903	14.01	8.16	1.00	1.71
1903–1904	13.49	8.02	1.00	1.68
1904–1905	13.69	7.99	1.00	1.71
1905–1906	13.90	7.91	1.00	1.75
1906–1907	13.56	7.70	1.00	1.76
1907–1908	13.82	8.61	1.00	1.60
1908–1909	13.93	8.67	1.00	1.60
1909–1910	15.05	8.47	1.00	1.77
1910–1911	16.33	8.90	1.00	1.83
1911–1912	19.13	10.80	1.00	1.77
1912–1913	20.05	11.07	1.00	1.81
1913–1914	19.95	10.41	1.00	1.91
1914–1915	20.09	10.03	1.00	2.00
1915–1916	20.84	10.36	1.00	2.01
1916–1917	21.68	11.00	1.00	1.97
1917–1918	20.83	11.36	1.00	1.83
1918–1919	18.29	11.50	1.00	1.59
1919–1920	19.98	12.19	1.00	1.63

TABLE XI (Cont.)

Year	Teachers' Salaries Expenditures Per Capita		Ratio Between Expenditures	
	White	Negro	Negro	White
1920–1921	$23.15	$13.59	$1.00	$1.70
1921–1922	23.14	13.21	1.00	1.75
1922–1923	23.83	13.43	1.00	1.77
1923–1924	23.21	13.53	1.00	1.71
1924–1925	20.90	13.15	1.00	1.58
1925–1926	22.28	14.60	1.00	1.52
1926–1927	22.19	14.13	1.00	1.57
1927–1928	22.99	15.40	1.00	1.49
1928–1929	23.93	15.94	1.00	1.50
1929–1930	25.17	16.84	1.00	1.49
1930–1931	27.86	17.68	1.00	1.58
1931–1932	27.55	17.25	1.00	1.59

TABLE XII[5]

TRENDS IN PER CAPITA EXPENDITURES, SCHOOL POPULATION AGED 6–20, FOR TEACHERS' SALARIES, BY RACE, IN FOUR ALABAMA COUNTIES

Expenditures for White Children Compared to Dollar Spent on Negroes

Year	Negro Child	White Child			
		Walker	Mobile	Jefferson	Lowndes
1908–1909	$1.00	$2.81	$7.21	$3.53	$16.84
1909–1910	1.00	2.18	5.55	6.53	23.92
1910–1911	1.00	2.48	4.38	5.27	29.39
1911–1912	1.00	1.34	5.83	4.15	30.37
1912–1913	1.00	1.95	4.35	5.38	33.40
1913–1914	1.00	1.92	4.54	5.32	25.16
1914–1915	1.00	1.67	4.30	5.17	23.95
1915–1916	1.00	1.39	4.34	4.86	30.08
1916–1917	1.00	1.02	4.54	4.54	22.91
1917–1918	1.00	1.26	4.31	4.25	26.84
1918–1919	1.00	0.93	3.56	4.84	26.01
1919–1920	1.00	0.93	3.19	3.88	28.08
1920–1921	1.00	0.84	2.82	4.35	33.22
1921–1922	1.00	1.13	3.19	3.49	26.27
1922–1923	1.00	1.34	3.22	3.09	27.57
1923–1924	1.00	1.37	3.16	3.37	32.44
1924–1925	1.00	1.32	3.15	3.25	33.14
1925–1926	1.00	1.35	3.10	3.17	29.50
1926–1927	1.00	1.52	2.64	3.45	29.65
1927–1928	1.00	1.44	2.61	3.15	28.99
1928–1929	1.00	1.35	2.67	3.02	26.75
1929–1930	1.00	1.52	2.57	3.00	25.26

[5] *Alabama State Reports, Department of Education.*

Specific counties. For purposes of comparison, we have selected four Alabama counties which in many ways are typical of the state. Jefferson County is an industrial area in which is located the city of Birmingham as well as numerous smaller industrial communities. Lowndes County is in many ways typical of the "black" counties, heavily populated by Negroes with a small white land-owning class. Mobile County represents a unified county-city system. Walker County is a semi-industrial county with a small Negro population.

The percentage of Negroes in the total school population of Jefferson County was 44.1 in 1910 and declined steadily to 36.6 in 1930. The percentage of Negroes in Lowndes County was 90.0 in 1910, and increased slightly to 91.2 in 1930. Negroes were 45.5 per cent of the population of Mobile County in 1910, but this proportion had declined to 33.6 per cent in 1930. Negroes were 13 per cent of the population of Walker County in 1910, but only 9.7 per cent in 1930.

At its peak, discrimination in Jefferson County resulted in $6.53 being spent on each white child, while $1 was being spent on each Negro child; in Lowndes County, the peak difference was in 1912, when for every dollar spent on a Negro child, $33.40 was spent on each white child; in Mobile County, $7.21 represented the greatest margin, in 1908; and in Walker County, in which for several years more money was spent on Negro than on white children, the greatest advantage for the white children was in 1908, when $2.81 was spent for each white child compared to $1 spent on every Negro child. The two semi-urban counties, Mobile and Jefferson, appear to show constant tendencies toward an equalization of expenditures for teachers' salaries over a long period of time. The fluctuations in Lowndes and Walker Counties could not well be given this interpretation. The addition of ten cents per capita to the yearly

budget for the Negro child in Lowndes County would explain these differences, so trivial is the initial amount spent
on Negro children.   The tendency to spend equal or even
greater amounts on Negro as compared to white children
in Walker County can be explained on several grounds:
(*a*) an impartial superintendent for a period of years

TABLE XIII [6]

TRENDS IN PER CAPITA EXPENDITURES, SCHOOL POPULATION AGED 6–20, FOR
TEACHERS' SALARIES, BY RACE, IN THE COUNTIES OF NORTH CAROLINA
ARRANGED ACCORDING TO THE PERCENTAGE NEGROES ARE
IN THE POPULATION

Ratio of Expenditures for White Child When Expenditure for Negro Child
Is Held Constant at $1

| | | In North Carolina Counties Where Negro Population Equals the Following Per Cent of the Total | | | |
Year	Negro Per Capita Payment	0–9.9%	10–24.9%	25–49.9%	Above 50%
1906–1907	$1.00	$0.95	$1.34	$2.18	$2.27
1907–1908	1.00	1.14	1.28	2.32	2.55
1908–1909	1.00	1.05	1.35	2.41	2.70
1909–1910	1.00	0.94	1.53	2.48	2.62
1910–1911	1.00	1.11	1.52	2.48	3.13
1911–1912	1.00	1.28	1.80	2.69	3.85
1912–1913	1.00	1.35	2.07	3.13	4.66
1913–1914	1.00	1.41	2.25	2.78	4.28
1914–1915	1.00	1.35	2.44	3.22	4.44
1915–1916	1.00	1.41	2.28	3.16	4.30
1916–1917	1.00	1.53	2.12	3.49	4.79
1917–1918	1.00	1.53	2.22	3.62	5.05
1918–1919	1.00	1.50	2.28	3.50	4.20
1919–1920	1.00	1.39	1.97	2.96	4.21
1920–1921	1.00	1.32	1.94	3.01	3.99
1921–1922	1.00	1.42	2.01	2.86	4.27
1922–1923	1.00	1.49	2.02	2.92	3.61
1923–1924	1.00	1.51	2.19	2.94	4.33
1924–1925	1.00	1.46	2.02	2.87	3.95
1925–1926	1.00	1.47	2.26	2.87	3.83
1926–1927	1.00	1.35	2.21	2.76	3.59
1927–1928	1.00	1.56	2.59	2.70	3.44
1928–1929	1.00	1.38	2.17	2.58	3.61
1929–1930	1.00	1.37	2.15	2.46	3.23

[6] *North Carolina School Reports.*

exercised as great a care for his Negro as for his white schools; (*b*) the small percentage of Negroes in the population has made discrimination a matter of no great advantage for the white children; (*c*) Walker County included during the period of equal expenditures a large number of coal-mining camps, in which the Negroes were principally employed. They took "cuts" from their weekly pay-checks which went to subsidize their schools and increase local and county funds for Negro schools.

A study of all of the counties in North Carolina from 1906–1907 to 1929–1930, in which these counties are divided into groups on the basis of the percentage of Negroes in the population, reflects interesting tendencies in expenditures, besides showing the likelihood that Negro children in counties in which there is a minority Negro population will receive a fairer proportion of the available funds than in counties where they constitute a majority.

Table XIII may be read: in 1906–1907, in counties where 50 per cent or more of the population was Negro, the ratio of expenditures was $1 for every Negro child to $2.27 for each white child; in counties with a Negro population from 25 to 49.9 per cent, this ratio was $1 to $2.18; in counties with a Negro population from 10 to 24.9 per cent, the ratio was $1 to $1.34; in counties with a Negro population below 10 per cent of the total population, the ratio was $1 to $0.95.

In general, it is seen that counties with a heavier Negro population reached a peak difference in expenditures between 1915 and 1920. Since then, there has been a consistent tendency for this expenditure to be equalized, although the general average shows that at the present time, expenditures for white children exceed those for Negroes two- and three-fold. The counties with a small Negro population show a less encouraging tendency toward equalization, although they have never shown the degree of

discrimination exhibited in the counties heavily populated
by Negroes.

The Effect of New Services Upon Expenditures for Negroes

So far, we have considered the simple index of teachers'
salaries as a basis for computing the trends in financing
schools for the two races.   In the instances studied, it appears that there has been a slight tendency for expenditures
for this item to be equalized within the last decade.   A more
important question is raised by a comparison of other items
of the school budget.   Has there been in expenditures for
buildings, equipment, and such new services as transportation a correspondingly definite tendency for educational
equalization?

An inspection of the itemized list of expenditures for the
State of North Carolina would indicate that the slight
tendency of teachers' salaries to be equalized is illusory.
Reducing all expenditures to the basis of 100.000 per cent
in 1909–1910, for the rural districts, 68.910 per cent of
all expenditures were specifically listed as for white children,
13.007 per cent for Negro children, and 18.083 per cent
unspecified as to the race upon which the expenditure was
made.   It is fair to assume that the "unspecified" expenditures, including General Control, Maintenance, Operation,
and Fixed Charges, Capital Outlay and Debt Service, were
principally for white children.   By 1929–1930, practically
all expenditures, with the exception of debt charges, were
listed by race.   The item of "General Control," including
expenditures for superintendents, and so forth, was in the
latter year prorated according to school population, and
therefore gives a much larger consideration theoretically to
the Negro children than would be represented by the actual
benefit which they received from these services.   Altogether,

in 1929–1930, Negro rural children received only 9.950 per cent of the school expenditures specified by race, while white children received 70.133 per cent of all specified expenditures. The "unspecified" expenditures in 1929–1930 were overwhelmingly chargeable to debt service, which in turn can be said to represent service upon prior capital outlays for white children in the ratio of about 90 per cent to 10 per cent incurred for capital outlay for Negro children.

During this period, the Negroes in the rural-school population decreased only from 31.2 per cent to 30.5 per cent of the total. It is plain that the slight tendency to equalize teachers' salaries has been overmatched by the expenditure in white schools of new funds, which might have been made available for the equalization of the education of Negro children, for new types of facilities demanding large expenditures.

Chief of the rivals for the Negro children's equal opportunity appears to be the building of rural schoolhouses for white children that are adequate and magnificent beyond the point of adequacy. Negro children, despite the work of the Rosenwald Fund, have not shared in this new avenue for expending school funds in any degree in the manner in which they have shared in expenditures for teachers' salaries. In 1924–1925, for example, $6,667,797 was spent on new buildings and sites for rural North Carolina white children, compared to $444,285 for the same purpose for rural Negro children. Per capita expenditures for teachers' salaries were proportionately three and one-quarter times as large for white children as for Negro children, but building expenditures were almost seven times as large for whites as for Negroes. In servicing a debt incurred largely through building schoolhouses for white children, rural North Carolina spent in 1924–1925 $6,875,870, a sum more than four times as large as the expenditures in the same

year for teachers' salaries for the thirty per cent of the
school population which was made up of Negroes.

Another item for expenditure, increasingly large in the
last few years, is that of transportation. In 1929–1930,
rural North Carolina spent $2,181,130 in transporting
172,286 white children to school, but almost two hundred
thousand dollars less for the salaries of teachers for 190,817
Negro children enrolled in North Carolina rural schools in
this year. Indeed, in 1929–1930, North Carolina spent
more money for school trucks for white children—$325,290
—than it did for new schools for Negro children—$209,911.
On repairs to furniture, apparatus, equipment, heating,
lighting, and plumbing, the white rural schools of North
Carolina spent in 1929–1930 several thousand more dollars
than was spent for all new buildings and sites for Negro
children.

North Carolina has not been taken here as a "horrible
example"; in fact, it presents probably the best present
situation in all of the Southern states with reference to the
"progress" of the Negro schools and the "equity" with
which school funds are expended. The figures here cited
simply show that new services mean that the Negro children
will receive a continuingly smaller proportion of the public-
school funds until these new services have been distributed
almost universally among the white schools. Not until
transportation places the school at the door of every white
child; not until a magnificent rural school greets the white
child when he steps from his bus; not until supplies and
equipment for the white school reach a level fairly comparable with existing situations in other counties and states, can
the Negro child expect to receive any consideration. In the
natural process of things, that time will never come; there
will never be a day, under our present dispensation, when
the schools of any locality will be satisfied to stop growing.
So long as the salary of the Negro teacher must compete

with demands for a better system of transportation of white
children, so long as new buildings for Negro children must
be weighed in the budget along with demands for new labora-
tories and gymnasiums for white children, so long may we
look forward to a continuation of the present inequalities.

The mad rush to equip every small school district with
school buildings for white children "as good as city children
have" has placed a fatal obstacle in the way of providing
adequate housing for Negro children, in spite of the best
efforts of philanthropic agencies. The assumption of the
load of local bonded indebtedness by a more centralized authority and the provision of a State Aid Building Fund
must precede any hopeful solution of the problem. School
buildings for Negro children in practically all rural areas,
and in most of the smaller cities, have been constructed by
funds furnished by the Rosenwald Fund, by individual contributions of white and Negro citizens, and by appropriations from local boards. These latter appropriations have
come from current funds, and have naturally limited the
amount of money which would be spent for teachers' salaries and other current expenses. It is for this reason that
debt service charges are not in any degree traceable to
schools for Negro children, and the point is also raised here
as to the wisdom of continuing a system of school construction which must feed upon interests as fundamental to the
operation of a school as the building itself. Mounting interest charges in both rural and urban communities, together
with the development of those new services, such as transportation, which are clearly without limit as to their future
expansion, clearly take away the margin which might have
been used for the equalization of expenditures for Negro
children.

The urban systems have not been forced to adopt transportation as a very important item in their budgets. However, a parallel with the rural schools is observable here:

special teachers, technical schools, capital outlay, and debt service successfully combine to raise a barrier to the more equable participation of the Negro child in the benefits of a public-school education. Without a greater degree of wise planning, without active centralization of authority in making expenditures for various purposes, there can be no hope that the Negro school will at any time in the near future even begin to achieve a greater measure of educational equality than that enjoyed for the last several decades, which is to say a bare pittance.

The Effect of the Depression on Schools for Negroes

Because of its unprecedented duration, the present depression beginning in 1929 is probably the first on record to result in definite curtailment of educational programs. A study of payments in the States of Alabama and North Carolina and in the city of Nashville, Tennessee, shows no decrease in expenditures during or immediately after the crucial "panic" years of 1893 and 1907.

Educational budgets in the South appear to have reached their peak level so far as construction was concerned in the years from 1925 to 1928. The size and salaries of the teaching staff did not begin to suffer until 1929–1930. Since that time, constructional activities have almost entirely stopped, and the teaching staff has undergone a rapid curtailment. The decline in educational expenditures has been progressive, with the severest effects coming in 1932–1933.

The State of Arkansas may be taken as an example of the effect our most recent decline in the business cycle has had upon schools. With numerous bank failures, short crops, low prices for farm commodities, and decrease in assessments and tax collections, no Southern state has suffered more than Arkansas. The comparative effects of the depression upon white and Negro schools in the state are outlined below:

Enrollment. The white enrollment in Arkansas elementary schools decreased from 286,651 in 1929–1930, to 286,328 in 1930–1931, and, more perceptibly, to 278,174 in 1931–1932. It is probable that this decrease is due more to the declining numbers of younger children in the state than to the effects of the depression. The Negro elementary enrollment increased from 101,805 in 1929–1930 to 105,174 in 1930–1931. There was a slight decrease of exactly 500 pupils enrolled from 1930–1931 to 1931–1932.[7]

White high-school pupils grew from 62,075 in 1929–1930 to 71,163 in 1930–1931, or 14.6 per cent. The Negro high-school enrollment increased from 3,829 in 1929–1930 to 4,944 in 1930–1931, or 29.1 per cent. For the next year, the high-school enrollment for both races remained practically stationary.

Teachers and teachers' salaries. The number of white elementary teachers dropped from 7,868 in 1929–1930 to 7,165 in 1931–1932. The number of Negro elementary teachers was cut from 2,244 in 1929–1930 to 2,112 in 1931–1932. White high-school teachers increased from 2,423 in 1929–1930 to 2,689 in 1930–1931. There was a decrease, however, in 1931–1932 to 2,548. Negro high-school teachers dropped steadily from 238 in 1929–1930 to 175 in 1931–1932.

The median salaries of white elementary-school teachers decreased 15.8 per cent in the year from 1930–1931 to 1931–1932, while the median salary for Negro elementary teachers fell 21.4 per cent. White high-school teachers had a median salary decrease of 11.3 per cent compared with 9.4 per cent for Negroes.

---

[7] These data are from a mimeographed pamphlet, "Summary Tables of a Survey of the Public Schools of Arkansas," authorized by the State Board of Education, March 12, 1932.

Negro share of all expenditures. Educational monies were spent as follows in Arkansas during the two years from 1930 to 1932:

	1930–1931 Amount	Per Cent	1931–1932 Amount	Per Cent
State Administration	$ 120,538	.8	$ 95,330	.76
County Administration	366,066	2.5	345,587	2.77
Local Administration	362,739	2.5	382,098	3.06
Payment on Bonds, Principal, and Int.	1,860,210	12.8	2,022,842	16.24
White Elem. Schools	6,655,077	46.1	5,486,847	44.05
White High Schools	3,861,322	26.7	3,080,291	24.73
Negro Elementary Schools	1,014,143	7.0	834,520	6.70
Negro High Schools	194,481	1.3	207,098	1.66

It appears, therefore, that Negro schools generally have not decreased their percentage of expenditures for the entire state during this period of depression. In 1930–1931, Negro children, who were 25.5 per cent of the school population, received 10.2 per cent of the money spent for schools excluding administration, general control, and debt service. Most of these expenditures, in addition, are directly chargeable to white rather than to Negro schools.

In 1931–1932, Negro children, with the same proportion in the school population, received 10.7 per cent of the money spent exclusive of general control, administration, and debt service.

These percentages, however, do not reveal the fact that the cuts in expenditures for Negro schools strike at a far more vital spot than equal and proportionate cuts for white school systems. The small payments for Negro schools are now principally devoted to the salaries of teachers. In Arkansas in 1930–1931, 86.3 per cent of the payments for Negro schools, as compared to 78.9 per cent of white payments, went to the payment of teachers. Retrenchment in the white schools can economize on transportation, building construction, maintenance, and many of the auxiliaries which have latterly been called "fads and frills." Because of the disproportionate amounts spent on Negro salaries as compared to other basic needs, school boards can cut only into the bone of the Negro teaching staff in effecting economies. White schools can be curtailed from ten to thirty per cent without reaching the foundation of instruction. The slightest decrease in payments for Negroes at once takes away from that essential figure in the schoolroom, the teacher.

It has been so throughout the South. School boards have instituted horizontal cuts of 10, 15, and even 55 per cent, affecting both white and Negro schools, and set forth confidently to the world that they are performing perfect justice. But the cut which might be met in the white school by a curtailment of extra-curricular activities must come in the shortening of terms, the discharge of teachers, or the closing of schools, where Negroes are concerned.

Summary

Whatever tendency to equalize expenditures for the two races is observable has been hopelessly delayed by the appearance of new educational services which have invited vast expenditures for the standardization of schools for white children. In the older types of expenditures, such as instructional services, it appears that there is some tendency to equalize expenditures for the two races. However, this trend is nullified by the development of such new avenues of educational expenditure as are represented by transportation, modern and super-modern school buildings, elaborate equipments, and auxiliaries of all sorts.

The extent of the encroachments of these new services upon the possibility of equalizing educational opportunity for Negro and white children is shown by the fact that while per capita expenditures for teachers' salaries in rural North Carolina in 1929–1930 for the white children exceeded pay-

ments for Negroes in the ratio of 3 to 1, the expenditures
for transportation for white children exceeded those for
Negro children by a ratio of more than 30 to 1.   The
rivalry between communities and states is such that there
cannot be much hope for alleviation of this situation aside
from drastic changes in the methods of providing for the
schools for Negro children, because new educational services
will always challenge communities to spend money for the
benefit of their children.   The result of two decades of competition between equalization for all children and new services has been that Negro children do now receive a smaller
proportion of the public funds in the Southern States than
they have at any time in past history.

CHAPTER IX

Literacy—The Leaven of Progress

IN the preceding chapters, an attempt has been made to consider the historical forces which have affected institutionalized efforts to educate Negroes. Save as influenced by economic trends which change the shading but not the sketchy outlines of the portrait, the pattern shows a consistency since the beginning of the present century which needs no new interpretation. The Negro in the South is a minority group, a distinct and inferior caste in many respects; and his education at public expense has undergone the vicissitudes which are the fate of any such politically and economically helpless fragment in any great population. Even more, the education of Negroes has been influenced by contrasting forces exerted by economic classes which have in the past stratified the dominant racial group.

This is not to say that the situation is exactly where it was thirty years ago. It would be difficult to show, relatively, that the educational status of the Negro has changed. But there have been absolute changes of profound significance. The remaining portion of this book will be devoted to an analysis of fundamental problems through which an understanding of the present situation may be reached. In this chapter, the index of literacy is taken to summarize the advance which has come from direct educational efforts, in a period extending from the ante-bellum period to the present.

So profound a student of the reality of ante-bellum life in the South as Francis Pendleton Gaines states that "the denial of educational opportunity to blacks" is a fact that "cannot be denied." [1] Chancellor Harper, of South Carolina, defended the existence of the laws which penalized the formal education of Negroes. In a speech in the Senate shortly before his resignation from that body, Jefferson Davis described the attitude of the South toward the education of Negro slaves, and his arguments may be considered authoritative:

> . . . When Cain, for the commission of the first great crime, was driven from the face of Adam, no longer the fit associate of those who were created to exercise dominion over the earth, he found in the land of Nod those to whom his crime had degraded him to an equality; and when the low and vulgar son of Noah, who laughed at his Father's exposure, sank by debasing himself and his lineage by a connection with an inferior race of men, he doomed his descendants to perpetual slavery. Noah spoke the decree, or prophecy, as gentlemen may choose to consider it, one or the other. [2]

In the foregoing paragraph, Senator Davis established the incapacity of the Negro to learn. His argument was current in the South at that time. That it was Biblical is typical of the times. At another period, the foundation for the argument would probably have been physiological, or rested upon the theory of intelligence tests.

Mr. Davis continued by saying that no one in the South would object to teaching Negroes ". . . if there were no incendiary publications to be put in their hands." He referred here to the great fear of slave insurrections that grew in the South after the uprising in Virginia led by Nat Turner. It was said at the time that Turner had been provoked to revolt against the established order by reading anti-

---

[1] Francis Pendleton Gaines, *The Southern Plantation*, Columbia University Press, New York, 1925, p. 235.

[2] *Remarks of the Honorable Jefferson Davis, Senator from Mississippi*, on the bill for the benefit of the schools in the District of Columbia, *Congressional Globe*, April 12, 1860.

slavery tracts published in the North. Southern people, said Mr. Davis, did not object to Negroes' reading the Bible: ". . . there is no apprehension of negroes who thus spell out the Bible being rendered worse to the master, and I know of no one who has any fear of their reading the holy truths of that sacred book." [3]   Among the more popular of the "holy truths" insisted upon by slave owners was the advice by the Apostle Paul to the slaves of his time: "Servants, obey your masters!" in his excellent study of *Philanthropy in Negro Education*,[4] Dr. U. W. Leavell has shown that Southern churches spent hundreds of thousands of dollars in sending missionaries to preach to Negro slaves. Gaines says, "It is likely that every master who was devoutly pious wanted his slaves to receive the benefit; and it is certain that many more worldly-minded masters offered religious training for its good effect on slave order." [5]   Bishop McTyeire, of the Southern Methodist Church, in a little book on the *Duties of Christian Masters*, stated that while he believed the laws against teaching Negroes to read and write were more severe than necessary, slavery as an institution had preceded books and schools, and good citizens should refrain from violating the law which prohibited the instruction of Negroes.

The messages of religious ministers, intended as they were to make the slaves more contented with their lot, and to make them more serviceable to their masters as producers, may be regarded as education of a sort, though hardly in the sense in which moderns would define the process under a free system. Senator Iverson, of Georgia, in the same debate in which the remarks of Jefferson Davis were made, even went so far as to say,

---

[3] *Ibid.*
[4] Pp. 1–56.
[5] Gaines, *The Southern Plantation*, p. 235.

There is no law in any Southern state, so far as I know, that prohibits the education of black children. Even the slaves in the State of Georgia are educated to that extent. They are not permitted to be taught to write, because that would be dangerous, certainly; for they might then carry on a correspondence, and combine; but they are permitted to be taught to read, and they go to our Sunday Schools.[6]

At that time, Georgia had on its statute books three laws forbidding Negroes an education: a law of 1770 prohibited teaching Negro slaves in the subjects of reading and writing, and imposed a fine of twenty pounds sterling for violation; another law of 1829 provided either a fine or whipping for teaching slaves to read or write; and still another law, of 1853, repeated the provisions of the prior laws. Savannah in 1818 enacted a city ordinance imposing a fine of thirty dollars for each such offense, with imprisonment for ten days and a whipping of not less than thirty-nine lashes.[7]

The Code of Virginia in 1849 stated that every assemblage of Negroes for the purpose of instruction in reading or writing "shall be an unlawful assembly." The punishment for violation of this ordinance was, for a Negro, whipping; for a white person, a jail sentence and a fine of five hundred dollars. In North Carolina, the teacher of slaves was liable to fine and imprisonment, if white, and to fine, imprisonment, and whipping, if Negro. The slave being instructed was also liable to not less than thirty-nine lashes.[8]

South Carolina had the first law on the subject; it was passed in 1740. This act was strengthened in 1800 and again in 1834. "Assemblies of slaves, free negroes, mulattoes, and mestizos, met together for the purpose of mental instruction in a confined or secret place" were prohibited,

---

[6] *Congressional Globe*, April 12, 1860.

[7] Speech of Henry Wilson, Senator from Massachusetts, in the Senate, as reported in *Congressional Globe*, April 12, 1860. Wilson cited Stroud, "Sketch of Laws Relating to Slavery."

[8] *Ibid.*

with fines, imprisonment, and whipping decreed as the punishment. Louisiana and Alabama had similar laws.[9]

It is clear that these laws were intended to keep the social order in a state of rest. Jefferson Davis reflected clearly the attitude of the ante-bellum period toward the education of Negroes when he said that there was no objection to teaching them anything that did not come in conflict with the cherished institution of the Old South. If cynics are correct in believing that the entire school system generally has been intended to bolster up the existing social order, the attitude of the South toward the education of Negroes was only more self-conscious in its aims.

To read the ferocious laws which appeared on the statute books, one might believe that Negroes were wholly without formal education in the South prior to the Civil War. The laws or the general sentiment which evoked them were tremendously effective so far as the masses of Negroes were concerned, for the census of 1870 showed that 81.4 per cent of the Negroes were illiterate, despite the number who had been taught in the schools in the first few years of freedom. There were rare exceptions, which probably have survived because of their rarity. Bishop Turner, of the African Methodist Church, was taught his alphabet by an otherwise cruel master,[10] and Nat Turner was taught how to read by his master.[11] The unhappy result of the latter educational experiment did more to strengthen the laws against the education of Negroes than anything else. Frederick Douglass "stole" a knowledge of the fundamentals, and was afterward aided by a member of his master's family in perfecting that knowledge.[12]

---

[9] *Ibid.*

[10] Simmons, *Men of Mark*, pp. 805 *ff.*

[11] William S. Drewry, *Slave Insurrections in Virginia*, Neale Co., Washington, 1900, p. 36.

[12] Frederick Douglass, *Life and Times of Frederick Douglass, Written by Himself*, DeWolfe, Fiske and Co., Boston, 1892.

In cities where free Negroes developed little islands of some wealth and culture, schools were maintained openly or "bootlegged." The Honorable J. C. Napier, formerly Registrar of the United States Treasury, tells of attending a school in Nashville for free Negro children before the Civil War. One morning, the children came to the school building to find it padlocked, with a policeman stationed at the door to inform them that the school was closed for good. Mr. Napier, in his further career, illustrates the manner in which a number of other free Negro children were educated. He was sent to Cincinnati, which became a center where well-to-do parents in the South sent their children to be educated free of restraint.

Many free Negroes in Charleston and New Orleans sent their children to Europe. In the latter city, a small group of Negro Creoles, possessed of exceptional talent and well educated, formed a literary *salon*, which they called the "Cordon Bleu." They published a volume of verse in French and produced from their number several men who attained distinction in literary circles in Paris.[13]

Perhaps the strangest commentary upon the education of Negroes in the ante-bellum South is to be found in the census figures for 1850. In spite of the fact that the laws of every Southern state proscribed the education of slaves, and that in several of these states the prohibition extended to free Negro children, Mississippi was the only state reporting no Negroes attending school in that year.

Considering the states with the largest population of free Negroes in 1850, the data with regard to illiteracy in those above 20 years of age will be found to correlate closely with the data given regarding school attendance.

The illiteracy of Negroes before the Civil War in certain Eastern states is shown to be less than that of the white

---

[13] Edward Laroque Tinker, "Les Cenelles—Afro-French Poetry in Louisiana," *The Colophon*, September, 1930.

TABLE XIV [14]

ILLITERACY AMONG WHITE AND FREE COLORED POPULATIONS AGED
TWENTY AND ABOVE, 1850

	Free States			Slave States	
	Per Cent of Illiteracy			*Per Cent of Illiteracy*	
State	*White*	*Free Colored*	*State*	*White*	*Free Colored*
Massachusetts	4.8	14.9	Delaware	13.2	69.5
Rhode Island	4.0	11.9	Maryland	9.9	56.6
Connecticut	2.2	12.8	D. C.	7.4	60.9
New York	5.6	26.3	Virginia	18.6	45.0
New Jersey	6.0	33.3	N. Carolina	29.2	56.9
Pennsylvania	5.0	36.9	S. Carolina	12.5	21.4
Illinois	....	46.2	Georgia	18.9	33.5
Indiana	17.1	45.0	Florida	18.1	57.8
Ohio	6.8	41.9	Alabama	18.9	20.7
			Mississippi	10.8	27.8
			Louisiana	15.8	37.4
			Arkansas	25.9	37.4
			Tennessee	24.5	37.6
			Kentucky	20.0	55.1
			Missouri	14.1	31.0

TABLE XV [15]

POPULATION, ILLITERACY, AND SCHOOL ENROLLMENT, 1850–1930

Year	Population Over 10	School Population* Aged 5–20	Percentage* Children 5–20 in School	Number Illiterate	Per Cent of Illiteracy
1850	....	1,426,716	1.9	....	......
1860	....	1,741,046	1.9	....	.....
1870	3,428,757	1,825,692	9.9	2,789,689	81.4
1880	4,601,207	2,531,661	33.8	3,220,878	70.0
1890	5,328,972	2,998,313	32.9	3,042,668	57.1
1900	6,415,581	3,499,187	31.0	2,853,194	44.5
1910	7,317,922	3,577,860	44.7	2,227,731	30.4
1920	8,053,225	3,796,957	53.4	1,842,161	22.9
1930	9,292,556	4,128,998	60.0	1,513,892	16.3

* To 1900, school population data are for the age-group 5–19; school enrollment, for all attending school.

[14] From various tables in *United States Census Report for 1850*.

[15] Bulletins of the *United States Census, 1930*, on *Illiteracy* and *School Attendance*.

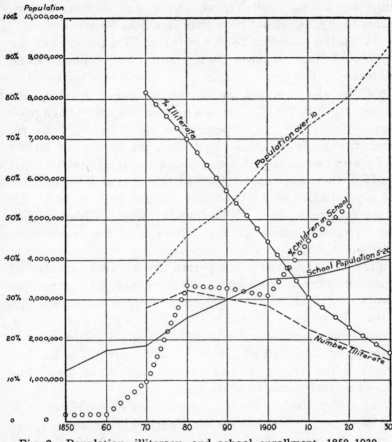

Fig. 2.—Population, illiteracy, and school enrollment, 1850–1930.

population of several Southern states. The general illiteracy of the Negro free population was slightly in excess of 50 per cent at the time of emancipation. Free Negroes then numbered approximately 500,000, or one-eighth of all those in the country. It is hardly probable that there was among the enslaved Negro population anywhere more than one out of a hundred who could read or write. The rate of illiteracy among adult Negroes at the time of emancipation, accordingly, could not have been less than 93 per cent.

When the census of 1870 was taken, 81.4 per cent of the 3,428,757 Negroes above the age of ten were reported to be illiterate. The gross number of illiterates had increased in 1880, by almost a half million, to the largest number ever reported, or 3,220,878 out of a population above the age of ten of 4,601,207. The percentage of illiteracy, however, decreased to 70.0. Since that time, the number of Negro illiterates has decreased both relatively and absolutely, until in 1930 there were only 1,513,892 reported as illiterates out of a population of 9,292,556, or a percentage of 16.3. In sixty-five years since emancipation, Negro illiteracy has been reduced from more than nine out of ten to less than two out of ten.

The actual decline in the percentage of Negro scholastics enrolled between 1880 and 1900 is regarded by some students as a fault of the child accounting in the census figures. It is more probable that these figures accurately reflect the stagnation of schools for Negroes in this period, previously described as one in which opportunities for Negro children were severely curtailed in order to give additional opportunities to white children.

By states, the heaviest concentration of Negro illiteracy is in those areas where schools for Negro children are farthest below American standards. A comparison of illiteracy data for 1920 with those for 1930 indicates that Negro illiteracy was reduced substantially within the decade in every state, excepting only Wisconsin. The slight increase in illiteracy in that state is easily explainable on the basis of an influx of illiterate Negroes from the South. Louisiana reduced the illiteracy of its Negro population to a greater degree than any other state, from 48.4 to 38.5 per cent. This substantial decrease is directly traceable to the vigorous efforts instituted by officials in the state coöperating with the Julius Rosenwald Fund to wipe out adult illiteracy by extension classes which have reached into the most remote sections.

The time when illiteracy may most effectively be reached, however, is in the period of school attendance. Appropriations for adult illiteracy work in several Southern states recently operated on a program which set aside $6 for teaching each white and $3 for teaching each Negro illiterate how to read and write. In thousands of cases, it was possible to teach adults long unaccustomed to habits of concentration these simple fundamentals through a course of lessons extending over a few weeks. The expenditure for this purpose doubled the per capita expenditure for teachers' salaries for regular school children, in many instances.

The greatest amount of illiteracy is concentrated in the upper age brackets. For the entire country, the age-group of those 65 years old and over constitutes but 4.01 per cent of the Negro population, and yet has 13.70 per cent of the Negro illiterates. On the other end of the age distribution, children 10–14 years old are 13.46 per cent of the population, and have only 4.37 per cent of the illiterates.

These data are given in more detail in Table XVI, wherewith is shown the percentage of illiteracy in each population group. It is plain that the illiterates of the older generation are a product of inferior schools. The discouraging feature of the situation is that 8.9 per cent of the age-group 15–19 years is illiterate. These children have not been reached by a school system within the last ten years, and their presence indicates that it will be a long process before illiteracy is entirely eliminated from among the Negro group.

It is significant that the general Negro population in 1890 showed an illiteracy rate of 57.1 per cent, approximately equal to that shown by the 65-and-over age-group in 1930. The *Census Report* states, "In general, the il-

TABLE XVI [16]

ILLITERACY DATA BY AGE-GROUPS FOR THE NEGRO POPULATION IN
THE UNITED STATES, 1930

Age-Group	Percentage in the Population	Percentage of all Illiterates Included in This Specific Age-Group	Percentage of Illiteracy within This Specific Age-Group
10–14	13.46	4.37	5.3
15–19	13.45	7.33	8.9
20–24	12.94	9.66	12.2
25–34	20.93	16.58	13.0
35–44	16.98	17.47	16.8
45–54	12.21	18.14	24.2
55–64	5.93	12.50	34.4
65–Over	4.01	13.70	55.7

literate population as shown by the census may be assumed
to comprise only those persons who have had no education
whatever." If there are yet a large number of Negro illiterates, there is but one reason for it, and that is inferior
educational opportunities. The direct effect of long-time
educational efficiency upon illiteracy rates may be observed
from Table XVII, which shows illiteracy data in thirty
counties in Alabama and Iowa. In Iowa, the five counties
with the highest and the five counties with the lowest per
capita expenditures for teachers' salaries in 1927 are shown
with illiteracy data for 1930 and 1910. In Alabama,
twenty counties for the two separate systems, white and
black, were selected, and are displayed in the same manner.
If in Alabama and other Southern states, there are today
counties in which more than one-third of the Negro population is unable to read or write, the cause of it is to be found
in the expenditure of pitiful sums for the education of Negro children, resulting in short school terms, poor teaching,
poor accommodations, and inferior schools or no schools
at all.

---

[16] Bulletin, *Illiteracy, United States Census, 1930.*

TABLE XVII [17]

COMPARISON OF THIRTY COUNTY SYSTEMS WITH REFERENCE TO PER CAPITA
EXPENDITURES AND ILLITERACY

County	Expenditures for Teachers' Salaries Per Capita Enrollment 1927	1887	Per Cent of Increase	Per Cent of Illiteracy 1930	1910
Sioux (Iowa)	$63.61	$11.25	465	0.2	0.5
Woodbury (Iowa)	62.10	9.32	566	0.2	0.4
O'Brien (Iowa)	61.86	10.25	603	0.2	0.1
Buena Vista (Iowa)	61.66	9.15	573	0.2	0.3
Dubuque (Iowa)	60.50	9.18	526	0.4	0.4
Lowndes (Alabama: White)	56.47	2.61	2063	1.7	3.7
Dallas (Alabama: White)	42.83	3.06	1299	2.4	7.9
Sumter (Alabama: White)	40.86	2.77	1375	1.0	1.8
Macon (Alabama: White)	40.42	3.22	1155	2.3	4.4
Bullock (Alabama: White)	39.45	2.54	1453	2.8	3.5
Marion (Iowa)	38.26	6.08	512	1.1	1.7
Davis (Iowa)	37.57	5.34	603	0.7	1.8
Lucas (Iowa)	37.42	4.55	722	0.6	2.0
Appanoose (Iowa)	37.29	5.98	523	1.0	2.2
Monroe (Iowa)	36.41	6.22	485	0.8	1.8
Cleburne (Alabama: White)	15.32	1.38	1010	9.4	16.1
Marshall (Alabama: White)	14.61	1.34	990	8.1	11.3
Coffee (Alabama: White)	14.20	2.01	606	10.2	16.2
Jackson (Alabama: White)	13.74	1.61	753	10.3	17.0
Mobile (Alabama: Negro)	12.96	3.40	281	20.4	28.9
De Kalb (Alabama: White)	12.68	1.25	914	6.4	18.3
Jefferson (Alabama: Negro)	12.48	2.25	454	16.5	25.4
Walker (Alabama: Negro)	10.05	1.04	866	20.6	30.4
Bibb (Alabama: Negro)	9.99	2.56	290	28.8	29.2
Baldwin (Alabama: Negro)	9.59	2.67	259	27.4	35.4
Macon (Alabama: Negro)	2.60	1.55	67	22.7	36.3
Choctaw (Alabama: Negro)	2.55	1.55	64	28.8	44.0
Monroe (Alabama: Negro)	2.25	1.54	46	25.8	48.4
Russell (Alabama: Negro)	2.19	0.97	125	21.2	45.8
Wilcox (Alabama: Negro)	1.88	1.58	12	36.2	44.5

Progress

The steady decline of illiteracy in the Negro population is solid progress. It reflects the slow, uncertain, and yet

[17] Reprinted from *School and Society*, August 13, 1932, p. 224. Data from Iowa and Alabama educational reports, and from United States Census returns for the years given.

TABLE XVIII [18]

ILLITERACY AND SCHOOL ATTENDANCE FOR NEGRO SCHOOL CHILDREN IN THE VARIOUS STATES

States with Separate School Systems	Percentage of Negro Children Illiterate in the Age-Group 10–14		Percentage of Negro Children Attending School			
			Ages 7–13		Ages 14–15	
	1930	1920	1930	1920	1930	1920
Alabama	9.4	15.8	80.7	69.2	74.6	66.0
Delaware	0.7	1.6	94.8	94.2	84.5	81.2
Maryland	1.4	5.9	96.5	84.0	74.1	68.8
District of Columbia	0.2	0.4	96.6	93.0	92.9	76.6
Virginia	5.2	9.8	86.8	78.1	76.6	69.1
West Virginia	1.5	2.2	93.5	88.6	86.3	80.4
North Carolina	5.4	7.9	88.8	81.8	76.9	74.4
South Carolina	10.6	9.0	79.7	82.3	70.3	74.8
Georgia	7.0	15.2	83.1	70.2	64.5	56.3
Florida	7.9	13.3	83.9	73.1	70.6	67.1
Kentucky	2.5	4.0	91.1	85.9	81.3	76.2
Tennessee	3.8	13.7	88.9	71.1	80.8	64.9
Mississippi	5.2	15.5	87.6	71.5	81.2	66.1
Arkansas	4.3	13.3	87.3	69.9	83.0	65.4
Louisiana	7.7	25.4	83.1	61.0	73.2	53.8
Oklahoma	2.1	5.1	91.4	77.8	87.9	74.8
Texas	2.7	4.5	87.9	84.0	84.3	80.4
Missouri	1.3	3.6	93.1	86.8	83.3	74.4
Typical Northern and Western States						
Massachusetts	0.1	0.4	97.4	95.9	91.8	82.5
New York	0.3	0.4	96.6	93.1	93.3	83.8
Pennsylvania	0.2	0.5	95.8	93.2	91.8	83.1
Ohio	0.4	0.5	97.1	95.8	94.2	85.8
Indiana	0.2	0.4	97.0	94.2	93.6	78.6
Illinois	0.2	0.5	96.8	93.7	91.1	82.5

final development of an educated population in the sense that Negro children are today in possession of the fundamentals of civilized intercourse as never before. The dramatic downward sweep of the illiteracy curve mirrors lengthened school terms, a greater percentage of children in attendance at school, and a general improvement of the educational system. It is instructive to note the distribu-

[18] From bulletin on *Illiteracy, United States Census*, 1930.

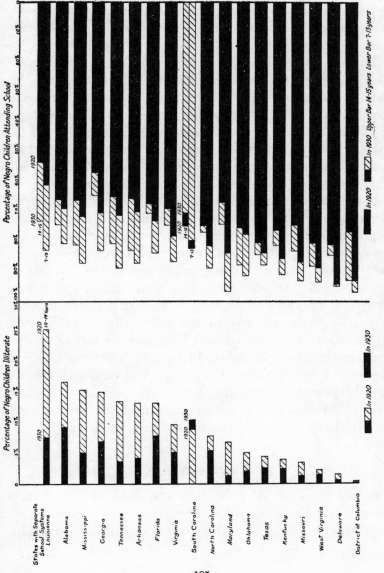

Fig. 3.—Percentage of Negro children enrolled in school, with percentage illiterate, 1930, for selected states.

tion of school attendance in the different age divisions for Negro children and to compare this factor with illiteracy figures, although the age-groups reported in the census are not equivalent. We have selected here the age-groups 7–13 and 14–15 with reference to school attendance, and have compared with these data the illiteracy data of Negro children in the age-group 10–14.

The only state showing an increase in Negro illiteracy in the age-group 10–14 between 1920 and 1930 is seen to be the state of South Carolina. It will also be seen that this state was the only one which showed a decrease in the percentage of Negro children in these age-groups in school. Manifestly, the schools in which Negro children are enrolled in South Carolina retrograded during the decade which in all other states witnessed tremendous strides forward.

If such states as Massachusetts, New York, Ohio, Indiana, Illinois, and Pennsylvania can reduce their illiteracy among Negro children to a minimum, the Southern states can do the same thing. The road to the eradication of illiteracy clearly leads toward including all of the children of school age in school. Of all age-groups, that including children from 7 to 13 years is the most vital. In 1930 there were 1,811,015 Negro children of this age-group in the United States, all of whom should have been in some sort of educational institution. However, 12.7 per cent of these children were out of school during the year. These children constitute the potential illiterates of the next generation. They are concentrated in the South, particularly in South Carolina, Alabama, Georgia, Mississippi, and Louisiana.

Summary

Before the Civil War, Negro slaves lived in an enforced ignorance. The ante-bellum opposition to the literacy of Negroes was logical, in that a literate population cannot be expected to remain slaves.   In a free system, literacy is as imperative as ignorance is necessary in a slave system.

Illiteracy statistics reflect the progress made in educating Negro children and adults since their emancipation.   They also point to the areas where greatest attention must be given.   The strategic point of attack in reducing illiteracy is in the early years of school attendance.   The illiteracy of children of school age is a clear indication that, for them, the school has not functioned.

There is a clear connection between low per capita expenditures for education and illiteracy.   The lack of adequate finance is at the root of the entire matter.   Since the Civil War, schools for Negro children have been consistently inferior to those for white children in the South.

Literacy, of course, is not an end in itself.   Beyond the bare ability to communicate with others through printed characters is the higher function of language as a means for communicating ideas.   It is probable that more than half of the Negro population are on the bare margin of a "mental illiteracy" which gives no great profit to the individual who possesses the crude skill with no facility in its use.   Schools for Negro children must extend their work so as to eliminate all elementary illiteracy.   They have done so in great measure in the past.   For the future, they must remove the marginal illiteracy which presents little advance over the old.   They must develop a definite facility in the use of the fundamentals, but even more they must direct aims and attitudes toward the profitable employment of these tools.   If they teach children how to read, they must direct their minds to good reading; if they teach children to write, they must develop skill in written expression.   For these purposes, the growth of school and municipal libraries and a general elevation in the taste of teachers and students must follow upon the final conquest of illiteracy in the Negro group.

Part II

ECONOMICS AND FINANCE

CHAPTER X

Migration, Industrialization, and Urbanization

Migration

GEORGE WASHINGTON took horse at Mount Vernon, early in 1789, preparatory to leaving for New York, where he was inaugurated the first President of the United States on April 30. At that time, the center of the Negro population, numbering 757,181 in a country with less than four million inhabitants, was located approximately one hundred and fifty miles southwest of his plantation on the Potomac. For the next one hundred and twenty years, the center of the Negro population moved steadily in a southwesterly direction, until in 1910 it was in northeastern Alabama, 628 miles southwest of Mount Vernon. From 1910 to 1920, this point "backtracked" for the first time in history, moving 9.4 miles east and 19.4 miles farther north, to the extreme northwestern portion of Georgia.[1] By 1930, it had moved again, this time to the northeast, coming to rest for the first time in history in the State of Tennessee.

The shifting locus of the imaginary point which represents the center of the Negro population carries with it a vivid portrayal of more than one hundred and forty years of the mobility of a people. Prior to the Civil War, this mobility was principally that directed by the economic cir-

---

[1] Monroe N. Work, *Negro Year Book, 1931-1932*, p. 343.

cumstances of slavery, a movement as if on a chess board
of so many million human pawns caught up in the inexorable
grasp of supply and demand. From 1790 up to 1910, one
hundred and twenty years, the dots on the map mark out
the progress of the Cotton Kingdom. The end of the Civil
War marked a slight acceleration of the westward movement
and a slight dropping away of the southerly trend; but the
story of the business cycles of the South and the Nation
could be written by these dots, if we knew how to place them
between the decennial periods.

As these centers of population march southward, we can
see the decay of New England slavery, written in the process
by which that section slowly emancipated its slaves or dis-
gorged them upon the South as they came to mean less and
less in returning real profits. We can see the Virginia and
North Carolina tidewater sections losing their dependence
upon slave labor as constant cultivation of the tobacco crop
reduced the fertility of their land for plantation purposes;
and we can see the slave owners of that section emancipating
their slaves, or selling them to the new Southwest, or taking
them with them into that new area of virgin soil, as the
centers stole decade by decade into South Carolina.

It is an astonishing fact that the catastrophe of the Civil
War did not immediately affect this phenomenon. As
though no Civil War had occurred, the period from 1860
to 1870 shows the same southwestward tendency of a century. Slavery had been abolished and the Negro was
theoretically no longer a bondsman; but neither war nor
law could stop the slow drift of population to the Southwest.
The planter of the eighteen thirties carried his slaves with
him from Virginia or North Carolina over the mountains,
through Tennessee, and down the Natchez Trail to the
Mississippi delta or the upper reaches of the Red River in
Louisiana. In the later eighteen sixties and early eighteen
seventies, no masters were abroad in the land; but labor
agents·from Texas and Louisiana sought out Negro peasants

in South Carolina, Georgia, and Alabama, and lured them
away to the still fertile lands of the West with stories of
bale-an-acre cotton and free labor paid the fabulous sum
of seventy-five cents a day for picking or chopping the
fibrous plant.

There were, it is true, occasional spurts of Negro migration following the Civil War that did not fit wholly into
this economic pattern.   Not all of the Negro migrants went
to Louisiana and Texas.   In 1879, a great wave of migration led to Western states, principally Kansas.   This migration is said to have transferred almost 100,000 Negroes from
Tennessee, Arkansas, Mississippi, Alabama, and southern
Louisiana to Kansas and Oklahoma as well as states even
further west.   Two spectacular leaders arose, Henry
Adams, of Louisiana, and Moses (Pap) Singleton, of Tennessee.   Singleton called himself the Moses of a new Exodus,
designed to set his people free by taking them out of the
land of Egypt into the promised land.[2]

Some historians have insisted that this movement was a
result of the oppressive measures adopted by the Democratic
legislatures in the South following the assumption of political power by that party after the years of Reconstruction
dominated by the Republican Party.   In retrospect, it is
not to be denied that the agitation of certain leaders for
political equality did accelerate the movement; but its basic
tendencies appear to lead straight to the fact that the migration was a direct response to economic pressure within the
regions involved.   The period was one of low prices for
cotton, and the removal of this large number of laborers left
no lasting impress upon the size of the cotton crop.   It is
therefore reasonable to believe that the migration consisted
of a surplus agricultural labor force.   This surplus had
been growing as Negroes increased in number, as free labor
demonstrated its superiority over slave labor in crop produc-

---

[2] Carter G. Woodson, *The Negro in Our History* (The Associated Publishers, Washington, 1927), p. 429.

tion, and as improved methods of agriculture replaced men with machines even in those early days. In 1860, the cotton crop of the United States, raised entirely in the Slave States, was 3,841,000 bales. In 1880, the crop was 6,357,000 bales, an increase of production of 65 per cent.[3] Meanwhile, the Negro population, who constituted the principal labor force in the cultivation of the cotton crop, had grown in the twenty years from 1860 to 1880 only 25 per cent. The migration of the Negroes, then, may be regarded as a means by which the labor surplus was forced outward as constantly growing cotton crops required fewer workers each year in proportion to the total amount raised.

A steady migration of Negroes from the South to the North had continued; but, as the shift in the center of population indicates, it was not until 1920 that the census figures showed a reverse movement of the general trend toward the Southwest. The continuation of this shift from 1920 to 1930 is shown by the further displacement of the center of population to the Northeast. The greatest migration of Negroes, accordingly, has taken place within the last twenty years. This movement is not only dramatic and charged with the spectacular; it has consequences that affect sharply the educational problems of all sections where the race is located, both those deserted and those adopted as a new home. It is essential to an understanding of the present educational problems of Negroes to consider the extent and implications of this more recent mobility of the Negro population.

Extent. Table XIX indicates the growth of Negro population in the last thirty years in three sections of the United States. From 1910 to 1930, the Negro population of the South increased less than seven per cent. During this time, the South was experiencing the most rapid gain

---

[3] *Reports of U. S. Department of Agriculture.*

of its white population in history.   The result has been a
steadily diminishing percentage of Negroes in the total
population.   This is shown in Table XX.   The only states

TABLE XIX [4]

INCREASE IN THE NEGRO POPULATION OF THE UNITED STATES, BY SECTIONS
AND PERCENTAGES, 1900–1930

| | | | | Percentage of Growth | | |
| | Total Population | | | 1920– | 1910– | 1900– |
Section	1930	1920	1910	1930	1920	1910
Total	11,891,143	10,463,131	9,827,763	13.6	6.5	11.2
The North	2,409,219	1,472,309	1,027,674	63.6	43.3	16.7
The South	9,361,577	8,912,231	8,749,427	5.0	1.9	10.4
The West	120,347	78,591	50,662	53.1	55.1	67.5

TABLE XX [5]

THE PERCENTAGE OF WHITE AND NEGRO IN THE POPULATION OF SOUTHERN
STATES, 1900–1930

| | Per Cent of Population for Each Race | | | | Decline | Gain |
| | 1930 | | 1900 | | Percentage | Percentage |
Division and State	White	Negro	White	Negro	Negro	Negro
The United States	88.7	9.7	87.9	11.6	1.9	
The South	73.1	24.7	67.4	32.3	7.6	
Delaware	86.3	13.7	83.4	16.6	2.9	
Maryland	83.0	16.9	80.2	19.8	2.9	
District of Columbia	72.7	27.1	68.7	31.1	4.0	
Virginia	73.1	26.8	64.3	35.6	6.8	
West Virginia	93.3	6.6	95.5	4.5		1.1
North Carolina	70.5	29.0	66.7	33.0	4.0	
South Carolina	54.3	45.6	41.6	58.4	12.8	
Georgia	63.2	36.8	53.3	46.7	9.9	
Florida	70.5	29.4	56.3	43.7	14.3	
Kentucky	91.3	8.6	86.7	13.3	4.7	
Tennessee	81.7	18.3	76.2	23.8	5.5	
Alabama	64.3	35.7	54.7	45.2	6.5	
Mississippi	49.6	50.2	41.3	58.5	8.3	
Arkansas	74.1	25.8	72.0	28.0	2.2	
Louisiana	62.7	36.9	52.8	47.1	10.2	
Oklahoma	88.6	7.2	84.8	7.0		0.2
Texas	73.5	14.7	79.6	20.4	7.5*	

* In 1930, Mexicans were separated from whites in the Texas returns. The
percentages given are accurate for the ratio of Negroes in the population, showing a definite decrease, as indicated in the table.

[4] Negro Year Book, 1931–1932, p. 338.
[5] Ibid., p. 339.

which have separate systems for the education of the races established by law which show an increase in the percentage of Negroes from 1900 to 1930 are Oklahoma and West Virginia; and in each of these states, the percentage of Negroes is less than eight per cent of the total.

Educational consequences. The public schools are supported by a public sentiment; and public-school officials expend funds derived from taxation, in the main, as they are guided by public sentiment. In a situation where Negroes constitute a minority voice in government, either through population ratio in the whole country or through disfranchisement, as in parts of the South, it is evident that schools for the education of Negroes must depend upon the public willingness to furnish education for Negro children at public expense. It is evident that in states and communities where there is a large proportion of Negro children to be educated, their schools will appear to be supported, not only at public expense, but at the expense of the schools for white children.

It is of the greatest importance to note that the proportion of Negroes in the population has decreased steadily in every Southern state with a considerable Negro population. It is true that this decrease would have to be continued over a century or more to reduce the proportion to that now existing in states like Kentucky and West Virginia, where Negro children do receive now in separate schools an equal benefit of the school funds to which their numbers entitle them.

When the First Census of the United States was taken, in 1790, 19.3 per cent of the population was made up of Negroes. Since that time, the percentage of the race in the population has decreased steadily with every census, with two exceptions. In the period from 1800 to 1810, the percentage rose one-tenth of one per cent, a fact probably due to the rush to import slaves before the closing off of the traffic by the Constitution, in 1808; and the other year

was 1880, a return probably affected by the fact that
members of the white race suffered many casualties in the
Civil War from 1860 to 1865 that were not endured by the
Negro. In 1930, Negroes constituted 9.7 per cent of the
population. In the course of one hundred and forty years,
the race has diminished its proportion in the population from
one in five to one in ten.

There are exceptions in many of the Southern states to
the general rule that a declining Negro population assures
fair expenditures. While there has been a tendency for
expenditures for teachers' salaries to become equalized during the last decade, this tendency is not apparent in other
items of expenditure. It may well be that there is a minimum point below which this hypothesis may be applied. In
Delaware, Kentucky, West Virginia, Oklahoma, Missouri,
and Maryland, where the Negro proportion in the population is less than twenty per cent, there is now a fair approximation between expenditures for whites and Negroes. However, a declining proportion of Negroes in Alabama and in
South Carolina has been accompanied by a declining proportion of public-school funds received far more exaggerated
than the population ratio decrease.

Industrialization and Urbanization

Migration has been referred to as one process, generated
largely by economic factors, which is tending to redistribute
the Negro population throughout the United States. At
the same time that the Negro has been on the move from
one state to another, he has been on the move to cities within
the South; and he has entered industries in those cities in
large numbers.

Whatever the hypothetical relation between intra-state
migration and educational expenditures, it is clear that the
processes of industrialization and urbanization must affect

all educational interests vitally. In the first place, industrialization adds more taxable wealth to a community or a state. This taxation may be turned into school funds, and a greater measure of educational efficiency may be made possible with more substantial funds.

The second effect of industrialization is that in so far as it concentrates a population within a small area, it tends to cheapen the cost of education. Of course, new services are hit upon by the social sense of the community as falling within the province of the school, and so urbanization increases as it diminishes the cost of education. Nevertheless, to give an equal amount of education to rural children, scattered over a large spatial area, will cost more per child than the same amount of education in an area where the educables are highly concentrated. Urbanization allows for centralization of administration, cuts down on the duplication of plant, and is economical in general maintenance of the plant equipment necessary for the school.

A third factor which touches a problem more specially belonging to the school program for Negroes is that the twin processes of industrialization and urbanization lead more and more in the direction of indirect taxation for the support of schools. In rural areas, where the electorate is also likely to be the taxpaying population, it is easy to see how great antipathy toward the support of schools for Negroes might exist on the part of men who control the administration of the schools generally and who pay directly through property taxes for the support of those schools. In the city, on the other hand, the distribution of funds is likely to be controlled either by men of a more liberal spirit, or by an electorate that pays for the support of schools only indirectly. The provision of fairly adequate educational opportunities for Negro children is, accordingly, less likely there to meet with instant opposition.

Another factor of no little importance is that the city focuses the need for education on the part of its disorganized elements. A Negro or white man may be densely ignorant of any of the fundamental processes and yet find no irremediable handicap in the way of performing serviceable functions in a rural community. In a city, however, illiteracy and ignorance bring immediate and spectacular penalties. Life is so highly organized, so complex in its machinery, that the uneducated man or woman finds it impossible to supplement necessary adjustments with "Mother-wit" or "horse-sense." The result is that no urban community is likely to tolerate, for its own self-protection, the wholesale ignorance of any proportion of the population.

The Degree of Urbanization

The migration of Negroes to the North has been a cityward movement, and in 1930 there were 25 Northern cities with a Negro population in excess of 10,000. In these cities, 1,513,834 Negroes were living. Nearly 90 per cent of the Negro population of the North was located in urban

TABLE XXI [6]

NUMBER AND PER CENT OF NEGROES IN THE SOUTH LIVING IN RURAL AND URBAN AREAS, 1890–1930

Year	Number of Rural Negroes in the South	Number of Urban Negroes in the South	Percentage of Southern Negroes in Rural Areas	Percentage of Southern Negroes Living in Urban Areas
1890	5,727,342	1,033,235	84.7	15.3
1900	6,558,173	1,364,796	82.8	17.2
1910	6,894,972	1,854,455	78.8	21.2
1920	6,661,332	2,250,899	74.7	25.3
1930	6,395,252	2,966,025	68.3	31.7

[6] Reports of the United States Census for respective years. *The Negro Year Book, 1931–1932*, and the United States Census' *Negro Population, 1790–1915* (Gov't Printing Office, Washington, 1918) together contain material of great value for those wishing to utilize summarized tables.

centers. We have thought of the South as being an area where Negroes were primarily and permanently rural. However, there are fewer Negroes living on the farms and in the villages of the South today than there were in 1900. Table XXI gives some salient facts with reference to the change in the composition of the South's Negro population.

There are 52 cities of the South in which more than 10,-000 Negroes live. These cities range from Baltimore, with a Negro population of 142,000, to Monroe, Louisiana, with slightly more than 10,000 Negroes. Altogether, 1,759,624 Negroes are living in these Southern cities with more than 10,000 Negro inhabitants.[7]

In 1930, the number of Negroes living in urban areas had increased to 5,193,913. This number represents 43.7 per cent of the Negro population for the entire country. From the fact that the curve of Negro migration appears just to be beginning in its country-to-city direction, it is probable that by 1950 the majority of Negroes in the South will be living in urban areas, and that a decade or so later, a still larger number may be in the cities. Programs having to do with the education of Negroes in the South have, in the past, assumed that they will continue to be a rural folk. A more intelligent provision of education must con-

---

[7] Frank Alexander Ross, "Urbanization and the Negro," Papers on Social Process, *Publications of the American Sociological Society*, August, 1932, Vol. XXVI, No. 3, pp. 115–128. Ross lists the following American cities as having more than 10,000 Negroes in 1930: in the West, Los Angeles; in the North, in order of the size of the Negro population, New York, Chicago, Philadelphia, Detroit, St. Louis, Cleveland, Pittsburgh, Cincinnati, Indianapolis, Newark, Kansas City (Mo.), Columbus (Ohio), Boston, Kansas City (Kan.), Gary, Dayton, Atlantic City, Youngstown, Buffalo, Toledo, Jersey City, East St. Louis, Camden, Omaha, Akron. In the South: Baltimore, Washington, New Orleans, Birmingham, Memphis, Atlanta, Houston, Richmond, Jacksonville, Louisville, Norfolk, Nashville, Savannah, Dallas, Chattanooga, Winston-Salem, Montgomery (Ala.), Charleston, Shreveport (La.), Charlotte (N. C.), Newport News, Galveston, Wilmington (N. C.), Lexington (Ky.), Petersburg (Va.), Raleigh (N. C.), Roanoke (Va.), Wilmington (Del.), Meridian (Miss.), Greenville (S. C.), Baton Rouge (La.), Port Arthur (Texas).

sider that probably more than half of the Negro children to
be educated in the decade 1930–1940 will have to make adjustments to the conditions of urban rather than rural existence.   It is estimated that 2,251,541 Negroes have moved
from the country to the city since 1900, more than a million
of this number having removed since 1920.   Even had the
rural schools provided an excellent education with reference
to adjustments to an agricultural economy, which they did
not, this vast number of migrants to the city would have
found themselves unprepared by education for their new
problems and difficulties.

Ross writes,

> Much has been said by writers on Negro migration of the
> effect of persecution and discrimination, the incursion of the
> boll weevil and the extraordinary demand for labor created
> by the Great War and our immigration restriction policy.
> These have been potent propulsive and attractive factors.
> The new Industrial Revolution, by supplanting hand proc-
> esses by semiautomatic machines, has drawn to our cities
> hundreds of thousands of Negroes by converting many proc-
> esses, previously too highly skilled for his untrained hands,
> into simple machine feeding.   Rumor has it that at last a
> practical cotton picking machine has been perfected.   If this
> be true, hundreds of thousands more Negroes will be forced
> from southern cotton farms.   A similar result will be an
> inevitable consequence of current legislative drives toward
> the limitation of cotton acreage.[8]

Summary

The geographic location of Negroes is a factor of the utmost importance in the education of the race.   The earlier
plantation economy centered the Negro population in the
lower South, with a constant drift to the Southwest.   The
high percentage of Negroes in the population of Northern
states in colonial days was sharply reduced in the half-century following the Revolutionary War.

---

[8] Ross, *op. cit.*, p. 127.

The last two Federal Censuses show a reversal of the drift of the Negro toward the Southwest. The current movement is Northward and cityward. When the proportion of Negroes in a community decreases, educational problems of support for a separate system become less complicated. Negroes are moving out of the rural South, where they have previously been concentrated, into the urban North and South. Wherever they go in the cities, they find improved educational facilities as compared to the schools of rural communities. However, the nature of city life presents even more difficult problems for human welfare, subsistence, and culture. The center of the Negro educational problem, if defined by numbers, should no longer be the rural South, but the urban South. It is probable that within but a few more decades, Negroes will live principally in cities. Schools which are now teaching rural and city children should bear in mind the abrupt shift in emphasis necessitated by this new direction of the population. The Negro child of today will be the worker in industrial plants tomorrow, as his fathers before him were agriculturists. The situation demands an intensification of techniques designed to initiate this vast population into the intricate demands of modern urban life.

CHAPTER XI

Economic Background of Education in the South

WE HAVE seen that in the first decades after the Civil War, the South witnessed an unprecedented revival of interest in education. The Reconstruction legislatures placed schools for the two races on an equal basis. The conservative representatives who succeeded them in power attempted to operate the systems for a time on the same basis of equality, although with a reduced expenditure for both systems. The rise of the small farmers in the South was accompanied by a growing realization that the public school system was the agency through which the vast majority of white children were to be educated. Expanding educational needs were restricted by a series of limitations placed upon school expenditures by conservatives. The natural result was to turn to the funds then being spent on schools for Negroes as a ready source of supply for the growing needs of white schools. The relation between wealth and education, between the growth of the school as an institution and the concomitant growth of the ability of the population to take advantage of it is, therefore, of paramount importance in the consideration of education in the South for both races, and we intend here to trace the various developments which are interwoven in the entire picture.

The Facts of Educational Expansion

The year 1895 may be taken as a general conclusion for the period in which Southern states struggled with the possibility of providing equal education for both races.   Discrimination against Negroes had been adopted in every Southern state by this date.   The white enrollment of ten Southern states had grown 250 per cent in the twenty years from 1875 to 1895, and the end of this explosive growth had not as yet come.   The first period of growth had been that of the first acceptance of a system and the inclusion of all children in it; the period following was to be the natural increase due to the inclusion of the younger generation in the school system, along with the expansion of educational services along all lines.

Since 1895, the enrollment of Negroes in ten selected Southern states—Alabama, Arkansas, Florida, Georgia, Louisiana, Mississippi, North and South Carolina, Tennessee, and Texas—has grown year by year, though not always with the same rapidity characteristic of the white school enrollment.   Table XXII gives these figures for both races.

TABLE XXII [1]

GROWTH IN ENROLLMENT FOR WHITE AND NEGRO CHILDREN IN TEN STATES OF THE SOUTH FOR THE PERIOD FROM 1895 TO 1930

Year	Enrollment		Percentage Increase over 1880	
	White	Negro	White	Negro
1880	1,053,025	714,884		
1895	2,176,464	1,142,500	106	159
1900	2,450,461	1,234,592	232	172
1905	2,692,597	1,317,881	255	184
1910	2,965,123	1,426,102	281	199
1915	3,438,865	1,609,983	326	225
1920	3,876,904	1,683,769	367	235
1925	4,414,797	1,828,290	424	255
1930	4,531,141	1,893,068	435	264

[1] *Ibid.*

Considering the educational responsibility shouldered by the states represented in Table XXII as the number of children actually in school, it is to be seen that this direct educational load has multiplied four times since 1880. As, in the last analysis, the relationship between the education of white children and that of Negro children presents mainly an inescapable financial problem, it is proper to note particularly the rapid growth of the needs as represented by a white school enrollment that has been multiplying much more rapidly than the Negro enrollment. It is true, of course, that a larger number of Negro children would be enrolled if their educational opportunities had expanded with the same rapidity as those of white children; but it is enough at this point to note that the period of stress so far as existing school facilities were concerned came early in the period surveyed, through a great development of educational needs for white children.

Another index of the increasing load upon the school system is furnished by the statistics showing high-school enrollment. These figures are rather inaccurate up to comparatively recent times. The available data, however, are exhibited in Table XXIII arranged by reports of public-school students over five-year periods since 1890, for the ten states mentioned above.

The white public high-school enrollment tripled between 1890 and 1895, and did not again attain this rate of growth until between 1915 and 1920, when the enrollment increased two and three-quarters times. The figures for Negro high schools show an increase in the five-year period from 1920 to 1925 which is immensely significant.

As great as the expansion of the system may appear when measured by enrollment figures, the expenditures furnish a final index which is yet more indicative of the tremendous attention being paid to education in the South. In Table XXIV are listed the total expenditures for public schools

The Education of the Negro

TABLE XXIII [2]

ENROLLMENT IN PUBLIC HIGH SCHOOLS IN TEN
SOUTHERN STATES, 1890–1930

Year	Enrollment	
	White	*Negro*
1890	10,361	981
1895	32,730	639
1900	49,203	2,659
1905	59,752	4,089
1910	95,337	3,600
1915	147,163	6,329
1920	412,061	8,585
1925	655,064	53,891
1930	739,891	79,388

in our ten selected states in the period from 1880 to 1930.

While this table does not include 1875, it is evident from a study of individual states that the year 1875 was marked by larger expenditures than that of 1880 in many instances. In Alabama, for example, it was not until 1885 that the state regained the level of expenditures which was reached in 1875. This may be taken as an example of the reaction which set in with reference to educational policy, following the assumption of political power by the conservative Democrats. Following the generous expenditures of that era, the schools, and indeed every aspect of governmental expenditures, were sharply curtailed. This represents the "crippling" of the school systems by the conservative reaction concerning which we have already quoted Knight.

As a final example of the expansion of education in the South between 1880 and 1930, Table XXIV also arranges the expenditures in the form of an index, with 1880 being taken as 100 per cent. This index indicates a cumulative expansion of school expenditures which could be matched by no other section.

---

[2] *Reports of the United States Commissioner of Education* for the respective years shown.

TABLE XXIV [3]

GROWTH OF EXPENDITURES FOR EDUCATION IN TEN
SELECTED SOUTHERN STATES WITH EXPENDITURES
FOR 1880 TAKEN AS 100%

Year	Expenditures	Index
1880	$ 4,666,427	100
1885	7,051,261	152
1890	11,188,632	241
1895	13,223,882	286
1900	15,531,760	336
1905	25,314,916	504
1910	36,203,662	786
1915	59,802,254	1,300
1920	112,249,885	2,439
1925	247,438,196	5,356
1930	292,588,109	6,270

Summary—Educational Expansion

We have indicated, through reference to public-school enrollment for both races and separately and by high-school enrollment as well as expenditures, that the school systems of the Southern States have had a tremendous expansion within the last fifty years. While the greatest expenditures have been made within the last two decades, the period from 1885 to 1900 was not proportionately lacking in progress, considering the original base. In order to interpret this progress, it becomes necessary to examine some of the fundamental factors upon which was based the economic structure of the social system which permitted this expansion.

The Fact of Industrial and Economic Development

Broadus Mitchell says, in the 1931 *Annals*, concerning the recent industrial history of the South:

---

[3] *Ibid.*

What the South needed throughout its prior history was productivity. This meant, first, abandonment of the expedient of mere exploitation,—chattel slavery, soil exhaustion, defrauding public and private creditors—: and second, the emergence of a wider margin between the cost of production and the price obtained for the product. The old South had no social surplus, and consequently was limited on every hand. The New South of industry mixed with agriculture begins to have riches, and in that measure, as a people, begins to live.[4]

We are interested here in the beginning of the "riches" which have aided the section in beginning "to live," not an inconsiderable feature of which, evidently, is the attention given to public school systems. The following table is taken from another recent essay on the industrialization of the South.

TABLE XXV [5]

GROWTH OF MANUFACTURING IN THE SOUTH WITH THE YEAR
1904 TAKEN AS AN INDEX EQUALLING 100

Year	Index for Alabama	Index for N. Carolina	Index for All South	Index for Other States
1904	100	100	100	100
1909	117	148	133	123
1914	135	183	147	141
1919	187	236	184	186
1923	226	322	218	208
1925	242	370	233	220

North Carolina is included here because it was the first Southern state to embark on a widespread industrial development; and Alabama, because it has recently matched the great textile and tobacco developments in North Carolina with other textile expansion, as well as with iron and steel

---

[4] "Growth of Manufacturing in the South," *Annals of the American Academy*, Vol. 153, p. 24.

[5] Table taken from James W. Martin, "Industrial Changes and Taxation Problems in the South," *Annals*, 1931, p. 225.

production. It will be noticed that these two states outstripped not only the average for the South at large, but
that for the Nation as well.

Another factor of great importance is that of tangible
wealth within the borders of certain states. Arranged for
ten-year periods, the wealth of the ten selected Southern
states is presented in Table XXVI.

TABLE XXVI [6]

WEALTH OF TEN SELECTED SOUTHERN STATES
FROM 1880 TO 1922 EXPRESSED IN THOUSANDS

Year	Wealth
1880	$4,489,000
1890	7,227,957
1900	8,489,867
1912	21,271,378
1922	38,580,510

Taking 1880 as an index of 100, the figure for 1890 is
161, for 1900, 189, for 1912, 474, and for 1922, 961.
The South, then, had in 1922 wealth which was 961 per
cent as great as that in 1880.

Another key to financial growth is furnished by figures of
per capita wealth, per school child. Table XXVII indicates the per capita wealth for children aged 5 to 14.

Of considerable interest in this connection is the fact that
in agricultural sections, the proportion of educable children
to working adults is considerably larger than in urban, industrial areas. Because of this fact, it has been demonstrated that such states as Mississippi and South Carolina
have many more children to educate per adult of working
age than more favorably situated industrial states.

The percentage of children of school age for both races
to adults is much larger in the South than in the Nation
at large; but this discrepancy is growing to be less for both

---

[6] Table taken from *Bulletin of Research Division, N. E. A.*, Vol. IV,
W. W. Norton, "The Ability of the States to Support Education," p. 75.

TABLE XXVII [7]

WEALTH PER CAPITA CHILD AGED 5–14 IN TEN SOUTHERN STATES

State	1880	1900	1922
Alabama	$1,218	$1,596	$4,860
Arkansas	1,264	1,707	5,777
Florida	1,622	2,708	11,208
Georgia	1,417	1,582	5,211
Louisiana	1,517	2,256	7,722
Mississippi	1,092	1,324	4,616
North Carolina	1,229	1,367	6,735
South Carolina	1,163	1,317	5,240
Tennessee	1,657	1,881	7,512
Texas	1,882	2,847	8,812

races. However, it is important, in assessing the influence
of this factor, to remember that the Southern states have
in the past been faced with a greater educational burden
than the other sections of the country. In 1900 in seven
of the ten selected states, there were more Negro children
proportionately to the total population than whites; while
there were only five such states in 1920 and only three in
1930.

In a relatively backward state of society, such as the
South has been from the standpoint of industrialization, one
would expect to find a large percentage of women gainfully
employed. In the South, the data show a rise in the number
of white women employed between 1900 and 1910 and a
general decrease thereafter, indicating that the section is
reaching a higher plane of economic stability. The decline
in Negro percentages came between 1920 and 1930. It is
significant that the decline of white women workers came
from 1910 to 1920, the period of the great expansion of
the white high-school enrollment, while the decline for Negro
women came a decade later, coincident with the expansion
of the Negro high-school enrollment. The figures in gross
show a very high percentage, due to the predominance of

[7] *Ibid.*, p. 56.

women working partially in agricultural occupations and the tendency of Negro women to work in proportions far beyond those of white women. The sharp rise in the employment of women from 1900 to 1910 and the sharp decrease in the next decennium were due to the rapid expansion of industry in the first decade, while in the second period, industry reached a higher plane, and, with the mechanization of production, could afford to employ men in larger proportion, as compared with the employment of women and children.

Another index to economic development may be found in the increased number of persons employed in manufacturing and mechanical occupations in the South. In Table XXVIII is presented a picture of the rapid increase in this type of employment.

TABLE XXVIII [8]

NUMBER AND PER CENT OF NEGRO AND WHITE MALES OVER TEN YEARS OF AGE GAINFULLY EMPLOYED IN MANUFACTURING AND MECHANICAL INDUSTRIES IN TEN SOUTHERN STATES, 1890–1930

	White				Negro			
	Number in Mechanical and Manuf. Industries		Per Cent of All White Male Workers in Mechanical and Manuf. Ind.		Number in Mechanical and Manuf. Industries		Per Cent of All Negro Male Workers in Mechanical and Manuf. Ind.	
State	1890	1930	1890	1930	1890	1930	1890	1930
Alabama	23,612	105,746	10.8	21.4	10,856	55,009	5.6	19.6
Arkansas	15,092	51,312	7.1	12.8	3,679	17,331	4.2	11.7
Florida	6,967	76,611	10.9	24.9	5,241	36,110	11.2	25.6
Georgia	36,156	124,258	13.8	23.0	18,523	64,149	7.5	20.6
Louisiana	12,312	85,976	7.9	22.1	11,223	43,013	9.0	18.3
Mississippi	10,533	40,789	7.5	13.7	6,487	30,339	3.2	9.6
No. Carolina	35,075	167,711	12.8	27.1	14,465	46,840	9.7	19.0
So. Carolina	16,961	79,814	13.6	29.8	12,188	31,969	6.5	15.0
Tennessee	39,578	128,011	11.2	20.8	11,546	32,583	9.5	22.1
Texas	33,448	236,168	6.9	18.0	6,249	38,607	5.0	14.5

[8] Data derived from *United States Census Reports, Occupations*, for the respective years given.

Mississippi shows the smallest percentage of male workers for both races employed in manufacturing and mechanical industries in 1890 and in 1930. Data not exhibited here, for 1920, show that the peak of Negro employment in manufacturing was reached in 1920. There were very small increases in the total number employed in Florida, Georgia, and North Carolina, with the remaining seven states shown here presenting an actual decrease in Negroes employed in these pursuits. The increases among whites were considerable in all states. In Florida, the number of whites so employed doubled between 1920 and 1930, while the number of Negroes increased less than five per cent. The number of whites gainfully employed in manufacturing and mechanical industries increased from 725,153 in 1920 to 1,098,396 in 1930 for the ten states here exhibited, or 51.4 per cent. The number of Negroes so employed decreased from 409,404 in 1920 to 395,950 in 1930, or 3.3 per cent, for the ten states exhibited.

The gross increase for the states reflects the transfer of populations from agricultural and rural to industrial and urban patterns of life. It also reflects growing wealth for the section, for greater industrial production means greater resources in these communities for all concerned. It reflects a growth in ability to support school systems and to support children enrolled in school.

For Negroes, the implications of the decrease in employment in these avenues are not so encouraging, save as the race stands to profit from general community progress in wealth. The declining proportion of Negroes employed in manufacturing and mechanical industries in these Southern states must mean a generally lower economic status and, consequently, poorer health, possibilities for education, and opportunities for the growth of the individual and the community.

Relationships Between Educational Expansion and Economic Development

Comparisons are made here by reducing educational items and the facts of economic expansion to indices which afford comparable data. Using 1880 as a point of departure, expenditures for education for the ten states and tangible wealth show the following indices:

	Expenditure	Wealth
1880	100	100
1890	241	161
1900	336	189
1910	786	
1912		
1920	2,439	
1922		961
1925	5,356	
1930	6,270	

Expenditures for education rose much faster than the tangible wealth, multiplying themselves by 24 in 1920, while the wealth index was increasing only 9 times.

It is also instructive to compare the enrollment of both races in high school with various criteria of wealth. With 1890 taken as a basal index of 100, the comparison then stands:

	Wealth	White H.-S. Enrollment	Negro H.-S. Enrollment
1890	100	100	100
1900	116	477	288
1910		925	400
1912	294		
1920		4,000	944
1922			
1925	534		
1930			

Here, again, the school expansion has far outstripped the development of the industrial resources, if one may judge from the criteria of wealth. A later comparison yields more similar rankings. Taking 1904 as the base for manufacturing and 1905 as the base for expenditures, the following comparison is possible:

Manufacturing in the South		*Expenditures for Education*	
1904	100	1905	100
1909	133	1910	112
1914	147	1915	256
1919	184	1920	481
1925	233	1925	1,618

The following figures relative to percentage increases show the same rapid development but continue to show an educational development far ahead of the industrial:

	1880–1890	1890–1900	1900–1912	1900–1910	1912–1922	1910–1920
Increase in Wealth	61%	17.4%	50.5%		81%	
Increase in Expend.	239%	38.8%		233.0%		310%
Total Enrollment	63%	27.4%		19.1%		26%
Total White Enroll.	77%	31.4%		21.0%		30%
White H.-S. Enroll.		474.0%		193.0%		432%
Negro H.-S. Enroll.		271.0%		35.3%		238%

From these summary comparisons, it will be seen that the greatest proportionate gain in wealth occurred between 1912 and 1922. This was the period, likewise, for the largest increase in expenditures. It is significant that the decade in which the next largest increase of wealth is registered (61 per cent, 1880–1890) was the period of the second relatively largest expenditure for education. Likewise, the decade 1880–1890 was remarkable for the largest increase in white enrollment. The fact that the next decade shows the largest increase in high-school enrollment for whites is obviously a result of the increased enrollment in the entire system registered in the preceding decade. While educational development in the South has been aided by an intensive industrial development, the educational system has grown far more rapidly than the industrial system, when measured on the basis of beginnings.

School Attendance and Occupations

We have been accustomed to thinking of school attendance as a relatively simple matter, including only two elements. The first of these is customarily thought of as the provision of a school which can be attended, and the second is the willingness of the child or his parents for him to attend school. A third factor may be legislation to compel attendance of the school established by the state as a measure falling within the police power of government, for it is considered right and just that the state, having established the school as an instrument of public policy, should demand attendance from the child.

The fact of legal compulsion is more frequently the antecedent of a high percentage of school attendance than its cause. In this, as in many other respects, the placing of a statute in the code is a gesture recognizing a fact already accomplished. The prime example of this tendency of social legislation to follow rather than lead in actual change is the recent adoption of a clause outlawing child labor in the National Textile Code adopted under the provisions of the National Industrial Recovery Act at a time when the economics of factory operation had already practically eliminated child labor. Where legislation is in advance of the crest of social conviction, it is simply not enforced, as in the case of compulsory education laws in the South in rural regions for whites and almost universally in the South for Negro children.

It is not too far-fetched to say that the most significant factor in the education of Negro children in the South in recent years has been the rapid rate at which these children have been withdrawn from employment. With the migration to cities, which has taken children from the necessity of working on cotton farms, and with the gradual mechanization of the South, which has made the labor of children non-

essential in urban and industrial areas, the net result has
been an emancipation of the child from daily labor.   The
primary reason why children do not attend school is not
their unwillingness, or the unwillingness of their parents
for them to do so.   It may be hazarded that it is not even
the lack of a school to which they can go.   If children
attend school today in the South or in the North, it is principally because there is no employment to which they might
be profitably assigned.   It is no accidental coincidence that
the percentage of Negro children aged 14 and 15 who were
attending school in 1930 was 78.1, compared with a school
attendance for white children in 1910 of 77.4 per cent for
the same age-group.   In 1930, the percentage of Negro
children aged 10–15 who were gainfully employed was 16.1.
In 1910, the percentage of white children aged 10–15 who
were gainfully employed was 14.3.   The index of school
attendance for the two races between 1910 and 1930 is not
merely the index of educational advancement which it appears to present; it is an index of correlation as to the consistent two-decade lag of Negroes behind whites from the
standpoint of economic advancement.   It is not wholly cyni-
cal to believe that industry has demanded—and obtained—
the labor of children as long as it was profitable to do so; nor
is it unreasonable to suppose that parents will permit and
even oblige their children to work as long as the children
can find employment which will add materially to the standard of living within the family.   The withdrawal of Negro
children from industry, accordingly, means both that
Negroes are better circumstanced, economically, than they
were thirty years ago, and also that the imperious demands
of industry, domestic employment, and agriculture are less
insistent than they were in former days.   Almost one-half—
46.6 per cent—of all Negro children aged 10–15 were gainfully employed in 1910.   By 1920, this percentage had
dropped sharply down to 21.8.   In the decade 1920–1930,

the decrease was less notable—to 16.1 per cent of the age-group.

The occupations in which Negro children are employed have shown little variation since 1910. In 1920, the largest number, 85.2 per cent of the age-group 10–15, were employed in agriculture. The next largest group was employed in the mechanical and manufacturing industries, where 3.9 per cent of the children were employed in 1920 and 3.4 per cent in 1930. The percentage of gainfully employed Negro children engaged in agriculture remained the same in the decade, although the entire number employed in all occupations decreased from 270,265 to 204,455.

There is very little "waste" in any of the younger age-groups among Negroes. Recent figures compiled by the Census Bureau in 1930 for the first time show that Negro children are either at work or in school, with a very small amount of overlapping between those employed and those who are attending school. The age-group 16–17 for both sexes shows the highest percentage of children who are neither employed nor in school. It is probable that these children are "finding themselves," for subsequent age-levels show a sharp diminution in this percentage. By the time the age of 21–24 is reached, 96 per cent of the Negro males in a state like Delaware are either in school or at work. In the State of Mississippi, 97.6 per cent of Negro males aged 21–24 are in school or at work. There is little room for further talk about the "shiftlessness" of Negro adolescents when we realize that even in times of unemployment, more than 95 per cent of young Negro males in Mississippi are at work or in school. At the same time, it is easy to see why high-school enrollment for Negroes should be much smaller proportionately for the race than among whites. White adolescents have long since been emancipated from the necessity for labor, and, as a result, they are in school,

The Education of the Negro

The same process is taking place among Negroes, with the "lag" which we have noted above.

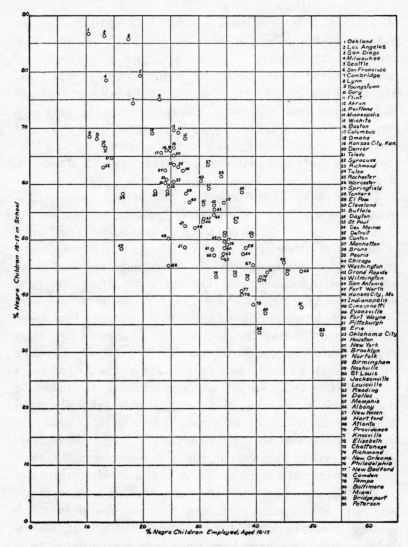

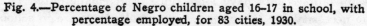

Fig. 4.—Percentage of Negro children aged 16–17 in school, with percentage employed, for 83 cities, 1930.

Figure 4 gives a scatter diagram in which the attendance of Negro children aged 16–17 is checked against the percentage of employment for this age-group in cities of 100,000 or more population in 1930. The correlation is almost perfect, showing that in those cities where the largest number of Negro adolescents are occupied, the percentage attending school is lowest, and vice versa. The cities showing the highest percentage of Negro children aged 16–17 in school are for the most part located on the Pacific Coast, Oakland, Los Angeles, and San Diego standing highest in this respect. In Los Angeles in 1930, 86.4 per cent of the Negro children aged 16–17 were attending school, while 13.4 per cent were employed.

The cities standing lowest in school enrollment and highest in the percentage of children of this age-group employed are not Southern cities, as one might think. Bridgeport, Connecticut, and Paterson, New Jersey, both show the small percentage of 33.3 per cent of Negro youths aged 16–17 attending school, while at Bridgeport 40.6 per cent and at Paterson 51.7 per cent of these children are employed. Both of these cities are readily identified as textile centers in which it is probable that the Negro children would be employed along with other races. Tampa and Miami, Florida, and Baltimore, Maryland, are the lowest cities in Negro school attendance for the South. The first two are centers of the cigar industry, which employs large numbers of Negro adolescents; while the percentage of Negroes engaged in domestic service is exceptionally high in the Maryland city.

Sex Differences in School Attendance

Every individual familiar with a high school in which large numbers of Negro children are enrolled has noted the excess of girls over boys in the upper grades. The writer

has heard numerous educators explain this difference by saying that "Negro girls are more ambitious than Negro boys."
Usually, the commentator is inclined to be quite disgusted
with the boys on this account.

The slightest attention to employment figures for the two
sexes might serve to show that girls exceed boys in Negro
high-school enrollments for the most part because boys can
be, and are, employed in greater degree than girls.   In
Northern cities, however, where Negro female adolescents
can find employment in domestic service, while Negro boys
cannot find employment in industry or trade, the percentage
of males in the upper age brackets attending school exceeds
that of females.   In New York and Ohio, for example, there
are more Negro males in school at each age-group than
females.   The same thing is true in New Jersey, Pennsylvania, Indiana, and Illinois for the age-groups 14–15,
16–17, and 18–20.   In Southern urban areas, the percentage of males attending school exceeds that of females, in
Delaware, for the age-groups 7–13, 14–15, and 16–17; in
Maryland, Virginia, and West Virginia, for the age-group
14–15; in South Carolina, Georgia, Florida, Texas, Louisiana, Arkansas, and Mississippi, for the age-group 18–20.
In other states showing an excess of females by percentage,
the greatest variation is in the age-group 16–17, with the
difference in the age-group 18–20 greatly reduced, though
still in favor of the females.

There is yet another factor which explains the great
excess of Negro females in high school aside from the fact
that the Negro males are employed in greater number at
these ages, and, as a result, are obliged to forego attendance
at school.   This factor is the decisive sex ratio in favor of
females, especially at the adolescent ages, a ratio which is
particularly low in Southern cities.   In 1930, in urban
centers in Texas, the percentage of Negro males aged 18–20
attending school exceeded that of females, being 16.3 for

the males and 14.2 for females. Yet, there were 1,795
females attending school in this age-group as compared to
1,374 males, an excess in absolute numbers of more than four
hundred, while the percentage of attendance was smaller.
In Texas in 1930, there were 2,754 males enumerated in
urban areas in the age-group 16–17 as compared to 3,892
females. In North Carolina in the same year, 2,643
females in this age-group, but only 1,740 males, were enumerated in urban areas; in Alabama, 1,957 males and 2,929
females.

The concentration of older female adolescents in cities as
contrasted to males of the same age-group is a social phenomenon well known to sociologists. Certainly we shall be
on safer ground in interpreting the low sex ratio characteristic of the Negro high-school enrollment in terms of
economic and sociological factors than on the basis of
"ambition" or "push," so much relied upon in the past as
an explanation, to the detriment of the opinion in which
the Negro boy is held by school administrators.

Rural-Urban Differences

With 85.2 per cent of all Negro children aged 10–15
gainfully occupied working in agricultural pursuits, together with the improved school opportunities which the city
has to offer, we should expect to find the attendance in
school higher for city children than for rural children.
In the South, generally, this is true of the lower age-
brackets; but in those states where the Negro population
is heavily rural, a larger percentage of older children are
in school in rural areas than in cities. In Delaware, for
example, 55.1 per cent of urban 16–17-year-old male Negro
children were in school, in 1930, as compared to 23.2 per
cent of the rural-farm children of the same sex- and age-
group. In Mississippi, a state with a notoriously inefficient

school system, 46.2 per cent of urban male Negroes aged 16–17 were in school, and 55.1 per cent of rural-farm children of the same age-sex group. In this case, it is clear that the attendance of Negro children in school in Mississippi is illusory as an index of progress; in fact, it is an index to the backwardness of the system and the high retardation of the children, which leaves over-age children in lower grades long beyond normal expectation.

Summary

Recent interpretation of the rapid growth of American educational institutions has emphasized the close correlation between educational growth and economic betterment. It is clear that the expansion of education in the South in recent decades could have come only as a result of intensive industrialization of the section, and it follows that the future will bring a like mutual relationship between the development of industrial resources and the expansion of educational institutions. It appears, however, that schools for Negroes have shared in this betterment only in a passive sense, gleaning as they have the crumbs which have fallen from the table of a greater economic affluence and stability. Statisticians have endeavored, where other classes of the population were concerned, to trace the greater symptoms of educational growth to easily discernible economic patterns. There are more children in high school, it is argued, because parents are now able to dispense with the labor of their adolescent offspring, and this in turn is due to a higher standard of living and larger real wages for the working population. Again, the increase in high-school enrollment is traceable to an improved ability of communities to build and support institutions for the education of adolescents.

The reciprocal effects of high-school attendance and high-school construction and availability make it uncertain, in any case, which comes first in importance. Where Negroes are concerned, it is probable that the greatest factor working upon the recent and prodigious increase of the Negro high-school enrollment has been the cloture of avenues of employment to Negro adolescents. The general economic advance of the South has provided communities with ability to provide high-school facilities for Negro children, though in no degree comparable with those afforded white children. For the rest, the mechanization of the section while Negroes were being rapidly urbanized has meant that the services of hundreds of thousands of Negro and white adolescents—in more recent years, particularly Negroes—have become superfluous. With nothing else to do, these children of the middle ages now attend school. In every Southern state, with the exception of Florida, Georgia, and North Carolina, the number of Negroes engaged in manufacturing and mechanical industries suffered a decline from 1920 to 1930, while the number of white persons so employed advanced rapidly. Even in the states where there was an increase, that for whites far outweighed that for Negroes. At the same time, the number of Negro women employed decreased in a proportion that was constant for every state, while the percentage of white females employed increased slightly in Florida, Georgia, Louisiana, and Texas. The decrease of Negro women workers is a reflection of the withdrawal of Negro women from agriculture, while the increase of white women workers compensated in industrial and clerical employment for those taken from the cotton farms of the South.

Ordinarily, we would suppose that the class or race showing the smallest proportion of women and child workers was the more favorably circumstanced economically. However, if the smaller percentages for Negroes reflect displacement by other population groups rather than advancement of the economic status of the group itself, the question presents a far different angle. We are not in a position to know whether the economic status of the Negro in the South has declined or advanced since 1920. We can say that so far as school attendance is concerned, economic and population changes have worked toward precipitating an increasingly larger number of Negroes into high and elementary schools.

CHAPTER XII

Financing Separate Systems

CONSTITUTIONAL and legal enactments establish systems which are generally made mandatory both as to "separation" and as to "equality." The first mandate of the school laws is universally respected, while the second is almost as universally disregarded. In a recent study, McCuistion reported an analysis of the current expenditures for Negro schools in typical Southern states, as shown in Table XXIX.

TABLE XXIX [1]

SUMMARY OF EXPENDITURES IN COLORED SCHOOLS

State	Total Expended	Additional Amount on Equal Basis	Fraction of Equal Expenditures Received by Negroes
Alabama	$1,964,524	$3,515,946	.36
Arkansas	1,443,306	2,141,680	.40
Florida	1,302,623	2,881,090	.31
Georgia	1,667,884	4,273,514	.28
Louisiana	2,542,213	5,028,664	.33
Maryland	2,230,857	912,928	.71
Mississippi	1,583,541	6,015,099	.21
North Carolina	4,086,792	4,409,217	.48
Oklahoma	1,657,544	432,544	.79
South Carolina	1,718,854	6,056,927	.22
Texas	3,263,821	4,020,443	.45
Total	$23,461,959	$39,688,052	.37

[1] Fred McCuistion, *Financing Schools in the South*, Chicago, Julius Rosenwald Fund, 1930, p. 18.

The mere statement that more than twenty-three million dollars was spent in educating Negroes by Southern states in 1930 is impressive. If we qualify this statement with the fact that the money actually spent represented only 37 per cent of what should have been spent had a fair distribution of funds been made, the amount decreases in significance, especially if the high-sounding constitutional declarations for equality be remembered. The actual situation is that vast sums of money are being spent upon the education of Negroes by Southern states; but when compared with the amount spent for white children in accordance with the American theory of equal opportunity, there is much to be hoped for from the future.

Can the South Support Equal Systems of High Quality for Both Races?

By whatever index we may measure the ability of a state to support education, the Southern states incline toward the bottom of the rankings including all states in the Union. Table XXX gives the rank of the states which have legal, separate systems in various indices of the ability to support education.

It is instructive to compare this table with the proportion actually spent on the education of Negroes in these states. Mississippi, the state showing the lowest percentage of equal expenditures received by Negroes, ranks forty-eighth, at the extreme lowest point, of all the states of the Union in its ability to provide a system of education for all of its children. The United States as a whole shows three times as much wealth per child as Mississippi; three times as much average annual total income per child; more than twice as much average annual income per child; more than three times as much ability as judged from the index of economic resources (total income plus 1/10 wealth per

TABLE XXX [2]

WEALTH, INCOME, AND INDEX OF ECONOMIC RESOURCES PER CHILD AGED 6–13
YEARS IN THE STATES HAVING SEPARATE SYSTEMS, COMPARED TO THE
AVERAGE FOR THE UNITED STATES AND THE FOUR QUARTILES

States	Wealth per Child	Average Annual Total Income per Child	Average Annual Current Income per Child	Index of Economic Resources (Total Income Plus 1/10 Wealth per Child)	Index of Economic Resources (Current Income Plus 1/10 Wealth per Child)
UNITED STATES	$17,618	$4,194	$3,840	$5,955	$5,602
First Quartile	24,329	6,429	5,853	8,862	8,286
Second Quartile	21,362	4,622	4,158	6,758	6,294
Maryland	17,407	4,900	4,536	6,641	6,277
Missouri	18,480	3,800	3,598	5,648	5,446
West Virginia	16,710	2,863	2,622	4,534	4,293
Texas	10,958	3,047	2,715	4,143	3,811
Florida	13,917	2,751	2,374	4,142	3,766
Third Quartile	16,606	3,470	3,183	5,130	4,844
Oklahoma	9,747	2,728	2,440	3,703	3,415
Virginia	10,811	2,331	2,154	3,412	3,235
Louisiana	9,571	2,306	2,149	3,263	3,107
Kentucky	7,964	2,074	2,114	2,870	2,911
Tennessee	9,367	1,930	1,844	2,867	2,781
North Carolina	8,449	1,796	1,694	2,641	2,539
Georgia	6,464	1,619	1,649	2,266	2,296
Arkansas	7,190	1,569	1,568	2,288	2,287
South Carolina	6,528	1,496	1,532	2,149	2,185
Alabama	5,889	1,544	1,462	2,133	2,051
Mississippi	5,776	1,331	1,316	1,909	1,894
Fourth Quartile	7,987	1,884	1,813	2,683	2,612

child) ; and more than twice as much ability as judged from
the index of economic resources (as measured by current
income plus 1/10 wealth per child).

[2] *Federal Relations to Education*, Report of the National Advisory Committee, p. 173.

The relationship between wealth and educational efficiency may be judged in another manner. Wealth means ability to pay taxes for the support of an educational program. Taking the average for the United States, and for selected states in the upper brackets of wealth, what in general would be the ratio between the necessary tax rate in these areas as compared to the Southern States? This question is answered in Table XXXI.

In general it follows from Table XXXI that a state like Mississippi would be obliged to levy taxes six times as great as those levied in California to maintain an educational system as efficient for *all* of the children in Mississippi as in California. Alabama in 1930 levied a three-mill state tax, a four-mill county tax, and a permissible tax of three mills in the district for the support of public education. Counting all forms of taxation thus provided for, the ten mills now levied in Alabama would have to be multiplied six times to afford as much money per child as California can provide through a ten-mill levy. In 1928, the payments on general property taxes in the State of New York amounted to $2.05 for each inhabitant of that state. To raise the same amount of money in Mississippi would require a tax from four to six times as great as the tax levied in New York State in 1928.

In general, approximately 40 per cent of all governmental expenditures in 1928 were devoted to public educational expenditures. If this ratio is to be held constant in, let us say, Mississippi and California, it is evident that a program of education in the former state will necessitate heavy increases in total governmental expenditures if the two state systems are equalized, holding all other expenditures equal. Approximately five per cent of the national income is devoted to education. The application of this principle of equalization to Southern states would mean that, as compared to California, Mississippi would have to devote from

TABLE XXXI[3]

TAX RATES NECESSARY TO MAINTAIN EQUALIZED EDUCATIONAL OPPORTUNITIES
FOR CHILDREN IN THE UNITED STATES, WITH THE UNITED STATES
AVERAGE TAKEN AS THE BASIC INDEX OF 100 PER CENT

		Ratio of tax levy necessary to maintain adequate educational opportunity with the United States Average taken as 100% according to:			
States	Wealth per Child	Average Annual Total Income per Child	Average Annual Current Income per Child	Index of Economic Resources (Total Income Plus 1/10 Wealth per Child)	Index of Economic Resources (Current Income Plus 1/10 Wealth per Child)
UNITED STATES	$1.00	$1.00	$1.00	$1.00	$1.00
California	.52	.47	.50	.48	.50
New York	.72	.56	.56	.60	.60
Iowa	.63	1.09	1.07	.90	.88
Maryland	1.01	.85	.85	.90	1.05
Missouri	.95	1.10	1.06	1.06	1.03
West Virginia	1.05	1.46	1.46	1.31	1.30
Texas	1.60	1.37	1.41	1.31	1.30
Florida	1.26	1.52	1.61	1.43	1.48
Oklahoma	1.80	1.53	1.57	1.61	1.64
Virginia	1.63	1.80	1.78	1.74	1.73
Louisiana	1.84	1.82	1.79	1.83	1.80
Kentucky	2.22	2.02	1.82	2.07	1.92
Tennessee	1.88	2.17	2.08	2.08	2.01
North Carolina	2.08	2.33	2.26	2.25	2.20
Georgia	2.72	2.59	2.32	2.63	2.43
Arkansas	2.45	2.67	2.45	2.60	2.45
South Carolina	2.69	2.80	2.50	2.77	2.56
Alabama	2.99	2.71	2.62	2.79	2.73
Mississippi	3.05	3.15	2.91	3.11	2.95

20 to 30 per cent of its total income from all purposes to education, and the other Southern states would have to do the same in but slightly smaller proportion. Not even our most advanced educational systems have found citizens willing to levy such an immense tax upon their resources in the provision of public schools for the children of their communities.

---

[3] From Norton, *Ability to Support Education*, p. 67.

TABLE XXXII [4]

PERCENTAGE INCREASE IN WEALTH PER CHILD AGED 5-14 INCLUSIVE FROM
1880 TO 1922

Quartile	Wealth Per Child Aged 5-14 Inclusive			Percentage of Increase		
	1880	1900	1922	1880-1900	1900-1922	1880-1922
First Quartile	$5,500	$8,007	$19,738	45	146	258
Second Quartile	4,483	6,618	17,201	25	159	283
Third Quartile	2,845	4,421	13,412	55	203	371
Fourth Quartile	1,470	1,937	6,472	31	233	340

The industrialization of the South has had its greatest growth within the last thirty years. Existing differences in the wealth per child of various states are due (1) to the actual poverty of some states and the wealth of others, and (2) to the high proportion of educable children in these conditions. As to the first, however, wealth is increasing in the South at a rate unprecedented elsewhere in the Nation. The overbalance of children is due to the high birth rate that always accompanies a general low economic status on the part of a population. With the development of economic resources, it is probable that the disproportion of children to adults will decrease to something of the ratio to be found in more highly developed industrialized and urban areas.

The relative ranking does not show the true trend of wealth and its concentration in various parts of our nation. While this relative position has not been disturbed to any large degree, the factual evidence shows that by comparison with thirty or fifty years ago, the South is more able today to maintain systems of education similar to those found in richer states than she was in the past. Nevertheless, this diminution of the ratio between the various sections is slow, if certain. It would be agreed by all, perhaps, that the South is not now and never has been able to main-

---

[4] Norton, *op. cit.*, p. 60.

tain a system of public education of the highest quality for the children of both races because of its inferior ability to support education when compared with states in other sections of the country.

The special burden of a dual system. We have been considering here the question of ability under the presumption that *all* children were embraced within the sphere of an equalitarian distribution of educational opportunity. If the South had an entirely homogeneous population, it would not be able to maintain schools of high quality for the children unless its states and local communities resorted to heavy, almost crushing rates of taxation. The situation is further complicated by the fact that a dual system is maintained. Considering the expenditures made for Negro schools, it is clear that the plaint frequently made that this dual system *is* a burden is hardly true; but it is also clear that if an honest attempt were made to maintain "equal, though separate schools," the burden would be impossible even beyond the limitations of existing poverty.

The problem involves the duplication of plant, of administration, and of supervision. There are several counties in North Carolina where the per capita expenditures for Negro children are higher than those for white children, and this situation could be duplicated in other states where there is a small number of Negroes in the population. It is said that in Missouri, where the state law calls for the establishment of a separate school wherever there are as many as fifteen Negro educables in a district, a check of census reports shows a large number of districts reporting only *fourteen* Negro children. This is, of course, an open subterfuge to evade the expense of setting up a school for these Negro children; but it is plain that such a subterfuge would not be necessary if the population was a homogeneous one. We have, unfortunately, no certain knowledge of the degree to which separate schools swell school expenditures.

In large cities, where residential segregation concentrates the Negro population in a few well-defined areas, there is little more expense connected with a segregated system than with one in which segregation does not exist. In smaller cities, many of the more expensive services must be duplicated for both races; and such activities as are included in library work, transportation, and special classes would, if duplicated for both races, create a definite problem. There are but few instances at present, however, where an effort has actually been made in separate school systems to duplicate the more expensive school facilities for the benefit of the Negro children.

The Cash Value of a Negro Child [5]

At the height of the "Negro Fever" in the South just before the Civil War, small Negro children were sold in the open market at astounding prices. A sale at Marshall Court House in Texas is typical: Caroline, aged 11, $1,100; Frank, 9, $805; Little Allick, 7, $810; Catharine, 10, $700; Flora, 5, $695; Sarah, 9, $890; Dick, 7, $650; Sam, 3, $450; Phœbe, 10, $655; Ben, 6, $405.[6]

The slave markets have long since been torn down, or, as in several instances of authentic record, been transformed into schools for Negro children. It is true today, nevertheless, that Negro children in the majority of the former slave states still have a definite cash value, especially for the white children of school age in these states. Many writers on education in the South are fond of speaking sacrificially of the "heavy burden" that section has to endure from having to support two separate systems of education for white and black. Knight gives as a partial explanation for the backwardness of the Southern states in

---

[5] Reprinted from *School and Society,* Vol. 37, No. 959, May 13, 1933.

[6] Frederic Bancroft, *Slave Trading in the Old South,* p. 358.

education the fact that they ". . . with limited funds, have had to provide two systems of education for large numbers of children scattered over wide areas." But only a cursory glance at official reports will show that the "two systems," far from carrying with their support an additional burden, are a device by which the purpose of equalizing educational opportunity for white children is forwarded.

Norton has given an extended study of wealth per child which disregards the fact of the separate systems in the South and the discriminations practised within those states in the support of the two systems. In this day, when the question of Federal equalization is being put more and more to the fore, it is necessary to remember that fifteen of the seventeen states in which there are legally mandatory, separate systems in practice eliminate a large part of their theoretical burden through racial discrimination. In these states, Negro children have a definite cash value for every white school child. They allow by their presence, and by accompanying discriminations, immense sums to be released for the benefit of the children of white parentage, sums which would normally be dispersed evenly.

Using Norton's figures [7] as the basis for the estimated wealth of the several states, the writer has attempted to discover here just how much every Negro child in states maintaining separate systems is worth to every white child from the point of view of making it possible for the state to equalize expenditures for its white children more in accordance with the national index of per capita wealth.

Table XXXIII may be read: In the entire group of seventeen states maintaining separate school systems, the theoretical burden upon the wealth of the states in the age-group 6–13, according to Norton, is 5,148,194 white and 1,828,328 Negro children, a total of 6,976,522. Estimated

---

[7] Norton, *The Ability of the States to Support Education*, p. 24.

in this fashion, white children constitute 73.8 per cent and Negro children 26.2 per cent of the educational load. However, Negro children receive but 11.0 per cent of the money expended for educational services in these states, and in practice may be regarded as constituting only 11 per cent of the educational burden actually assumed. This is equivalent to saying that racial discrimination in expending school funds releases wealth that otherwise would have been shared by $1,197,416 children, all of whom, in the nature of things, are Negro children. It pays to discriminate; a residual burden of 5,780,175 children is left instead of the theoretical burden of 6,976,522 children counted by Norton. The resulting value of Negro children to these states is shown in Table XXXIV.

Table XXXIV may be read: The South has an estimated wealth of $64,774,518,000. Theoretically, this wealth gives a per capita valuation for each child aged 6–13 of $9,283. As shown in Table XXXIII, however, these states so discriminate in the expenditure of funds that to all practical intents, Negroes constitute only 11 per cent of the school population for whom a burden is actually assumed by the states. This reduces the educational load of these states by the equivalent of 1,197,416 children. Readjusting the per capita wealth of the section to this reduced burden, as occurs in actual practice, we have a real per capita wealth of $11,205. On account of racial discrimination, the sum of $1,922 is released to increase the wealth available for the education of each white child in the South. Each Negro child in the section adds $5,791 to the potential wealth which may be tapped in the support of a system for white children.

Negro children may be said to fetch the highest price in Florida, where each white child has added to the wealth available for his education the sum of $6,119, on account of discrimination, and where each Negro child, accordingly,

TABLE XXXIII

THEORETICAL AND ACTUAL EDUCATIONAL BURDEN OF STATES MAINTAINING SEPARATE SCHOOL SYSTEMS

State	No. of Children Aged 6–13 (Theoretical Burden)			Per Cent in Population (as Shown by Theoretical Burden)		(As Shown by Burden Assumed)		Negro Children for Whom Burden is Not Assumed	Residual Burden
	White	Negro	Total	White	Negro	White	Negro		
Alabama	301,273	193,428	494,701	60.9	39.1	89.9	10.1	159,581	335,120
Arkansas	266,662	93,205	359,867	74.1	25.9	82.0	18.0	34,670	325,197
Delaware*	28,287	4,797	33,084	85.5	14.5	85.0	15.0	194	33,278
Florida	114,425	60,269	174,694	65.5	34.5	94.4	5.6	53,882	120,812
Georgia	338,618	259,647	598,265	56.6	43.4	86.0	14.0	204,524	393,741
Kentucky	409,970	36,621	446,591	91.8	8.2	92.0	8.0	972	445,619
Louisiana	215,565	138,983	354,548	60.8	39.2	87.9	12.1	109,310	245,238
Maryland	185,667	40,481	226,148	82.1	17.9	88.3	11.7	16,880	209,268
Mississippi	176,997	199,592	376,559	47.0	53.0	80.0	20.0	155,343	221,246
Missouri	517,563	22,127	539,690	95.9	4.1	96.1	3.9	1,123	538,567
N. Carolina	366,992	167,982	534,974	68.6	31.4	87.4	12.6	115,075	419,899
Oklahoma	379,107	29,854	408,961	92.7	7.3	94.9	5.1	9,470	399,491
S. Carolina	164,901	199,925	364,826	45.2	54.8	89.7	10.3	180,990	183,836
Tennessee	366,966	83,299	450,265	81.5	18.5	87.0	13.0	28,645	421,620
Texas	747,904	146,719	894,623	83.6	16.4	86.1	13.9	25,978	868,645
Virginia	302,194	138,322	440,516	68.6	31.4	89.0	11.0	100,973	339,543
W. Virginia*	265,103	13,074	278,177	95.3	4.7	95.0	5.0	878	279,055
Total	5,148,194	1,828,325	6,976,519	73.8	26.2	89.0	11.0	1,197,416	5,780,175

*Delaware and West Virginia are exceptions, Negroes receiving more money in these states than warranted by their percentage in the population.

is worth $11,617 to the resources behind the general white school population.   In Kentucky, Negro children are worth hardly anything; each white child profits only to the extent of having $17 more of wealth released for his schooling, so that each Negro child accordingly is worth only $194.   In Delaware and West Virginia only can Negro children be considered as liabilities and not as assets.   So large is the contribution of Negro children to the economic ability of Florida to support schools for white children that its revised rank would rise from thirty-fifth in the Nation to twenty-third.   Maryland moves up six places from thirty-first rank to twenty-fifth, past Wisconsin, Maine, Indiana, Missouri, Delaware, and Idaho.   The complete abolition of all schools for Negro children and the release of all wealth for the benefit of schools for white children in the states here mentioned would add but $1,491 to the wealth per white child in the section, a sum less than that now furnished.   The resulting wealth would be $13,553 per child, compared to a theoretical $9,283, assuming equality in burden, and $11,205 under existing discriminations.   In other words, the states involved have already done most of what was possible in equalizing the wealth of their communities with that of others throughout the Nation: a complete abolition of schools for Negroes in Florida, for example, would add but $1,189 to the $20,058 of wealth available for each white child, an inconsiderable amount compared to the $6,119 already gained through the segregated, inferior system.

The cash value of Negro children today goes to increase educational opportunities for white children, rather than into the pockets of slave speculators; but not even the doughty Texan who in 1857 bid in "Sam, 3," for $450, and "Carolina, 11," for $1,100, could well afford to quarrel with the prices offered for similar commodities in the modern market.

TABLE XXXIV

The Cash Value of Negro Children in States Using Racial Discrimination in School Expenditures as a Means of Equalizing Educational Opportunity for White Children

State	Estimated* Wealth of States (000's Omitted)	Wealth Per Child		The Cash Value of Negro Children in Terms of—	
		(With* Theoretical Assumption of Equal Expenditures)	(Eliminating Negro Children for Whom Burden is Not Assumed)	Amount Available for Each White Child in State Due to Discrimination	Amount Contributed by Each Negro Child
Alabama	$2,913,467	$5,889	$8,693	$2,804	$4,368
Arkansas	2,587,642	7,190	7,957	2,767	2,182
Delaware	617,217†	18,655†	18,547††	108†	643†
Florida	2,431,235	13,917	20,058	6,119	11,617
Georgia	3,867,489	6,464	9,822	3,357	4,379
Kentucky	3,356,843	7,964	7,981	17	194
Louisiana	3,393,690	9,571	13,838	4,266	6,570
Maryland	3,936,717	17,407	18,721	1,314	6,029
Mississippi	2,175,530	5,776	9,832	4,056	3,590
Missouri	9,973,901	18,480	18,519	39	801
North Carolina	4,520,052	8,449	10,764	2,315	5,058
Oklahoma	3,996,341	9,747	9,978	231	2,937
South Carolina	2,381,674	16,528	12,955	6,427	5,201
Tennessee	4,217,940	9,367	9,999	632	2,784
Texas	9,803,548	10,958	11,286	328	1,670
Virginia	4,762,633	10,811	14,026	3,215	7,024
West Virginia	4,648,599†	16,710†	16,658††	52†	1,066†
Total	$64,774,518	$9,283	$11,205	$1,922	$5,791
United States	$310,042,785	$17,618	$18,902	......	......

*Norton, op. cit.
†Delaware and West Virginia are exceptions, Delaware spending 15.0 per cent of its school funds on 14.5 per cent of its school population which is Negro, and West Virginia spending 5.0 per cent of its school funds on the 4.7 per cent of its school population which is Negro.

The Rôle of the Negro Child in County School Finance

Negro children have a "value" for white children so far as great state systems are concerned. When we examine the expenditures by race within individual counties of Southern states, we find that the problem of financing both white and Negro schools is inextricably bound up with the proportion of Negroes in the total school population. This fact is due principally to the existence of large state apportionments which were instituted years ago on the principle of per capita payments according to school population. More modern funds have decried the per capita apportionment as unscientific, and have devised equalization plans on the basis of attendance, teacher and pupil units, and other criteria; but the facility with which per capita apportionments in the South have lent themselves to racial discrimination and to the peculiar advantage of small white populations in heavily populated Negro areas is largely the explanation for the delay of the section in exploring the possibilities of more equable means of state appropriations. The history of many of these funds and apportionments goes back beyond the Civil War, and at that time, both in the South and elsewhere in the Nation, the method of per capita appropriation and expenditure appealed to legislatures as the fairest method of handling state school funds. After the Civil War and for a brief time during and after Reconstruction, we have seen that these state funds, the prime source of educational support, were in large measure fairly expended for the two races. The next step we have seen to be the change in the laws to permit discrimination against Negro children in order to conserve the advantages of funds for white children. This step was followed by the belated adoption of local taxation.

In an unpublished master's thesis at Fisk University, Miss Helen L. Merriwether [8] analyzed the expenditures for teachers' salaries for each of the counties in Maryland, North Carolina, South Carolina, Georgia, Florida, Alabama, and Louisiana. These expenditures by race were reduced to per capita expenditures by obtaining the number of white and Negro children in the respective counties aged 5–19. These per capita indexes were then arranged by race for states and for the total of the seven states. They show a wide range in expenditures for both races, with the expenditures for white counties far in excess of those for Negroes. They also show, when arranged according to the percentage that Negro scholastics are of the total population, that the expenditures for Negro children are lowest in the counties where members of the race are most heavily concentrated, and are highest where Negroes are in a small minority. For the whites, the tables show significantly that the reverse is true: where there are fewest Negroes in the total population, expenditures for white children are lowest. All states do not show the same decisive pattern, but the trend is evident in each state. A general table which includes findings for all of the states that were covered in this study is shown on pages 240 and 241.

The summary Table XXXV may be read: In 1929–1930 in the seven states studied, there were 75 counties with a Negro population between 0.0 and 12.4 per cent of the total population aged 5–19. The median of per capita payments for teachers' salaries for Negro children in these counties was $8.62, while that for whites was $14.31. In the 96 counties where the proportion of Negroes in the population ranged from 12.5 to 24.9 per cent, per capita payments for Negro children showed a median of $5.28, while those for whites showed a median of $16.87.

---

[8] *The Per Capita Expenditure by Race for Teachers' Salaries and Racial Population Ratios in Southern States.*

TABLE XXXV

THE DISTRIBUTION OF 526 COUNTIES IN SEVEN SOUTHERN STATES ACCORDING TO THE PER CAPITA EXPENDITURES AND PROPORTION OF TEACHERS' SALARIES, FOR THE SCHOOL POPULATION AGED 5-19, BY RACE

Expenditures	0–12.4 N.	W.	12.5–24.9 N.	W.	25.0–37.4 N.	W.	37.5–49.9 N.	W.	50.0–62.4 N.	W.	62.5–74.9 N.	W.	75.0–87.4 N.	W.	87.5–99.9 N.	W.	Total N.	W.
$0.00– 1.49			3		5		8		5		2		2				25	0
1.50– 2.99	4		14		28		21		35		25		11		1		139	0
3.00– 4.49	11		17		23		20		16		14		4				105	0
4.50– 5.99	8		20	(1)	14		11	(1)	14		4		1				72	2
6.00– 7.49	5	(3)	7		9	(1)	15		5		2						43	4
7.50– 8.99	8	(3)	10	(2)	12	(3)	12		3		1						46	9
9.00–10.49	7	(8)	5	(7)	5	(1)	5	(1)	3		1	(1)		(1)			26	22
10.50–11.99	9	(7)	2	(4)	6	(7)	3	(1)		(1)		(1)		(1)			20	20
12.00–13.49	4	(10)	5	(10)	6	(13)	1	(5)		(2)		(2)					16	36
13.50–14.99	1	(12)	5	(10)	1	(5)	1	(1)		(1)							8	37
15.00–16.49	2	(10)	3	(12)	2	(10)		(6)		(10)		(1)					7	50
16.50–17.99	2	(5)	3	(8)	1	(12)		(7)		(7)		(2)		(1)			6	44
18.00–19.49	2	(3)		(7)		(9)		(10)		(9)				(1)			2	34
19.50–20.99	2	(5)		(3)		(4)		(5)		(6)		(3)		(1)			2	31
21.00–22.49	2			(6)		(6)		(11)		(4)		(4)		(1)			2	32
22.50–23.99				(5)		(8)		(6)		(8)		(1)					0	29
24.00–25.49	1	(3)	2	(2)		(6)		(11)		(7)		(7)		(1)			1	37
25.50–26.99		(3)	6	(6)		(3)		(9)		(7)		(7)					0	33
27.00–28.49		(1)				(5)		(9)		(4)		(4)		(3)			0	24
28.50–29.99				(3)		(3)		(1)		(7)		(4)		(1)			0	17
30.00–31.49		(2)				(1)		(3)		(5)		(4)		(2)			0	13
31.50–32.99				(2)		(3)				(2)		(3)					0	10
33.00–34.49				(2)		(5)		(2)		(2)		(3)		(1)			0	15

240

34.50–35.99																	0	5
36.00–37.49		1	(1)		(2)		(1)		(1)		(2)		(1)				1	4
37.50–38.99			(1)		(1)		(1)		(1)				(1)				0	4
39.00–40.49					(1)		(1)		(1)				(2)				0	5
40.50–41.99					(1)		(1)										0	1
42.00–43.49			(1)		(1)												0	3
43.50–44.99					(1)						(1)						0	2
45.00–46.49																	0	1
46.50–47.99																		
48.00–49.49											(1)				(1)		0	2
Total	68	75	95	93	112	112	97	97	81	81	49	49	18	18	1	1	521	526
N. Median	$8.62		$5.28		$5.56		$4.46		$3.05		$2.85		$2.12		($2.56)			
W. Median		$14.31		$16.87		$21.25		$21.25		$22.58		$26.25		$28.50		($48.57)		

241

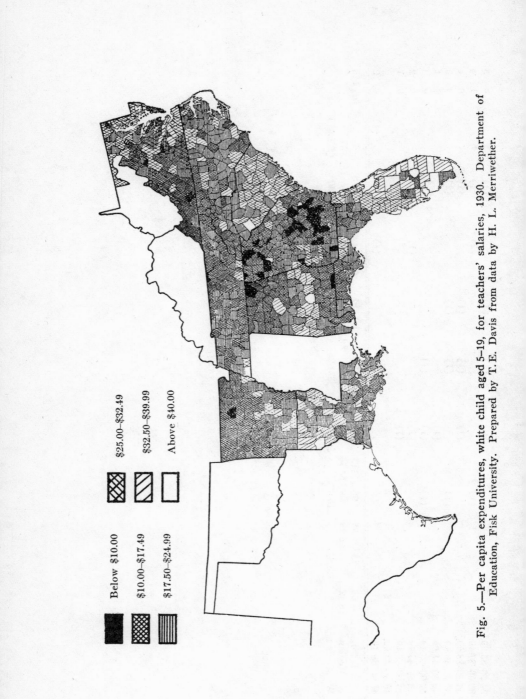

Fig. 5.—Per capita expenditures, white child aged 5–19, for teachers' salaries, 1930. Department of Education, Fisk University. Prepared by T. E. Davis from data by H. L. Merriwether.

Below $10.00

$10.00–$17.49

$17.50–$24.99

$25.00–$32.49

$32.50–$39.99

Above $40.00

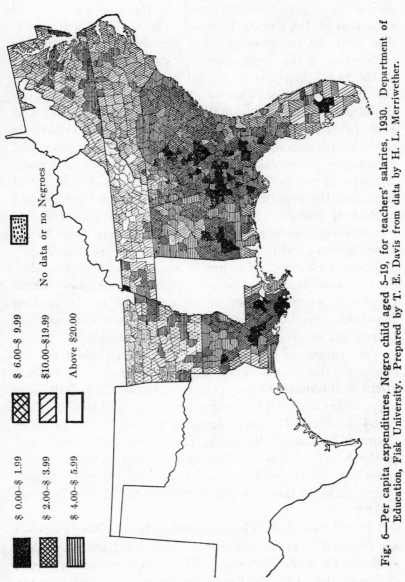

$ 0.00–$ 1.99

$ 2.00–$ 3.99

$ 4.00–$ 5.99

$ 6.00–$ 9.99

$10.00–$19.99

Above $20.00

No data or no Negroes

Fig. 6—Per capita expenditures, Negro child aged 5-19, for teachers' salaries, 1930. Department of Education, Fisk University. Prepared by T. E. Davis from data by H. L. Merriwether.

In any other section of America, we should refer our discussion of per capita payments to the wealth or assessed valuation of the county involved. In the South, it is evident that the factor of greatest significance is the number of Negroes in the population. A student of school finance in the South might be reminded of the legend of Cornelia, the Roman matron, who pointed to her children as her proudest adornments. In the present case, however, it is doubtful if the Southern schoolman would point with pride to the multitudes of Negro children who nevertheless are the foundation upon which the system of school finance rests, and who, if not precisely "jewels," are the most substantial asset that the county or state can possess under the present method of finance. The sums available for the education of white children are greatest where there are most Negro children, and, while the median expenditure for Negro children in no population group equals that for white children, expenditures for Negro children are highest where there are fewest Negroes and come closer to the median for white expenditures in counties where there is the smallest percentage of Negroes in the total population.

The range of expenditures for Negro children for teachers' salaries, per capita population aged 5–19, is from $0.29 in Randolph County, Georgia, to $36.57 in Baltimore City, Maryland. The range for white children is from $5.64 in Cobb County, Georgia, to $48.57 in Lowndes County, Alabama. Baltimore City is the only school unit in the South with a separate system where more money is spent per capita for teachers' salaries for the education of Negro children than for whites, the white per capita being $33.22.

The old formula will bear repetition here. Negro schools are financed from the fragments which fall from the budget made up for white children. Where there are many Negro children, the available funds are given principally to the

small white minority.   Besides depressing expenditures for
Negro children, expenditures for white children in these
heavily populated Negro counties are far above the median
for the entire state.   In counties with a small Negro population, where there is no great advantage in parcelling out
funds as in the "black" counties, there is a greater inclina-
tion to let the children "share and share alike" in state and
local funds.   The result is that in "white" counties expenditures for Negro children are far above those for children of
the same race in "black" counties, while expenditures for
white children are far below those for white children in
"black" counties because all of the available funds must be
distributed to all of the children.

Typical Budgets

The source of funds for Negro schools is, theoretically,
the same as that for all children in the public schools.   The
examination of typical school budgets for several units may
help clarify the existing situation.   For this purpose, we
have selected Lowndes County, in Alabama, a fairly typical
"black" county of the South-Central section; Winston
County, also typical of the "white" counties of north Alabama; and the cities of Birmingham, in Jefferson County,
and Montgomery, in Montgomery County.   It is not believed that the problems of finance here displayed make
these units unexceptionable in the South for their particular
class.   The expenditure for teachers' salaries in Lowndes
County for Negroes is $2.56 per child aged 5–19, and as
reported above, 164 out of 526 counties in seven Southern
states showed a per capita expenditure for this item of less
than $3.

The assessed valuation of Lowndes County in 1930 was
$6,485,309, giving, with its total of 11,014 black and white
children between the ages of 6 and 20, a per capita valua-

tion of $588. Jackson County had in the same year an assessed valuation of almost twice as much, $11,826,064, giving a valuation per capita for the 12,474 Negro and white children in the county of $948. In any scientific system of equalization, the expert would be inclined to regard Lowndes as the "poor" county and Jackson, by comparison, as a relatively "rich" county.

However, when we turn to a list of expenditures by race, we find that the white children of Jackson County enrolled in school in 1929–1930 had total expenditures per capita of only $24.72, while the white children of Lowndes County had total per capita expenditures of $95.93. The per capitas for Negro children in the two counties show the reversed standing, with Jackson County paying $7.79 for each of the Negro children enrolled while Lowndes County paid only $4.76 for each Negro child enrolled.

But the paradox is not as astonishing as it would appear. As suggested above, the wealth as shown by assessed valuation here is illusory so far as reflecting the true capacity of the two counties to support schools for their *white* children. The Negro children of Lowndes County furnish the explanation for the tremendous total payment made for white children in the county. There were enumerated in

TABLE XXXVI [9]

RECEIPTS FOR TWO ALABAMA SCHOOL UNITS, 1929–1930

Receipts (Source)	Jackson County Amount	Per Cent	Lowndes County Amount	Per Cent
Revenue Receipts:				
General Apport.	$62,933	25.98	$53,525	50.30
Bonus Fund	4,000	1.65	3,000	2.82
Revolving Fund	394	0.16	0	0.00
Illiteracy Fund	1,677	0.69	164	0.15
Erection, Rep., and Equip. Fund	4,512	1.86	355	0.33

[9] *Annual Report of the State Superintendent of Education of the State of Alabama, 1929–1930.*

Receipts (Source)	Jackson County Amount	Per Cent	Lowndes County Amount	Per Cent
Revenue Receipts:				
Library Fund	480	0.19	0	
County H.-S. Fund	4,500	1.85	4,500	4.23
Attendance Fund	9,831	4.09	5,466	5.13
High-School Fund	6,077	2.50	5,205	4.89
Equalization Fund	9,351	3.86	0	
State Funds for Vocational Education	3,690	1.52	780	0.73
Total State Funds and Apportion.	$107,445	44.36	$72,995	68.82
Federal Funds for Voc. Ed.	$1,475	0.60	$480	0.45
County Tax	$46,502	19.20	$19,367	18.20
District Tax	23,219	9.58	4,203	3.95
Poll Tax	4,053	16.73	1,183	1.11
Total Local Tax Funds	$73,774	30.45	$24,753	23.27
Appropriations from Co. Bd. of Revenue	$ 0		$2,960	2.78
Matriculation and Incidental Fees	2,311	0.95	1,257	1.18
Gifts, Bequests, Cont. from Local Sources	10,879	4.49	82	0.07
Philanthropy	0		182	0.17
Rent, Interest, and other Revenue Receipts	0		259	0.24
Total Revenue Rec.	$195,884	80.88	$102,968	96.80
Non-Revenue Receipts:				
Loans, Bonds, Sales, Unpaid Warrants	$29,507	12.18	0	
Total Non-Revenue Receipts	$29,507		0	
GRAND TOTAL RECEIPTS	$225,391		$102,968	
Appropriations from Co. Bd. of Ed. Bal. Prev. Yr.	$16,770		$3,400	
Net Amount Available within Unit	$242,161	100.00	$106,368	100.00

1930 at the time of the biennial school census, 975 white
and 10,059 Negro children between the ages of 6 and 20.

The state apportionment in that year amounted to $4.86 per child of school age from the state school fund, and, for the 11,014 children of both races, amounted to $53,525 for Lowndes County—$4,739 on account of the 975 white children, and $48,786 on account of the 10,039 Negro scholastics.

The solution of Lowndes County's educational problem becomes clear. By spending a total of $22,049 of the amount derived from the state apportionment on all schools for Negro children, there is left a residue of $26,737, which, it appears, comes as a bonus for having so many Negro children in the county. In order to spend $80,103 for the white children of the county, therefore, the aforesaid sum of $26,737 is already in hand. To this may be added the $4,739 received as a state apportionment on the basis of the number of white educables. A state "bonus" fund for high-school attendance adds $3,000, a state illiteracy fund $164 more. A state erection, repair, and equipment fund gives an additional $355. A state county high-school grant of $4,500, made uniformly to each of the sixty-seven counties of the state, is another item. An elementary-school attendance fund of $5,466, contributed to in some degree by the attendance of Negro children; an attendance fund based on high-school enrollment and attendance, amounting to $5,205; and state funds for vocational education amounting to $780, with Federal funds to the sum of $480, give a total of $51,426, which in itself would provide a per capita payment for the white children of the county, without the levy of a single local tax, twice as large as the total payments made in Jackson County for white children. Lowndes County, however, does the generous thing by its white children by levying local taxes in the ratio of one dollar for school purposes to every $251.80 of assessed valuation, while Jackson County, with a per capita payment for white children almost four times smaller than Lowndes, is forced to raise locally one dollar to every $160.36 of assessed valuation.

TABLE XXXVII [10]

EXPENDITURES IN TWO ALABAMA COUNTIES FOR EDUCATIONAL PURPOSES, BY
RACE, 1929–1930

	Jackson County				Lowndes County			
	Money Spent		Expenditure Per Capita Child Enrolled		Money Spent		Expenditure Per Capita Child Enrolled	
Expenditure *(Purpose)*	*White*	*Negro*	*White*	*Negro*	*White*	*Negro*	*White*	*Negro*
I. General Control, School Boards, Superintendents, Compulsory Attendance	$7,136	$132	$0.80	$0.19	$4,382	$1,782	$5.24	$0.38
II. Instruction in Day Schools, Teachers' Salaries, Supplies, etc.	127,727	2,330	14.30	3.41	49,014	19,944	58.69	4.30
III. Operation of School Plant, Janitors, Fuel, Light, Water, etc.	3,447	0	0.38	0	1,258	0	1.50	0
IV. Maintenance of School Plant	2,292	0	0.25	0	0	0	0	0
V. Auxiliary Agencies, Transportation, Libraries, Lunchrooms, etc.	15,759	0	1.76	0	20,199	188	24.19	0.04
VI. Capital Outlay, New Grounds and Buildings, New Equipment	17,005	2,871	1.90	4.20	5,250	75	6.29	0.02
VII. Fixed Charges, Rent, Insurance, etc.	1,797	0	0.20	0	0	0	0	0
VIII. Instruction in Night Schools	3,176	0	0.35	0	60	0	0	0.02
IX. Debt Service	42,435	0	4.75	0	0	0	0	0

	Jackson County		Lowndes County	
	White	*Negro*	*White*	*Negro*
Total Enrollment	8,931	684	835	4,634
Total Payments	$220,774	$5,333	$80,103	$22,049
Total Payments Per Child Enrolled	$24.72	$7.79	$95.93	$4.76

[10] *Annual Report of the State Superintendent of Education for the State of Alabama, 1929–1930.*

It is probable that the school board members of Lowndes County would object to the payment of larger sums for the education of Negro children on the ground that the Negro parents do not pay any taxes. In this connection, it is interesting to note that in 1930, Lowndes County paid, altogether, $58,730.32 into the State Treasury of Alabama, and received back from the state for pensions and schools alone, $60,664.68.[11] Furthermore, of the property assessed in the county, $1,674,082 represented public utility corporation valuations of property which, comprised principally by such corporations as the Louisville and Nashville Rail Road, the Western Railway of Alabama, and the Alabama Power Company, was probably owned by "foreign" stock and bondholders not even resident in the state. Assuming that all other property in the county was owned by white people resident there, we have a "native tax" of $43,572.03, in return for which, as pointed out above, $60,664.68 was returned to the county for schools and pensions alone, not counting other services of the state, such as highways, courts, and so forth. Logically, the white school children of Lowndes County are being educated at the expense of outside interests, as it might be claimed that Negro children are educated at the expense of the white people of Lowndes County. It is, of course, too much to ask of prejudiced self-interest that it be logical.

That the county does do handsomely by the white children is seen by an examination of the data showing expenditures. A per capita of $24.19 was paid for the transportation, alone, of white children, compared to a per capita payment of $4.76 for all expenses for the Negro schools; and, in fact, Lowndes County spent in 1929–1930 only slightly less per capita for the transportation of each white child than Jackson County spent for all expenses for the education of its

---

[11] *Auditor's Report, State of Alabama, 1930.*

white children.   The per capita expenditures for fuel, light, and water for the white high-school children was $3.36, seventy per cent of the total per capita expenditures for Negro children.

The situation in Jackson County has been noted by implication.   The only fund which it shares to the exclusion of Lowndes County is the Equalization Fund, which adds but $9,831 to the resources of the county.   It is of the greatest significance that we note here that each of the state funds, with the exception of the Attendance and Equalization Funds, gave approximately equal payments to the counties irrespective of burden.   This is due to the fact that the politically dominant "Black Belt" counties until very recent years forced all payments to be made on a blanket county scale.   The Equalization Fund was specifically devised in Alabama to meet the requirements of white children in the "white" counties.

The net result of this peculiar set-up, unique in the respect that it could occur only in Southern states, is that a "poor" county like Lowndes has a per capita payment for white children four times as high as that in Jackson County, which has assessed wealth twice as great.   Another peculiar feature is that the equalization law, by an ironic twist, is obliged to "equalize" education in the state by giving money to a county with an assessed valuation of $948 per educable while the county with an assessed valuation of $588 is levying very low local taxes and refuses the offer of "equalization" because it would cost too much to put it into effect!

Sample budgets for the cities of Birmingham and Montgomery are shown to indicate the wide variations in payments for services rendered to Negro and white children. In Jackson County, and in Birmingham and Montgomery, more money is spent on Negro children than is received by the unit in state apportionments.

TABLE XXXVIII [12]

EXPENDITURES IN TWO ALABAMA CITIES FOR EDUCATIONAL PURPOSES, BY RACE, 1929–1930

Expenditure (Purpose)	Birmingham Money Spent White	Negro	Birmingham Money Spent Per Capita Child Enrolled White	Negro	Montgomery Money Spent White	Negro	Montgomery Money Spent Per Capita Child Enrolled White	Negro
I. General Control, School Boards, Superintendents, Compulsory Attendance	$65,860	$12,769	$2.00	$0.68	$15,978	$2,360	$2.07	$0.44
II. Instruction in Day Schools, Salaries, Supervision, etc.	1,924,221	399,822	58.65	21.27	344,936	49,973	44.71	9.29
III. Operation of School Plant, Janitors, Fuel, Light, Heat, Water, etc.	134,616	31,930	4.10	1.70	28,935	4,714	9.74	0.88
IV. Maintenance of School Plant	158,251	33,674	4.82	1.79	6,873	622	0.89	0.11
V. Auxiliary Agencies, Transportation, Libraries, Lunchrooms, etc.	10,237	4,968	0.31	0.26	12,533	120	1.62	0.02
VI. Capital Outlay, New Buildings, New Grounds, New Equipment	728,019	66,762	22.16	3.55	320,813	6,495	41.59	1.21
VII. Fixed Charges, Rent, Insurance, etc.	19,377	5,693	0.59	0.30	6,063	2,666	0.78	0.49
VIII. Instruction in Night Schools	28,264	6,424	0.86	0.34	2,181	0	0.28	0.00
IX. Debt Service	50,470	242	1.54	0.01	0	0	0	0

	Birmingham White	Negro	Montgomery White	Negro
Total Enrollment	32,805	18,796	7,714	5,375
Total Payments	$3,118,315	$562,284	$738,312	$66,950
Total Payments per Child Enrolled	$95.05	$29.91	$95.71	$12.45

[12] *Annual Report of the State Superintendent of Education for the State of Alabama, 1929–1930.*

State Equalization and Negro Schools

In the majority of Southern states which have adopted "equalization" laws, the term "equalized" cannot be applied to schools for Negro children save in a farcical sense. These laws have come principally because of the righteous indignation of the "white" counties, who have seen an unconscionable amount of state money sent into "black" counties under the old per capita apportionment system with results similar to those we have noted in the illustration offered by Jackson and Lowndes Counties. The "equalization" laws, accordingly, have been ingeniously framed by experts who wished to focus the benefit of the new funds upon the counties heavily populated by white children and sparsely populated by Negroes as an offset to the advantage hitherto enjoyed by the "black" counties in the disposition of state funds. In approved equalization schemes, the expert begins by estimating the ability of the local community to support schools, a standard according to a "defensible" instructional program. In the South, this would mean that the counties with the heavy Negro rural populations would fall within the category, in most cases, of the counties to be aided. In the "scientific" method of constructing equalization schemes, the authorities set up certain minimum requirements for support, in the way of local effort and aid, which is to be supplemented to a greater or smaller degree by state funds to the amount necessary to meet the minimum program.

In the South, the same superficial steps have been used in planning, but the joker is found in the setting up of minimum requirements which for Negroes are far below the requirements for the white children. This may mean separate salary scales or separately-sized teacher-units. A minimum salary for a white teacher, accordingly, may be set at $900 while the minimum for Negro teachers is set at $300.

At the same time, the size of the teacher-unit for white elementary-school children may be regarded as 30 white children enrolled while the teacher-unit for Negroes is set at 45 children.

TABLE XXXIX [13]

TENTATIVE VALUES OF THE VARIOUS TEACHER-UNITS FOR THE 1929–1930
ALABAMA STATE MINIMUM PROGRAM

Kind of Unit	Salary Portion of Each Unit	Maximum Value of Entire Unit
WHITE		
Elem. Teacher	$ 550.00	$ 687.50
High-School Teacher	1,050.00	1,312.50
Helping Teacher		2,400.00
Additional Amounts for Special Services*		
Elem. Principal	800.00	1,000.00
High Principal	1,200.00	1,500.00
Voc. Agr. Teacher	1,200.00	1,500.00
COLORED		
Elem. Teacher	275.00	343.75
High-School Teacher	525.00	656.25
Helping Teacher		1,200.00
Additional Amounts for Special Services*		
Elem. Principal	400.00	500.00
High Principal	600.00	750.00
Voc. Agr. Teacher	600.00	750.00

* These amounts apply only to certain teacher-units.

A tragic insight into the condition of Negro schools is given by the fact that, as low as the minimum requirements are for Negro children, but few counties with a considerable Negro population find it worthwhile to qualify for the desired state aid. In Alabama, the equalization law of the state is actually doing what it was intended to do—aid the "white" counties as compared to the "black" counties. The minimum program for white children in these counties, however, by no means compares favorably with the high expendi-

[13] Bulletin of the State Department of Education, *Equalization in Alabama 1929–1930*, State Printers, Montgomery, 1930, p. 5.

ture for those in "black" counties, and there is much agitation yet on the part of the people from the "white" counties
to remedy the situation of unequal advantage among members of the same race but in different counties which has
been perpetuated. The extent of this bitterness may be
gauged from a debate occurring in the Alabama Senate in
1933. A representative from a "white" county attempted
to change the method of apportionment so as to take away
from the "black" counties the monies now spent almost entirely on white children there and distribute them more
equably throughout the state for the benefit of all of the
white children. A "black" county representative angrily
retorted that if north Alabama attempted such a thing, the
white people of the "black" counties would take their
Negroes to the ballot boxes and vote them as they did in the
period just after Reconstruction, so as to exercise complete
control over state-wide referenda on the question. "You
know we haven't forgotten how to count Negroes, yet," was
the defiance of the "black" county man; and this challenge
effectively squelched all further agitation on the matter.

North Carolina had an equalization system similar to that
of Alabama here mentioned prior to its recent adoption of
what is considered by educators everywhere one of the most
advanced systems of state aid in existence. Under the old
system, the state board of equalization set a salary scale
and required that a six-months term be supported by local
funds, the state contributing to extensions of terms and to
meeting the salary minimum requirements. The minimum
salary requirements for Negro teachers were approximately
30 per cent below those for white teachers. Much latitude
was allowed to local authorities, however, with the result that
the laws as to state certification and minimum salaries were
frequently disregarded where Negroes were concerned. In
1930, the writer found in Union County, North Carolina,
that no less than ten of thirty-three Negro rural teachers

possessed no certificate at all, at a time when it was claimed
that every teacher in the state was required to have a state
certificate.   Furthermore, these teachers were being paid in
several cases less than $30 per month, when the state sched-
ule called for a minimum of $55 for each monthly check.
The authorities here, obviously, were saving money for white
schools by employing wretchedly trained and utterly incompetent Negro teachers, in contradistinction to the printed
expression of the equalization law.

The recent legislation of North Carolina places the responsibility for the entire support of the minimum six-month
term upon the state, with the assumption by the larger system of local bonded indebtednesses.   Local communities are
to apply local taxes to an enrichment of the state minimal
program.   A more recent attempt to extend the state support to eight months was hedged around by the clause, "the
seventh and eighth months may be run concurrently with
the fifth and sixth months"; *i.e.*, leaving a considerable
loophole which would logically be used first by those wishing to discriminate against Negro children.   The North
Carolina experiment will be deserving of the greatest attention in the future.

State equalization in Maryland has proven relatively advantageous to the Negro schools, although this state has the
peculiar distinction of being the only one in the South to set
separate salary scales by law for white and Negro teachers.
This clause is probably unconstitutional and challenges a
test of the issue involved.   In West Virginia, Negro teachers are protected by an equal-pay clause in the state law
providing for equalization.

An interesting application of equalization has recently
been made to Negro schools in Missouri.   In this state, a
large influx of Negro cotton tenants into the southwestern
section created a distinct problem for separate schools in districts already heavily indebted for buildings for white chil-

dren. By special grant of the state board of education, a
portion of the state funds were released to aid these districts
in caring for Negro scholastics. Although the total number of Negroes in the population of the state is inconsiderable, compared to the heavy concentrations in other states,
the principle has great significance for the future of schools
in the South for Negro children.

Summary

The South is the section of the country least able to support even a single system. As compared to the Nation at
large, it may be said categorically that Southern states are
not able to support systems for the two races comparing
favorably with national norms of achievement. The result
is that Negro children are discriminated against universally
in states with a heavy Negro population, all available funds
being devoted as far as possible to the needs of white school
children.

The county system of administration combines with ante-
dated methods of apportioning school funds to make Negro
children one of the most important factors in school finance
in the South. Besides keeping expenditures for Negro
schools down to a bare pittance, the easy availability of state
apportionments in "black" counties has thwarted effort after
effort to extend local taxation in the past, and state aid in
the present, to all sections of the state. The present method
of expending funds creates inequalities between white children almost as marked as those between white and black
children.

Per capita expenditures for teachers' salaries increase for
white children with the increase of Negro children in the
total proportion of Negroes to whites, and decrease for Negro children with a mounting ratio of Negroes in the population. This process indicates that the extension of the

proportion of state aid will be of doubtful value to the education of Negro children unless hedged about by rigid restrictions as to expenditure by race.

A study of county and city budgets will show that Negroes receive far less in expenditures for all items than white children, with the greatest diversity appearing in what may be classified as "new services," such as transportation.   Ordinarily, more of the school budget goes to these "auxiliaries" for white children than to all purposes for Negro children, even where Negroes are in a large majority in the population.

Equalization funds in the South have meant little to Negro children because they were intended, not to "equalize" education in the broader sense, but to offset by the provision of new state aid for "white" counties the old system, so advantageous to the "black" counties, by which apportionments were made on a per capita population basis but spent at the discretion of local authorities.

Perhaps the best conclusion of any discussion of the present status of financing schools for Negroes in the South today are the words of W. P. Keith, a liberal-minded superintendent of education of Jefferson County, Arkansas.

> I started out on the theory that the county superintendent is superintendent of Negro schools as well as white, but that, being a white man, I should first take care of the white schools. After I had done all I could for them, I would then take hold of the Negro schools. That may be a selfish policy. No doubt it is. However, this is the only policy with which a county superintendent may work in the South, especially in Arkansas.
>
> Well, we followed that policy and when we had done what we could for the white schools, we began to work on the Negro schools. When you start on a thing like that you had better make a resolution and stand by it. You will get criticism enough. You will be called, as Dr. Moton said last night, a "nigger lover." Take your stand and stay there and show by your work that you can get things done. We have done some building among the Negro schools and the

progress in school affairs among the Negroes has been more
pronounced than it has been with the whites. They have
outstripped us. . . .[14]

We may repeat here what was said above concerning the
obvious truth of Mr. Keith's statement of policy. The difficulty with the situation is that it is impossible to stop when
one has "done all I could for them," for there is always
something more to be done—county high schools, consolidated schools, transportation, special teachers, higher salaries, smaller classes. If the junior-college movement took
firm root in the South, the consequences it would have for
Negro schools are obvious. Until the budget for the education of Negro children can be planned on a basis of coöperative development for both whites and Negroes, assuring
eventual equality in expenditures, there can be no immediate hope for an equality of opportunity for Negro children.

---

[14] "A Job For the County Superintendent," *Education and Race Adjustment*, Atlanta, Inter-racial Commission, 1932, p. 50.

Part III

CURRENT PROBLEMS

CHAPTER XIII

The Teacher

A RECENT critic of our educational system took his text from the ideal university where Mark Hopkins sat on one end of the log and a student sat on the other. The log, said the critic, had put forth numerous shoots, and branches, and leaves, and finally became a forest, and in this wilderness of growth from the physical standpoint, sight had been lost almost entirely of Mark Hopkins and the student as well.

The criticism may not be entirely true of schools for Negroes. In one of his plaintive dialogues, the great Negro comedian, Bert Williams, was asked by his interlocutor what he needed. With a supreme gesture of despair, Williams would say, "What I needs? Why, man, I needs everything!" Certainly the deficiencies of separate systems for the instruction of Negroes are so manifold that no one division may be selected as particularly in need of improvement. Everything is needed.

The place of the teacher is one, however, that is axiomatic in its importance, and it presents a sphere where any program of improvement may find ready application. The schools have steadily evolved in the direction of accepting greater delegations of authority from other social agencies designed to fit the growing child into the social order. Negro children usually come to the school from environments, both at home and in their immediate neighborhoods, which fail to supply certain facilities for personal growth that are matter of course in other economic groups. The teacher of Negro boys and girls has, therefore, a tremendous responsibility along lines which make the task complex in nature.

In the earliest periods of organized attempts to educate Negroes, men and women of the highest character devoted themselves to a missionary life of teaching Negro children. In the South, there were white men and women of good family from the section itself, as well as from the North, who entered private and public schools as teachers. The expansion of systematic efforts soon demanded a native teaching force. The early colleges furnished this teaching force, and in more recent years, the states have assumed the task of supplying teachers for the three million Negro school children in the South. In 1930, there were nearly fifty thousand Negro teachers in the District of Columbia and the seventeen states in which separate systems are mandatory by law.

Teacher Supply

Excluding West Virginia, Delaware, and the District of Columbia, McCuistion [1] reported in 1930 that there were 47,426 Negro teachers certified in fifteen Southern states. Many persons are engaged in teaching, even in the best states with the most rigid requirements, as in North Carolina, who possess no certificate; in one county in North Carolina in 1930, the writer found, out of 33 teachers, ten who possessed no certificate of any description. These teachers, some of whom had never been beyond the fifth grade in school, had been employed by the County Superintendent because it was cheaper to hire Negro teachers with substandard requirements and pay these teachers very low salaries than it was to employ Negro teachers meeting the

---

[1] Fred McCuistion, *The South's Negro Teaching Force*, Julius Rosenwald Fund, Chicago, 1932, p. 18.

state requirements for certificates. In addition, it is to be remembered that in many localities in which short terms are conducted in the Negro schools, teachers frequently teach two different schools in one session.

As a standard of school excellence, it is generally agreed that the number of pupils in average daily attendance per teacher should not exceed from 25 to 30. The ratio of children to teachers in daily attendance is far larger in Negro schools. When the number of children enrolled per teacher is considered, it appears that there is much room for improvement. McCuistion reports that the situation has improved greatly in recent years, the number of children enrolled per teacher being 67 in 1912–13, 50 in 1921–22, and 47 in 1928–1929.[2] In Negro schools, it is true that the percentage of attendance is much less than among white children. Much of the poor attendance could be remedied by the provision of an adequate teaching staff, which would work back along all lines in the improvement of instruction and in rendering the school more attractive to prospective students. In 1924–1925, the average number of pupils enrolled per teacher in the entire United States was 31.94. Only Kentucky and the District of Columbia among systems for Negro children showed a smaller number in 1929–30.

If Negro teachers were supplied for the children of Southern states in the ratio characteristic of the Nation at large, the following numbers of teachers would be needed to supplement the Negro teaching staff immediately:

Alabama, with 3,473 teachers, would need 6,069, or 2,596 more.
Arkansas, with 2,383 teachers, would need 3,805, or 1,422 more.
Florida, with 2,148 teachers, would need 3,117, or 969 more.
Georgia, with 4,934 teachers, would need 8,062, or 3,068 more.
Kentucky, with 1,339 teachers, would need 1,342, or 3 more.
Louisiana, with 2,700 teachers, would need 4,487, or 1,787 more.
Mississippi, with 5,125 teachers, would need 9,164, or 4,039 more.

---

[2] McCuistion, *op. cit.*, p. 24.

North Carolina, with 5,815 teachers, would need 8,436, or 2,621 more.

Oklahoma, with 1,275 teachers, would need 1,646, or 371 more.

South Carolina, with 4,339 teachers, would need 7,494, or 3,035 more.

Tennessee, with 2,721 teachers, would need 3,753, or 1,032 more.

Texas, with 3,859 teachers, would need 6,625, or 2,766 more.[3]

This would mean supplying teachers for the more than 1,000,000 Negro children who were not enrolled in any school during 1929–1930. In these twelve states, where 40,111 Negro teachers are listed, 23,729 additional teachers would be needed to supply a teacher-coverage similar to that found in the Nation at large.

A more practical basis of planning appears from an actual study of the manner in which teaching positions are being opened for Negro teachers in Southern states. It is estimated that the following numbers of Negro teachers are needed annually in these states: Alabama, 500; Arkansas, 400; Florida, 300; Georgia, 750; Kentucky, 100; Louisiana, 400; Maryland, 210; Mississippi, 500; Missouri, 300; North Carolina, 600; Oklahoma, 300; South Carolina, 450; Tennessee, 400; Texas, 600; Virginia, 500. This gives a total of 6,310 positions which become open for additions to the Southern Negro teaching staff in the course of every year.

It is a significant fact that the Negro school population, like the white school population, is entering a period in which there promises to be no great increases in the total burden. If present population trends continue, we shall within another generation reach a stable school population. The white schools have already reached this point in the lowest school grades. There is yet a large provision to be made for an increasing population for Negro schools, but twenty years should transfer the great burden of teacher

---

[3] Johnson, *The Negro in American Civilization*, pp. 245-246.

demand from the elementary-school grades to the higher
grades among Negroes as well as among whites.

Teacher Supply and Demand

It is frequently the case that an official in charge of employing Negro teachers will insist that there is no reason for
offering larger salaries to Negroes in the public schools.
It is said that there is available at all times a large supply
of teachers for the Negro schools, and when one has ten applicants for a job paying $25 a month for five months, why
pay $50 a month for the same job?   If we believe that the
process of employing teachers is no more than fitting a human automaton into a particular niche, and signing salary
checks drawn to this individual for a stipulated length of
time, the question is unanswerable.

If one conceives of the selection of teachers as the means
by which the best-trained men and women can be obtained
for the positions opened, the easy supply of Negro teachers
is less obvious.   In all too many instances, the employment
of teachers for Negro schools is performed under the assumption that the duty of the superintendent is finished
when he has driven the hardest and shrewdest bargain that
will staff the Negro schools.   The result is that thousands
of candidates for positions become available which would
under any system of higher standards suffice to balance the
supply with the demand.

In 1930, McCuistion reported that more than one-third
—18,130—of the Negro teachers working in fifteen Southern states possessed less than high-school training.   He also
pointed out that 58 per cent of these Negro teachers had
less than two years of college training, "which is commonly
considered the minimum professional training for elementary
teachers." [4]   So long as the Negro man or woman who en-

---

[4] McCuistion, *The South's Negro Teaching Force*, p. 21.

ters the profession with two or more years of college work is obliged to compete with thousands who have never advanced even to the point of high-school education, it can be said that there will be an oversupply of Negro teachers.

The turnover in Negro schools in the South, together with deaths, retirements, and so forth, is estimated to furnish the need for approximately six thousand new teachers annually. If the entry of new personnel into the field could be limited to those meeting minimum requirements, including all graduates of Negro colleges and two-year teacher-training departments in the South there would be approximately 2,400 candidates available for the six thousand jobs. It is obvious, then, that under existing circumstances the supply of Negro teachers with two or more years of college work would have to be supplemented by additions from the ranks of high-school graduates, of which class from four to five thousand become available annually. In a state like Alabama, for example, it is estimated that 500 jobs are opened annually in the Negro schools. In 1929–1930, to supply this demand, there were 24 graduates of four-year teachers' colleges and 186 graduates of two-year colleges, or a total of 210 persons with the minimum requirement. This would leave a shortage of almost three hundred teachers. However, there are several hundred high-school graduates who become eligible to teach either by graduation from high school, in some counties, or by spending six weeks in a summer school immediately following graduation. The writer knows of a "Black Belt" county in Alabama where it is the custom of the Superintendent, three or four weeks before the Negro schools are to open, to send the Negro supervisor of his county to Birmingham, commissioned to recruit teachers for the Negro schools at a salary of $25 monthly for five months. The type of teacher thus solicited, the resulting turnover, and the educational results obtainable may be imagined.

In many states, the authorities have struggled bravely with the task of imposing higher standards upon local communities in the employment of Negro teachers.   In as many instances, however, they have lacked coercive influence in effecting any drastic changes, and even where equalization laws have been passed, their requirements have been modified so greatly with reference to Negro salaries as to make a rigid selection of Negro teachers barely operative.   In Louisiana, for example, at a time when the average annual salary of Negro teachers within the state was $293, the state salary scale set as an average salary total for Negro teachers the sum of $300 per annum, while the minimum payment for white teaching units was set under the equalization requirements at three times that amount.   The low standards required of Negro teachers and the slight stimulation presented to prompt them to carry on their professional training, with the low salaries generally paid, constitute a vicious circle that shows no immediate signs of being broken.[5]

The salary of a Negro teacher may range anywhere from $100 per annum for a four-months term to $1800 for a nine-months term within the same state.   The range by states is from $306 per year in Georgia to $947 in Maryland, for Negroes, as compared to a range for white teachers of from $667 in Arkansas to $1,406 in North Carolina. In sixteen fairly typical counties in the South surveyed in 1928–1931, the salaries for Negro teachers were found to be as shown on page 270.[6]

From the time when the Peabody Fund first inaugurated a differential system of payments to schools for white and colored pupils and explained its action by saying that "it did not cost as much to operate a Negro school as it did a

---

[5] See *Report of the State Superintendent of Education of Louisiana*, 1930.

[6] Foreman, *Environmental Factors in Negro Elementary Education*, see Appendix.

Counties	Average Length of Term in Months	No. of Teachers	Average Monthly Salary
Alabama			
Jefferson	8.7	371	$ 67.86
Mobile	9.0	164	51.77
Dekalb	7.0	6	51.25
Baldwin	7.2	28	47.30
Limestone	7.1	44	43.26
Montgomery	6.9	183	44.84
Wilcox	5.0	59	25.00
Louisiana			
Orleans	9.0*	327	126.02
Webster	6.1	65	56.17
Desoto	4.3	96	37.70
Tensas	6.5	43	50.35
St. James	7.0	18	41.11
North Carolina			
New Hanover	9.0	70	91.51
Durham	8.6	98	87.32
Edgecombe	6.4	90	68.49
Union	6.2	58	56.39

* Orleans Parish is coextensive with the city of New Orleans. The term is for nine months, but salary payments were for ten months.

white school," various explanations have been given for paying Negro teachers smaller salaries than are paid to white teachers. A reason not often mentioned but perhaps of greatest importance is simply the great saving in school funds effected by discriminating against the Negro teachers, in no small degree influenced by the practical impossibility of maintaining two systems with high salary scales without imposing an impossible tax upon the resources of the communities affected. In many instances, of course, the salaries of the Negro teachers are sacrificed to the end that no local tax at all need be levied, the entire expenses of employing white teachers at salaries well above the state medians being met from payments from the general school funds paid on the basis of the general school population, white and black.

It is also generally believed (a) that Negro teachers are inferior to white teachers, and therefore should be paid at lower rates, and (*b*), that the living cost for Negro teachers is lower than that for whites, and that therefore they can live respectably on sums which would not support the white teacher in a decent manner. The first reason is hardly susceptible to extended argument, being a matter more of judgment, prejudiced or not, than of experiential fact. The second reason carries more weight because it is frequently observed that a much larger number of Negroes will seek employment as teachers, even when as graduates from colleges they are offered greatly inferior wages, than would be the case among white candidates.

It is generally true that the number of "white collar" jobs open to Negro graduates are inferior in variety or in rewards to those open to white men and women. The white college graduate in normal times had numerous choices— among clerical work, salesmanship in stores, banks, and securities houses, while the Negro college and normal-school graduate is restricted to a few narrow lines of endeavor most promising of which is the teaching profession. It is another question, however, when we come to the opinion that the public educational system should capitalize upon the prejudice which bars Negroes from other occupations by forcing Negro school graduates to seek employment at pitiable wages. Certainly it is a debatable issue whether or not the school system should take shrewd advantage of the extremities of the race, and whether or not the individual should, for equal hours of labor, and for equal types of services, be given inferior wages.

In the city of Nashville, Tennessee, in 1930, a differential salary schedule was in effect for teachers of the two races. Table XL indicates the result of this system.

The Constitution of the State of Tennessee, under which the Charter of Nashville has been granted and under which, consequently, the school system is operated, states that "A public school system shall be maintained . . . for the equal

TABLE XL [7]

MONTHLY SALARIES OF THE VARIOUS TYPES OF NASHVILLE TEACHERS AND
PRINCIPALS, MAY, 1930

	No.	Range	Median	Mode
White				
Teachers: Elementary-School	262	$ 60.00–$175.00	$128.03	$125.00
Teachers: Junior-High-School	129	80.00– 170.00	134.86	135.00
Teachers: Senior-High-School	52	80.00– 220.00	172.50	170.00
Principals: Elementary-School	12	155.00– 203.00	173.90	
Principals: Junior-High-School	10	203.00– 269.00	245.50	
Principals: Senior-High-School	1	400.00		
Negro				
Teachers: Elementary-School	96	$ 40.00–$135.00	$101.50	$ 95.00
Teachers: Junior-High-School	30	60.00– 120.00	107.27	105.00
Teachers: Senior-High-School	14	110.00– 125.00	117.22	115.00
Principals: Elementary-School	9	125.00– 145.00	131.66	
Principals: Junior-High-School	3	137.00– 153.00	143.33	
Principals: Senior-High-School	1	165.00		

benefit of all the citizens" of the state. In addition, there are the stipulations of the United States Constitution under the fourteenth amendment with reference to "due process" and discrimination on the basis of race, color, or previous condition. The Nashville schedule of differential salaries has been in vogue as a result of special rulings of the city board of education, which has laid down a specific salary schedule which differentiates the maximum and minimum salaries to be received by the white and Negro teachers of the city, not on the basis of training, but on the basis of color.

The probable explanation that would be given, of course, is that Negro teachers can live more cheaply than white teachers. A study of the cost of living, however, indicates that there is little difference between the basic requirements for livelihood of teachers of the two races. Eighty-three white teachers boarding out reported a cost of room and

[7] Frank P. Bachman, *A Survey of the Public Schools of Nashville, Tennessee,* George Peabody College for Teachers, Nashville, 1931, p. 219.

board of $558 per year, while 96 Negro teachers reported
a cost of $548 per year.   One hundred and fifty-two white
teachers reported the cost of room and board when living
at home of $532, while 45 Negro teachers living at home
reported this cost as $456.   A great difference was shown
in the matter of householders, 192 white teachers reporting
an annual cost of $1,353 for self and family when keeping
house while 94 Negro teachers reported a cost of $984 for
self and family when keeping house.[8]   The last figures indicate, of course, that the Negro teachers have been obliged
to adapt their standard of living to the income received,
while the first figures showing cost of board and room when
living away from home are nearly identical for the two
groups.   No enlightened public policy could well afford to
continue a discrimination in the payment of its servants
engaged in the work of the public weal which consigned a
portion of them to an inferior standard of living on account
of race.

For example, the maximum salary payable to the principal of the Negro high school was $165 per month, which
was less than the median salary paid to white junior-high-
school teachers.   The maximum salary paid to the principal
of the white senior high school was $400.   It might be said
that the Negro high-school principal could live more cheaply
and therefore maintain a higher standard on $165 per month
than the white high-school principal could maintain on $400
per month; but a plain inspection of the facts indicates that
what actually happens is that the Negro school principal is
obliged to restrict his standard of living to his income, while
the white high-school principal must similarly restrict his
standard of living to what $400 per month might purchase
in the way of subsistence and provision for his family in a
city like Nashville.   By setting up a separate salary sched-

---

[8] *Ibid.*, pp. 228–230.

ule, the public-school authorities not only decide as to the relative needs of various groups in the population; they also exercise a dictatorial influence in setting up separate standards of decency and living in two groups of the citizenry.   In a state which took its democratic principles seriously, such discrimination would be unthinkable.

Efficiency of the Negro Teacher

Certainly the Negro teaching staff lacks a full share of that effectiveness which it might possess under more favorable conditions.   As an example of one of these handicaps, it is pointed out by McCuistion that in 1928–1929, expenditures for teaching equipment in Georgia white schools were 99 per cent of the total expended for this purpose and the share of the Negroes, 1 per cent.   Negroes constituted 34 per cent of the school population.   In five states where Negroes were 31 per cent of the population, only 9 per cent of the expenditures for teaching equipment went to the Negro schools.   Standard tests of pupils are valueless in determining the true efficiency of the Negro teaching force. An investigator enters a school building which is a broken-down shack and finds there a teacher with from 50 to 75 children in attendance, seated on rough benches, with no blackboards in the room and a total dearth, in fact, of any kind of equipment.   The children for the most part come from homes in the lower economic brackets.   Their parents in a rural region may show an illiteracy as high as 65 per cent, and not less, even in cities, than 15 per cent.

These children have attended school irregularly and for terms in rural areas seldom exceeding six months.   There are no libraries, no newspapers, no stimulating conversation or contacts of any kind which might aid the school in its enlightening work.   The result of a test administered to such a group under such conditions is less a test of the efficiency of the school than it is an index to the entire complex of social, economic, and educational factors which play upon the group. In the same way, the teachers must be regarded as products of a system similar to that which has brought their pupils to the school. The teacher may come from a middle-class home and, through a process of elimination and selection, represent a somewhat higher level of environmental origin than his typical student. If the same standards of training are insisted upon for white and Negro teachers, it may well be that the Negro teachers may be equal, and, because of the lack of other opportunities for bright young Negroes, be superior to, comparable groups of white teachers. In no case should we diminish our expectations as to what the teacher should achieve; but, on the other hand, it is absurd to expect the school to be able to overcome the accumulated deficiencies of generations of inferior social and economic status within a school generation. The Negro teacher has a greater opportunity for working the miracles of education demonstrably possible than has the teacher in a white school, as shown by the results of a few years of work by the early white missionaries from the North immediately after the Civil War. At the same time, his possibilities are more severely restricted by the crushing weight of general social maladjustment.

In the summer of 1931, the writer administered the Stanford Achievement Test in reading and arithmetic to 306 Negro teachers enrolled in summer school within that state who had been actively engaged in teaching in the school year 1930–1931. These teachers represented six Alabama counties in which the same test had been administered to 5,126 children in the third and sixth grades. In order to determine what effect additional training had upon the command these teachers possessed of the fundamentals, they were grouped into four classes with reference to preparation: Class A, those with two or more years of college work; Class

B, those with high-school graduation and some additional
college work; Class C, those with high-school graduation but
with no additional training; and Class D, those who had not
graduated from high school. In Table XLI, the educational ages equivalent to the scores registered by these
teachers are compared with the educational ages represented
by the scores made by the Negro children in the several
Alabama counties tested.

TABLE XLI

A COMPARISON OF THE EDUCATIONAL AGES OF ALABAMA TEACHERS AND
THIRD- AND SIXTH-GRADE NEGRO CHILDREN, AS SHOWN BY SCORES IN
THE STANFORD ACHIEVEMENT TEST

Group		Educational Age
Teachers		
Class A (Two or more years college)		15 years, 8 months
Class B (High school and some college)		13 years, 11 months
Class C (High school but no college)		13 years, 11 months
Class D (Not high-school graduates)		13 years, 5 months
Children		
Jefferson County	third grade	8 years, 3 months
	sixth grade	11 years, 0 months
Limestone County	third grade	8 years, 3 months
	sixth grade	10 years, 11 months
Baldwin County	third grade	7 years, 8 months
	sixth grade	10 years, 7 months
Mobile County	third grade	7 years, 8 months
	sixth grade	10 years, 6 months
Montgomery County	third grade	7 years, 6 months
	sixth grade	10 years, 6 months
Wilcox County	third grade	7 years, 8 months
	sixth grade	10 years, 3 months
National Standards	third grade	9 years, 2 months
	sixth grade	12 years, 3 months
	seventh grade	13 years, 3 months
	eighth grade	14 years, 7 months

With the tendency for less well prepared teachers to be
found where the achievement test scores of the children are

inferior, and for the best prepared teachers to be found in communities where the scores are higher, it is apparent that the typical teacher in a Negro school rates from two to three years educationally ahead of his pupils in the advanced grades. In other words, a typical Jefferson County, Alabama, Negro teacher shows an educational achievement equivalent to a middle-eighth-grade class, while her sixth-grade class which she has in daily charge shows an educational age of eleven years, corresponding to a school grade of about the fifth grade.

It is fair to state also that this evidence indicates that the teachers tested, who were 38.7 per cent of the 870 Negro teachers employed in the counties visited, were inferior in attainment generally to the achievement one is led to expect from the national standards for ninth-grade children. An arrangement of scores by the ages of the teachers tested indicated that the scores in achievement advanced as the ages of the subjects decreased, leading one to believe that the younger generation of Negro teachers is more able than the older generation. It is worthy of note, however, that the highest score made by any of the 306 teachers in two reading tests and two arithmetic tests was 498 out of a possible 517 points, a score achieved by a teacher who had graduated from the Broad Street Academy in 1892 and who had been teaching ever since. This school was equivalent to a present-day two-year high school.

Better Teachers

If intelligence and sincerity were applied to the problem of the Negro school-teacher, progress would be possible. Both local and state educational organizations could cooperate in enforcing a gradual but certain improvement in the condition of the Negro teaching staff. Such a movement would first attempt to take the selection of Negro teachers from the familiar though nebulous aura of "general acquaintance" and place it upon a higher though less informal and more systematic basis of fitting the prepared individual into the job.

Because Negroes do not participate in politics in many Southern states, it is frequently believed that the selection of teachers of Negro schools is on a much more impersonal plane so far as "favoritism" is concerned. Nothing could be farther from the truth. In all too many instances, preferment comes to the Negro candidate or teacher because the white patrons are able to make themselves felt as well as heard in the direction of school affairs. In a Louisiana parish, the writer found six persons teaching who were members of one Negro family. Not one of these teachers had ever attended high school, although the Superintendent publicly stated that it was his intention to have only persons with a minimum of high-school training teaching in the Negro schools. The inconsistency was explained in this way: during the Reconstruction troubles, this family of Negroes had aided the white conservatives in their effort to wrest the control of the parish from the "carpetbaggers" and "scalawags." Grateful for the successful efforts of their Negro co-workers, prominent white men in the parish had pledged themselves to see to it that members of the G—— family should never fail to find employment in that parish. The result was that sixty years after Reconstruction, the gratitude of one race to one family of another race resulted in foisting six immensely inadequate Negro teachers upon Negro school children.

The writer knows of another instance in which a county superintendent, after being nursed through a terrific illness by a faithful Negro retainer, promptly appointed his bodyguard as principal of the Negro county training school as a reward for his services. In both of these instances, the motive prompting the employment of these Negroes was undoubtedly very precious and highly laudable; but when we consider the effect upon the educational future of several thousand Negro children, and the proper expenditure of the public funds, the means adopted for exhibiting gratitude seem at least open to serious question. It has been said humorously that the means by which the balance in race relations is maintained in the South are that every white man has "his Negro," whom he believes in and trusts in spite of a possible abhorrence of the race as a race, and that every Negro in the South has "his white man," to whom he can look for protection and patronage in troublous times. There is much truth in this statement, but the Negro teaching problem would be moved considerably nearer to a solution if familial relations of this sort were subordinated in the employment of teachers for schools where Negro children are to be educated at public expense.

It has become the public policy of most Southern states to assign the task of training teachers for the state system to the normal schools and teachers' colleges established and maintained by the state. No Southern state now possesses the machinery by which all of the necessary replacements for its Negro system could be furnished by the state schools alone. That this machinery should be placed in operation by the state and maintained by it, even if it necessitates the exclusion of private endowments and foundations, is highly reasonable. Beginning with a satisfactory salary schedule, state-wide in extent, it should be possible to make surveys of the teaching needs and replacements of the entire state, as is now done in many of our cities. The number of Negro graduates could then be adjusted to the number of positions which open up. Such a plan is far more feasible where the Negro schools are concerned than it would be for white schools. The administration of Negro schools for the most part is out of the range of local control and of a centralized nature which makes such a project possible

here where it would be impossible where the white schools
are concerned.

Specific knowledge. For better or worse, the program
of schools in which Negroes are enrolled in preparation for
teaching have adopted the curricular provisions found in
our largest centers.   The requirements for state certificates
recently enacted are in most cases identical for members of
the two races.   This fact gives rise to a most perplexing
problem.   The state may, for example, require that the
teacher who presents herself as a candidate for certification
on completion of the two-year college program shall have
had certain definite courses included in her course of training.   The typical program of a state college for Negro
teachers in training for elementary-school certificates was
as follows in 1931:

> Seventy-two semester-hours required for two-year course.
> Eight hours required for general methods.
> Eight hours required for general and educational psychology.
> Twenty-four hours required for special methods courses, in-
>   cluding methods in the general school subjects, and in
>   methods of administering tests, etc.
> Four hours of physical education required.
> Four hours of music required.
> Twelve hours required for history and English courses.
> Twelve hours of electives.

The students to whom this course was offered were fairly
typical examples of the upper-level graduates of a school
system in the South for Negro children.   Measured by
national standards, the typical member of this normal class
had accumulated a backwardness in the fundamental subjects of approximately a year and a half in reading and
arithmetic by the completion of the eighth grade.   By the
time of graduation from high schools, whose programs for
the most part represented a sharp break from subjects
taught in the elementary schools, their retardation measured
by grade in the fundamental subjects would easily approxi-

mate from two to three years. They are then projected
into the college or normal school, bringing with them a fatal
weakness in the simple, everyday matters of a fundamental
instruction. Upon this faulty foundation is superimposed
a structure made up of all kinds of psychologies—general,
educational, adolescent, subnormal, and so forth. In the
same way, a second-year teachers'-college student whose
achievement in geography, when measured by national
standards, is that of a sixth-grade pupil in a standard school
system, is obliged to enroll for a course in methods of teaching geography.

It is true that the same problem must be met in Southern
colleges for whites, for which data show that typical normal-
school and teachers'-college students rank, in terms of
national norms, below corresponding groups in other sections
of the country. The problem is particularly important in
schools for Negroes because the general level of the group
from which prospective teachers are drawn is likely, as a
whole, to be as ill-circumstanced by comparison with white
students from the same section as these white students in
turn are likely to be below standards for Northern states.

It would certainly be opposed to permanent public policy
to set up for members of the two races different standards
of teacher-training which might in time come to be the
"dead hands" of a tradition that securely barred the way
to any further advance in methodology and material. One
way of meeting the situation would be to exercise in teacher-
training schools for Negroes an even higher degree of selection than is characteristic of the schools for white candidates
for teaching positions. If the abilities, so far as a command of the fundamental school subjects is concerned,
of two groups, one of white teachers'-college students
in the South and the other of Negro teachers'-college students, were projected in the form of two normal curves, it
is probable that the two would largely overlap. However,

the median for the white group would be higher than the corresponding median for the Negro group. The Negro teaching profession, then, if recruited from the upper fourth of the possible candidates, as compared to a white teaching force recruited from the upper half of the white distribution, would be likely to be similar in abilities and standards of achievement. Exercise of the closest selective inspection of candidates for the teaching profession among Negroes would, therefore, result in a group comparable to any in those qualities which make for good teaching. Where the white school can afford to reject fifty out of a hundred, the Negro school, to maintain the same caliber in its graduates at the present time, must reject perhaps seventy-five out of a hundred candidates.

Certainly this severe selection of teaching personnel is preferable to a normal or college curriculum which is such only in name, and which occupies its time in making up deficiencies in fundamentals which the student brings to college from elementary or high school. The development of method, an acquaintance with the nature and purpose of curricular objectives, and an appreciation of the psychological problems involved in teacher-student relations is highly necessary for the teacher; but the teachers' college can never hope to be both a good grammar school and a good college. Either the one or the other must be sacrificed.

Summary

The Negro teacher is the center of the problem of giving an education to Negro children. The number of Negro teachers is far too small for the number of Negro children actually enrolled in school, and is still more inadequate in view of the number of educables not enrolled in school.

Teacher demand among Negroes, however, is not determined by need, but by the practical considerations of a slowly expanding system. Artificial conditions of differential salary schedules and lower standards permit the ranks of Negro teachers to be filled with incompetent and poorly trained persons, who degrade the general level of the profession and make even more difficult the plight of the well-trained, competent applicant for a position.

The improvement of personnel among Negro teachers can come only through the provision of adequate salaries to encourage entrance into the field of properly trained individuals. At present, the efficiency of the Negro teacher is qualified by conditions beyond her control—equipment, length of term, attendance, and the faulty preparation of students, which has even deeper roots. In spite of these deterrent factors, the efficiency of Negro teachers could be greatly improved through effective supervision. The improvement of personnel must depend upon a greater degree of selection exercised in teacher-training institutions with regard to persons certified by them for teaching positions. The success of any program of selection will depend upon the coöperation of public-school authorities with teacher-training officials. No corps of teachers in training can be expected to subject themselves to the rigors of a strenuous scholastic discipline unless there are appropriate rewards for the employment of their faculties.

CHAPTER XIV

The Forgotten Child

THE echo of Professor Summer's dramatic phrase, "The Forgotten Man," by President Franklin D. Roosevelt promises to achieve immortality. It is no mere statement, however, to say that there is in America today a forgotten child. He is a child whose parents bear, in the majority of instances, the accumulated ignorance and poverty of centuries of labor, toil for which they were not requited. He is born into circumstances of disease and degradation and grows up to attend schools which are, for the most part, the most miserable provided in any civilized country for the generation of tomorrow. His father and mother do not usually have any influence upon the dictation of political or educational policies, through ignorance, disfranchisement, or lack of the interest to be found in more cultivated circumstances, or through a combination of all three factors. Certainly this is the forgotten child—and he is the Negro child of our Nation.

Social Background

If we were to select an assortment of one hundred Negro children as a hypothetical basis for making comparisons, we should find, to begin with, that twenty-three of these children lived in Northern cities, and that only two lived in rural areas in the North. From the standpoint of educational advantages, this first group of children had much the better start in life in comparison with the other seventy-five who live in the South.   Two of these children live in Chicago and two in New York, while another lives in Philadelphia.   In these cities, they were attending schools which were in fact, if not in law, separate schools, attended wholly or principally by children of their own race.   Residential segregation separated the elementary schools and in some cases created separate high schools.   Little or no inequality, however, was to be found in the school facilities provided for Negro children of this Northern group and those provided for Northern white children.

Of the remaining seventy-five children, one lived in Baltimore, one in Washington, one in Birmingham, and one in New Orleans.   In the first two cities named, school facilities comparing favorably in most respects with the best available for children of any racial group were provided. Sixteen children lived in various cities of the South where school facilities were inferior to those provided for white children, though vastly superior to those available for the remaining fifty-five children, who lived on farms in the South.   Of all of our forgotten children, the last group is by far the most neglected.

Only two of the children living in the North came from homes where both parents were illiterate, and one came from a home where one parent could not read or write.   Of the twenty children living in Southern cities, three came from homes where both parents were illiterate, and one from a home where one parent did not have either of the essential tools of a formal education.

Of the fifty-five children living on Southern farms, twelve came from homes where both parents were totally illiterate, and eight from homes where either the father or the mother could not read the school lessons of the child or write a note to the teacher excusing an absence or giving suggestions for the education of his child.

Of the twenty-five Northern Negro children, eleven came from homes where the parents made the family livelihood by being employed in some kind of manufacturing or industrial occupation. Even during the most prosperous periods, in the homes of two children neither parent was employed, and charity or relief funds of some other character were relied upon to furnish food, clothing, housing, and school for these children. In 1933, this number had been swelled to seven. The twelve remaining children came from homes supported by the labor of parents as domestic or personal servants. In seven of these Northern homes, both parents were away all day engaged in some gainful occupation to eke out a narrow existence. The family lived in cramped conditions with an average of one-half room for each person and paid exorbitant rentals for quarters usually overcrowded, unsanitary, and unattractive.

One child of the entire hundred came from a "professional" home, where the head of the family was doctor, lawyer, teacher, or the like; and this child probably lived in the South.

Of the rural Southern children, not more than fourteen out of fifty-five came from the homes of farm-owners. The remainder came from the homes of tenant farmers, almost all of whom were cotton-farm tenants. The cotton-farm tenant families have an extremely low scale of living, but the owners are but little better off. Table XLII shows the budget of the typical Negro farm family in certain Southern states.

Tenants rely less and less upon goods furnished by the farm itself, and this "is a diagnostic sign of the one-crop system with cotton for cash." Negro owners will be found in the uplands, the river bottoms being largely monopolized by the great landowners with access to fluid capital.

A recent survey of American living conditions stated that $2,000 was the minimum upon which an American standard

TABLE XLII [1]

BUDGETS OF NEGRO FAMILIES IN KENTUCKY, TENNESSEE, AND TEXAS

Per Cent Items	Furnished	Purchased	Total
Food	$178.6	$148.1	$326.7
Clothing	—	107.1	107.1
Rent	41.0	—	41.0
Furnishings	—	4.5	4.5
Operating	20.1	35.7	55.8
Health	—	24.8	24.8
Advancement	—	28.3	28.3
Personal	—	8.9	8.9
Insurance	—	14.0	14.0
	$239.7	$371.4	$611.1

of living could be maintained. What may we say of this majority Negro rural population? Simply that they fall far below all standards for decency in American family life, for each child regarded here comes from a family of approximately five persons.

Another study shows that "Croppers, with the lowest standards of living, buy the most groceries, $310, to $296 for cash tenants and $294 for owners." [2]

The cash income of the tenant classes is distressingly low. Branson and Dickey report the money income for 329 North Carolina farm families, as shown in Table XLIII.

TABLE XLIII

MONEY INCOME OF NORTH CAROLINA FARM FAMILIES

Class	Family Cash Income Per Year	Per Cent of White Owners' Income	Daily Cash Income Per Person
135 white owners	$626	100.0	34 cents
41 black owners	597	95.6	32 cents
66 black renters	289	44.4	16 cents
38 white renters	251	40.1	14 cents
36 black croppers	197	31.4	10 cents
13 white croppers	153	24.2	8 cents

[1] Rupert B. Vance, *Human Factors in Cotton Culture*, University of North Carolina Press, Chapel Hill, 1929, p. 226.

[2] Cited in Vance, *Human Factors in Cotton Culture*, p. 231.

Our typical rural Negro child, accordingly, will come from a tenant family where the daily cash income to supply books, means of advancement, and the clothes and other equipment necessary for his well-being as a student must be purchased from a budget of less than twelve cents a day. This sum must also furnish almost one-half of the food and other expenses incident to keeping the child alive.

The child, furthermore, comes from a home which in almost no instance has an indoor toilet or a bathtub. More than seventy-five per cent of the tenant families will be found to have no toilets of any sort, and the bodily refuse is voided indiscriminately to become the source of typhoid and hookworm infection. The average child will come from a home where it is almost an even chance that one parent, at least, is wholly illiterate; and the father will have received less than one grade of education. If five children have been born in the family, the probability is that one or more will have died before reaching school age.

In the cities, a larger family income will be found. In Southern cities, one out of every four Negro school children will come from homes owned by their parents, in contrast to almost one out of every two white school children. In Northern cities, the Negro children in nine out of ten cases will live in run-down apartment-house areas, and only one out of ten will come from a home owned by his parents. In Southern cities, the school child arriving for his first day has already seen three out of ten children born on his birthday die, while in Northern cities the percentage will be more than two out of every ten.

Eighty per cent of the rural children will have been "gainfully employed" from the time when their little fingers were agile enough to grasp and strip a cotton boll, and this skill is utilized before school age and during the first months of the short school term. Only an inconsiderable proportion of the city children will be employed at any occupation during the first years.   However, forty per cent of the urban children will come from homes where both parents are away from the home all day supporting the meager resources of the family, and the child is obliged to stay at home to take care of younger children, or he is obliged to play in the streets until night brings his parents homeward. In a city like Nashville, Tennessee, the Negro child may be one in three of the city's child population, but he has only one-tenth of one per cent of the play and park space devoted to his interests.[3]

Enrollment

The ratio which school enrollment bears to school population indicates that a very large proportion of Negro educables are not enrolled in school at all. By Table XLIV, in Delaware, Texas, Kentucky, West Virginia, and the District of Columbia, the ratio of Negroes enrolled exceeds that of whites, while in Tennessee it is equal to that of whites.   This fact may be explained on the basis of the over-ageness of Negro pupils, especially in rural districts, indicating that the apparent advantage is after all a disadvantage; for example, it does not mean that more Negro children of comparable ages are attending school in Texas than whites, but it does mean that there are more eighteen-, nineteen-, and twenty-year-old Negroes enrolled in elementary grades for Negroes than for whites, thus bringing up the ratio in an excessive degree.   The white children have already been enrolled in the lower grades and left the school at a lower age-level than have the Negro children.

If we consider the "school population" as including additional age-groups above 17, we find that the percentage of white eligibles enrolled in school was 81.8 per cent in 1930, while the percentage of Negroes was 68.8 per cent.   Almost

[3] Unpublished survey of Charles S. Johnson, Fisk University.

TABLE XLIV [4]

STATISTICS OF WHITE AND OF NEGRO SCHOOL POPULATION, ENROLLMENT, AND TEACHERS IN 18 STATES, 1929–1930

State	Population 5-17 Years of Age, Inclusive		Per Cent of School Population		Total School Enrollment		Ratio of Enrollment in Public Schools to School Population		Number of Teachers Employed	
	White	Negro	White	Negro	White	Negro	White	Negro	White	Negro
Alabama	456,352	294,238	60.8	39.2	428,257	194,731	.934	.662	12,903	4,227
Arkansas	374,584	139,210	72.9	27.1	351,076	105,109	.937	.755	10,593	2,397
Delaware	45,399	8,017	85.0	15.0	35,629	6,731	.785	.840	1,217	203
Dist. of Columbia	54,804	26,185	67.7	32.3	53,934	27,031	.984	1.043	1,850	872
Florida	235,876	112,740	67.7	32.3	254,575	91,859	1.079	.815	8,654	2,306
Georgia	479,909	345,302	58.2	41.8	468,249	245,041	.976	.710	13,742	5,329
Kentucky	634,409	54,550	92.1	7.9	540,818	47,536	.852	.871	13,962	1,361
Louisiana	380,062	226,256	62.7	37.3	277,707	156,850	.731	.693	9,145	3,028
Maryland	300,287	70,004	81.1	18.9	225,769	51,690	.752	.738	7,250	1,495
Mississippi	248,515	313,828	44.2	55.8	302,640	292,809	1.218	.933	9,206	5,932
Missouri	747,050	45,120	94.3	5.7	619,854	36,219	.830	.803	22,940	1,260
North Carolina	624,907	317,559	66.3	33.7	607,344	259,595	.972	.817	17,489	5,886
Oklahoma	589,377	49,139	92.3	7.7	633,369	49,281	1.075	1.003	18,323	1,484
South Carolina	252,218	292,066	46.3	53.7	248,200	221,170	.984	.757	8,888	4,510
Tennessee	623,425	128,748	82.9	17.1	514,345	113,402	.825	.825	16,110	2,221
Texas	1,386,415	241,421	85.2	14.8	1,104,288	153,646	.794	.735	30,526	5,141
Virginia	449,242	209,084	68.2	31.8	409,310	203,740	.911	.844	12,674	3,803
West Virginia	446,083	29,190	93.9	6.1	369,367	26,138	.828	.895		
TOTAL	8,328,914	2,902,567	74.2	25.8	7,444,731	2,282,578	0.894	0.786	215,472	51,455

[4] *Biennial Survey of Education, 1928–1930*, p. 82.

a third of the Negro children in the states referred to above, or a total of 1,037,093 children, did not attend any school during the year 1929–1930. The lowest percentage was in Mississippi, where four out of every ten Negro children, a total of 192,828 children out of 482,410, did not attend school. The corresponding percentage for whites in Mississippi was 17.8 per cent. The age-group 5–17 shows a high enrollment percentage for whites and Negroes in the State of Mississippi as expressed in terms of ratio of school enrollment to the population group. Here, again, the high ratios for both races are probably due to the extreme over-age location in lower grades of many children outside of the age-group 5–17, and this is, accordingly, a sign of deficiency rather than of progress.

Attendance and Length of Term

The enrollment figures must be qualified with reference to the frequency of attendance and the length of the school term, if we are to form an adequate picture of the education received by the typical Negro child. Attendance figures found in published reports are themselves susceptible to numerous faults, and their indices should be taken with more than the accustomed grain of salt. In counties which are unsupervised, receiving at most from one to two visits from a school official during the school year and in some cases not even one visit, the attendance figures cannot be expected to be at all accurate.

Terms of three and four months' duration are by no means uncommon in the states of the "Old South." That the averages are as high as they are is due more to the recent concentration of Negro children in cities where nine-month terms are usual than to the improvement of term-lengths for rural children.

The short term is frequently justified by school officials and citizens on the ground that the low attendance of Negro children does not justify an extension of school opportunities. If Negro children only go to school for four months when a five-month term is offered, why extend the term to six, or eight, or even nine months? Apparently, this reasoning is based on a belief that the rate of attendance represents the entire educational ambition of Negro children.

But there is much reason for thinking that this belief is more a rationalization, originating from a real desire to save school money at the expense of the Negro children, than a sincere opinion. Dr. Ullin W. Leavell tells of visiting a Mississippi plantation where the landlord had recently placed screens in all of his Negro cabins. The landlord was much discouraged because the Negroes had promptly kicked all of the screens out. It developed on inquiry that the school term on this plantation had averaged two months per year for the last decade or more. Now, the disappointment of the landlord has as much reason as the plaint of school officials who state that Negroes will not appreciate greater school facilities. Poor attendance is a complex, certainly, of many factors, and reaches into the home, the education of the parents, and the efficiency and attractiveness of the schools themselves. The writer has frequently been in Negro schools in the South where on cold days it was much more agreeable to remain outside of the school in order to keep warm, than to stay inside. The fact that in almost every Negro rural community a well-built, weatherproof church may be found, in contrast, usually, to a dilapidated school structure, is another example of the effect of old, traditional patterns upon social currents. Whatever its faults, the Negro rural church has fastened itself upon the life of the community, and it has fostered and received the support of that community. The Negro school prior to the coming of the Rosenwald Fund had no such active

leadership to energize the united will and educational ambitions of the community as preachers have cultivated and
utilized the religious feeling of rural Negroes.

Sickness plays an important part in curtailing the regular attendance of Negro school children.   In an Alabama
county located in the Alabama River valley, the writer found
the schools practically deserted for several weeks.   The
usual explanation given by teachers and those children who
did come to school was that Mary, or Jim, or Zack, "had
the chills and fevers."   Malaria was expected in this community every fall as a natural part of the pattern of life.
The excessive morbidity of Negroes is found in children to
an even greater degree than among adults, by comparison
with their healthier—and, it may be added, better-educated
—white neighbors.   Seasonal occupations play a large rôle
in attendance.   Throughout the cotton belt, a "late" cotton picking season may empty the schools for white and
colored as effectively as a plague.   In the Northern cotton
belt, running through North Carolina, southern Tennessee,
northern Alabama, northern Mississippi, Louisiana, Texas,
Arkansas, Oklahoma, and southern Missouri, the divided-
session plan is frequently adopted to provide from two to
three months of schooling for children in the summer "off-
season" between "planting" and "picking," with the balance
of what rarely exceeds a seven-month term in the winter
interlude.   This system has its special disabilities in the
attendance and learning of children, white as well as black.
Tenants and cotton farmers generally must live before they
go to school, and the employment of a child in the cotton
field is a harsh necessity more imperative than school attendance.

In addition to these major disturbances of school attendance, there are a variety of causes which arise from a general economic pressure from within and without coupled
with an absence of that appreciation of the value of regular

school attendance which comes only with greater leisure and intelligence. Negro mothers, as well as white mothers of the poorer class, think it no injustice to the child to call for his services in carrying a bundle of clothes to a house, or picking "greens," or running errands to the store. The lack of a compulsory education law, or, at least, of willingness to think of applying it in such instances, leaves the question almost hopeless of solution. Few Negro teachers would be inclined to protest the absence of a child from school when he was called upon to carry the weekly wash to the home of a local white board member.

In a general fashion, we may hit upon several things that need to be done in improving the attendance and enrollment of Negro children in school. (1) The Negro parent needs to become conscious in a greater measure of the values of education. During the Reconstruction Period, education was a passion with Negroes. That spirit needs to be recreated, and the teacher must furnish the means for organizing this interest and rearousing it, by coöperation with the Church and the press and through personal contacts. (2) The Negro school must be made more attractive to children. This implies improvement of the teaching staff, provision of better buildings, re-location of many schools, and consolidation in order to bring schools nearer to the children of tender ages. (3) The compulsion of the law must be called upon to enforce the pressure of moral and social suasion. Throughout the North and West, no white or black parent can flaunt the law which demands the presence of the child at the school for the preservation of society. In most localities in the South, the same is true for white parents. To the end that a people with no tradition of school-seeking shall be led to the school, and that no parent shall be allowed to take advantage of the dependent nature of the child, compulsory education must come to mean for Negro children what it means for all other children.

The immediate rectification of school inequalities in the South to provide the most effective sort of schools would not in a day, or a month, or a year remove the uncertain attendance and the low enrollment ratios of Negro and white children in the section.   The school represents in a very great degree the general cultural level of the community, and these cultural factors are of prime importance for estimating the accumulated deficiencies of that community.   On the other hand, it is certain that the school can become the instrument for accelerating change in this, as in all other matters; and with its aid, we may expect to do in a generation what might otherwise require several centuries.

Grade Placement

The even progress of children through the grades is, like the ratio of attendance and enrollment, an excellent index to two factors which, while parallel, are not identical.   In the first place, the distribution of children through all the grades reflects the efficiency of the school system and its power to retain children at successively higher levels as well as to forward their progress in the mastery of subject matter.   At the same time, grade-distribution mirrors the relative advancement of the community in economic and social matters.   In England, all plans for disseminating secondary education to the masses have been predicated on the fact that the labor of adolescents becomes profitable to families at about the fourteenth year; and, accordingly, the state has sought to free promising children for this higher education, not only by the provision of free secondary schools, but also by subsidizing families which are deprived of the labor of children who go on to school at the upper levels. It has not been necessary for American educators to contemplate this system, for in our own land mechanization has done for the adolescent what it is proposed to do for him in England by social legislation.

TABLE XLV [5]

ENROLLMENT OF WHITE AND NEGRO CHILDREN IN 18 STATES, ACCORDING TO YEARS OF ADVANCEMENT, 1929–1930

Grade	White Pupils		Negro Pupils	
	Number	Per Cent	Number	Per Cent
Kindergarten	56,167	0.8	3,970	0.2
First	1,425,252	19.1	785,281	34.4
Second	875,462	11.8	334,756	14.7
Third	853,905	11.5	293,014	12.8
Fourth	799,815	10.7	257,264	11.3
Fifth	714,411	9.6	202,341	8.9
Sixth	654,884	8.8	150,463	6.6
Seventh	567,914	7.6	105,504	4.6
Eighth	303,257	4.1	37,399	1.6
First Year High	429,894	5.8	47,765	2.1
Second " "	327,589	4.4	31,004	1.3
Third " "	247,255	3.3	20,045	.9
Fourth " "	188,926	2.5	13,772	.6

The last decade has witnessed an unprecedented increase in the number of Negro high-school students, and, as a result, a more even distribution of Negro children throughout the grades. It is true that the high schools available for Negro children have increased from 64 in 1916 to more than 1200 in 1932. It should be plain that more is involved in the increase of Negro high-school students in the same period, which exceeded 600 per cent, than the bare fact of a larger number of schools. The two increases have been reciprocal. A wider provision for Negro high-school students has increased the number of such students, and the increase in those clamoring for a high-school education has precipitated a tremendous development of secondary schools for Negroes. There is a definite saturation point in grade progress, which advances as the general level of the community is raised and as its economic resources become more

---

[5] *Biennial Survey of Education*, 1929–1930, p. 84.

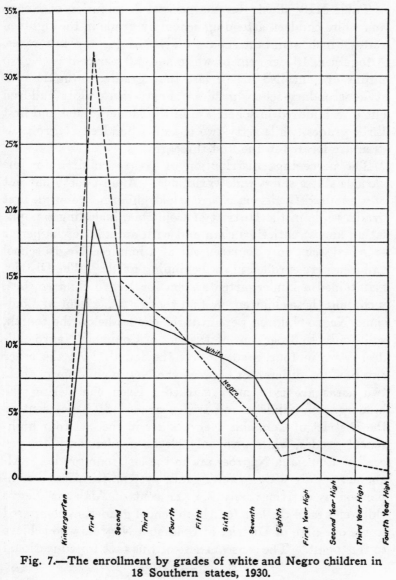

Fig. 7.—The enrollment by grades of white and Negro children in 18 Southern states, 1930.

297

able, not only to support more schools as a financial matter of taxes and appropriations, but also as a financial matter of supporting more "idle" secondary-school pupils.

Table XLV illustrates the general distribution of Negro and white children attending school by grade in the eighteen states which maintain separate systems for the two races. Altogether, 16 per cent of white and 4.9 per cent of Negro pupils are enrolled in the last four grades, or in the old-style secondary-school grades. Forty-three white children out of a hundred in school are in the kindergarten and first three grades, while sixty-two out of a hundred Negro children are located in the first three grades.

The percentage distribution of Negro children for the various states shows wide variations. Almost forty-one out of a hundred Louisiana Negro school children are in the first grade, while in the District of Columbia, including a population almost entirely urban and with an infinitely superior school system, only fourteen out of a hundred Negro school children were enrolled in the beginning grade. The District maintained a kindergarten system for Negro children, but, including these children, we find that 68.2 per cent of Louisiana Negro children were in three grades below the fourth, while only 43.3 per cent of District of Columbia Negro children were in four grades below the fourth. At the other extreme, the differences between the Negro children in these two areas are even more marked. Even considering the kindergarten children and twelve grades, 20.0 per cent of the District of Columbia Negroes are in the last four high-school grades, while with only eleven grades, only 4.2 per cent of Louisiana Negroes are in the last four grades. Alabama, a state with a twelve-grade system, furnishes a comparison as extreme: only 2.4 per cent of Alabama Negro children are in the last four high-school grades, as compared to the one-fifth of District of Columbia Negroes who achieve to this point. The consequences of this fact for educational

and social leadership are startling, as that leadership undoubtedly will come from those in the higher ranks of school
attainment.   Alabama, with 294,238 Negro children aged
5–17, had in 1929–1930, 824 Negro high-school seniors,
while the District of Columbia, with 26,185 Negro children
aged 5–17, had in the same year 615 high-school seniors.
The proportion is, for Alabama, one high-school senior to
357 Negro children aged 5–17 in the state; for the District,
one senior to 43 children aged 5–17.   In proportion to the
population, eight times as many Negro children reach the
senior year of high school in the District as in Alabama,
and the index roughly parallels both the efficiency of the
schools provided for the children of the two units and the
relative advancement of the two racial groups.

As unfavorable as the present situation of such a state as
Alabama is, the state has made giant strides in the improvement of grade-placement among Negro school children in
the last decade.   Alabama is not alone in this respect; the
figures already presented showing the startling increase in
Negro secondary-school students in recent years indicate
that the trend is characteristic of every Southern state.   In
ten years, Alabama has increased the percentage of Negroes
enrolled in the ninth, tenth, and eleventh grades from forty-
six hundredths of one per cent to 3.2 per cent, an increase
of 695 per cent in a decade.

It is noticeable, in Table XLVI, that the percentage of
children in the first grade reached its maximum in 1927–
1928, and that the increase in the number of children in the
upper grades has come principally through reducing the
number and per cent of those in the middle grades.   A very
significant conjecture may be permitted on the basis of these
figures: that the Alabama school system during the period
here covered improved principally in the direction of enrolling a larger proportion of the Negro children, while not
improving its efficiency so far as these entrants were con-

TABLE XLVI[6]

PERCENTAGE DISTRIBUTION OF NEGRO CHILDREN IN ALABAMA, BY GRADE, IN THE DECADE 1920–1921 TO 1929–1930

Grade	1920–1921	1921–1922	1922–1923	1923–1924	1924–1925	1925–1926	1926–1927	1927–1928	1928–1929	1929–1930
First	38.9	38.4	39.6	39.6	37.5	38.1	36.9	40.2	38.8	38.2
Second	18.8	18.7	17.2	16.8	16.1	15.5	15.3	15.3	14.5	14.4
Third	14.8	15.0	14.4	14.8	14.3	14.0	13.8	12.3	13.0	13.1
Fourth	11.9	11.7	12.1	12.5	12.3	11.0	11.9	10.5	11.0	11.0
Fifth	7.7	7.8	7.9	7.5	8.8	8.9	8.7	8.3	8.3	8.5
Sixth	4.7	4.8	4.9	4.7	6.0	6.4	6.6	6.3	6.3	6.5
Seventh	2.1	2.4	2.5	2.7	2.4	2.7	2.7	2.7	3.2	3.0
Eighth					1.3	1.5	1.7	1.8	1.9	2.1
First H.S.	0.60	0.67	0.80	0.8	0.7	0.9	1.0	1.2	1.4	1.4
Second H.S.	0.30	0.30	0.30	0.3	0.3	0.6	0.6	0.7	0.9	0.9
Third H.S.	0.13	0.16	0.20	0.2	0.2	0.3	0.3	0.4	0.4	0.5
Fourth H.S.	0.06	0.07	0.10	0.10	0.1	0.2	0.3	0.3	0.3	0.4
Total	100.00	100.00	100.00	100.00	100.00	100.00	100.00	100.00	100.00	100.00

cerned; and that the improvement in the provision of higher opportunities for older children was not duplicated by the lower-grade schools. Expenditures for Negro teachers' salaries in the elementary school increased 71 per cent from 1921 to 1930, but the expenditures for Negro high-school teachers increased 525 per cent.

North Carolina shows the same peculiar feature. In 1923–1924, 38.7 per cent of the Negro school children in that state were in the first grade. In 1929–1930, an even larger per cent, 39.7, were enrolled in the first grade. Meanwhile, the percentage enrolled in high-school grades had increased from 2.3 per cent to 5.85 per cent. Manifestly, the lower grades have not profited from the recent advances made in either Alabama or North Carolina as have the high-school grades. The emphasis upon the secondary school was long needed; but in the same manner, it appears that the spectacular achievements in these schools for older

---

[6] *Annual Reports of the State Superintendent of Education of Alabama* for the respective years.

children have diverted our attention from what Miss Anna Jeanes called "the little country schools." The county training schools have brought high-school opportunity to the Negro children in more than three hundred rural counties, and the elementary schools now enroll a much larger proportion of educables than formerly, but the concentration of Negro rural children in the first grade does not seem to have been materially affected.

The violent contrasts afforded by counties and cities within the same state are striking. In a decade, the city of Birmingham, in Alabama, has decreased the percentage of Negro children enrolled in the first grade from 35.5 per cent to 23.3 per cent. In the same state, the rural county of Autauga, a highly typical cotton belt county, actually shows the same percentage enrolled in the first grade in 1929–1930 as in 1920–1921. The fact that Autauga

TABLE XLVII [7]

PERCENTAGE DISTRIBUTION OF NEGRO AND WHITE CHILDREN ENROLLED IN TWO ALABAMA SCHOOL SYSTEMS

	Birmingham (City)				Autauga County			
	White		Negro		White		Negro	
	1929–30	1920–21	1929–30	1920–21	1929–30	1920–21	1929–30	1920–21
Grade	%	%	%	%	%	%	%	%
First	15.2	20.3	23.3	35.5	20.9	24.1	47.2	47.3
Second	10.5	11.3	12.9	17.2	11.9	11.9	14.7	16.0
Third	10.3	11.3	12.0	14.7	12.4	13.4	11.2	11.8
Fourth	10.0	12.6	10.3	11.8	11.0	10.4	10.1	9.4
Fifth	8.7	11.0	8.4	7.5	8.6	11.3	7.1	9.1
Sixth	8.0	10.8	7.1	4.7	11.3	9.2	5.4	3.7
Seventh	6.8	8.2	5.6	3.4	7.3	7.7	2.9	1.3
Eighth	6.7	6.6	5.5	2.0	5.1	4.9	0.8	1.4
Ninth	7.0	4.1	4.8	1.1	4.3	3.2	0.4	......
Tenth	6.0	2.0	4.4	0.8	3.7	2.5	0.0	......
Eleventh	5.3	1.2	3.9	0.6	1.9	1.4	0.2	......
Twelfth	3.6	......	3.0	......	1.6	......	......	......
No. Enrolled	32,805	22,614	18,796	12,584	2,210	2,538	2,482	1,436

[7] *Annual Reports of the State Superintendent of Education of the State of Alabama* for the respective years shown.

County almost doubled the number of Negro school children enrolled in this decade while the school population aged 6–20 increased only 6 per cent indicates that the county had progressed in the direction of including more children in the school, but not in eliminating the retardation of these children. The rapid adjustment which has taken place in the city of Birmingham is indicative of the results of a rapidly improving city school system.

Retardation

The data which give the retardation of children in terms of the concentration in the first few grades show that there exists a far higher degree of over-ageness among Negro children than among white children. The differences between rural and urban Negroes, however, are quite as pronounced as those between discrete racial groups. Elsewhere (in Chapter XVI) data are presented to show the retardation of Negro children measured both by age and by achievement.

Figures invariably show that the degree of retardation among Negro children far exceeds that among white children. If comparisons were restricted to comparable social and economic groups, rather than to racial groups, it would be clear that Negro children suffer from retardation to the extent that they are identified with the lower economic strata. It is also true that such comparisons as are usually made neglect the fact that Negro children because of their location in the submerged social classes are liable more than any other racial group to the factors causative of backwardness. They suffer more frequently from ill-health, and are more apt likely to be unemployed both seasonally and permanently. The employment and family regimen of their parents are likewise more irregular. The schools have short terms, poor teachers, and poor accommodations. To the inferior schools come children with inferior social backgrounds. The result is a high rate of retardation. That it is being decreased in progressive systems is shown by the data quoted above from the city of Birmingham. The improvement in this industrial city, however, should not be credited altogether to the virtues of the school. Much credit is due to the general improvement in social and economic status of the Negro population. In the ten-year period in which the number of Negro children enrolled in the first grade decreased from thirty-five per cent to twenty-three per cent of the total enrollment, the parents of these children had been initiated into an urban existence. They had been freed from the necessity of employing their children around the house or on the farm. They had become accustomed to regularity and order, both in school and out. They had developed habits of school attendance. An improved rural school can strike at many of the causes of retardation, but the basic factors must await the changing status of the patrons, which is enmeshed in the general cultural pattern of the community.

Summary

The Negro child is neglected and forgotten by the conscience of administrative officials and of the ordinary citizen. When prejudices, hatred, and actual discrimination are added to the fearful social barriers which stand in the way of fulfillment for the Negro child, it is apparent that the Negro children of America constitute its most unfortunate class.

The social background of Negro children shows an almost unvarying pattern of difficulties in the way of decent physical and personal growth. These factors work along with inferior educational advantages to reduce the enrollment of Negro children in school and to make attendance uncertain and vagrant.

The placement of Negro children in grades indicates that more than sixty per cent are in the first three grades. The picture reflects an immense degree of retardation and poor attendance. In order to strike at the root of this matter, teachers, patrons, and administrators must look both to an improvement of the efficiency of the school, and to an improvement in the social and economic status of the Negro parent and in the Negro community generally.

CHAPTER XV

Capacity

IN ANSWER to the question, "Does the average Negro pupil have as much capacity to learn as the average white pupil?", nineteen North Carolina city and county superintendents are reported to have said, "Yes." [1] Eighty-five answered the question by an emphatic "No!" The reasons for believing Negroes incapable of learning are of interest, although they can be regarded only as a conscious statement that may, or may not, be a rationalization of true states of mind.

Replies	Evidence Given to Corroborate Statements	Number of Superintendents
No	My general observation and association with Negroes	57
No	(No reason given)	9
No	His whole background is primitive, but it is developing fast	7
No	Observation and results of research work	5
No	In this county, the money spent for the Negro has shown nothing	1
No	Their inability to progress	1
No	Results of standard group tests	1
No	He has more capacity when mixed with white blood	1
No	The Negro is a child race	1
No	By inheritance	1
No	I supervise both white and Negro schools	1

Even the results of "scientific" studies may actually reflect no more than the deep-seated prejudices of the individual who, as Pintner says, uses the test as an entirely sincere

---

[1] Dennis Hargrove Cooke, *The White Superintendent and the Negro School in North Carolina*, George Peabody College for Teachers, Nashville, 1930, p. 126.

but nevertheless patent rationalization of convictions already firmly grounded and impervious to "pure reason." [2]   Woodworth has said,

> There are race prejudices standing in the way of a fair view of the facts.   And the facts themselves are often misleading.   There are so many factors besides sheer mental ability that enter into the racial question.   Even the personal equation, the difference between one individual and another of the same race and culture, is beset with curious influences that lower an individual's record below the level where it should be; and when we endeavor to compare races, the equation is still more difficult to make out.   Language differences, habits of thought and action, group ideals and attitudes, are all likely to distort the facts or to make the facts as they are actually found at the present time misleading to anyone who is not on his guard. [3]

From the first entrance of the Negro into America, it was necessary for the good men of the time, to justify his retention in slavery, to invent reasons where none existed.   It was at first stated, accordingly, that slavery was designed to induct the heathen into Christianity and was an institution divinely appointed of God for this purpose.   The complete evangelization of Negroes soon destroyed this plea, and other reasons were sought for—and found—to justify the institution of human bondage.   Through the early part of the nineteenth century, as Negro slavery became more and more a strictly commercial enterprise designed to exploit the labor of many for the benefit of a few, the efforts of apologists to find justification became more and more fervid.   We make a mistake if we believe that any considerable proportion of slaveholders were men inordinately vicious or wicked; rather, they were perhaps typical of human beings faced with a problem which challenged fundamental convictions of right

[2] R. Pintner, *Educational Psychology*, Henry Holt and Co., New York, 1929.

[3] In the introduction to Thomas R. Garth, *Race Psychology*, McGraw-Hill Book Co., New York, 1931, p. xiii.

and justice and who sought a solution of their conflicts by seeking adequate explanations for a profitable system.

The result was that a final conclusion was generally agreed upon—that Negroes were an inferior race of men, consigned by the Almighty, because of the curse levelled at Ham by Noah, to be "drawers of water and hewers of wood" for the more respectful sons of the builder of the Ark.   It was a religious age, and the reasons put forward for the enslavement of Negroes and for their incapacity were religious reasons.   If the reasons put forth today for the limitation of the educational opportunity of Negro children are "scientific," it is no more than an old human tendency clothed in modern terminology.   Jefferson Davis argued against the education of Negro children on the basis of their inferiority and enforced his argument by quoting from the Holy Scriptures; and our present-day contemporaries who would limit the education of Negro children on the basis of their alleged mental inferiority and quote intelligence tests as the foundation for their opinion are the spiritual descendants of the first and only President of the Southern Confederacy.

Explanations of Racial Differences

At first sight, there are definite differences that appear when we inspect different racial groups.   These more superficial differences are in the main those of physical configuration: color, facial features, body structure, hair, eyes. There are many cultural differences that are frequently confused as racial differences; for example, it is the natural tendency to read a definite racial difference into the type of clothing worn by such Orientals as the Chinese as compared to Occidental dress; or one may reason that because Africans wear rings in their noses while Englishmen wear rings on their fingers, the difference is a typical racial difference.

In large, however, the study of "racial differences" must

begin with a strict definition of race. Despite the propaganda of particular enthusiasts for one kind of race superiority rather than another, anthropologists are generally
agreed that there is no such thing as a pure race. If we
talk about the "white race," we are including individuals
as diverse as a typical tall blond of Scandinavia and a typically short, brunette Italian from southern Europe. There
are many Europeans darker than many persons usually
classified without question as Negroes in America. Within
the white "race," there are Italians who claim the superiority
of the Latin over all other peoples, and there are Germans
who protest that the Teuton is the superior "race."

The American Negro is first of all a combination of many
different subracial stocks derived from the mother continent. Since the beginning of Negro residence in America, there has been a steady infiltration of blood from various European sources—French, Scotch, Irish, German,
Italian, Spanish, and so on. To this racial mélange, we
must add a considerable proportion of admixture from
American Indian sources. It is common knowledge among
anthropologists, as Dr. Robert E. Park has expressed it,
that the American Indian probably was not exterminated—
rather, he was swallowed up in the Negro through three centuries of miscegenation. One of the principal motives leading to the sequestration of Indians of the Choctaw and
Cherokee tribes west of the Mississippi was the fact that
Negro runaways often found a ready asylum in Indian en-
campments bordering upon white settlements.

The need for rationalizing any discrimination practiced
against any considerable proportion of the population has
been mentioned. These rationalizations have taken various
forms where differences in intelligence, the most important
racial differences for our purposes, are concerned. Biblical arguments were early reinforced by pseudo-scientific
arguments which purported to base slavery upon the find-

ings of early experimentation. It was argued, accordingly, in the days when the multiplicity of cerebral convolutions was held to be indicative of the degree of intelligence, that Negro brains showed fewer of these striations than white brains. When brain specialists were much more certain of the localization of various "faculties" in different portions of the brain than they now are, it was argued that Negroes were peculiarly deficient in those areas where the "higher faculties" were located. One experiment of a more recent period is of interest as showing the degree to which scientific judgment can be turned awry even when the most careful precautions are taken to avoid prejudice.

In 1906, Dr. R. B. Bean, a noted brain specialist attached to the Medical School of the Johns Hopkins University, in Baltimore, reported that he had made a careful study of a large sampling of brains from white and Negro cadavers.[4] Apparently with the most exacting scientific detail, Dr. Bean carefully weighed the brains and subjected them to a detailed examination with reference to their complexity of structure. He reported that the Negro brains were far inferior to the white brains both in structure and in gross proportions, and concluded that all of the inferior capacities which other writers had assigned to Negroes found their location in these cerebral deficiencies. The study was reported in a highly reputable journal and was quoted widely because of the care which the prestige and scientific authority of the investigator guaranteed in the study.

A few years later, Dr. F. P. Mall, also of Johns Hopkins University, repeated the study of Doctor Bean.[5] In the first investigation, Doctor Bean had labelled the brains studied according to race. In his repetition, Doctor Mall

---

[4] R. B. Bean, "Some Racial Peculiarities of the Negro Brain," *American Journal of Anatomy*, Vol. 5, pp. 353–433 (September, 1906).

[5] F. P. Mall, "On Several Anatomical Characters of the Human Brain Said to Vary According to Race and Sex," *American Journal of Anatomy*, Vol. 9, pp. 1–32 (February, 1909).

concealed from himself the race of the specimen which he was studying, identifying it only at the end of the study for purposes of conclusions. The result was that the differences found by Bean largely disappeared, and Mall was forced to the conclusion that the personal equation had misled even so painstaking an investigator as Doctor Bean, and that nothing conclusive could be said regarding the mentality of Negroes or whites on the basis of the data which were obtained in the second experiment.

Studies of Intelligence

The study of the psychological differences which may exist between races has developed along with the science of psychology. The first crude attempts were directed toward an investigation of differences in sensory abilities. In 1895, Bache experimented with the reaction time of a small group which included 12 whites, 11 Negroes, and 11 Indians.[6] He reported that the Negroes were the median group, the Indians the quickest, and the whites slowest. The group, of course, was too small for serious consideration in evaluating race differences. Stetson administered simple memory tests to 500 whites and 500 Negroes in 1897.[7] He reported that Negroes were superior to the whites, but discounted this superiority on the basis that the Negroes tested were older.

The study of Mayo in 1913, based upon the school marks of Negro children in a Northern city school system compared with those of white children, ended with the conclusion that the Negro children were 75 per cent as effective as the white children in their school work.[8] Baldwin used a

---

[6] R. Meade Bache, "Reaction Time with Reference to Race," *Psychological Review*, Vol. 2, pp. 474–486.

[7] B. R. Stetson, "A Memory Test of Colored and White Children," *Psychological Review*, Vol. 4, pp. 285–289.

[8] M. J. Mayo, "The Mental Capacity of the American Negro," *Archives of Psychology*, Vol. 5, pp. 109–146.

learning test to experiment with 37 white and 33 Negro girls in a Pennsylvania reformatory,[9] and came to a conclusion that, considering the small number of individuals tested and the dubious nature of their previous environment, was entirely unjustified by the study itself—that the smaller degree of accuracy in the Negro girls reflected a real racial difference. In the same study, Baldwin stated, with a sweeping gesture all too frequent in later studies, that the *laissez-faire* attitude of the Negro girls taking the test "appeared to be a racial characteristic."

The tests developed by the French psychologist Alfred Binet, intended originally to segregate feeble-minded children in the Paris schools, consisted of a series of problems arranged to present a "ladder" of growing difficulty at successive stages. Decroly and Degand, of Belgium, administered the Binet tests to Belgian children as early as 1910, and commented at that time on the fact that scores appeared to be affected by the social status of the child tested.[10] The Binet tests were enthusiastically received in this country, where several revisions were made and the tests were standardized to fit the new language and environmental requirements. The most notable of these revisions were those by Kuhlmann, Goddard, of the Vineland Training School of New Jersey, and Terman, of Leland Stanford University. The Terman revision has achieved the widest use, and has been employed in most studies where individual tests have been desired in the study of racial differences.

One of the first uses of the Binet scale in racial psychology was that of Strong, who in 1913 measured 350 white and

---

[9] B. T. Baldwin, "The Learning of Delinquent Adolescent Girls as Shown by Substitution Tests," *Journal of Educational Psychology*, Vol. 4, pp. 317–332.

[10] Decroly and Degand, "La mesure de l'Intelligence chez des enfants normaux," *Archives de Psychologie*, 1910, Vol. 9, pp. 81–108.

colored children in a South Carolina town.[11]   Strong reported that, as a whole, the Negro children were 29 per cent below the level attained by the typical white child; however, when the white children were divided into social classes, one of which was made up of children whose parents worked in a cotton mill, she found that the differences between the Negroes and the white mill children were inconsiderable.

Pyle devised scales for testing what he called "intelligence," and administered them to 500 Negro children in Columbia, Missouri. The Negro children fell considerably below the standards achieved by the white children.[12]   Pyle introduced an interpretative note which has been echoed by many investigators since that time.   He stated that the tests were not influenced by environment, because the school opportunities for the Negroes in Columbia were as good as those for white children.   This naïve belief, that the school represents the sum total of the cultural factors which act to stimulate a growing child, has been a favorite plea of other investigators, who by this conclusion abruptly sweep into insignificance the accumulation of several centuries of illiteracy, intellectual stagnation, family disorganization, and low occupational and economic status.   It is also interesting to note that Pyle does not report data in full for rural white children, although such material is published for urban whites and Negroes and for rural Negroes.   Similar studies where both groups have been taken into account and where the results have been published indicate that the urban white children are far in advance of the urban Negroes, but that the urban Negroes are not far below, if they do not equal, the rural white children.

---

[11] Alice C. Strong, "Three Hundred Fifty White and Colored Children Measured by the Binet-Simon Scale of Intelligence," *Pedagogical Seminar*, Vol. 20, pp. 485–515.

[12] William Henry Pyle, "The Mentality of the Negro Child Compared with Whites," *Psychological Bulletin*, Vol. 12, pp. 12 and 71, January and February, 1915.

Ferguson in 1917 reported the result of studies made in 1916 under the ambitious title, "The Psychology of the American Negro," although the basic data were confined to a comparison of 421 white and 486 Negro children in Virginia.[13] On the basis of tests which were supposed to be tests of "the higher mental processes," Ferguson came to quite extravagant conclusions concerning the intellectual, physical, and moral nature of the Negro. He introduced the technique of comparing groups of Negro children divided according to skin color. Herskovits and others have since shown that this index is highly unreliable in determining the degree of racial admixture within Negro groups, but upon this basis, Ferguson believed that he found a successive increase of intelligence with an increase of white blood. Sociologists have since emphasized the need for remembering that the fact of mulatto ancestry may be coexistent with an advantage of this class in social environment over pure-blooded Negroes; moreover, this coincidence has further been ascribed to factors which are more traceable to cultural than to genetic factors. It is a well-known fact that the free-Negro group prior to the Civil War was preëminently a mulatto group, in no small degree because the Negroes manumitted by their masters were likely to be the children of the men who emancipated them. To this initial advantage over the purer Negroes is the fact that mulattoes were usually preferred for service around the "big house," where they were in a position to profit more largely from the stimulation of cultural contacts than the purer Negroes who labored in the fields. Park has pointed, also, to the fact that the "marginal" location of the mulatto may have given to him an intangible advantage in the eyes of both the slave class and the master class, from which he sprang, and before

---

[13] C. O. Ferguson, "The Psychology of the Negro," *Archives of Psychology*, No. 36, Columbia University Press, New York, 1917.

and after emancipation may have given him a greater urge for achievement than would otherwise have been the case.

Pressey administered his own test to Negro and white children, and reported the Negro children inferior by approximately 15 per cent to the intelligence quotient of the white children.[14] Pressey has also done much testing work in comparing rural and urban Indiana white children. In this latter comparison, he found that the urban white children scored above the rural white children by margins almost as large as those between the typical white and Negro child.

In 1919, Garth made a comparative study of "work curves" in white, Indian, and Negro children which was the forerunner of extensive research in this field by him.[15] He found that the Negro children tired more easily than children of other races in performing a task calling for mental exertion, and attached great significance to the factor of mental fatigue as a possible factor in all tests of intelligence. The implication is that Negroes may be unaccustomed to tasks requiring sustained application, while white children, habituated through a lifetime of stimulation, which extends its pattern from the home to the school, tend to make higher scores in all tests, partially because of this factor. Now, these racial habits of work, in Garth's opinion, were due to environment. Experimentation with Indian children showed the same difference within this racial group when groups from different environments were tested. Early in the period, and at a time when other writers were declaring without equivocation their belief in the results of intelligence tests as the final proof of the inferiority of the Negro, Garth developed a formula which he suggested be

[14] S. L. Pressey and G. P. Teter, "A Comparison of Colored and White Children by Means of a Group Scale of Intelligence," *Journal of Applied Psychology*, Vol. 3, pp. 277–282.

[15] T. R. Garth, "White, Indian and Negro Work Curves," *Journal of Applied Psychology*, Vol. 5, pp. 14–25.

applied to all studies purporting to establish racial differences:

> The elements in a study of racial mental similarities or differences must be these: (1) two so-called races R_1 and R_2; (2) an equal amount of educational opportunity E which would include social pressure and cultural patterns of thought; and (3) psychological tests D within the grasp of both racial groups. As a result of the experiment, R_1ED would be equal to, greater than, or less than R_2ED. In this experiment the only unknown elements should be R_1 and R_2. If E could be held constant, the experiment could be worked.[16]

It may be well to say here that in his summary of the entire field of "race psychology," published in 1931, Garth finds no reason to believe that any investigator has "equalized E," and that he concludes the book with these words: "Much of the difference found in the results of studies of racial differences in mental traits is due to differences in natural factors, and the rest is due to racial mobility, so that one race has a temporary advantage over another." [17] The work of Adler and other "newer school" psychologists in establishing the definitive nature of the very first years of a child's life in determining character and intelligence pushes still farther into the future the time when any psychologist may fairly lay claim to having equalized the educational factor in the study of racial differences.

In 1920, Derrick reported a study of the intelligence of 52 Negro and 75 white college students in North Carolina.[18] The Negro I.Q. median was found to be 103, and that of the white students, 112. Arlitt made a comparative study of 71 Negro and 191 white children in 1921, using the Stan-

---

[16] Garth, T. R., "Mental Fatigue during the Continuous Exercise of a Single Function," *Archives of Psychology*, No. 41, Vol. 26, No. 2.

[17] Garth, *Race Psychology*, p. 221.

[18] S. M. Derrick, "A Comparative Study of Seventy-five White and Fifty-two Colored College Students by the Stanford Revision of the Binet-Simon Scale," *Journal of Applied Psychology*, Vol. 4, pp. 316–329.

ford Revision of the Binet intelligence test.[19]   Miss Arlitt's study is significant in that she emphasized the "necessity for caution" in setting up norms for racial achievement in intelligence tests.   The differences between racial groups which she reported were in favor of white children; but when she compared her groups by social status, it was found that the variations between children of the same race on different environmental levels were greater than differences between races.

A Study of American Intelligence, published in 1923 by Carl C. Brigham, presented the vast amount of material made available by the intelligence tests administered to the draftees incorporated into the American Army during the World War.[20]   The "Alpha" test was designed for literate soldiers, and the second, for illiterate native Americans or for foreign-born soldiers unable to deal successfully with English.   The second test was a "performance" test, as it was believed that reaction to it depended entirely on ability to solve simple problems not involving any language capacity.

Brigham's book presented the data of the Army tests according to race, country of origin of the foreign-born, and state of residence.   He found that the mental age of the typical white, American-born recruit was that "of a thirteen-year-old child," while that of Negro recruits was three years lower.   Classifying the median scores by race and nationality, he placed in the fore the soldiers of North European descent, then those from the southern countries of Europe, and finally the Negro.

---

[19] Ada H. Arlitt, "The Relation of Intelligence to Age in Negro Children," *Proceedings Thirtieth Annual Meeting, American Psychological Association*, p. 14.

[20] Carl C. Brigham, *A Study of American Intelligence*, Princeton University Press, Princeton, 1922.

In his argument, Brigham sought to meet the contention
that scores on the Army Intelligence Tests were influenced
by environment by showing that if Negro and white soldiers
of the same grade standing in school were compared, the
white soldiers maintained a substantial advantage in score.
This argument ignored the vast discrepancy between the
efficiency of Negro and white schools in the South. At a
time when the average length of term for the Negro child
in the South was less than five months and that for white
children more than seven months, Brigham assumed that a
fifth-grade Negro child had received an education comparable to that of a fifth-grade child who was white. The
assumption also ignored differentials in the preparation of
teachers, in equipment of school buildings, in supervision,
and, in fact, every factor conducive to actual equalization
of educational opportunity. This unfortunate omission was,
perhaps, not so critical for the validity of the comparison
as the repetition of the naïve belief, referred to previously
in connection with Pyle's earlier study, that the school constitutes the sole measure of environmental equality. In the
face of an illiteracy among Southern Negroes three times as
great as that among whites, and in disregard of the fact
that the Negroes were overwhelmingly from rural areas and
from isolated cotton farms where tenantry was the rule,
Brigham asserted that the environment of the two groups
thus compared was equal.

The publication of the book was soon followed by other
studies which sought to separate American groups with the
same fidelity which had characterized Brigham's attack
upon the problem of nationality and race groups. Bagley,
Bond, and Long reported the scores for native-born American soldiers by state, and there immediately developed an
anomaly in the conclusions of Brigham which in time threw
grave doubt upon their authenticity. Brigham had argued

that the North European stock—Scotch, Irish, English, and
Scandinavian—was the superior racial group in this country. When the states are listed in order of the scores made
by soldiers from these states in the Army tests, it was found
that the Southern white soldiers made the lowest scores of
any registered by white soldiers in America. Now, the
South has the highest percentage of white people of Scotch,
Irish, and English ancestry in the country, with an inconsiderable number of foreign-born of any nationality. On
the other hand, states like Massachusetts and Connecticut,
with the heaviest proportion of foreign-born in the country,
made scores much higher than states such as Georgia, Kentucky, and South Carolina, where the white population is
almost "99 44/100 per cent" pure "Nordic" in origin.
According to Brigham's theory of racial superiority, the
Southern white soldiers should have made the best scores
among white Americans; actually, they made the lowest
scores.

An even more striking fact was found on further investigation. If the scores made by Negro soldiers be separated,
state by state, and ranked in order, the same succession of
superiority becomes apparent, with the Negro soldiers from
the North making scores considerably above those from the
South. Nor is this all; the Negro soldiers from certain
Northern states made scores higher than the white soldiers
from Southern states.

TABLE XLVIII

SCORE OF WHITE RECRUITS OF SOUTHERN STATES COMPARED WITH SCORE OF
NEGRO RECRUITS OF NORTHERN STATES IN THE ARMY ALPHA TEST

Southern States	Median Scores of White Recruits	Northern States	Median Scores of Negro Recruits
Mississippi	41.25	Ohio	49.50
Kentucky	41.50	Pennsylvania	42.00
Arkansas	41.55	New York	45.02
Georgia	42.12	Illinois	47.35

The meaning of the figures in Table XLVIII presents an alternative: either we must admit that Northern Negroes are biologically superior to Southern whites, or we must believe that Northern Negroes are superior or equal to Southern whites because of superior environmental conditions.   In the one case, the Army Alpha test finds justification as an excellent test of "native intelligence"; in the other, it is evident that it was simply an excellent gauge of educational and environmental advantages enjoyed by different social groups.   If we believe the former, well and good; if we believe the latter, it becomes reasonable that the superiority of the Southern whites over Southern Negroes as shown by the Army tests may be due to the vast advantage which the whites of the South possess over the Negroes of the section.   If we adopt the latter explanation, we can then explain the inferiority of the Southern white recruits to Northern white recruits on the same basis, *i.e.*, that of environment.   If not, we must believe that the Northern white recruits, with their large percentage of foreign-born, are biologically and racially superior to the Southern whites with their almost pure Anglo-Saxon heritage.

Now, we do know that the schools, and other sources of mental and cultural stimulation, available for white soldiers in the South at the time of their childhood were inferior to the same facilities provided for Northern recruits during their childhood.   The first five state school systems, in the ranking of 1900 of the Ayers Index, which rates the efficiency of school systems in the various states, ranked 9th, 19th, 3rd, 4th, and 7th in the Army tests administered in 1917–1918.   The last five states in the Ayers ranking for efficiency of schools in 1900 ranked 44th, 46th, 38th, 40th, and 42nd in the Army tests administered in 1917–1918.   The index of correlation for the entire list of states in school efficiency and in rank in the Army tests for white soldiers was excessively high—giving a correlation coefficient of .74. The correlation of Army test rank with the per cent of literacy gives a correlation of .64; with the average wage for farm labor, .83; and with the per cent of urban population, .62.

The conclusion cannot be escaped that the Army Intelligence Tests were excellent measures of environment and educational experience.

Some writers have been led to grant the superiority of Northern Negroes to Southern whites in order to maintain the validity of the tests as tests of intelligence. They state that the Northern Negroes are exceptions, and that they represent the "cream of the race," because the migration of Negroes to the North took the most intelligent Negroes from the South and concentrated Negro intelligence in that section. This argument has also been advanced by later investigators who have been disturbed by finding that Northern Negro children invariably test at a higher level than Southern Negro children, and who are unwilling to admit that the intelligence tests can be affected by a superior or inferior environment. The assumption involved, it has been suggested by Freeman, is entirely gratuitous; and Klineberg has more recently dissolved this despairing claim, which was never more than an unwarranted surmise. Klineberg found a definite advantage for Northern Negro children over Southern Negro children in intelligence tests. To check up on the theory that the migration involved the most intelligent class among Negroes, he visited the schools in the South from which many of his Northern subjects had come. Inspecting the school grades made in Southern elementary schools by these migrant children, he found that they were by this index inferior, on the whole, to the children who had remained in the South while their apparently duller fellows went to the North. Certainly, if the Negroes from Nashville, Birmingham, and New Orleans who migrated

to the North in the period from 1915 to 1925 had been
inherently superior to the other Negroes whom they left
behind, their children should have made marks in school
superior to the children of the Negro parents who did not
migrate.   Such was not the case.   It is more reasonable to
believe that the migration of Negroes to the North was on
the whole a fair sample of the population, although one
might expect the successful, intelligent Negroes, who had
achieved some substance and a secure place in their Southern
communities through intelligence and character, to remain
where they were, while their less successful, and accordingly
less intelligent brothers moved away to find a new home.

In 1921, Peterson began a series of studies of the intelligence of Negro and white children.   Peterson at first used
standard group intelligence tests.   The Pressey test gave
an I.Q. for Negro children of 75, the Otis test, an I.Q. of
58, and the Haggerty test, an I.Q. of 92.   In these first
studies, Peterson considered the probable effect of environment, but believed that he had discounted this sufficiently
by selecting Negro pupils from social areas which he believed
to be superior for the race to the areas represented by his
white selection were for whites.   In Nashville, he stated, the
Negro schools were as good as those for white children, and
the Negro children in the Knowles School, in the neighborhood of Fisk University, came from a superior residence area
for Negroes.

Peterson's error lay, first, in assuming that because white
university neighborhoods are generally the focus for a highly
selected population with superior social and economic status,
the same would be true of a Negro university area.   H. W.
Gilmore, in a Vanderbilt University doctoral thesis, emphasized the fact that Negro social areas in Nashville showed
no degree of the stratification characteristic of white neighborhoods.   White areas are usually well defined on the basis
of economic ability and social status, but every Negro urban

community shows every variety of occupational level in its residences. The Fisk University area, for this reason, was typical not of a highly selected Negro population, as would doubtless have been the case with a white residence area, but merely of all strata of the Nashville Negro population.

Furthermore, there was in operation at the time of Peterson's experiments a private school in the neighborhood of Fisk University which was attended by the children of the "best" Negro families. In testing the public school in this neighborhood, Peterson touched not a population selected for superior intelligence, but one which actually did not contain the younger children of the families of the better class.

In 1925, Peterson, discarding the group intelligence test as too likely to be affected by educational factors, turned to a test of his own devising which he called a "Rational Learning Test." This test consisted of a series of performance items thought to be devoid of language facilities and depending entirely upon native intelligence. This test was administered to Nashville whites and Negroes and children of both races in Chicago and New York. The Northern Negro children were superior, not only to the Southern Negro children, but also to the Northern white children studied. Peterson reasoned from this finding that the Negro children in the North were a highly selected group, superior in native intelligence even to the Northern white children.

Koch and Simmons reported in 1926 the findings of intelligence tests given as a part of the technique of the Texas School Survey. Mexicans, Negroes, and whites were tested. For all racial groups, the city children excelled the rural children, and the white children were far above the Negro children. However, the difference between the city and rural whites was as appreciable as that between the city whites and city Negroes, and there was very little difference in performance between the city Negroes and the rural whites.[21]

Bond, in 1926, reported the results of individual tests administered to a group of highly selected Negro children whose parents were college professors.[22] A small group of 37 children yielded a median I.Q. of 122. Five children made scores above 135. According to the norms for the Stanford Revision of the Binet Test, which was employed in this investigation, these five children were in the "near-genius" and "genius" class.

It may be of interest to note here the results of the tests administered in 1932 to college students in institutions throughout the country under the auspices of the American Council on Education.[23] One hundred and seventy-three colleges are reported in all sections of the country, including the results of tests taken by 36,665 students. Two Negro colleges were at the bottom of the entire list. The median score of a Negro woman's college is exceeded by 95 per cent of the students who took the test, and the median score of the other Negro college is exceeded by almost 90 per cent of the students to whom the examination was given.

However, it is significant that of thirty-three Southern white colleges, only three reported a median score equalling or exceeding the national median. One Southern white college made a median score that is exceeded by 90 per cent of students taking the test; two, a median score exceeded by 85 per cent of the students in the Nation at large; three, a score exceeded by 80 per cent of all students; seven schools, a score exceeded by 75 per cent of students exam-

---

[21] Helen Lois Koch and R. Simmons, "A study of the Test-performance of American, Mexican, and Negro Children," *Psychological Monographs*, Vol. 35, No. 5.

[22] Horace M. Bond, "Some Exceptional Negro Children," *The Crisis*, September, 1926.

[23] L. L. Thurstone and T. G. Thurstone, *Educational Record*, April, 1933, pp. 184–193.

ined; eight, by 69 per cent; five, by 62 per cent; three, by 56 per cent; one, by 50 per cent; and two, by 43 per cent.

In 1929, 1930, and 1931, Fisk University freshmen, all Negroes, made gross median scores superior to those shown by freshmen at such Southern white colleges as the University of Alabama, the University of South Carolina, and the University of Georgia.

If the results of this psychological examination, one of the most carefully designed of any, are to be taken as a true index to the inherited intellectual capacity of those taking the test, the inferiority of the Negro students is undeniable. At the same time, it must be admitted also that the white students in Southern colleges are unmistakably inferior to students in Northern colleges, and that the white "race" in the South is probably the least intelligent of any of our racial groups, with the exception of the American Negro. The author would prefer to believe that the current psychological examination which portrays the intelligence of Southern Negro college students—and Southern white college students—in such an unfavorable light, is an excellent measure of the variety and strength of cultural, educational, and other environmental factors, but is no more a test of "native" intelligence than the Army Alpha test.

Non-Intellectual Traits

Downey devised a test which she called the "Will-Temperament" Test. She proposed that the intangible yet highly important characteristics of the individual which are not intellectual be measured through the medium of a series of tests based principally upon the motor reactions involved in handwriting.[24] McFadden and Dashiell applied the Downey test to racial differences in a study involving 77

---

[24] June Downey, *The Will-Temperament and Its Testing*, World Book Company, Yonkers-on-Hudson, 1923.

college students from each race in North Carolina. They
reported that the white students showed a stronger profile
of the "will-temperament." Herskovits gave the Downey
test to a number of Howard University students. His conclusions were that the test was of no value in estimating
the strength or weakness of the traits which it purported
to measure.

Bond made a study in 1926 of the non-intellectual traits
of several hundred Negro adults.[25] He used the Downey
test, both group and individual forms, the Pressey Cross-Out
Test of Emotional Susceptibility, and the Woodworth Scale
for Emotional Stability. A small sample of the Brotemarkle
Ethical Discrimination Test was also obtained. The results
for all tests were negative, so far as any decisive racial differences were concerned. The reaction to "modal choices"
in the Pressey X-O Test was clearly modified by peculiar
language habits and verbal mannerisms, and the Downey
test gave no reliable profile of "will-temperament" when
these findings were contrasted with the judgment of teachers
and fellow-students. The Woodworth test gave no significant results.

There is a profound conviction in the popular mind that
Negroes in America possess a distinctive racial talent for
musical rhythmic expression. The Seashore Music Tests
have been devised to measure musical talent as exhibited
by reaction to experiments calling for a sense of pitch, intensity, time, memory, and rhythm. Johnson,[26] Lenoir,[27]
and Peterson [28] have investigated this aspect of the problem,

[25] Horace M. Bond, "An Investigation of the Non-Intellectual Traits of
a Group of Negro Adults," *Journal of Abnormal Psychology*, Vol. 21
(1926), pp. 267–276.

[26] Guy B. Johnson, "A Study of the Musical Talent of the American
Negro," unpublished manuscript, quoted in Garth, *Race Psychology, op. cit.*

[27] Zaid D. Lenoir, *Racial Differences in Certain Mental and Educational
Abilities*, unpublished master's thesis, University of Iowa, 1921.

[28] Peterson and Lanier, "Studies in the Comparative Abilities of Whites
and Negroes," *op. cit.*, pp. 138 *ff*.

but in none of the studies does a clearly defined difference appear. It has been the observation of the author that Negro students suffer from the same handicap in responding to the Seashore test which is to be found in any test requiring sustained application: namely, a disposition to make scores below their actual abilities because of an inability to understand directions and sustain patterns of reaction which call for immediate responses.

Summary and Conclusion

We have purposely avoided defining "intelligence" until this portion of our discussion was reached. With no clear definition of intelligence, tests were devised to measure the "capacity" which all believed to be present, much as instruments for the measurement of electricity were devised before any certain definition could be agreed upon.

In the past, men were content to let results speak for the intelligence of individuals, but in an age which wished to subject all observable phenomena to measures as exact as possible, the development of the "intelligence" test was inevitable. It was highly uneconomical to test a man's intelligence over a long period of years of behavior, if this judgment could be foreshortened into a series of reactions to set situations which would be standard for all and shed light upon the probable success of the individual in relation to wider spheres of behavior. In performing this task, it can hardly be denied that psychologists have been remarkably successful. Intelligence tests do make possible prophecy as to ability to perform those tasks involved in school and other activities to a great degree. In so far as they accomplish this end, they must become a part of the technique used by all school administrators. Long after intelligence tests were devised and put into actual use, a committee of American psychologists agreed that the capacity should be delimited as follows: "(*a*) ability to learn and to utilize in new situations knowledge or skill acquired by learning; (*b*) selective adaptation through acquired knowledge."

In so far as Negro children in Southern states almost without exception show on intelligence tests scores inferior to those of white children of the same locality, as is the case, we must agree that the test is accurate in showing a lesser "ability to learn and to utilize in new situations knowledge or skill acquired by learning," on the part of these children. To say this is not to voice a belief, however, that the difference thus shown for the two gross groups compared is permanent and ineradicable. Burks summarized a number of investigations of the intelligence of the Negro by saying,

> Home environment contributes about 17 per cent of variance in I.Q.; parental intelligence about 33 per cent. . . . The maximal contribution of the best home environment to intelligence is apparently 20 I.Q. points, or less. . . . The least cultured, least stimulating kind of American home environment may depress the I.Q. as much as 20 I.Q. points. But situations as extreme as these occur only once or twice in a thousand times in American communities.[29]

It is the author's belief that Miss Burks' estimate—for it is only an estimate—of the underprivileged American homes in which the "I.Q. . . . may be depressed as much as 20 I.Q. points" is far too meager. No one familiar with the isolated tenant farms and dismal slum areas, in which more than eighty per cent of all Negro children live, could believe that these "extreme situations" occurred so infrequently, if not in "American communities," at least in the typical Negro community. In thinking of "environment," we should not be so naïve as to believe that the present school, or the

---

[29] Barbara S. Burks, "The Relative Influence of Nature and Nurture upon Mental Development," *Twenty-Seventh Yearbook, National Society for the Study of Education* (1928), Part I, pp. 219–316.

present home, or the present play associations mark the limits of the societal setting of the Negro or any other child. We should also include in the picture the record of education and literacy of parents and other members of the immediate family, the presence or absence for generations back of various instruments of cultural stimulation, such as books, the press, and even, in a later day, the moving picture.

Sherman recently made an investigation of a group of isolated mountain whites in Virginia located hardly a hundred miles from the National Capitol. These whites—of almost pure Anglo-Saxon ancestry—had been left aside, high and dry on their little peaks, by the onward rush of civilization. The level of intelligence which the children of these mountain white families registered would classify them by any intelligence test as definitely feeble-minded. It has already been pointed out that Southern white recruits in the World War, and Southern college students of the white race today, make inferior showings on intelligence tests as compared to soldiers and students of the same race from the North. Until more proof is put forward, we state here that the case is as strong for these differences between members of the same race, and also between different races, to be due to patterns of social environment as it is for them to be due to any inherited factor of intelligence.

If Negro children make low scores in intelligence tests, as they do; if white college students in the South, or mountain whites in Virginia, make scores inferior to those attained by groups in other sections of the country, as they do; we hold these data to indicate an imperative necessity, not for the limitation of educational opportunity, but for the immediate and active reinforcement of such opportunity. It is even highly probable that the "intelligence quotient" of most Negro children could be measurably increased by the improvement of any one of a series of factors which now tend to lower it. McAlpin reports that Negro children

who migrated to the city of Washington from more southerly points showed a definite rise in I.Q. after a few years
in the improved environment;[30] and Freeman and Holzin-
ger, in studying the constancy of the intelligence quotient
of white and Negro children transferred from their own to
foster homes by placement agencies in Chicago, found a
definite tendency of the I.Q. to be affected after only a few
years by the new home surroundings.[31]

Many writers have suggested that the curriculum for
Negro children should be modified in accordance with the
findings of intelligence tests. Two facts stand out unchallenged: as Freemen has insisted, all so-called "racial differences" discovered have been quantitative, but not qualitative, differences. If Negro children differ from white
children in intelligence, it is not in kind, but in degree.
Furthermore, there is an immense amount of overlapping in
every racial comparison; there will be found Negro children
as able as the best among the white children, and there will
be found white children whose scores are as low as any made
by Negro children. There is no more reason for teaching
Negro children a certain kind of arithmetic, or reading, or
history, on the basis of their lower scores taken in the gross
than there would be to have a special curriculum for the
white rural children of the South as compared to the urban
white children of the section or of the North. It is as
reasonable to suggest a specified curriculum assumed to be
proper for an inferior Negro intellect as it would be to
suggest that the white colleges of the South no longer attempt the same sort of program pursued by Northern colleges of similar pretensions. A differentiated curriculum

[30] Alice S. McAlpin, "Changes in the Intelligence Quotients of Negro
Children," *Journal of Negro Education*, Vol. 1, No. 1 (April, 1932),
pp. 44–49.

[31] F. N. Freeman *et al.*, "The Influence of Environment on the Intelligence, School Achievement, and Conduct of Foster Children," *Twenty-
Seventh Year Book, N. S. S. E.*, Part I, pp. 103–317.

must find its only justification in a clear demonstration of a unique social and occupational need. This justification cannot be found in intelligence tests. Not until the yawning deficiencies in the elementary education of Negro children are remedied can we afford to begin to talk about curricula on higher levels which may properly be modifiable according to racial needs.

In his study of California children of "genius," discovered by an intensive "intelligence survey" of that state, Terman found several Negro children of surpassing ability.[32] That fact should hold a lesson for the Negro teacher. The strong and conscientious teacher can do much for all of her pupils. For those who by some strange quirk of nature or nurture are of exceptional promise, the teacher can do more. From the elementary school to the college, persons interested in the future of the American Negro should bend every effort to increasing the opportunity for mental growth on the part of all of the children, but especially on the part of promising children and youths. It is to be hoped that the loss of these promising youngsters in the elementary school and the high school may be minimized, and that the colleges will be readier to extend aid in the form of scholarships and free tuition to Negro boys and girls of great promise. The marginal economic status of the Negro in all too many instances allows the talented child to drop out of school in the face of an imperious economic necessity. The school can exert itself more than it has in the past to minimize the wastage which has been so prevalent in this sphere.

[32] Lewis M. Terman *et al.*, *Genetic Studies of Genius*, Vol. I, Stanford University Press, Palo Alto, 1925.

CHAPTER XVI

The Achievement of Negro Children

THE school as at present constituted cannot be expected to do everything. The fact has been stressed that most Negro children come to the school from low-income groups, from the lower economic and occupational levels, and from surroundings which are not generally conducive to study or sustained application. We are interested here in the degree to which the school can affect these surroundings and elevate the generation now in school above the level, cultural and economic, from which the parents were drawn. The school for Negro children cannot hope to obviate in one school cycle the intellectual poverty of generations, but it can do much. We intend here to see what it has done and what it is doing with reference to the improvement of children in the fundamental subjects of instruction.

Direct studies of the achievement of Negro children have not been numerous. Intelligence tests have attracted far more attention than tests in fundamental school subjects. School surveys which have used extensive testing programs yield considerable material. These surveys have found, for the most part, that Negro children are inferior in scholastic achievement. One exception is furnished by the Memphis survey, which discovered the fact that in the Stone Reasoning Tests of arithmetic, the Negro children of this Tennessee city surpassed the white children.

In Mississippi, O'Shea administered tests to Negro and white children in urban and rural communities through the state, checking the achievement of the children by means of a standard intelligence test.[1]   In the intelligence test, O'Shea found that the Negro children were only 55 per cent as efficient as the white children; but in the test of standard school achievement, he found that the Negro children were 75 per cent as efficient as the white children.   He found a difference of the same significant sort between the rural and urban Negro children, and the rural and urban white children.   Comparing the rural and urban groups, O'Shea regarded the intelligence tests administered as true indices to the ability of the children tested, so far as scholastic achievement was concerned.   He therefore came to the conclusion, since the Negro children made higher scores in achievement than in intelligence tests, that the Negro children of the state were putting forward far more effort than the white children, considering their limited attainments.

The absurdity of this statement did not prevent O'Shea from saying the same thing about the white rural and urban children when he compared these groups.   According to the intelligence test, the children enrolled in the urban white school systems had an ability that may be expressed by the index, 100 per cent.   However, he found that according to the achievement tests the city white children had only an efficiency in the neighborhood of 90 per cent, while the white rural children had an efficiency quotient in excess of 110 per cent.

In some counties, O'Shea found what he called the "achievement quotient" for Negro children to be as high as 165 per cent, indicating that the Negro children in these counties were performing their school work with 65 per cent more efficiency than was warranted by their intelligence. Of the white and Negro children who were thus supposedly working above the expectation shown by their intelligence tests, O'Shea used these remarkable words:

[1] M. V. O'Shea, *A State Educational System at Work,* Bernard B. Jones Fund, Washington, 1927.

This suggests that pupils in rural districts may be less distracted from school work than are pupils in larger communities, and they may possess greater interest in school work and greater endurance, industry, and ambition to succeed, since they have rather meager educational opportunities as compared with pupils in the larger places.[2]

Now it is almost impossible for anyone familiar with the psychological aura of the typical Mississippi plantation to see how O'Shea could have believed that the "poor (in intellect) but deserving and industrious" rural child should put forth superior effort in order to compensate for inferior intellect. The fact is that all intelligence and achievement tests, wherever administered, show this inversion of the achievement quotient. The writer has investigated the correlation between achievement and intelligence in two schools in and around the city of Chicago in which were enrolled white children at the opposite nadirs of ability. The children of the Elementary School of the University of Chicago show a median I.Q. of above 118. At the Lincoln State School, an institution for feeble-minded children, the I.Q. range is from below 50 to 75, while the I.Q. range at the University of Chicago Elementary School is from 84 to 158 with a median as indicated.

Records were available for both groups in the Stanford Revision of the Binet Test, an intelligence test, and in the Stanford Achievement Test by subjects. Beginning at the lowest I.Q. grouping, achievement quotients steadily decrease, the children of the lowest I.Q.'s having achievement scores far above their expected intelligence. Brown and Lind [3] explain this as owing to the retarded children's having had more training than those on the higher levels; however, when we compare children enrolled in a short-term

[2] O'Shea, *A State Educational System*, p. 349.

[3] Andrew W. Brown and Christine Lind, "School Achievement in Relation to Mental Age," *Journal of Educational Psychology*, Vol. 22 (November, 1931), pp. 561–576.

system with children in a long-term system, where the length
of term for the advantaged children outweighs the fact that
the retarded children have been in a grade longer, the same
phenomenon is apparent.

Now, in the definitely feeble-minded children of the Lincoln School, the achievement quotient declined with rising
intelligence test scores, and the same phenomenon is apparent with the University of Chicago Elementary School children.   Dividing the total score by subject, it was found that
the great advancement of the University of Chicago children
was more apparent in reading than in arithmetic.   With
the most nearly perfect educational conditions available in
any American school system, it was found that the highly
advantaged University of Chicago children made a much
less favorable index of achievement in arithmetic than in
reading; and, as well, their achievement quotients for both
subjects were inferior to those of children in the institution
for the feeble-minded.

We can adopt O'Shea's explanation, and apply it to this
situation.   Perhaps the feeble-minded children at Lincoln
School are "less distracted from school work" than the children at the University of Chicago Elementary School or
"possess greater interest in school work and greater endurance, industry, and ambition to succeed."   Another alternative is to regard the difference as due to the fact that the
intelligence and educational tests *do* test widely different
factors.   But this does violence to our notion that the intelligence test furnishes an excellent indicator of the degree
to which an individual can learn subject matter, an idea
fundamental in all work with intelligence tests.

To the author, there is a third alternative opinion with
regard to these findings which appears to be, at the least,
more logical.   It is that the feeble-minded children of the
Lincoln School in Chicago, as compared to the children at

the University of Chicago Elementary School; the rural
white children of Mississippi, as compared to the urban
white children of that state; and the Negro children, as
compared to the white children of Mississippi, make higher
achievement quotients because the intelligence test is only a
refined test of environment. The intelligence test was
standardized in such a manner as to avoid the more obvious
effects of direct educability, but in doing so, it plumbed
depths which were none the less susceptible to the effect of
environment. The range in educational achievement is
much narrower and more compact than the range in intelligence test scores: *i. e.*, the feeble-minded children are much
nearer to the exceptional children in reading and arithmetic
than they are in the intelligence test scores. The school
has parcelled out and made as its own province the correction
of deficiencies in the fundamental subjects, and tests of
school achievement show that this has been done to a large
degree. In those provinces less directly susceptible to the
teaching process, or, at least, which extend over a less tangible field of application, the school is shown, by the results
obtained from giving these tests to these different classes of
children, to have but a limited scope.

Even within the educational test itself, there are to be
found wide variations for each subject. The third grade
at the University of Chicago Elementary School, as we have
seen, had a range in intelligence quotients which was fairly
well restricted to the upper levels of intelligence. The
lowest score was 84, which is within the limits of normality;
while the lower fourth of the class showed an I.Q. of 109,
and the upper fourth, one of 128, with the highest score,
158. The children in the upper quartile of intelligence
quotients made an average reading score of 5 points, equivalent to a six-months educational-age advantage, above the
average arithmetic score. The second and third quartiles

had the same six-months advantage in their reading as compared to their arithmetic scores; and the only group to show a larger arithmetic score than reading score was composed of children in the lower fourth of the distribution according to intelligence test scores. This fact was standard for each grade, with the upper grades showing as much as a year's advancement in their reading as compared to their arithmetic scores.

The meaning of this phenomenon is not entirely clear. It is certainly absurd to say that the University of Chicago children in the higher brackets in intelligence have higher achievement quotients in reading as compared to arithmetic because they are better taught in the one than they are in the other, or because they are more industrious in the one as compared to the other, while the less intelligent children who have higher achievement quotients in arithmetic than in reading reverse the picture. The wide range in intelligence quotients corresponds with the wide range in reading scores, but does not correspond with the narrow range in arithmetic achievement. Is it not reasonable to conclude that arithmetic represents a variety of information which it is possible to compress and to teach with great success to all children, while reading does not offer the same opportunity for equalizing opportunity? Efficiency in reading depends upon intangibles which the school cannot affect so directly as it does the mechanics of arithmetic. The same application may be made to the problem of differential achievement quotients between children with high and low intelligence test scores. The intelligence test may be regarded in much the same light as the reading test; it is based on factors so selected that it escapes from a narrow compression of materials which may be directly taught. The achievement test, on the other hand, is so arranged as to yield results which reflect the effect of the educative process.

The Efficiency of the School and Educational Achievement

The most extensive study of the achievement of Negro children has been conducted by the Julius Rosenwald Fund. A survey of the schools and of the achievement of the children was made in 1929–1931 by Clark Foreman, assisted by H. M. Bond and Roy K. Davenport.[4] The survey first selected counties in Alabama, Louisiana, and North Carolina on the basis of per capita expenditures and geographical location. These states have three characteristic portions, from each of which a high-expenditure county and a low-expenditure county were selected as the centers for study. Limestone and Dekalb Counties in northern Alabama and Webster and DeSoto Parishes in northern Louisiana were taken as samples of the moderately high-altitude belt that runs through the South from the East to the Southwest. No hill county in North Carolina had enough Negro children to justify a special study.

St. James Parish in Louisiana was selected as a typical Mississippi Delta county, in which the chief agricultural resource is sugar cane cultivation. Tensas Parish, also located on the Mississippi River, is highly typical of the cotton-raising section of the middle delta region. In Alabama, Wilcox County and Montgomery County were selected for study as typical of the "Black Belt" area, where the entire life of the community centers in cotton production. In North Carolina, Union and Durham Counties were selected for study as typical counties of the piedmont tableland.

Mobile and Baldwin Counties are adjoining in southern Alabama, and were selected for the way in which they mirror the general characteristics of the Gulf-coast section.

---

[4] Foreman, *Environmental Factors in Negro Elementary Education*, published for the Julius Rosenwald Fund by W. W. Norton, New York, 1932.

Edgecombe and New Hanover Counties in North Carolina present a similar contrast in the tidewater section of that state. The Parish of Orleans in Louisiana and Jefferson County in Alabama, the first including the city of New Orleans and the second that of Birmingham, were selected as typical urban communities with a highly variegated industrial development.

In the following discussion, the author has relied first upon the materials reported by Doctor Foreman in his book, *Environmental Factors in Negro Elementary Education*. To the data concerning the achievement of Negro children assembled there, the author has applied a technique devised by Dr. Charles Thompson, of Howard University, for the measurement of the relative efficiency of a school system and the achievement of children within the system compared to national norms.[5] This technique involves rating the school system to be studied in accordance with approved items of importance, and determining what percentage of efficiency the school system shows of the efficiency of American schools generally. The percentage of efficiency of the school children enrolled is then estimated by comparing their scores in standard tests with national standards.

Thompson reports an application of this principle to tests administered by Pressey to Indiana white children, and by Peterson to Tennessee Negro and white children. Taking the Indiana white system as 100 per cent, and the scores made by Indiana white children as 100, Thompson computed the relative efficiency of the systems and children tested in these systems. He found a close correlation between the efficiency of children in standard tests and the efficiency of the school system. Thompson says,

[5] Charles H. Thompson, "The Educational Achievements of Negro Children," *The Annals of the American Academy*, Vol. CXXX, November, 1928, The American Academy of Political and Social Science, Philadelphia, 1928, pp. 193–208.

It is perfectly obvious from this analysis that we have a situation whose cause is not only more logically explained by difference in environment, but could by no reasonable stretch of the imagination be interpreted as "a real race difference." However, this is the usual interpretation of such facts.[6]

Not all survey data show the close correlation indicated by Thompson's analysis of the Peterson material. The Virginia School Survey reports the results of tests administered to large numbers of urban and rural Virginia children of both races in 1920. The educational achievement rank agrees with the school efficiency rank. However, the disparity between school efficiency for the rural Negroes and for children in the other systems is much greater than the difference between their achievement and the achievement of the other groups. In other words, it appears that the Negro children make scores in educational tests which far exceed expectation on the basis of the efficiency of the school system. We shall refer to this phenomenon later.

The Rosenwald Survey

A total of 10,023 children—6,516 third-grade, and 3,507 sixth-grade—were given the Stanford Achievement Test in reading and arithmetic. All schools in the counties selected for study were visited, and the test was administered to all children present on the day of the inspection. It is of interest to note that the general attendance found by this check was much smaller than that reported in official statements.

The data discovered by the test may be approached for interpretation in one of three ways. We can take the chronological age reported and say that the child, if normal in achievement according to national standards, should have

---

[6] *Ibid.*, pp. 193 ff.

TABLE XLIX [7]

ENROLLMENT IN THIRD AND SIXTH GRADES, BY COUNTY, WITH NUMBER
TESTED IN EACH GRADE AND MEDIAN ACTUAL AND EDUCATIONAL AGES

County	Enrolled 3rd Grade	6th Grade	Tested 3rd Grade	6th Grade	Median Chronological Age 3rd Grade	6th Grade	Median Educational Age 3rd Grade	6th Grade
Mobile	878	491	581	327	9–11	14–9	7–8	10–6
Baldwin	198	130	79	75	12–21	14–9	7–8	10–7
Montgomery	1561	869	728	434	10–11	14–0	7–6	10–6
Wilcox	343	117	165	50	12–9	15–10	7–8	10–3
Dekalb	22	15	9	4	11–0	14–6	7–8	10–4
Limestone	359	98	76	20	11–9	15–4	8–3	10–11
Jefferson	4324	2566	1611	968	10–3	13–2	8–3	11–00
Webster	438	196	223	105	12–9	15–11	8–4	10–9
DeSoto	788	320	361	132	12–5	15–7	7–11	10–5
Tensas	309	70	103	37	12–0	15–1	7–10	10–8
St. James	143	54	122	34	12–1	13–11	8–1	10–6
Orleans	2310	2424	1078	613	10–3	13–3	7–11	10–10
New Hanover	446	231	316	169	10–8	13–10	8–10	11–1
Edgecombe	612	329	324	132	12–1	14–10	10–8	12–1
Durham	694	309	617	283	10–4	13–4	7–11	10–11
Union	409	252	232	124	12–0	14–10	8–0	10–9
TOTAL	13,834	7580	6516	3507				

an educational age exactly the same as his stated span in
years lived. The Stanford test is calibrated by experiment
to carry these equivalents up to the age 14 years and 4
months, and an extrapolation of values above this point
gives a slight difference above. In other words, a child in
Mobile County in the third grade, typically 9 years and 11
months old, should have an educational age of 9 years and
11 months. However, these children are shown by the test
to have an educational age of only 7 years and 8 months,
and accordingly, this comparison would show an educational
retardation of 2 years and 3 months for the median Mobile
County child.

---

[7] Foreman, *Environmental Factors in Negro Elementary Education*, Appendix B.

A second method of comparison would be to eliminate age as a factor, as Thompson did in reviewing the achievement of Negro children, and compare their achievement by grade with that of children in the same grade according to national standards. The Mobile County children, accordingly, would be judged according to this method by the degree to which they reached, exceeded, or fell below grade standards. The comparable grade standard in this instance would be that for the third grade in the second month. The median score achieved by the Mobile County children gives a grade standing of a second-grade class in the sixth month; eliminating the age factor, the Mobile County children would be only four-tenths of a grade behind national standards.

The third method of measuring the efficiency of the children in achievement would be a combination of the two preceding methods. We should then find the median chronological age of the child tested, and, by reference to national standards, find out what grade this child should be in. We would then locate the child's achievement score with reference to the grade he is actually in and determine his achievement in terms of this combination of age and grade factors. According to his chronological age as given, the median Mobile County child should be classified, if normal, in the 4.1 grade. Actually, the score of this child is that of a child (according to national standards) in the 2.6 grade. The Age-grade Achievement Index, as we may call it, would then show a percentage of efficiency of 63.4; the Mobile County child, looked at in this way, has this percentage of efficiency in tests of fundamental school subjects. The age factor is too important as a gauge of school efficiency and individual progress, in the opinion of the writer, to be discarded. The data, therefore, have been rearranged with this index kept in mind as a true index of the relative efficiency of the school children tested. Table L may be read: The median United States child in the third grade is 9 years and

3 months of age.   The median sixth-grade child is 12 years and 4 months of age.   We should expect these children to make scores in standard achievement tests equivalent to grades of 3.5 for the third grade and 6.5 for the sixth grade. This would give a percentage of efficiency of 100 per cent for both children.

TABLE L

PERCENTAGE OF ACHIEVEMENT EFFICIENCY OF NEGRO CHILDREN

County	Chronological Age		Expected Grade		Achieved Grade		Percentage of Efficiency in Terms of National Norms	
	3rd Gr.	6th Gr.	3rd Gr.	6th Gr.	3rd Gr.	6th Gr.	3rd Gr.	6th Gr.
(United States)	9–3	12–4	3.5	6.5	3.5	6.5	100.0	100.0
New Hanover, N.C.	10–8	13–10	4.7	8.0	3.2	5.2	68.0	65.0
Jefferson, Ala.	10–3	13–2	4.3	7.5	2.9	5.1	67.4	68.0
Mobile, Ala.	9–11	14–9	4.1	8.7	2.6	4.6	63.4	52.8
Orleans, La.	10–3	13–3	4.3	7.5	2.7	4.9	62.8	65.3
Durham, N. C.	10–4	13–4	4.4	7.6	2.7	5.0	61.4	65.8
Montgomery, Ala.	10–11	14–0	5.0	8.1	2.6	4.6	52.0	56.8
Dekalb, Ala.	11–0	14–6	5.1	8.4	2.6	4.4	51.0	52.4
Limestone, Ala.	11–8	15–4	5.8	9.0	2.9	5.0	50.0	55.6
Union, N. C.	12–0	14–10	6.2	8.7	2.8	4.8	45.2	55.2
Edgecombe, N. C.	12–1	14–10	6.2	8.7	2.8	4.7	45.2	54.0
Tensas, La.	12–0	15–1	6.2	8.9	2.7	4.7	43.5	52.8
Webster, La.	12–9	15–11	7.0	9.2	2.9	4.8	41.44	52.2
Baldwin, Ala.	12–2	14–9	6.3	8.7	2.6	4.6	41.3	52.9
DeSoto, La.	12–5	15–7	6.6	9.0	2.7	4.4	40.9	48.9
Wilcox, Ala.	12–9	15–10	7.0	9.1	2.6	4.3	37.1	47.3

In New Hanover County, North Carolina, the median Negro child in the third grade is 10 years and 8 months old, or 1 year and 5 months older than the median for the United States.   The sixth-grade Negro child in New Hanover County is 13 years and 10 months old, or 1 year and 6 months older than the typical United States school child enrolled in this grade.   Considering the age of these children, we should expect the third-grade Negro child in New Hanover County to be in a higher grade and to make on a standard test an educational age equivalent to that grade, or 4.7. The sixth-grade child, also, if normally advanced, should be in the beginning eighth grade, according to his age, and should make a test score equivalent to this advancement. However, the third-grade child in New Hanover County typically achieves a grade of only 3.2 in a standard test, and the sixth-grade child makes a score equivalent only to the 5.2 grade. Since these children are retarded, not only in age, but also in achievement, their percentage of efficiency compared to national norms is 68.0 per cent for the third grade, and 65.0 per cent for the sixth grade.

If we disregard the age factor, and judge these children only on the basis of achievement, their achievement is seen to be more nearly up to standard. The third grade in New Hanover County would be only two-tenths, or approximately 2 months, behind the national norm; while the sixth grade would be 1 year and 3 months behind the national standard in grade achievement.

The amount of retardation in both age and achievement may be judged from an inspection of the table. The third-grade children in Webster Parish, La., and Wilcox County, Alabama, are of the age of children who more properly should be enrolled in the seventh grade. However, both of these counties show scores on achievement tests inferior to those attained by typical third-grade children. The third-grade children of Wilcox County are 3 years and 6 months older than they should be for their grade, and make scores on achievement tests nearly a year behind United States standards for third-grade children. By age-grade achievement, the Negro children of Wilcox County who are enrolled in the third grade have only 37.1 per cent of the efficiency of the median United States child. The efficiency of the third-grade children in the best counties is nearly twice as great as that for the Negro children in the worst counties.

The sixth grade does not show such a decisive pattern, the range between the achievement indexes of the various counties not being so wide. It is believed that this may be accounted for by a selective influence working in the poorer counties, whereby those children in the rural sections who continue in school are of a much higher social level, comparatively speaking, than children who continue their education through the grades in the better systems. In Wilcox County, for example, four times as many children in the entire number tested in the sixth grade reported homeownership on the part of their parents as did third-grade children. The city child may go on to the sixth grade because there is nothing for him to do; however, in a county where farm tenantry is customary and not more than three per cent of the children go as far as the sixth grade, only those families who can afford to deprive themselves of the labor of a valuable economic unit in cotton culture will or can permit the attendance of an older child in school.

School Efficiency and Achievement Efficiency

Ayers and Phillips [8] have devised a scheme by which the relative efficiency of school systems may be measured. The ranking of schools according to this system depends upon ten points, each of which is so arranged as to give 100.0 per cent for a maximum index of efficiency. The ten items are listed below:

1. Per cent of school population (school population including those aged 5–18) attending school daily.
2. Average number of days attended by each child of school age—divided by two. (Obtained by dividing the average daily attendance by the number of children of school

---

[8] Frank M. Phillips, "Educational Ranking of States by Two Methods," *American School Board Journal*, December, 1924.

age and multiplying by the length of the school term).

3.   Average number of days school was kept open, divided by two. (A condition of maximum efficiency would exist where the schools were kept open 200 days.)

4.   Per cent that high-school attendance is of total attendance, multiplied by 4 in 8–4 systems, and by 2.75 in 7–4 systems.

5.   Per cent that boys are of girls in high schools.

6.   Average annual expenditure for child attending.

7.   Average annual expenditure for child of school age.

8.   Average annual expenditure per teacher employed, divided by 24.

9.   Expenditure per pupil for purposes other than teachers' salaries, multiplied by two.

10.   Expenditure per teacher for salary, annual salary divided by twelve.

The county systems studied were arranged according to their percentage of efficiency in each of these items, the United States average being taken as 100.0 per cent of expectation.   The rating of Phillips for the schools in 1922 was taken as a standard of comparison, for the results of tests administered in 1929–1931 were interpreted on the basis of tests standardized prior to this time.   It was therefore believed that the average of efficiency for United States schools in general reported in 1922 would be comparable to the efficiency of the school children reported as normal in the Stanford Achievement Tests employed.

In order to determine the direct relationships between each of these factors and the efficiency of the school children tested, simple rank correlations were made for both the third- and the sixth-grade rankings by which the efficiency of the school children was compared in turn to the ten factors of school efficiency.   In both grades, the coefficients of correlation thus obtained are all positive, with those for the third grade on the whole much higher than those for the sixth grade.

The length of school term and the average daily attendance appear to be the most important factors in the achievement of Negro school children of both grades. Expenditure factors follow next in importance. Length of school term and attendance vary directly with the amount of money invested in systems for Negro children.

School and Child Efficiency—The Rosenwald Survey

The comparison of school efficiency and child efficiency as shown in the Virginia School Survey indicated close correlation between these factors, with the exception of the rural Negro children, who, with a ratio between the efficiency of their schools and that of the schools of urban white school children of only 49.9 per cent, show an efficiency index in achievement of from 73.1 per cent in spelling to 93.5 per cent in handwriting. The Negro children might be said to show an effectiveness in school achievement far above the efficiency of the school system.

When the counties studied in the Rosenwald survey are ranked in order of school efficiency and child achievement efficiency, the same phenomena appear: the children from the poorest counties, when school conditions are considered, do far better than one would expect, while the children from the better-school counties do not do as well as we are led to expect. In other words, the wide range in efficiency of schools is not duplicated by a corresponding wide range in child achievement.

A rank-order correlation will show a decided tendency of the efficiency of the children to coincide with the efficiency of the school system. However, the relationship is much more marked for the third grade than for the sixth grade; and there are three counties—New Hanover, Durham, and

TABLE LI

RANK OF COUNTIES IN RATIO OF SCHOOL EFFICIENCY TO UNITED STATES
AVERAGE, COMPARED TO RATIO OF CHILD EFFICIENCY MEASURED IN TERMS
OF AGE-GRADE ACHIEVEMENT IN READING AND ARITHMETIC

| | Percentage of Efficiency in Terms of National Norms | | | |
| | Third Grade | | Sixth Grade | |
County	School	Child	School	Child
(United States)	100.0	100.0	100.0	100.0
New Hanover, N. C.	82.9	68.0	82.9	65.0
Durham, N. C.	74.7	61.4	74.7	65.8
Orleans, La.	72.0	62.8	72.0	65.3
Jefferson, Ala.	66.1	67.4	66.1	68.0
Mobile, Ala.	56.8	63.4	56.8	52.8
Edgecombe, N. C.	46.7	45.2	46.7	54.0
Webster, La.	43.7	41.4	43.7	52.2
Montgomery, Ala.	42.0	52.0	42.0	56.8
Union, N. C.	41.6	45.2	41.6	55.2
Baldwin, Ala.	40.6	41.3	40.6	52.9
Tensas, La.	34.1	43.5	34.1	52.8
Dekalb, Ala.	32.3	51.0	32.3	52.4
Limestone, Ala.	28.5	50.0	28.5	55.6
DeSoto, La.	24.5	40.9	24.5	48.9
St. James, La.	24.1	45.2	24.1	55.6
Wilcox, Ala.	17.1	37.1	17.1	47.3

Orleans—where the school systems compare more favorably
with national norms than do the achievement ratios of the
children studied.   In New Hanover County, for example,
our estimate shows the efficiency of the school to be 82.9
per cent of the national average, while the achievement of
the third-grade Negro school children of this county is estimated to be only 68.0 per cent of national standards.   At
the other end of the scale, the children have a higher
achievement index than school index, Wilcox County having
a Negro school system that rates but 17.1 per cent of national standards, while the third-grade children display a
percentage of efficiency twenty points higher—37.1.

This difference probably occurs because the method of
applying efficiency rates for an entire system to the efficiency of the children enrolled is faulty because of the selective factor.   Certainly, the lack of close correlation in

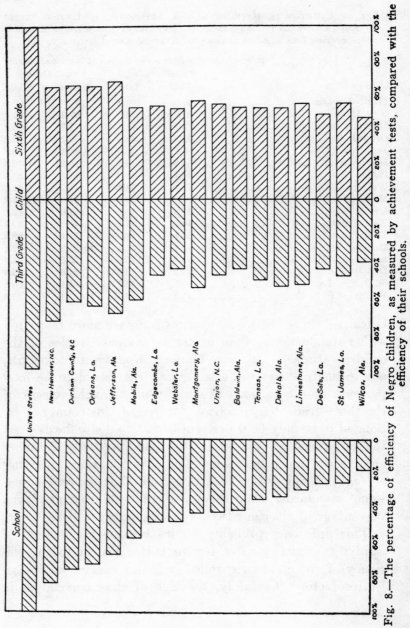

Fig. 8.—The percentage of efficiency of Negro children, as measured by achievement tests, compared with the efficiency of their schools.

the sixth grade, a selected group, as compared to the third grade, would incline to this opinion. For example, Wilcox County shows a large variation between the efficiency of the school and that of the child. But the figures for school efficiency in Wilcox County are based upon the entire school population, whereas only thirty per cent of this school population is in school. It would be expected that these children who were thus selected for school attendance would represent superior environmental status and a correspondingly higher level of efficiency in the tests than would be true of all of the children in the county.

With regard to those counties which show achievement inferior to school opportunity ratios, it is probable that the superior services of the schools are spread out over a larger number of children of inferior social status as compared to the counties with greatly inferior systems.

Jefferson County and T. C. I. Schools

The most striking example of the effect of improved educational and environmental patterns upon the achievement of Negro children reported by the Rosenwald survey is to be found in the differentiation between scores made by children in Jefferson County, Alabama. This county includes the city of Birmingham, with a separate school organization; a county school system, in which are enrolled children whose parents work on farms and in small industrial plants; and the school system operated by the Tennessee Coal and Iron Company, which maintains several large plants in the section. The T. C. I. Company supervises its industrial settlements which supply Negro labor with a strictness that amounts to paternalism. The schools are excellently managed, equipped, and supervised, and altogether, this is probably the best system for Negro children in the entire South. In addition to the schools, recreational and health services

are maintained by the company, and the housing conditions
maintained in the company housing areas approach the ideal
for a working-class population.

Apart from their distinctly superior educational and environmental advantages, the Negroes who live in the T. C. I.
plants are certainly no different from the typical laboring-
class Negro of the South. Yet the children tested show the
highest educational age of any group tested in the South.
The third grade equals the national norms for achievement
in reading and arithmetic and but for a median retardation
of one year in age would be normal. The sixth grade shows
a slight disadvantage compared to national standards, and
these sixth-grade children as a whole have not been wholly
trained in the T. C. I. schools and plants, as have the third-
grade children almost without exception.

TABLE LII [9]

COMPARATIVE SCORES OF CHILDREN IN SCHOOLS OF JEFFERSON COUNTY AND
OF THE SOUTH

Grades	Score		Chron. Age		Educa. Age		Retarda-tion (Grade Factor Elim'd.)		Age-Grade Index of Efficiency	
	3	6	3	6	3	6	3	6	3	6
United States							0–0		100.0	100.0
All Sixteen Co.....	26	58	10–11	13–5	8–1	10–6	2–10	2–11	56.0	60.5
Jefferson County:										
Urban	25	61	10–2	12–9	8–0	10–9	2–2	2–0	65.1	67.6
T. C. I. System	41	71	10–4	13–8	9–3	11–7	1–1	2–1	79.5	73.0
Other Non-Ur.	29	60	10–4	13–9	8–4	10–8	2–0	3–1	65.9	59.4

The schools operated for Negro children by the Tennessee
Coal and Iron Company are a testimonial to the manner in
which improved educational and environmental conditions
can raise the standard of achievement in a group of Negro
children. The two factors—education and environment—

---

[9] Foreman, *op. cit.*, p. 29.

are separated here to remind the reader that caution must
be maintained in believing the school in itself entirely responsible for superiority or efficiency of school children.
We usually find a good school in a good community, but it
is not altogether true that because these institutions are
found together on an equal status, an improvement or decrease in the efficiency of the one or the other will immediately have a corresponding effect on the other one.   In the
case of the T. C. I. schools, the entire credit for the excellent
showing of the Negro children enrolled there cannot be laid
entirely to the excellent schools.   Rather, it is the entire
complex which is involved, for the industrial company man-
aging these plants has not restricted its program of social
betterment to schooling alone.   Conversely, we have seen
that in many counties, Negro children appear to be superior
to the schools in which they are enrolled.   The sacrificial
devotion of the teachers working in these schools is one important factor involved in this circumstance, together with
the factor of selection already mentioned; but it is also probable that the schools are far more wretched by comparison
than the social status of the children enrolled.

Rural and Urban Differences

The results of the tests employed showed a definite advantage for urban children in counties where both rural and
city children were tested.   It is significant that in the four
counties listed in Table LIII, the rural children in the third
grade were in each case not only older in years than the
urban children, but also made lower educational-age scores.

It will be noted that the last column, giving the index of
efficiency for the achievement of the children in the two
grades, shows in every county a marked advantage of the
city children over the rural children.   The urban children
are younger than the rural children in each county and each

TABLE LIII [10]

RELATIVE SHOWING OF URBAN AND RURAL SCHOOLS IN FOUR COUNTIES OF
THE SOUTH

County	Gr.	Educational Age in Years		Chronological Age in Years		Retardation in Years (Grade Disregarded)		Age-Grade Index of Efficiency	
		Urban	Rural	Urban	Rural	Urban	Rural	Urban	Rural
(National Norm)						0–0		100.0	100.0
New Hanover, N.C.	3	8–10	8–7	10–7	10–8	1–9	2–1	69.5	65.9
	6	11–1	10–11	13–5	13–11	2–4	3–0	68.4	61.7
Mobile, Ala.	3	7–10	7–6	9–6	9–11	1–8	2–5	72.9	55.3
	6	10–6	10–2	12–11	13–4	2–5	3–1	63.8	56.5
Durham, N. C.	3	8–2	7–11	10–2	11–5	2–0	3–6	65.1	48.2
	6	10–5	10–7	13–0	13–11	2–7	3–4	59.4	58.0
Montgomery, Ala.	3	7–10	7–6	10–6	11–5	2–8	3–11	58.6	48.2
	6	10–1	10–2	13–2	14–6	3–1	4–4	57.3	50.6

grade, and, with the exception of the sixth grade in Montgomery and Durham Counties, make higher scores on the test. The greatest difference is between the rural and urban children of Mobile County, Alabama, where a unified county and city system gives apparently the same degree of efficiency between rural and urban schools.

It would appear from these data that the school is no mean factor in Negro school achievement where city-country differences are regarded, but it is also clear that even here the school is but one aspect of a widely variegated environment working in the achievement of the children.

Parental Occupation and Achievement

By far the greater number of Negroes who are gainfully employed find placement in unskilled occupations or in agriculture. In the Rosenwald survey, the percentage of Negroes gainfully employed who were engaged in agriculture ranged from 87.1 per cent in Wilcox County, Louisiana, to

---

[10] *Ibid.*, p. 26.

1.2 per cent in Orleans Parish, a unit that includes the city of New Orleans and is almost entirely urban. From the first, studies of intelligence and achievement have shown that children from poorly circumstanced homes make inferior scores, and the low level of life in agricultural areas makes this factor especially important where Negroes are concerned. Besides agriculture, the next most important classification for occupations of Negroes in the areas studied was domestic and personal service. In the urban areas, domestic and personal service was the largest classification. In general, it may be said that the proportion of Negroes engaged in agriculture and in domestic and personal service will serve as an index to the relative advancement of the groups studied, for these occupations are universally recognized as belonging to the lowest social status. Here we strike upon another facet of the many-sided factor which must be taken into consideration in the interpretation of test results. We know that Negro children in Northern cities, where the parents are employed more largely in industrial occupations than is the case in the South, achieve higher scores; but at the same time, these children have better schooling. Children of parents employed in industry have the great advantage of a higher wage scale and, consequently, a higher standard of living than the children of parents employed in domestic or personal service or in agriculture.

In addition, Doctor Frazier, of Fisk University, has pointed out the fact that the proportion of Negro women employed decreases as the proportion of men engaged in industry rises. The employment of married women necessarily deprives a home of that stability and central bond which is a powerful, however intangible, factor in the school work of children. In Southern cities, a large proportion of married Negro women will be found to be employed in domestic and personal service, and to deprive the family of the female head is bound to have an effect upon the achievement of the children.

In an unpublished master's dissertation at Columbia University, R. K. Davenport attempted to study the effect of occupation and other social factors upon the achievement of a group of Negro school children in New Orleans. Three hundred and forty-six children were divided into six main divisions on the basis of the occupation in which the head of the family was engaged. The mean indexes of efficiency, figured on an age-grade basis, are shown in Table LIV.

TABLE LIV [11]

AGE-GRADE EFFICIENCY OF NEW ORLEANS NEGRO CHILDREN ACCORDING TO PARENTAL OCCUPATION

Class	No. of Cases	Score Range	Chronological Age	Educational Age	Index of Efficiency
(National Standard)					100.0
Unskilled	114	21–75	13–2	10–8	62.6
Semi-skilled	114	22–75	12–11	10–7	63.8
Skilled	80	32–81	13–0	10–8	63.5
Farmers	8	15–69	13–4	10–1	55.2
Clerical and Business	25	42–73	12–11	10–8	65.2
Professional	5	59–80	12–0	11–2	85.4

The data shown here indicate that the children whose fathers were engaged in agriculture had a much lower "index of efficiency" than any other group. Their mean chronological age shows them to be older, on the average, than the other children, and to this initial retardation was added the fact that they made a score showing the lowest educational age of all children surveyed. The comparisons are limited, of course, by the small number of cases studied; however, the distribution is fairly representative of what might be expected in the city of New Orleans.

The small group of children whose parents fell into the "Professional" category showed the highest index of ef-

---

[11] From the manuscript of R. K. Davenport.

ficiency. Not only was their mean chronological age lower than that of any other group; their mean score on the tests was higher. There was not much differentiation on the lower levels shown by this general grouping; however, when the major groups are separated into sub-groups, more significant differences appear. Fifty-four children, for example, reported that their fathers were "porters." Dividing this group into "train porters" and "porters" engaged in menial work within the city, it was found that the train porters' children had an efficiency index ratio of 67.6 compared to 63.5 for the city porters' children. Regarding a similar group of Negro children in Los Angeles who made scores superior to the local white children, Peterson interpreted the high scores of the Negro children as due to the fact that "they were the children of parents who had travelled widely."

A study of the achievement of 97 children from families in which the mother was the sole source of support, owing to the death, desertion, or unemployment of the father, showed that this group of children had the highest retardation in both chronological and educational age, with the exception only of the eight children from agricultural families. Their index of efficiency falls to 61.8, only six points above the "Farmers" class, and twenty-four points below the mean for the "Professional" class.

The division of the children of the homes where mothers were employed showed that those children whose mothers were laundresses had the lowest index of efficiency of any group, less even than that of the agricultural group. They were followed in ascending order of achievement ratios by the children of houseworkers and those of cooks. Davenport states,

> When grouped by paternal occupations, it appears that the higher up the scale the paternal occupation is, the less will be the effect of maternal occupation upon the achievement of

the child, while the lower down on the scale the paternal occupation falls, the more will the occupation of the mother
affect the achievement of the child.[12]

The ranges of scores attained by New Orleans children
show that even in the poorest circumstances, there are Negro
children whose achievement is equal to that of the children
from the best environment. Occasionally, the child of a
laundress whose husband is dead or has deserted his family
will make as high a score as the brightest child from the
most stable family. The upper-middle-class Negro families
do now and probably will continue to furnish the great majority of leaders of the race from these children who are as
a general rule above their fellows in achievement. However,
there are yet Negro children who, like Booker T. Washington, come to the school from the most dismal surroundings
and yet have the promise of excelling in the world of affairs.
To all children, but particularly to these children, the Negro teacher has a grave responsibility which is as challeng-
ing as that of any preceptor of youth in America today.

Summary

As they are now constituted, schools for Negro children
are in a position to raise very definitely the level of compre-
hension represented by their achievement in standard tests.
Studies of achievement, however, point to the fact that instruction in the fundamental subjects which goes on in the
classroom cannot be divorced from the total social life of
the school child. Achievement in reading and arithmetic,
and in any other teachable subject, comprises far more than
the strict relationships of teacher-and-student. The individual efforts of students or teachers may draw the child
upward to illimitable heights from the muck of the lowest

---

[12] Davenport, *op. cit.*, p. 8.

type of social origin, but this can happen only in isolated cases. For the most part, the process of teaching involves a slow and tedious raising of standards of knowledge. It goes hand in hand with improvement in family organization, health, attendance, and economic and social status, and with the general extension on all sides of the civilizing process. The school does not, and should not, attempt to work in a vacuum. So long as the efforts of educators are restricted to an improvement of the method and means of instruction, we must resign ourselves to several centuries of continued struggle before the ultimate will be even in sight.

Fortunately, "the very stars in their courses" are fighting the battles of the educator. Instruments for the communication of ideas arising from man's inventive genius, such as printing presses, radios, and telegraphy, make their contribution. Machines which free men and women from degrading toil add their tithe. The wider dissemination of wealth and human comfort bring their gift as well. The teacher will oversimplify the complexity of her task if she believes that the limited control now exercised over the life of a child can in one or even several school generations revolutionize the world; but it is expressing no defeatist philosophy to admit that the schoolroom is but one of many places where human intelligence is being affected, and further to extend the true function of the educational process to agencies less formally constituted. The earnest teacher, in the efficient system, may count herself fortunate if she has been the lever by which even an infinitesimal portion of the load is lifted. This and more the teacher of Negro children can do, and in this is her proper function.

CHAPTER XVII

Higher Education for Negroes [1]

A GENERATION that takes Carrie Nation as its stock example of the moral crusader finds it difficult to realize that the anti-slavery agitation of a century ago liberated in its New England devotees a spiritual ardor which could add intelligence to passion. Not all of that New England suffered from the sharp disillusionment of Henry Adams. Some few of its colleges, at least, produced not only a "type," but also a "will," and this still ingenuous portion believed devoutly in the New England common school and in the New England college as the indispensable instruments of civilization.

---

[1] A brief bibliography of higher education for Negroes would include the following titles: Samuel Chapman Armstrong, *Twenty-Two Years' Work of Hampton Institute*, Normal School Press, Hampton, 1893; Ambrose Caliver: *Personnel Study of Negro College Students*, Columbia University, Teachers College Press, New York, 1930; *Background Study of Negro College Students*, Bulletin, Office of Education, Government Printing Office, Washington, 1933; W. E. B. Du Bois: *The College Bred Negro*, Atlanta University Publications, 1900, 1910; "Education for Life," *Journal of Negro Education*, Vol. 1, No. 1, April, 1932; "The Field and Function of the Negro College," *Fisk University Herald*, 1933; Fred McCuistion, *Higher Education of Negroes*, Southern Association of Colleges and Secondary Schools, Nashville, 1933; Gustavus Pike, *The Fisk Jubilee Singers or the Singing Campaign for Ten Thousand Pounds*, American Missionary Association, Boston, 1876; Francis Greenwood Peabody, *Education for Life, the story of Hampton Institute*, Doubleday, Page and Co., New York, 1918; Thomas Jesse Jones, *Survey of Negro Education*, Bulletin No. 38 of the U. S. Bureau of Education, 1916; *Survey of Negro Colleges and Universities*, U. S. Office of Education, 1928; Reports of the U. S. Commissioner of Education, 1870— (Vol. ii for 1901 has a survey of higher education for Negroes by Kelly Miller.).

To this abolitionist mind, the Civil War was a prelude, necessary but incomplete, to the work of assisting in what Mr. Beecher called "the greater providence of God." The actual fighting over, men and women offered themselves and their means of social salvation to the newly emancipated Negroes of the South. Augustus F. Beard, of the Yale Class of 1857, was engaged by the American Missionary Association as its general field agent for the location of schools, from whose active management he has but recently retired. Samuel Chapman Armstrong graduated from Williams College in 1862. After the War, he left the command of a brigade of Negro soldiers to found Hampton Institute in Virginia. Erastus Milo Cravath left the Federal Army to become an agent for the American Missionary Association in 1866 and President of Fisk University in 1875. Edmund Asa Ware and Horace Bumstead graduated at Yale in 1863. Bumstead's brief army service carried him to the crater at Petersburg and the command of a regiment under Grant. He studied for two years at Tubingen, and in 1875 came to Atlanta to join Ware, who had founded a "university" there in 1867. Helen Clarissa Morgan, like Cravath, a graduate of Oberlin, came to Fisk to teach Latin. Her first classroom was a dirt-floored barrack abandoned by the Army. General Swayne opened a college for Negroes in an ante-bellum academy building at Talladega, Alabama, and one of the first graduates was an ex-slave who had laid brick in the building intended for the sons of slave-owners. General O. O. Howard, of the Bowdoin class of 1850, established thousands of schools of all sorts for Negroes in his post-war capacity as head of the Freedmen's Bureau. In 1869, he founded Howard University, at Washington, D. C.

The early charters provided for the immediate establishment of a faculty of letters and anticipated the development of faculties of theology, law, and medicine as need should arise. These ambitious plans were not as pretentious as

they may now appear.   Northern missionary societies were
in the full flush of enthusiasm for the "uplift," and the
Freedmen's Bureau promised an inexhaustible source of
revenue for expansion.

But the North soon wearied of the enthusiasm of peace as
it had tired ten years before of the prolonged fever of war.
Philanthropic subsidies dwindled soon after the abolition of
the Freedmen's Bureau in 1870 left the new colleges sus-
pended over a mass of ignorance.   State systems were slow
in developing: it was not until well after 1910 that Southern states assumed any considerable responsibility for the
secondary education of Negroes.   The mission school was
obliged to become elementary school, high school, and college in turn.   There were no eligible Negro students at
Howard University when it opened in 1869, and the first
class was made up of five young white women, all of whom
were daughters of local trustees, and two white boys from
Louisiana.   In truth, the founders of these colleges were led
by their optimism to an extreme catholicity.   Armstrong
intended to have an institution where he could "directly help
the whites of the South by giving them an industrial education at Hampton."   Berea college, under John G. Fee, had
provided in its first charter, formulated in 1858, for the "coeducation of the races," and Cassius M. Clay made this his
sole objection to becoming a trustee.   Berea did maintain
an open door for Negroes as well as for whites until 1907,
when the Kentucky Day Law of 1904, proscribing "mixed"
schools, was declared constitutional.

Deflated hopes and stringent finances forced a compact
organization upon the schools.   A recent critic of higher
education for Negroes has said that the early graduates
"with their little Latin and their less Greek" were but poorly
prepared for the practical necessities of life.   No provision
was made in the curriculum for electives.   Latin and Greek
these Negro colleges did have, but what they had was neither

"small" nor "less."   Cicero, Livy, Horace, Quintilian, Tacitus, and Prose Composition afforded a rather full fare in Latin, while Greek could hardly be said to suffer neglect when every student was expected to read Xenophon's *Memorabilia*, Homer's *Iliad*, Sophocles' *Antigone*, "and other Greek tragedies," the New Testament in Greek, Thucydides, Plato's *Apology* and the *Crito*, and Demosthenes's *On the Crown*.   Mathematics courses were as extensive as those in the classical languages, and the few classes in history, natural science, and moral philosophy were organized and taught in the approved fashion of the time.

The missionary teachers who taught these subjects were liberally educated in the current scholarship of the period, and as undergraduates had often been among the best scholars in their colleges.   They made no concession to inferiority, assumed or real; the number of students allowed to enter upon or complete the college course was rigidly restricted.   Exceptional as was their attainment as masters of subject matter, the superior social order from which they were descended gave them an even greater advantage in contact with students who possessed no intellectual tradition. They did not, however, for this reason patronize the men and women they taught, but treated them as human beings. Deeply religious, they infused something of their own Puritan code into those about them.

The institutions maintained internally a strict discipline that gave order to minds and bodies unaccustomed to any sort of regimentation.   The inspiration of the teachers gave even more than order.   The institution of slavery, whatever its more idyllic aspects, was never intended to make men of its chattels.   Boys and girls came from the environment of slavery and were transported to a place where the students of Mark Hopkins, Theodore Woolseley, Charles Finney, and Henry Fairchild sought to do with Negro students what these men had done with them.   They succeeded in an uncommon way. If the colleges took students from "life," it was from a life in which there was no idealism and very little intelligence. The teachers insisted that the institutions they managed should have both.

The life of the missionary was a lonely one, and his only associations were with the students of the college community, for the "Yankees" were ostracized by the native white population. Early suspicion changed to ridicule as it became apparent that the work could make no revolutionary impress upon the system. "Mandy, is yo' did yo' Greek yit?" The classical tongues were the province of a gentleman's study, an acquaintance with Latin or Greek being a lesser *droit* of a caste. To see a former chattel whose expected rôle was that of a field-hand or house-boy seriously engaged in the study of Quintilian was an immense shock to one's sense of propriety. But the times have changed; a Southern city board of education recently voted unanimously to retain Latin in the curriculum of a Negro high school, while instituting new vocational courses in the white high school to displace the classical tongue. The Latin was much less expensive to teach.

There was more sincerity in a controversy that arose forty years ago as to what should constitute the higher education of the Negro. General Armstrong, the founder of Hampton Institute, was the only missionary leader whose early background was alien to New England. A native of Hawaii, he was familiar with the Hilo Manual Labor School in the islands, and he observed that ". . . it had turned out men less brilliant than the advanced schools, but more solid." While Cravath's students at Fisk and Ware's students at Atlanta were translating Latin, Armstrong set his pupils to work at "useful trades and occupations." There is significance, however, in the fact that at Fisk Cravath, in addition to being president, was professor of moral philosophy; and that at Hampton Armstrong reserved as his prerogative the instruction of senior students in the same subject. Armstrong had been enrolled in a class in moral philosophy taught by Mark Hopkins at Williams, and as a textbook in the Negro school he used Hopkins's "Outline Study of Man."

Booker T. Washington was Hampton's most prominent graduate, and soon after his monumental achievement at Tuskegee attracted national attention, he became the arbiter of such matters as affected the education of his race. Washington said, "I would set no limits to the attainment of the Negro in arts, in letters or statesmanship; but I believe the surest way to reach those ends is by laying the foundations in the little things of life that lie immediately at one's door." W. E. B. DuBois, a Fisk University graduate who took his doctorate at Harvard in 1895, insisted that inversion had always been the rule in the development of culture, and that it was as inevitable as it was necessary. "The Negro race is going to be saved by its exceptional men. . . . if we make money the object of man-training, we shall make moneymakers but not necessarily men; if we make technical skill the object of education, we may possess artisans but not, in nature, men."

The age was one in which the "vocationalism" so abhorrent to Mr. Nock had seized upon the American college. Appreciating the magic in Washington's personality and his visible good works at Tuskegee, the practical men of the day upon whose philanthropy the higher education of the Negro depended were convinced that it was the alchemy of "industrial training" which had produced so great a marvel. Now, part of the mystery, at least, lay in the alchemy of Mark Hopkins filtered through the hand and brain of Samuel Chapman Armstrong. But philanthropy henceforth preferred to concentrate its efforts on "industrial training," to the neglect of Charles Eliot's plea: "The only way to have good primary schools and grammar schools

in Massachusetts is to have high and normal schools and
colleges, in which the higher teachers are trained. It must
be so throughout the South; the Negro race needs absolutely
these higher facilities of education." The cause of higher
education for Negroes was further embarrassed by a multitude of inferior institutions that sprang up everywhere in
the South, and flooded the section with "cheap degrees and
cheaper people."

The old controversy has no great significance today.
Hampton and Tuskegee Institutes, the creations of Armstrong and Washington, have recently established themselves as degree-granting colleges. This circumstance
reflects the transformation that has taken place. The machine has done much for the Negro, perhaps as much as
Abraham Lincoln did. The limitations set by Bernard De
Mandeville for the education of persons "who are to remain
and end their days in a Laborious, Tiresome and Painful
Station of Life" have no present application to all members
of a racial group numbering twelve million souls.

Philanthropy has recently renewed its interest in the
higher education of Negroes. The great foundations are
assisting promising students to enroll in the graduate departments of the best Northern universities. Northern colleges have known the Negro since John Chavis, a North
Carolina free Negro, was sent to Princeton in 1797 by two
Granville County gentlemen "to see if a Negro could take a
college education." Lemuel Haynes, a Negro Congrega-
tional minister, who achieved wide repute as a theological
disputant, received one of Middlebury's first honorary degrees in 1804. John Baptist Russworm graduated from
Bowdoin in 1826, in the class following that of Hawthorne
and Longfellow.

Southern states provide for the education of the Negro on
every level with the exception of the university. Missouri
and West Virginia now pay tuition fees in other institutions

making no discrimination for such of their Negro citizens as
may desire advanced study and are barred by law from the
local state universities.   At this writing, a Durham Negro, a
college graduate, has pending a mandamus action against
the officials of the University of North Carolina to force the
university to show cause why he should not be admitted.
This action promises to precipitate in North Carolina the
question now met by out-of-state subsidies on the part of
Missouri and West Virginia.   University education is too
costly to think of duplicating state services for the two races.
New university centers for Atlanta, Washington, Nashville,
and New Orleans are planned by the great private foundations to absorb existing colleges in these cities.   When the
Southern Association of Colleges agreed in 1928 to extend
accreditation to Negro colleges within its province, the disappearance of the worthless diploma-mills which did so
much to bring disrepute upon the entire enterprise of higher
education for Negroes was assured.   Endowments are still
pitiably small: the combined productive funds of all Negro
colleges amount to less than the endowment of any one of
a score or more Northern universities.

With the exception of adequate finance, which is, to be
sure, no small consideration, the problem of higher education for the Negro is not far from that of higher education
for white Americans.   DuBois believes with characteristic
pessimism that the Negro undergraduate of today "has swallowed hook, line and sinker, the dead bait of the white undergraduate, who, born in an industrial machine, does not have
to think, and does not think."   The faculties of institutions
specifically for Negroes are taking on much of the highly
standardized aspect of other schools.   Whether the new
recruits from Northern and European universities will carry
on the "great tradition" is quite another question.   There
are even those who regret the passing of the old days with
their shabby buildings and controversial curricula.   Faintly

ridiculous to some, the time of the gently-bred woman of fine scholarship who taught Latin to ex-slaves on a dirt floor, recalls a golden age to others. The task of higher education in which she was engaged needs little justification today, and the great faith in her lonely mission which made it highly effective deserves at the least to be perpetuated.

CHAPTER XVIII

Education of Negroes in the North

COTTON MATHER'S *Magnalia* reveals the fact that as early as 1675 a great spirit had protested against the prejudices which deprived Negroes in the Plymouth Bay Colony of an education. John Eliot, the Apostle to the Indians,

> . . . had long lamented it with a Bleeding and Burning Passion, that the English used their Negro's but as their Horses or their *Oxen*, and that so little care was taken about their immortal Sould; he looked upon it as a Prodigy, that any wearing the *Name* of *Christians* should so much have the *Heart* of *Devils* in them, as to prevent and hinder the Instruction of the poor *Blackamores*, and confine the souls of their miserable Slaves to a *Destroying Ignorance*, merely for fear of thereby losing the Benefit of their Vassalage; but now he made a motion to the English within two or three Miles of him, that at such a time and Place they would send their *Negro's* once a week to him; For he would then catechize them, and *Enlighten* them, to the utmost of his Power in the Things of their Everlasting Peace: however, he did not live to make much Progress in this Undertaking.[1]

The education which the Apostle wished to give Negroes partook strongly of the religious impression of the time, but this was typical of educational efforts for all classes of the population. Instruction in the New England Theocracy was designed to fit human souls for their salvation, and all other objectives were secondary. Cotton Mather published

---

[1] Cited in G. W. Moore, *Notes on Slavery in Massachusetts*, D. Appleton & Co., New York, 1866, p. 37.

in 1693 his *Rules for the Society of Negroes,* in which he inveighed against the Massachusetts planters who believed black men were created by Almighty God "only to serve the Lusts of Epicures, or the Gains of Mammonists." [2]   Chief Justice Sewall of the Massachusetts Colony was another strong defender of the right of the Negro to religious instruction.

Among religious sects, that of the Quakers furnished the most devoted friends of the education of Negroes in the North in these colonial times.   William Penn frowned upon the institution of slavery in the colony established by him and advocated the emancipation of such Negroes as were enslaved in order that they might enjoy the intellectual and moral advantages of freemen.   The Quakers themselves were intolerant of slavery, and one among their number, Benjamin Lay, believed that education should accompany and precede emancipation.   The Friends, he said, should "bring up their Negroes to some Learning, Reading and Writing," in addition to giving religious instruction.

Anthony Benezet, a Huguenot refugee from the persecution of the Bourbons in France, became interested in the condition of Negroes while conducting a female seminary in Philadelphia.   Associating himself with the Quakers, he agitated for the education of the slaves and at his death left a sum of money to be used for this purpose.   A schoolhouse was erected in Philadelphia in 1787, supplementary funds being contributed by members of the Society of Friends and by Thomas Sydney, a Negro of Philadelphia.   The curriculum of this school reflected the influence of the rising academy movement, including the subjects of reading, writing, arithmetic, plain accounts, and sewing.[3]

---

[2] Cited in C. G. Woodson, *The Education of the Negro Prior to 1861,* Association for the Study of Negro Life and History, Washington, 1919, p. 39.

[3] Woodson, *op. cit.,* p. 79.

The first school regularly established for Negroes in the North, however, appears to have been that of Elias Neau in New York City, who began his labors in 1704. Neau was an agent of the Society for the Propagation of the Gospel in Foreign Parts, a missionary auxiliary to the Anglican Church communion. This society was active in establishing schools for Negroes, principally for religious instruction, in the Southern Colonies as well as in the North.

In the Goose Creek Parish, of South Carolina, the Reverend Samuel Thomas by 1705 had twenty Negro communicants whom he had instructed in the common branches. The Moravians, in Pennsylvania, the Presbyterians, in New Jersey, and the other religious sects of the Northern Colonies all put forward some effort to give Negroes within their reach religious and secular training in fundamentals.[4]

The development of a revolutionary spirit in the Colonies, culminating in the Declaration of Independence and the formation of a constitutional republic, affected markedly the social status of the Northern Negro. The theory of the "natural rights of man" filtered down from French and English philosophers through the minds of the early Revolutionaries and was ultimately diffused throughout the Colonies. In New England, slavery had gradually disappeared, and even in the South it was clearly seen by the foremost leaders of the Revolution against Britain that the institution of human slavery was inconsistent with the newly established American system of democracy. James Otis declaimed against slavery in Massachusetts; Thomas Jefferson in Virginia could make no apology for it; and the trend of the generation from 1775 to 1800 was unmistakably in the direction of a gradual but complete abolition of slavery in all of the land.[5]

---

[4] Leavell, *Philanthropy in Negro Education*, p. 5.

[5] Ezra B. Chase, *Teachings of Patriots and Statesmen, or, The Founders of the Republic on Slavery*, J. W. Bradley, Philadelphia, 1860.

The rise of abolitionist and colonization societies also gave impetus to efforts to educate Negroes. The religious societies continued to aid, and schools supported by religious associations and private philanthropies were established in all of the cities where there was a concentration of Negro freedmen. The Negroes themselves in many instances established mutual benefit associations whose prime interest was the provision of an education for their children. There were sixteen schools for colored children in Philadelphia alone in 1822, and eleven of these were taught by Negro teachers.[6] In New York, an "African Free School" was founded in 1787 by the "Society for Promoting the Manumission of Slaves." Besides the fundamental subjects of instruction, needlework was taught to the girls after 1791. By 1820, several hundred children were enrolled. When Lafayette returned to America in 1824 on his triumphal tour of the country, he visited the school and remarked upon its good discipline.

Another Revolutionary hero, the Polish general Kosciusko, asked that Thomas Jefferson act as the executor of his estate in order to buy Negroes, to give them an education in the trades or in other respects, "and in having them instructed for their new condition in the duties of morality." The will does not appear to have been executed.

In the New England States, immediately after the formation of the Federal Union, separate schools were maintained by Negroes for their children. Many of the separate schools maintained by Negroes were not enforced so much by prejudice as by the tradition of private schools, the public schools being regarded "pauper institutions." The Negroes were advised by some friends not to avail themselves of the public school system because they would be accused of

---

[6] Woodson, *The Education of the Negro Prior to 1861*, p. 146.

being charges upon the public, but rather to support their
own schools.

Several higher schools for Negroes were projected, and
four actually were established and flourished in the ante-
bellum period.   Avery College, at Pittsburgh, operated successfully from 1852 until after the Civil War.   It was the
first school of designedly higher level to employ an all-Negro
faculty.   Ashmun Institute was located in Chester County,
Pennsylvania, by a resolution of the Presbytery of New Cas-
tle.   The school was designed to train religious leaders for
service in Liberia and in America; it was renamed Lincoln
University in 1866.[7]

Wilberforce University was established at Tawawa
Springs, near Xenia, Ohio, in 1854 by the Cincinnati Conference of the Methodist Episcopal Church.   The locality
was one where numerous Southern planters had settled their
mulatto offspring and other manumitted servants on farms.
The African Methodist Episcopal Church acquired the property in 1862.[8]

There were few communities in the North ready to receive
Negroes in large numbers, whatever the attitude of individual abolitionists.   A schoolhouse for Negro boys at New
Canaan, New Hampshire, was dragged into a swamp by outraged villagers.   At Canterbury, Connecticut, Miss Pru-
dence Crandall conducted a school for white girls.   When a
colored girl by the name of Sarah Harris applied for admission, she was admitted.   The other white students left
the school, and Miss Crandall advertised for colored girls to
take their places.   A number of girls from New York, Boston, and other cities put in their appearance at the school.
The opposition within the town to the school was so virulent
that boycotts, annoyances, and actual violence multiplied.

---

[7] George W. Williams, *History of the Negro Race in America* (popular
edition), G. P. Putnam's Sons, New York, 1882, p. 178.

[8] Woodson, *Education of the Negro*, p. 272.

A tragic picture of the state of civilization in Connecticut at that time is reflected by a description of one night in the school when the girls cowered frightened and helpless as a mob stood without, cursing, catcalling, and pelting the structure with missiles of every description. The state legislature passed a law outlawing any school maintained in the state from without the state for Negroes, and making the permission of local authorities a condition precedent to the establishment of a school of any sort for Negroes, whether native or not.[9]

Miss Crandall was arrested and jailed as a law violator when she stubbornly refused to close her school. Convicted in the lower courts, she was finally freed when the court of errors quashed the indictment on technical grounds.

In other places, the opposition to schools for Negroes was frequently focused by outbreaks of mob violence directed against the race in general. Successive riots in Washington, Baltimore, and New York invariably found the school buildings for Negroes made one of the objects of mob violence. In settlements in Ohio and Indiana, schools for Negro children were occasionally destroyed.

Despite all opposition, the schools flourished and were responsible for the training of a distinguished leadership for Negroes both before and after the Civil War. Charles Reason, Alexander Crummell, John M. Langston, Henry Highland Garnett, Ira Aldridge, and other notable men received their first training in the private schools established by philanthropists or by Negro parents for Negro children.[10]

Public Schools for Negroes in the North

The period in which private schools dominated the educational picture of Northern Negroes was one in which the

---

[9] Williams, *History of the Negro Race*, pp. 149–156.
[10] *Vide* biographical sketches in Simmons, *Men of Mark*.

battle for free schools for white children was being waged in
that section.   The abolitionist was likely to be fighting
not only for the rights of Negroes, but also for prohibition,
or for women's suffrage, or for socialism, or for any one of
many other varieties of the reform movements which characterized the nineteenth century.   In Massachusetts, Horace
Mann won the battle for free schools and went to Congress
thereafter on an anti-slavery platform; and in Pennsylvania,
Thaddeus Stevens was called a "radical" long before Reconstruction days, because he fought a winning battle in the
Pennsylvania Legislature against "pauper" and parochial
schools.

The result was that the struggle of Negroes in the North
for education which should be supported by public taxation
was part and parcel of the great humanitarian movements
of the day.   The process generally followed these steps: first,
the creation of a public school system for all white children;
second, the provision of separate schools for Negro children
at public expense; and, at last, the prohibition of separate
schools on the expressed grounds that they were undemocratic in principle.

In the year 1933, there appears a startling similitude in
the educational problems of the Negroes to many of the
problems of education of Negroes in the North which were
violently argued in the decade before and the one after 1833.
There is no index to shifting trends of racial relations more
reliable than the agitation regarding separate schools, for
the training of the child, dear to the hearts of parents of
both races, has always been one of the first of social relations to find its way into legislation and litigation.   At the
present time, and for the last few years, there has been a
growing tendency to segregate Negro children enrolled in
Northern cities.   To date, the tendency has not found its
way into legislation, but it is reflected in numerous actions
of boards of education, city superintendents, and patrons,

black and white. Stephenson, writing in 1910, stated that
there were seven states which formerly had separate schools
but now prohibited them: Illinois, Massachusetts, Nevada,
New Jersey, New York, Ohio, and Pennsylvania.[11] When
we reflect upon the changes in social theory represented by
these changing statutes, when we remember that in southern
Illinois, Ohio, and New Jersey, there are separate schools
for the two races today, and that the elementary schools for
Negroes in Philadelphia and in other smaller communities
throughout a large portion of southern Pennsylvania are
separate, it is plain that the school codes do not always do
justice to actual educational practice.

Various changes in the pattern are traced below:

> **Massachusetts.** A separate school for colored children
> was established as a part of the Boston public school sys-
> tem in 1820. Separate schools for Negroes existed in other
> Massachusetts cities at the same time, although no specific
> legislative action was involved. In the case of *Roberts* vs.
> *the City of Boston*, brought to test the legality of maintain-
> ing a separate system for Negroes, the Supreme Court of
> Massachusetts said in 1849: "For half a century, separate
> schools have been kept in Boston for colored children, and
> the primary school in Belknap street was established in 1820,
> and has been kept there ever since." [12] At New Bedford in
> 1838, at Nantucket in 1843, and in other Massachusetts
> towns by 1846, with the exception of Boston, Negro children
> had been admitted to the public schools without distinction.[13]
>
> In 1846, George Putnam and other Negroes of Boston
> petitioned the school committee to abolish separate schools
> for Negroes. The board answered this petition by stating
> that they deemed separate schools not only "legal and just"
> but also "best adapted to promote the education of that
> class (*i.e.*, Negroes) of our population." Wendell Phillips

[11] Gilbert T. Stephenson, *Race Distinctions in American Law*, D. Appleton and Co., New York, 1910. This work, together with Woodson, *The
Education of the Negro prior to 1861*, and Williams, *History of the Negro
Race in America*, constitute available sources for most of the material discussed in this chapter.

[12] Cited in Stephenson, *Race Distinctions in American Law*, p. 167.

[13] Woodson, *Education of the Negro Prior to 1861*, pp. 320–321.

aided the Negroes in their agitation. In the case brought by Roberts, cited above, the Massachusetts court held that the complaining Negro patron had no cause to object to separate schools so long as the school maintained for Negroes met the same educational requirements as other public schools and afforded opportunities similar to those maintained in other public schools. The court added an enlightening note: "Schools for colored children were originally established at the request of the colored citizens, whose children could not attend the public schools on account of the prejudice then existing against them." [14]

Charles Sumner was the attorney for the plaintiff in this action. The Massachusetts Legislature in 1857 passed a law, after long agitation by Sumner, Phillips, and other abolitionists, requiring school committees to exercise no discrimination, in admitting children to schools, on account of "race, creed, or previous condition of servitude." A penal clause was attached to the bill, which also provided that offended parties might recover damages if they could establish discrimination.

The passage of a law, however, settles no question in Massachusetts any more than it does in any other state. There have been sporadic outbreaks of segregation in several Massachusetts towns and cities within the last two decades. In 1907, Charles W. Eliot, at that time President of Harvard University, stated in a speech at Boston: "If the numbers of white and blacks were more nearly equal (in Boston) we might feel like segregating the one from the other in our schools. It may be that as large and generous a work can be done for the Negro in this way as in mixed schools. So the separation of the races in the Berea schools is not really an abandonment of the principle, although it may be a departure from the original purpose.

"Perhaps if there were as many Negroes here as there we might think it better for them to be in separate schools. At present, Harvard has about five thousand white students and about thirty of the colored races. The latter are hidden in the great mass and are not noticeable. If they were equal in numbers or in a majority, we might deem a separation necessary." [15]

The reader will remember that within the last decade the Board of Overseers of Harvard University seriously con-

---

[14] Stephenson, *loc. cit.,* p. 167.
[15] Stephenson, *op. cit.,* p. 162.

sidered restricting the number of Jews in the college population to a designated quota, and that Doctor Eliot's successor, Lawrence A. Lowell, approved the protest of a white freshman from the South who objected to the presence of a Negro in the college dormitory where both resided.

Connecticut. The first recorded provision for separate public schools in Connecticut, similar to that in Massachusetts, followed the petition of a group of Negro patrons to the School Society of Hartford, asking that the school fund due Negro children be used to establish a separate school. Lacking authorization in the existing statutes for such action, the School Society appealed to the state legislature. The result was a law which permitted the establishment of several separate schools for Negroes in various cities of the state. Just as the minority white populations in certain "black" counties of the South found out after the Civil War that the school fund was inadequate to support schools for their scattered white school children, the Negro minority in Connecticut found the pro rata apportionment of the state too inconsiderable to maintain separate schools in view of the small Negro population. This complaint was set forth in an appeal to the School Society of Hartford in 1846. Attention was also called to the fact that school officials did not concern themselves with supervising the Negro school after the apportionment had been paid.

In answer to this appeal, the School Society continued to maintain a separate school, but did allow Negroes to participate in local taxation. Soon afterward, the Negroes of Hartford petitioned again for improved school facilities. The abolitionists were, at the time, agitating for a mixed system of instruction in the North. At a public meeting called by the School Society to determine the question, the Negroes voted in favor of a continuance of a separate system if these schools were maintained on an equal basis with those for whites. It was not until 1868, at a time when the Reconstructionists were providing for a mixed school system in Mississippi and South Carolina, that Connecticut by law prohibited the further continuance of separate schools.

New York. At the beginning of the New York public school system, school funds were distributed through private associations and denominational organizations for the support of the schools. The African Free Schools in the city of New York received the portion of money allotted to Negro children. The powerful benevolent and parochial societies, in fact, fought the development of a real public school system at every step. It is probable that the administrators of schools for Negroes were one with these antagonistic elements for selfish reasons. In 1841, the establishment of a separate school was authorized in every district which voted to have one in preference to a mixed school. More than 5,000 Negro children were enrolled in separate schools in 1847. Appropriately enough as a foreshadowing of later events in the South, a New York State commissioner of education protested about this time at the practice of diverting public tax funds from separate Negro schools to those for white children.

The administration of the African Free Schools was placed under the New York Public School Society in 1834. In 1853, the semi-private School Society relinquished its authority in turn to the New York City Board of Education.

The revised code of New York in 1864 made the establishment of separate schools for Negro children discretionary with local boards. The courts decided in 1869 that the action of the city of Buffalo in maintaining separate schools for Negroes was valid in that the right to attend public schools is derived from legislative rather than from Constitutional guarantees. A separate school case from Albany in 1872, the oft-quoted case of *People* vs. *Gallagher* in 1883, and litigation arising from alleged discrimination in the Borough of Queens in 1899 were all decided by the courts in favor of the right of the school board to segregate children of different races so long as equal educational facilities were maintained by the authorities for Negroes. These decisions were based upon the law of 1864, which was re-enacted in 1894. In 1900, during the governorship of Theodore Roosevelt, the previous statute was repealed and separate schools were prohibited in the state.

Pennsylvania. Early legislation to establish a public school system in the state was hindered, as in New York, by the cry of "pauper schools" on one hand and the antagonism of entrenched private and parochial school interests on the other. The private schools in which Negroes were enrolled fought for their portion of the school fund and against a public school system that might encroach upon their prerogatives. Separate public schools, however, were established ultimately in Philadelphia in 1822, 1833, and 1841. Harrisburg first had a separate school, but when the Lancastrian system was introduced there in 1832 for the purpose of curtailing school expenses, all children were required to attend this school or go to private schools. The revised school law of 1854 placed the Pennsylvania system on a firm, tax-supported basis for the first time. Thaddeus Stevens played an important rôle in the enactment of this law. Separate schools were made discretionary with local officials wherever there were as many as 20 Negro children in a district. Negro children were refused admittance to the sub-district schools of Pittsburgh in 1869, but the local law permitting this exclusion was repealed in 1872. The law of 1854 was repealed in 1881, and it was thereafter, at least in theory, unlawful to maintain separate schools in the state.

In spite of the law, local sentiment has resulted in the provision of separate elementary schools for Negro children in many towns and villages of southern Pennsylvania. The elementary schools of Philadelphia, largely through district "gerrymanders," have been separate since their incorporation into the public system. No separate high schools have as yet been provided for Negroes.

Within the last few years, the question of segregation has been rife in Pennsylvania. The Cheyney Normal School was made a state institution in 1925. The school is not designated as a "Negro" school, but its long history of devotion to the interests of that race, added to the fact that no white students appear to have taken advantage of its facilities, indicate that it is intended to be a separate school for the training of Negro teachers. Rayford W. Logan, among other critics of this recent development, believes that ". . . this policy will lead to separate public schools."[16]

At Berwyn, a suburb of Philadelphia, the school board has recently constructed a new school building and designated the old structure as a separate school for Negro children. In 1932, the Negro patrons, on the advice of counsel, refused to send their children to the "Negro" school. It has been said that the board intends to base its defense in the courts not on the basis of the necessity for racial separation, but on the grounds that the Negro children are inferior in intelligence to the white children and as a group demand special classes for optimum educational results. The attempt to segregate Negro children at a high school in Pittsburgh has also been widely publicized within the last two years (1931–1933).

[16] "Educational Segregation in the North," *The Journal of Negro Education*, Vol. ii, No. 1, p. 67.

New Jersey.   No provision was made for separate schools for Negroes in 1844 by the constitution of that year.   The state funds were declared for the equal benefit of all of the people, a favorite phrase of the legislators even in those states where separate schools are taken for granted.   In 1881, a statute was enacted by the general assembly making it unlawful to exclude any pupil on account of "religion, nationality, or color."   In 1904, the public schools of East Orange, New Jersey, kept Negro and white children in the same building but in separate classes.   The experiment was abandoned soon afterward, one school official having been reported to say, "it seemed like going back to old ideas." Other New Jersey officials have not been reluctant to "go back to old ideas," in this particular, at least.   Throughout southern New Jersey, the practice is to maintain separate schools, sometimes separate classes, in a few cases in different wings of the same building.   The playgrounds are fenced off from one another in these cases by high wire partitions.

In 1924, Trenton built the New Lincoln School to replace several smaller schools used by Negro children.   The structure "cost when completed nearly a million dollars and is one of the most beautiful school buildings occupied exclusively by Negroes anywhere in the United States. . . . It is evident that the desire of the school board has been in the direction of separation, and they have been willing to pay handsomely for it." [17]

New Jersey, like Pennsylvania, maintains a separate school for the advanced training of Negroes, the Bordentown Manual Training School.

Ohio.   In 1829, Ohio passed a law expressly forbidding the attendance of black and mulatto children in public schools.   The property of Negroes was exempted from school taxes.   A broadside statute of 1848 levied a tax upon the property of Negroes for the support of Negro schools if white people in any locality objected to the attendance of Negro children.   No money raised from taxation upon white people was to be used for the support of Negro schools, unless such appropriation was agreeable to the white taxpayers.   Repealed in 1849, this law was followed by another which appropriated to colored schools the taxes paid

---

[17] Payne, George E., "Negroes in the Public Schools of the North," *Annals of the American Academy*, November, 1928, p. 229.

by Negroes as the sole source of support for the separate
system.

The Constitution of Ohio at that time restricted the electorate to white persons and prevented any Negro from holding public office, but Negroes were held by the courts not to
be barred from the office of school director, and in one case
it was held that a person with more white than Negro blood
might be admitted to the white schools. John Mercer
Langston, a mulatto, who graduated from Oberlin College
in 1849 and was admitted to the Ohio Bar in 1855, was
elected Clerk of Brownhelm Township in 1857 and school
visitor shortly thereafter.

In Cincinnati, by 1855, four public schools for Negroes
had been established. In 1858, Nicholas Longworth erected
a building which he leased to Negroes at a nominal rental
for public-school purposes.

Ohio boards of education were given discretionary power
to establish separate schools for Negroes in 1878. This law
was repealed in 1887 and another statute enacted prohibiting
separate schools. However, Cincinnati has maintained for
years a peculiar system in which one-half of the Negro children are enrolled in separate schools, and the remainder in
mixed schools. The high schools are mixed. The recent
influx of Negroes into other Ohio cities has resulted in a
marked trend toward separation.

In Dayton and Columbus, separation has been effected by
gerrymandering districts within the city where Negroes and
whites reside together, one device being to draw district
lines so as to include a single Negro family in a block in a
separate district. In 1933, Dayton plans to open a junior
high school specifically for Negro children, although litigation has been instituted by Negro citizens to prevent the
action of the board.

By annual contributions to the "Industrial" or "State"
Department of Wilberforce University, the Ohio Legislature
helps in maintaining a separate higher school for Negroes.
There have been several cases of discrimination involving
the Ohio State University at Columbus, the most recent of
which was that of a Negro student in the Home Economics
Department who was denied admittance to the "model" home
maintained by that division. The lower courts have sustained the action of the university, but in spite of the fact
that the young woman has now graduated from the school,
an appeal to the higher courts is proposed by the Negro
litigants.

Indiana. Two trends of migration are discernible in the early history and, to some extent, the present traditions, of the State of Indiana. The northern section of the state was peopled from New England and the Middle States. The southern section was populated principally by migrants who followed the old "Wilderness Trail" out of Virginia and the Carolinas, through the Cumberland Gap into Tennessee and Kentucky, and from there northward across the Ohio into Indiana.

The Indiana law of 1837 included white people only as members of the local school corporations. In 1841, a petition of Negroes asking that a portion of the school funds be designated to their needs was declared "inexpedient" by the legislative committee appointed to consider it. In 1850, the public-school law excluded Negroes from the tax lists. It was held by the courts in a test case that Negroes should not be admitted to any white school if any white patron objected. The decision of the court said in part, "This (exclusion) has not been done because they do not need any education, nor because their wealth was such as to render aid undesirable, but because black children were deemed unfit associates of white, as school companions."

An effort to include Negroes in the benefits of the public-school act in 1853 failed by a large negative vote. Following the Civil War, in 1869, school boards were required to organize equal but separate schools for Negro children. The Indiana law was revised in 1877 to allow boards to establish separate schools or mixed schools, within their discretion.

Separate schools have always been general in southern Indiana, in both the lower and higher grades. The schools of Gary were formerly mixed, but with the increasing Americanization of the foreign-born white working population, separatist tendencies grew apace. In 1928, the white students of a Gary high school organized a strike as a protest against the presence of fifteen Negro students in a school numbering more than one thousand pupils. A new high school was built for Negro children immediately to pacify the Negroes, and the entire system is now separate.

In Indianapolis, the Attucks High School was opened for Negro pupils in 1929 after the elementary schools of the city had been separate for some time. In Indianapolis, as in Gary, the first building erected as a separate school for Negroes was a magnificent structure.

A peculiar trend in the direction of separation has lately (1933) been reported to the writer. In several small towns of southern Indiana and Illinois, where separate schools have existed for years, the depression has brought school finances to the point where several separate schools for Negroes have been closed and the Negro children admitted to the white schools in order to save the extra expense.

Illinois. The constitution of 1847 referred to "white" school children throughout the section on education, and thus by implication excluded Negro children from the benefits of the public school system. The money collected from Negroes in school taxes was returnable to that race. Chicago established separate schools for Negro children in 1864, but the number of such children was so small that the provision of separate schools soon proved impracticable. Negroes were then incorporated into the entire school system. The state legislature specified a mixed system in 1874. A separate school established in Quincy in 1882 was held to be unconstitutional when submitted to the courts. In 1886, the township board of Upper Alton excluded Negroes in the elementary grades from going to school with white children. The courts again decided against the action of the board. In 1899, the council of Alton set aside a school for Negro children, but this action was held to be unconstitutional. A third case from Alton in 1908 was declared by the courts to be unwarranted in law.

In more recent years, despite almost unanimous decisions by the superior courts holding against such discriminations, separate schools for Negroes have been established in many parts of Illinois, particularly in the southern portion familiarly known as "Little Egypt." Fitful attempts at litigation have been made for years by the Negro citizens of Morgan Park, a suburban area of the city of Chicago, where a separate elementary school has been established for Negro elementary-school children. In the city of Chicago itself, there has been achieved a close approximation to segregation because of the heavy concentration of Negroes in the "Black Belt" of the city. This area runs from 12th Street southward to 67th Street, and from Wentworth Avenue on the west to Cottage Grove Avenue on the east. Within this highly congested strip, fifty-five blocks long but only twelve blocks wide, 186,000 of the 225,000 Negroes resident in Cook County lived in 1930.

The Wendell Phillips High School, located in 39th Street, has within fifteen years changed its complexion from white to black. The extension of the Negro population southward has brought considerable numbers of the Negro population into the high-school districts served by the Englewood High School, at 62nd Street, and the Hyde Park High School twenty blocks to the east.   The Chicago School Board included in its plans for construction in 1929 a new high-school building at 59th Street on State.   Obviously, this building was planned to enable the school board the convenience of redrawing district lines so as to include the large Negro population which was beginning to annoy many white patrons of the Englewood and Hyde Park High Schools.   The general financial stringency affecting the Chicago system, however, forced the school board to discontinue work on the proposed building after most of the steel superstructure had been completed.   To date (1933), no further progress has been made on this project.

An Evaluation of Separate Schools for Negroes in the North

In one sense, the discussion of the merits or demerits of a separate school system for Negroes in the North resolves itself into a purely academic question.   Students of race relations should have learned by now that the question of ultimate "right" seldom disturbs a majority in its disposition of the fate of a minority group.   Whether due to the action of local boards, state legislatures, constitutional bodies, or courts of inferior and superior jurisdiction, the separate school for Negroes will receive sanction ultimately if the majority white population deems it necessary for whatever purpose—race purity, economy, or other real or alleged reason.   Even if the separate school is wrong in principle, no amount of "protest" from Negroes will avail to prevent it, in the long run, if the majority wishes to have separation.

Most of the arguments given in favor of the separation of black and white in public schools are either rationalizations of more fundamental motives or *post-mortem* analyses designed to justify the course of action taken.   Since the phenomenon of a separate school in a democratic state is of great significance, the minds of students should be clear about its implications.

Pechstein, after reviewing the literature, reports the following arguments:

> Those who oppose segregation hold (*a*) that segregation involves separate and inferior schools, (*b*) that separate schools are created by self-interested race-leaders, (*c*) that separate schools are responsible for race troubles, and (*d*) that separate schools lead to general segregation. Those who favor segregation hold that (*a*) great mass movements are handled better in segregated groups, (*b*) that separate schools have far-reaching social effects, (*c*) that there are more negro graduates of separate high schools than of mixed high schools, (*d*) that negro schools in Northern cities are not inferior to mixed schools, and (*e*) that negroes in mixed schools do not receive inspiration.[18]

In neither case does Pechstein exhaust points of argument. Continuing the list of reasons given by those opposed to separate schools, it is fair to say that the most important argument against them is that they denominate one portion of the population as being inferior to other portions. In the words of the old Indiana decision, whether used in America, as in that case, or in Germany, as more recently, the separate school means that the segregated class, Negroes or Jews, "are not deemed fit associates" of white or gentile children. In addition, it is not to be denied that the separate school is an anomaly in a democracy supposedly dedicated to the proposition that all men are created equal. Again, it is undeniable that the separate school is economically unsound.

In defense of separate schools, we may add the argument that they furnish employment for Negroes who would not be employed in mixed schools.

---

[18] L. A. Pechstein, "The Problem of Negro Education in Northern and Border Cities," *The Elementary School Journal*, Vol. XXX, No. 3, p. 192.

However school boards may invest initial sums of impressive size in separate schools, it would be difficult to find, North or South, a separate system more than a generation old in which the schools for Negroes are not inferior to those for white children. It is also true that the greatest proponents of separate schools, among Negroes, are either citizens with sons or daughters to employ, or politicians looking for extra opportunities for petty graft and patronage. Separate schools are probably not a cause of race troubles, but a symptom of them. However, all social psychology teaches that early contact with members of diverse racial groups is more conducive toward interracial amiability than total separation up to adulthood.

Separate schools probably are a concurrent and not a cause of general segregation. They do imply the inferiority of the Negro child, for the arguments that the move is inspired primarily for the benefit of the Negro child smack of hypocrisy. Separate schools are anomalous in our theoretically equalitarian state. Finally, no duplication of staff, buildings, equipment, and other facilities which segregation implies could possibly be called sound economics.

On the affirmative side, the implication that there are to be mass movements in Negro schools separate and distinct from those which would find motivation in a mixed school makes a permanent concession to an American school system in which different racial groups take definitely different directions in life. The belief that separate schools have a far-reaching social effect is a case of *double entendre.* Does it mean that the separate school is to be the instrument for perpetuating an American Ghetto?

The belief that there are more Negro graduates from separate than from mixed high schools may mean that (*a*) the standards of the separate school are inferior, or (*b*), that there has been a faulty interpretation of data from too small a sample.   The highest percentage of Negro boys and girls, aged 15–19, attending school in this country, is to be found in certain Pacific Coast cities where mixed schools are maintained.   (See Figure 4, page 218.)

To the belief that separate schools in the North are not inferior to white schools, apply the test of a generation, and it will evaporate. Gary, Indianapolis, Dayton, and Chicago are among cities which have made magnificent gestures in the direction of an equal separate system.   The final answer must come several decades in the future, when the easy promises of equality have been forgotten by the white populace.

The idea that Negroes in mixed schools do not receive inspiration for advancement because all of their teachers are white is found to be absurd when it is remembered that Booker T. Washington, William Edward Burghardt DuBois, Henry H. Proctor, and, in fact, practically every Negro college graduate of the generation before 1900— attended schools where all of the teachers were white.   The difficulty is with those brutal white teachers, met with frequently by Negroes both in high school and college, who lose no opportunity to browbeat their Negro students, and with a student opinion, frequently created by such teachers, which aids in the distortion of the personality of Negro children.   If this type of behavior is to be expected of a mixed school, there need hardly be any other argument for the existence of separate schools.

The matter of giving employment to Negro teachers involves also that of giving inspiration to Negro boys and girls. Several Northern cities, notably New York, have adopted the principle of employing Negro teachers and scattering them through the entire school system without reference to the race of the children taught.   It would appear that this is a reasonable focus for the activity of

Negro citizens desirous both of giving employment to qualified Negro teachers and of furnishing inspiration to Negroes in the sight of members of their own race occupying tutorial chairs.

Summary—Specific Problems of Northern Negro Children

In his incisive analysis of the Negro community in Chicago, Dr. E. Franklin Frazier has recently shown [19] that it is a mistake to regard the Negro population as possessing the blanket homogeneity which common usage of the term "Negro" usually implies. The Negro community shows most of the degrees of social stratification to be found in any other population; and in Northern cities, these social strata follow a pattern of geographic location in precisely the same manner as is exhibited by other racial groups. When we speak of "specific Negro problems," therefore, it is with all possible caution, for these are likely to be related to the Negro population more from economic than from racial reasons.

(1) Negroes generally belong to the lowest-income group. In this they resemble recent immigrants of South European stock. Primarily as a result of their low economic status, (*a*) they are poorly housed; (*b*) they are the victims of a tremendously excessive mortality and morbidity rate; (*c*) they suffer from all sorts of social disorganization to a disproportionate degree where racial comparisons are made; and (*d*) they possess a high degree of economic instability. They have few opportunities to lay aside a surplus during periods of employment and are usually among the first victims of unemployment during depression periods.

[19] E. Franklin Frazier, *The Negro Family in Chicago*, University of Chicago Press, Chicago, 1932.

(2) In that they are Negroes, differing from the immigrant in that they cannot so easily slough off the stigmas of their past and present economic status, (*a*) they find difficulty in improving their housing facilities on account of residential segregation; (*b*) they have a fearful background of illiteracy and low cultural status which they inherit as an incubus from the wretched school and cultural advantages afforded them in the South; and (*c*) because of discriminations in the ranks of organized labor based on color, the prejudice of employers, and their own ignorance and ineptitude for the complex skills of the modern machine age, they find the avenues to advancement along all lines sharply curtailed.

The primary problems of Negro children in the North, accordingly, appear to be those which find their roots in economic problems, affected to a greater or smaller degree by the fact that the race is separate and unassimilable. Theorists frequently preach the necessity for teachers of Negro children understanding the Negro child's "racial psychology"; and in Mississippi, a committee interested in adapting a curriculum for use in the separate schools of that state referred to the "Negro environment." The existence of qualitative differences between children of any race has not as yet been determined, outside of the pages of bathetic fiction. The evidence of intelligence and other tests seems to show that the problem of the "Negro intellect" is not one *per se* of race, but rather that of a poorly circumstanced group, the analogue of which can be found in any other racial stock. The typical "Negro environment" in Mississippi or in Chicago is simply the environment of human beings living on a subsistence level of existence.

It would seem more important to have, in the schoolroom and in the administrative offices, intelligent and sympathetic personalities consecrated to the problems of the

children with whom they come in contact than to staff these
offices with exponents of a pseudo-scientific "racial psychology" that has no real existence. The teacher who
deals successfully with the Negro child does not need to
know a special brand of Negro psychology, or Negro economics, or Negro health, any more than Jane Addams at
Hull House needed particularized training in the psychology of West Side Italian groups. Miss Addams brought
a New England conscience and intelligence, and an all-
pervasive human sympathy and patience to the slum where
she established herself more than forty years ago.

There is, unfortunately, no "overproduction" apparent
in the field of human relations such as might lead us to
hope that our classrooms could be filled with such personalities as those of Jane Addams and Mary McDowell. It
is perhaps true that the kind of sympathetic understanding
necessary can be found more frequently in Negro than in
white teachers. The admission that mixed schools are
filled with white teachers who assist in the mental crucifixion
of a Negro child minority is a frightful indictment of the
"profession" of teaching. Nevertheless, if it is true, the
situation clearly calls for separate schools, if for no other
reason than to protect the Negro children from such individuals.

On the high-school level, a great difficulty connected with
Negro school children in mixed systems is their social isolation, as well as the lack of vocational and educational guidance which results from ignorant, careless, and sometimes
contemptuous administration where these children are concerned. The program of vocational guidance recently begun in New York City high schools discovered that counsellors were not giving adequate attention to Negro boys
and girls. The counsellors were neither altogether prejudiced nor wholly indifferent. In many cases, the difficulty lay in the ignorance of these advisors as to the voca-

tional possibilities in fields open to Negro adults. A survey was initiated through which the opportunities open to Negroes were carefully examined. This survey unearthed possibilities of placement which were, in the words of a participant, "amazing." The New York City program suggests one way in which a mixed system can adapt itself to the specific problems of Negro children. Negro teachers in the system were called in for consultation and were largely responsible for the initial success of the project. No separate system has undertaken such an intelligent project as yet.

CHAPTER XIX

Problems of Administration and Guidance

IN THIS discussion of the problems incident to the education of Negroes, it has been assumed that the principles necessary to the correct administration, control, or teaching of such schools as enroll Negroes, either in mixed or separate systems, are not unique in themselves, so as to constitute an educational discipline any different from that which would be called upon in dealing with any group of children so circumstanced culturally and economically. The fact of a separate system, however, presents aspects which, if not specifically "Negroid," are at least complicated in so far as they concern a segregated racial group. It is proposed here to explore some few of these specific problems which a separate system evokes in the practical application to the educational process.

Administration and Control

The control of Negro schools was frequently assigned to Negroes in the ante-bellum period in the North, when monies for these schools were derived solely from taxes upon Negroes. Kentucky, Maryland, and Delaware instituted this system after emancipation, although this separate management has persisted only in Kentucky. In Arkansas and other Southern states where the district form of organization prevailed, district lines were usually drawn by white citizens to include in a district all of the property owned by whites, for support of the white schools, and in Negro districts, all

Negro property. This patchwork districting gradually resulted in the assumption by the county unit of what responsibility was actually taken for the education of Negroes. Negro trustees and school directors in districts in Mississippi, Louisiana, Alabama, and Arkansas usually functioned more as service committees in supplementing county funds by community efforts, than as actual agencies of control.

In the usual Southern county, the control of the Negro schools is vested entirely in the hands of the county superintendent. He prepares the budget for the schools for both races, and the county board of education, the county court, or the county police jury approves or modifies this budget. In many rural counties, the practice is to make a lump appropriation for the support of Negro schools, at a stipulated sum per teacher, per room, or per community. In one "Black Belt" county, the writer recently observed a county board of education considering the budget for the next school year. There were less than 1,500 white educables in the county, but more than 7,000 Negro educables. A budget in excess of $75,000 for the white schools was carefully deliberated for several hours. When this business was finished, the county superintendent announced that he had allotted $200 each to the forty-four Negro schools in the county, "the same allotment as for the last few years." Assent was given *viva voce* and the meeting adjourned without further query.

In those counties where training schools are located, the county superintendent usually allows the Negro principal to select teachers for the school, although the salary scale is fixed by the county superintendent. If a Jeanes supervisor is employed, her function is not "supervisory" in any strict application of the word. She is at the same time an *ex-officio* assistant superintendent for the Negro schools and a clerk responsible for the weekly or monthly reports from the Negro schools. She may have the responsibility for the employment and discharge of teachers. She makes daily schedules, plans for holidays, field-days, and special occasions of all sorts, and performs most or all of the routine that is connected with the management of the Negro schools.

In cities, the local superintendent, acting with the authority vested in him by the city board of education, is the dominant factor in the management of the Negro schools. In certain cities, assistant superintendents are specifically in charge of the Negro schools. In other cities, a Negro supervisor is actually the assistant superintendent in charge of the separate Negro systems. Birmingham, Alabama, has an assistant to the superintendent who is specifically entrusted with the management of the schools for Negro children and, in addition, employs a Negro supervisor who is a liaison officer between the city office and the Negro teaching staff.

In smaller cities, it is not infrequently the case that the principal of the Negro high school is also either officially or unofficially the head of the system for Negro children. In Durham, North Carolina, the principal of the Negro high school is unofficially dubbed an "assistant superintendent" in charge of schools for Negro children. In Wilmington, North Carolina, the principal of the Negro high school has official responsibility for supervising the work of the entire system, while the principal of one of the elementary schools is in charge of all elementary-school work.

State systems, through the aid given by the general education board, have attached to their staffs directors of Negro education who might be likened to assistant superintendents in their general function. N. C. Newbold, in North Carolina, D. E. Williams, in Florida, G. T. Bloodworth, in Texas, and other men of notable caliber have made their offices the focus of much of the educational work for Negroes ·in those states, with an influence in their particular field surpassing that enjoyed by other state workers in their specialties.

The state Jeanes and vocational agriculture workers are among the more important administrative officials where Negro schools are concerned. Because of the weight of the Federal subsidy in supplementing the meager funds available for Negro children, these agencies have exercised a disproportionately powerful influence upon the determination of policies in schools for Negroes as compared with those for white children.

Oklahoma has a peculiar system under which, by law, the separate school of the race which has a majority of the population within a district is called a "majority" school and draws its revenue and control from the local district, while the school for the race which is in the minority is supported by county funds derived from a levy not to exceed two mills and controlled by the office of the county superintendent. In practice, this works well for Negro-majority districts in counties with a small Negro population and a high assessed valuation, but poorly in districts located in poor counties with a large number of Negroes to be educated within the limits set by the two-mill tax restriction. Another statute, however, provides that the county superintendent may denominate a school as a "minority" school even if the population warrants that it be in the other classification. This legislation, of course, was designed to permit county superintendents to give white children the advantage of local tax funds where these were more substantial than the funds furnished by the county levy.

In all respects, it is clear that two reforms are needed in the administration of schools for Negroes. In the first place, some provision should be made for representation of the race upon boards and councils which determine policies and regulate expenditures. In a section where the first answer to an awakening of political consciousness

among Negroes has been legal or extra-legal steps toward
disfranchisement, Negro representation is unthinkable to
many persons. It has been suggested that the political
aspect of the matter be softened by allowing Negroes nonpolitical representation on boards of education, in the form
of advisory members or councils selected by Negroes but
without official status in law. West Virginia has a supervisor of Negro schools, and a Negro board of education
established by statute but having only the right to rec-
ommend policies to the state board of education.

There is always the greatest difficulty in staffing boards
of education among whites with nonfactional representation. The difficulty is even greater among Negroes, in
which case white administrators are frequently content to
get rid of an inconvenient situation by allowing the Negroes
to "handle their own affairs." The result is that, while
the membership on regular boards may be tempered by
nonpolitical appointments through active parental interest
and public criticism, Negro representatives may be merely
the most vocal of a political faction that is barred from
the "natural spoils" of post-office, civic, and county offices and grasps eagerly at the opportunity of spoliating the
schools as the only available bit of "Negro patronage."
Certainly, it is impossible to consider a separate system as
in any degree democratic when almost 25 per cent of the
school children in Southern states attend schools in which
their destinies are guided by not a single elective official of
their own race.

Another reform which is well under way is the centralization of control for separate systems with the state as the
unit for the entire system. The apathy among Negro patrons in Southern states, together with the carelessness with
which affairs concerning Negro children are sometimes regarded by county and city superintendents, has given an
opportunity to state agencies which has resulted in a much

greater degree of centralization of administration in schools for Negroes than is yet practicable in white schools.

The complete centralization of the administration of Negro schools on a state basis is open to but one objection. This is that the Negro children in some sections of every Southern state now enjoy educational advantages far above the level attained in those areas where the majority of the population lives. To place the Negro schools on a state basis might mean that the administrative officers, if dominated by sentiments appropriate to the "Black Belt," would set a state standard which would be far inferior to the level already reached in certain counties and cities. The example of Louisiana, where state equalization set a minimum standard of $300 for the yearly salary of Negro teachers at a time when the state average was $293 is a case in point. The tendency in that state has been for school officials in counties which have paid above the state minimum to reduce their expenditures to conform with it, while in the counties which have paid from $100 to $200 per year, the amount of state equalization required to bring Negro teachers' salaries to the state minimum was not worth the amount of state subsidy offered.

Supervision

Mr. Leo M. Favrot has shown that there are more than 700 counties in the South without supervision where the size of the Negro population would warrant such special services. This situation is shown to exist in spite of the fact that the Jeanes Fund in 1929 aided in furnishing supervision for Negroes in 311 counties.[1]

The extensive study of the relations existing between the white superintendent and the Negro school in North Car-

---

[1] Leo M. Favrot, *A Study of the County Training Schools for Negroes in the South,* John F. Slater Fund, Charlottesville, 1923.

olina by Dr. Dennis H. Cooke reveals a considerable lack of a feeling of responsibility for Negro schools.[2] In some exceptional cases, superintendents believe that their responsibility to Negro schools is as great as that to white schools; but in the majority of instances, this interest is secondary. One cannot, indeed, expect much more in a situation where the county superintendent in the majority of cases is an elective official, and, even in those instances where he is an appointive officer, is responsible to a county board which is seriously affected by political considerations. The first responsibility of the county or city superintendent is to the white children, represented by a board of education elected by the patrons of the white and not of the Negro children. The disfranchisement of the Negro was rationalized at the time when it was accomplished by the statement that the white man would be better able to take care of the interests of the Negro than the black man could himself. There is no field in which this apology fails more thoroughly than that of educational supervision.

The finest record in the South is that made by county and city superintendents who have had a live interest in the problems of their schools for Negroes as well as in those of their white schools. Probably the best work in the South was accomplished in Henrico County, Virginia, when Jackson Davis was superintendent and Virginia Randolph was supervisor. This county had all of the ingredients necessary for the work which was initiated here: a superintendent with intelligence, tact, courage, and sympathy for Negroes; a white population above the average in intelligence and gentility; a Negro population only 29.2 per cent of the population in 1910 and owning 310 of the 383 farmhouses occupied by Negroes in the county; and a Negro

<hr>

[2] Cooke, *The White Superintendent and the Negro School in North Carolina.*

supervisor with all of the qualities which make for success in establishing helpful human qualities.

In more recent times, the best work in the South has been done in Webster Parish, Louisiana. Here, between 1920 and 1933, Superintendent E. S. Richardson, together with a Negro supervisor, the Reverend A. S. Moore, has developed a system of schools for Negroes which is without doubt the best in the state and one of the best in the entire South. The Negro population has decreased from 51.5 per cent of the total in 1910 to 44.4 per cent in 1930. The parish is blessed with an assessed valuation (1931) of more than $16,000, per capita educable, which places it in the upper quartile of counties in the state in ability to support schools through direct taxation. Thirty-seven per cent of the Negro farmers own their own farms, and, while smaller than that in Henrico County, this percentage is high enough to afford small nuclei of Negro owners throughout the parish who are more likely to be responsive to efforts aimed at their improvement than are the tenant farmers. The small city of Minden employs many Negroes in industrial shops in skilled as well as unskilled work.

With this happy combination of factors, Webster Parish has stressed racial coöperation in terms of better opportunities for the Negro school child. The Negro supervisor does very little "supervisory" detail work in the commonly accepted use of the term. No amount of supervision can improve the work of ignorant, poorly trained teachers; and, on the other hand, an ounce of administrative care in selecting teachers will go farther toward attaining good teachers than a pound of detailed supervision. It is upon this principle that Webster Parish has operated. The Negroes have been organized into associations, and these associations have an agreement with the board of education for the parish whereby the board matches by appropriations every dollar raised by the Negroes for school improvement.

The chief method of raising money has been that of coöperative farm projects, Negroes and white people in the vicinity of a school donating five or ten acres of land, which is planted to cotton or some other cash crop and farmed coöperatively by the Negro patrons with labor, fertilizer, work animals, seed, tools, and other requirements donated by various persons.

One result has been the building of twenty-two Rosenwald schools in the county, with a total of thirty-six Negro schools. But these Rosenwald buildings are not of the melancholy sort so frequently seen in the South, built two or three years ago but already decaying, unpainted, unfenced, and unfurnished. The Rosenwald schools in Webster Parish in all cases have stout and attractive fences. Their grounds are planted to shrubbery and flowers and attractive walks decorate the premises, while in the spring, flower boxes appear on all of the window sills. Within, the kitchen room is equipped with a large range, and visitors at any time can find that these ranges are not used for extra storage space or in some cases for heating the teacher's lunch, as is so often true of the rural schools which are so equipped, but for the actual preparation of food as a demonstration and actual utility to the children. The classrooms all have jacketed stoves, clean blackboards, and patented desks, and the windows are curtained with cheerful cloths and shaded with easy-rolling shades. The teaching, while not by any means perfect, is far above that which is found in the typical Louisiana rural school. The teachers are paid from two to three times as much as Negro teachers in neighboring parishes.

The care and attention to schoolroom and grounds are coöperative enterprises; the furnishing of the building is coöperative; and the continuation of community interest in the school beyond the mere construction of a building is felt in a genuine interest on the part of the patrons in the

welfare of the school—an experience which is almost strange
to a visitor in the typical Negro community in the South.
The writer believes that this communal working together,
this neatness and cleanliness, this cheerfulness of attitude
and schoolroom, is the maximal point in the educational
process.

One might cavil at the fact that in Webster Parish the
expenditures for each white educable exceed those for
Negroes by more than 300 per cent. It is true that the
Negro teachers in the parish are underpaid by comparison
with the white teachers; and that in equipment, consolidation, transportation, and supervision in the fundamental
subjects there is no equality of educational opportunity in
the parish. But by contrast with the hundreds of other
counties in the South where it would be easily possible to
raise Negro schools to the standard achieved in Webster
Parish, and where it would be possible to enlist the coöperation of whites and Negroes, the parish system is a phenomenon.

As suggested above, the technical classroom supervision
of Negro rural supervisors in the South is purely nominal.
In many counties, these employees have been used to rid
the white superintendent of the inconvenience of the Negro
schools. The writer knows of one supervisor who was expected to employ teachers for a county system with 77
isolated, rural, one- and two-teacher schools. It was also
her duty to prepare the reports from these schools, work
for which she was given less than ten dollars per month for
clerical service. She was also entrusted with the task of
raising money in the communities to supplement the thirty-
dollar monthly salary, paid for five months, which was the
emolument received by her teachers. She had also to ar-
range for teachers' institutes, field-days, and a host of the
other minute particulars connected with the administration
of the schools. The preparation of monthly reports alone

consumed three full days of the week with hours which no
industrial code would sanction. Fully one-fourth of her
schools were located in out-of-the-way districts which were
inaccessible for an automobile during rainy weather in
three of the five school months. The schools themselves—
three "two-teacher" schools were taught in single-roomed
shacks—with the exception of three Rosenwald schools had
no equipment. Manifestly, "supervision" in this county
was a mockery. Cases of this sort, unfortunately, are not
exceptional.

If supervision is to mean anything where Negro rural
schools are concerned, it would be well to divorce the administrative from the supervisory functions of workers and
employ two individuals to do the two separate tasks. As
it is in many instances today, the two tasks conflict sharply.
The necessity for raising money in order to "put over programs" places the supervisor in the situation of having to
rely upon the good will of teachers to a degree that is not
conducive to even helpful criticism. In addition, the low
salaries paid Negro teachers make it impossible to select
teachers who are amenable even to the highest arts of cor-
rective supervision.

Supervision in cities varies in efficiency with localities.
In most instances, the principal of the high school is in
general responsible for supervising the work of the elementary schools. Nashville and Durham employ supervisors
for special subjects. The Negro schools in Birmingham
have the advantage of an excellent department of tests and
measurements which extends its services to all schools, white
and Negro. Birmingham furnishes progress reports in the
fundamental subjects to each school. New Orleans in 1931
employed only one Negro supervisor in the fundamental
subjects for a system enrolling more than 15,000 children.

The device of measuring the achievement of Negro children as an instrument of supervision is unknown to all but

a very few systems in the South. In many rural communities, the cost of a testing service would equal, if it did not exceed, the total expenditures for all other purposes.

Vocational Education

Whether as slave or freeman, the Negro in America has suffered from peculiar economic disadvantages. The result has been that in all generations, those who have interested themselves in his advancement have looked to some form of trade or industrial education as the primary lever for his elevation in the American system. Thomas Jefferson provided in his will for the education of his Negro slaves, who were to be manumitted, in "useful trades and occupations," and Kosciusko had before left in his will a sum of money to be used for the purchase and trade education of Negroes, with Jefferson as administrator. Pestalozzi's experiments at Fellenburg and Hofwyl were soon transmitted to America, and emancipationists saw in what the Swiss had done for the orphan children of Europe a hope for the solution of the Negro's problems in this country.

At Philadelphia in 1831, a convention of Negroes, with Bishop Richard Allen, founder of the African Methodist Episcopal Church, presiding, adopted a resolution "that it was expedient to establish a collegiate school on the manual labor system." Arthur Tappan, the abolitionist, purchased several acres of land in New Haven for the purpose, but the opposition of the townspeople defeated the project. Another convention in 1833 approved the plan of William Lloyd Garrison to raise money in England for a manual-labor school. At Rochester, New York, in 1853, Frederick Douglass was president of a convention which drew up a plan for the conduct of a manual-labor school. It was proposed that Harriet Beecher Stowe, author of *Uncle Tom's Cabin*, go to England to raise money for the pro-

posed institution. It was believed by the convention that
"The successful establishment and conduct of such an institution of learning would train youth to be self-reliant
and skilled workmen, fitted to hold their own in the struggle
of life in the conditions prevailing here." [3]

The creation of Hampton Institute by Samuel C. Armstrong, who had known in his youth of the Hilo Manual
Labor School for Hawaiian natives, has been described elsewhere, as well as the development of Tuskegee Institute on
the pattern set by Armstrong at Hampton. Theoretically,
the dominant interest of school officials, both public and
private, in the field of the education of Negroes has been
until quite recently that of vocational education. In practice, sums available for the development of an efficient system of vocational education for Negroes in the South have
been wholly lacking.

At the present time, the need for skilled workmen among
Negroes is felt as keenly by the friends and members of the
race as it was more than a century ago. Much of the great
vogue for vocational education for Negroes in the South
has been derived from the conception of the race as the
predestined "hewers of wood and drawers of water" for the
section, a notion derived both from the psychological belief
in the inability of the Negro to learn tasks calling for the
exercise of abstract intelligence, and from the social conviction that the South might be in the future as in the past
an aristocracy of white intellectuals and "brain-workers"
resting upon a foundation of Negro artisans and laborers.
At the time when men of influence in the South, of no great
good will toward the Negro, were urging a complete stop-
page of all educational effort that was not vocational, many

---

[3] John Wesley Cromwell, *The Negro in American History*, The Ameri-
can Negro Academy, Washington, 1914. *Vide* chapter on "The Early
Negro Convention Movement." Also printed separately as Occasional
Paper No. 6 of the American Negro Academy, Washington, 1904.

Negroes were bitterly opposed to the principle. Now, by one of the choicest bits of irony it is possible to imagine, there is little opposition to giving an academic training to Negroes anywhere in the South, while Negroes themselves are feeling more and more the need for training in the vocational pursuits of modern life. Thirty years ago, school boards were contemptuous of Latin, French, and German in schools for Negroes, insisting on industrial courses instead, although, to be sure, they appropriated very little money to institute these courses. Today, the Negro high school may have Latin, Greek, or any other subject which it wishes that calls for no equipment or expensive construction; but the large appropriations for the installation of machinery go to the white schools.

At times of great economic stress, the matter of vocational education for any portion of the population demands careful inquiry both as to its objectives and as to its methods. In most of the discussions of the problem, it is assumed that the training of young people for making a livelihood is a proper function of the school. There have been recent voices raised to insist that the school should function only in giving what has been called a "general education" to all children, and that it is better to leave to industry both the responsibility and the expense of training its workers. In the last analysis, of course, industry must pay the bill; but the example furnished by such industrial enterprises as conduct their own training schools, by its narrowness, its extreme specialization, and its attitude toward the worker as a mere cog in the machine, is not an attractive one.

There is also the objection that vocational training of the sort which the schools have given is hopelessly outmoded in modern life. Vocational education in schools for Negroes has been principally motivated by the aim of producing craftsmen. Printing, shoemaking, bricklaying and

carpentry have been favorite subjects in these schools.
They represent one of the most unfortunate assortments
of subjects which could have been made.   The equipment
for teaching printing visible in most shops for Negro students was purchased originally at secondhand and was at
the time hopelessly outmoded.   Technological improvements have been so rapid and the initial expense of purchase so great that not even Tuskegee and Hampton have
been able to keep step in their shops with advances made
in actual practice.   The apparatus for teaching shoemaking in the typical Negro school is as antiquated as that of
a medieval cobbler.   The construction trades known of old
have witnessed a constant rise in rate and amount of production with a steady diminution in the number of workers.

In addition to these difficulties, there exist in all of the
trades-unions which dominate these occupations a more or
less severe restriction upon the membership of Negroes.
The typical Negro student was taught by inefficient teachers
in a poorly equipped shop.   He had received no instruction which would have enabled him to participate in collective bargaining; and, indeed, the spirit of these schools
fostered a sturdy individualism that was as unsympathetic
toward organized labor as labor was toward him.   The
writer can think of no device better calculated to inculcate
disrespect for labor than the mockeries incident to "industrial education" as practiced in most Negro high schools
and colleges.

Instruction in agriculture and home economics has maintained a much higher standard, principally because of
standards enforced by the Federal Government.   When it
is realized that more than 20 per cent of Negro males and
80 per cent of Negro females who are gainfully employed
are engaged in domestic and personal service, the implications for special training in at least one field become
clearer.   It must be remembered, however, that however

unintelligent Negro domestic labor may be today, it is employed as widely as it is because it is "dirt cheap." It is believed by many that education would raise the working conditions of Negroes in domestic service, but it is more probable that specific training, by raising the price of such labor, would make it too expensive for employment in the South. So long as it is current practice in the South, even in "good times," to pay Negro help from $20 to $30 per month for seventy- and eighty-hour weeks, home economics education can hardly hope to be the gateway to a new day for Negro domestics. This must come, if at all, from circumstances but remotely connected with the school. Negro domestic labor has been displaced almost universally in the North, so far as the most remunerative fields are concerned, by various European racial groups—English, Italian, French, and Scandinavian, for the most part. The success of the latter groups of workers has not resulted from a specific educational advantage obtained from the classroom. Rather, it was bound up with the habits, traditions, and mannerisms of individuals accustomed to service for generations and with the products of a long apprenticeship in the field. It would be possible, of course, to foreshorten this process in the South, but to do so would involve an educational expenditure far beyond the present sums available.

The example of the textile industry in the South, by means of which literally millions of untrained and poorly educated mountain whites have been inducted into an industry which is highly mechanized, without any extensive training, indicates that modern machine feeding can dispense with a large degree of technical training. What Negroes lack on a grand scale in the way of vocational equipment is what has been called "the instinct for the machine." It is said that the success of the Russian Five Year Plan of mechanization was largely threatened because the Russian people were primarily peasants, fresh from the soil and unacquainted even with the simplest forms of machinery. The average American white boy has tinkered with watches, clocks, radios, automobile motors, and all sorts of mechanical gadgets. This has developed in the population, if not an "instinct," at least a feeling of familiarity with mechanical processes. Like the Russian peasant, the American Negro has his roots in the soil and is accustomed to the most primitive forms of power machinery, if with any at all. The school can function in developing this "mechanical intelligence" by the provision of opportunities through which children and youths can come in contact, and familiarize themselves with, mechanical contrivances of the basic sort. Exploration of this kind is as fundamental as acquaintance with letters and figures.

For more definite plans for vocational education, six current experiments present highly intelligent attempts to work out a solution of the problem. At the Bordentown School, in New Jersey, the industrial work has recently been revised with an end to acquainting the students with a wide range of mechanical techniques rather than isolating departmental work, which it was characteristic to do in teaching the older crafts, in which the separate fields were kept in utter isolation from one another. The authorities of this school have also explored the vocational possibilities for Negroes in the state. Among other fields, for example, they found that Negroes frequently found employment as janitors and caretakers in large apartment houses, an occupation latterly glorified under the name of "building engineer." The modern janitor is no longer a mere polisher of brass or a scrubber of floors. He must know something of steamfitting, of electricity, of plumbing, of carpentry, of boilermaking, and a host of other knacks which do not represent too great a degree of specialization. The Bordentown School has not only made an initial "job-analysis," but has changed its curriculum to meet the situation.

At Tuskegee Institute, in Alabama, an arrangement was worked out by which a selected number of students were allowed to enter the plants of the Tennessee Coal and Iron Company in the vicinity of Birmingham. Here they worked as apprentices for brief periods under foremen, the Institute maintaining contact with them through weekly conferences, reports as to efficiency, and correlations between shop practice and the theoretical instruction furnished by the school. At the end of a period of training the students returned to the Institute for further theoretical work, their places being taken by another group of students. The plan here outlined has been developed with exceptional success by Antioch College and the University of Cincinnati in Ohio. Certainly the vocational course for Negroes or anyone else which continues to work in isolation from employees actually working at the job is foredoomed to failure.

At the Paul Laurence Dunbar High School, in Little Rock, Arkansas, courses in auto mechanics have been instituted with excellent equipment and teachers. One of the difficulties with older vocational courses was that the teachers were likely to be either school-trained men and women with ability to teach but with no clear knowledge of the specific demands of the job in action, or, if the teachers were good craftsmen, they were deficient in teaching skill or experience. The Little Rock school has attempted to staff the vocational courses with persons possessed of both teaching and occupational efficiency. The white city supervisor of trade automobile mechanics assisted the Negro teachers in developing a course in which the materials, methods, and objectives were clearly defined. The course was divided into five sections, "Service," "Body and Running Gear," "Power Generator," "Power Transmission and Control," and "Electrical System." Under each of these sections, there were from four to six units, subdivided into lessons

bearing on more detailed elements of the process.   The first
lesson is reproduced here with slight modifications: [4]

SECTION I
UNIT I
LESSON No. I

WASHING A CAR

SPECIFIC OBJECTIVE

To acquaint pupils with procedure of washing a car.

TOOLS AND EQUIPMENT

Water under pressure, kerosene, soap, chamois, sponge,
brush.

SUBJECT MATTER AND PROCEDURE

1. Prepare car wash, clean interior, vacuum clean
   upholstering, let up glasses, cover motor, etc.

2. Starting places for wash on different types of
   bodies.

3. Cleaning chassis, removing grease and dirt from
   axles and under fenders.

4. Cleaning car shackles; chamois used to clean glasses
   and nickel finish.

5. Soaping and washing body; cleaning running gear.

REFERENCES

Car Manual
Dykes
Wright

Through each of the units and lessons, there runs a systematic procedure and definite statement of objectives in

---

[4] "Trade Automobile Mechanics," *Special Edition of Course of Study
Monographs For the Paul Laurence Dunbar High School*, p. 7.

terms of abilities and understandings. The technique, of
course, is not any specific "Negro vocational education"—
it is intelligent vocational education of the sort that should
find emulation in all schools for all races.

In the city of New York, the board for vocational education began with a survey of opportunities open to Negroes.
The information so derived discovered numerous openings
for Negroes which vocational counselors previously had not
imagined to exist. To these counselors who had before
considered the vocational future of Negro boys and girls
as a hopeless blind alley, this information was given in order
to allow Negroes in New York high schools to profit from
the excellent vocational opportunities of the system. The
essential features of the New York experiment were to survey possible fields, to transfer this knowledge to active vocational guidance in the schools, and to establish contacts
with employers.

New Orleans has conducted a number of surveys in recent
years to discover employment possibilities for Negro high-
school graduates, with a view to modifying the program of
vocational education in the Negro high school accordingly.
So far, the failure of the city to provide funds for efficient
instruction for Negroes in vocational fields leaves the
Negroes of the city without any effective program. Meanwhile, the exceptionally equipped Delgado Trade School for
white youths in the city has established itself firmly with
employers and trades unions. Political pressure brought
by white workers upon city officials has resulted in a practical "color bar" in the employment of labor for municipal,
state, and Federal construction projects, and it is doubtful
if the powerful influence represented by this action would
favor the establishment of an effective trade school for
Negroes in the city. Disfranchised by ignorance, law, and
custom, the Negroes themselves are not in a position to help
themselves.

At the Fort Valley High and Industrial School in Georgia, Principal H. A. Hunt has developed a school which has remained in close touch with the community, a feat which has not been achieved in many other schools of the same type as they have become more highly institutionalized. Before recent difficulties affected financial stability, the Snow Hill Normal and Industrial School in Alabama, an offshoot of Tuskegee, maintained the same valuable function. Schools of this sort with an elastic program and in close touch with their communities are needed in every Southern county with a large Negro population, but private philanthropy has been able to maintain but scattered examples of them here and there in the "Black Belt."

Summary

To summarize the virtues of the plans referred to above, it is clear that the following steps would be helpful in achieving a program of instruction in vocations for Negroes:

1. The provision of adequate facilities in buildings, equipment, and teachers, involving a much greater expense than is to be found anywhere in the South today with the exception of the Little Rock investment.

2. A careful survey to discover vocational opportunities which shall not, however, regard the occupational status of the Negro as irretrievably fixed in the grooves now apparent. Flexibility should be maintained both because of possible technological changes and because of social changes such as possible migratory shifts which may change the Negro status overnight.

3. The establishment of rapport between employers and the school and of coöperative training where possible, leading to the induction of youths into industry as evenly as possible.

4. The maintenance of a close contact with the local community, involving correlations with all other possible agencies of social improvement.

5. The development of specific aims and objectives to supplant the hit-or-miss methods of older days.

In most of the discussions of vocational education for Negroes, the tendency has been to regard the problem as one by which a natural resource may be utilized for the benefit of the community or state. This tendency in great part has represented the strategy by which ancient prejudices have been overridden. The writer would insist, however, that whatever the demands of strategy may be, the interest of the Negro child should be paramount. The frequent argument for vocational education of Negroes on the grounds that they will be more valuable to the state, or to the white people of any state, if so educated, is unanswerable; but when this is the only argument which is made, it smacks too much of the exploitation of children and of race of which we have already had too much in this country.

CHAPTER XX

The Social Setting

Land Tenure

THE experience of history teaches without exception
that all social problems of rural populations are subsidi-
ary to that of land tenure, and that until it is disposed of, no
other question of policy can be settled satisfactorily. The
agrarian problem was the basis for the French and Russian
Revolutions, as it was basic in England before the Industrial Revolution transformed that nation from an agricultural to a manufacturing and processing economy. The
bitter experience of Ireland has for centuries revolved
around the difficult relations between absentee owners and
native tenants, however complicated by other differences of
race or religion.

The Negro population of the South is being transformed
rapidly, so far as such changes can be measured, from a
rural into an urban group. From 1890 to 1930, the percentage of Negroes living in rural areas decreased from
84.7 to 68.3 per cent of the total, with a marked acceleration of the process of urbanization in the last two decades
of the period. Nevertheless, there were 6,395,252 Negroes,
or more than one-half of the total Negro population in
America, living on Southern farms in 1930. Of the 882,-
850 farm operators represented in this population, 181,016
were owners, operating 11,198,893 acres, valued, with buildings, at $334,451,396. Nine hundred and twenty-three
Negro managers operated 249,072 acres, valued at $14,-

844,767.   Negro tenants numbered 700,911, operating 26,-
149,167 acres of land, valued at $1,053,649,636.[1]

These figures represented in 1930 the ebbing of a wave
of land acquisition which began immediately after emancipation.   The cry of the freedmen for "forty acres and a
mule," ridiculed as it has been even in school textbooks, was
the deep expression of a social need echoing that of landless
French, Irish, and Russian peasants of generations before
and after theirs.   The progress of Negroes in acquiring
farm lands was prodigious for the four decades after emancipation.   By 1910, Negro owners were operating almost
sixteen million acres of land in the South.   The doctrine
of land ownership preached by Booker T. Washington found
a responsive answer in the heart of many Negroes.   Those
who were unable to purchase the "bottom land" comprised
in the old plantations went up into the "piney woods" and
bought the cheaper lands there.[2]

In spite of occasional exceptions, Negroes never managed
to get a start in landownership in the richer alluvial areas,
where the great masses of the race remained as tenants.
The continual extension of the frontier of cotton production to the Southwest made it more and more impossible
for the submarginal uplands to sustain the life of a farming
family.   The result was that as soon as farm prices in the
South began to fall below even the minimum they had held
previously and opportunities opened up in industrial sections of the North and South, the small Negro farm-owner
began to sell his land or was obliged to leave it by the crush
of heavy mortgages and high interest charges or remain
only as a tenant.   The phenomenon, of course, was not
confined to Negroes; but the ownership of Negroes suffered
more largely because their purchases had been principally

---

[1] Preliminary Bulletin on Agriculture, *United States Census*, 1930.
[2] For a good description of attitudes of whites toward this movement,
see the *Debates in the Alabama Constitutional Convention of 1901.*

in the nonproductive areas of the South. The number of
Negro owners decreased from 218,612 in 1920 to 181,016
in 1930, a falling off of 17.2 per cent in ten years. Meanwhile, Negro tenants decreased only from 705,070 to 700,-
911.

TABLE LV[3]

RURAL NEGRO POPULATION AND ACREAGE OPERATED, 1910–1930

	1910	1930	% Decrease
Rural Population	6,894,972	6,395,252	7.3
Acres Operated, Owners	15,691,536	10,860,998	30.8
Acres Operated, Tenants	26,567,802	25,919,619	2.5

During this time, the average size of farm operated by
tenants has increased but slightly. It is evident that those
Negroes who remain on the farm in the South have fallen
in recent years more and more into the tenant class. The
same phenomenon is apparent with white tenants. It has
been the policy of numerous large plantation owners in the
Mississippi Delta within the last several years to replace or
displace Negroes with white tenants from the surrounding
hill country. Throughout Texas, Louisiana, and Arkansas,
there is a rising tide of Mexican farm tenantry which promises, if unchecked, to displace Negro tenants entirely within
the next few decades.

In addition to the factors working against the Negro
owner which are common to all agricultural groups which
have purchased nonproductive lands in the face of a falling
commodity market, he has profited but little in the South
from legislative devices intended to aid his general class.
Coöperatives and farm loan associations do not usually include Negro owners, and they have not shared in the subsidies from these sources which have enabled white farmers
to hold their land.

---

[3] *United States Census Reports* for respective years.

The different problems here outlined may be summarized as follows: the Negro farmer in the South is tending inevitably toward tenantry to a greater degree than ever in the past; in the ordinary process, the entire Negro rural population will be a tenant class; and it is possible that Mexican immigration, the mechanization of agricultural production, and the higher capitalization of agriculture may combine with artificial crop reduction schemes to displace a vast number of Negroes from Southern farms. It is obvious that the cities, already congested with large numbers of unemployed and unassimilated Negroes, must receive into their none too hospitable bosoms a much larger number, if the trend continues.

The School and Farm Ownership

Any person whose experience has brought him into contact with the Negro rural school has realized that the land problem is an insuperable barrier to any permanent scheme for improvement. Under the present system of land ownership, the tenant family and child are on the plantation to be exploited for profit, and not for the purpose of receiving an education. The owner will vote the school taxes, select school officials, and determine what and how much shall be taught for how long a period. This is as true for white as it is for Negro children, although, to be sure, the white tenant is always a potential voter. The writer was told frankly by a plantation owner in Louisiana that he objected to displacing Negro with white tenants in the Delta because whatever advantages might be gained in cutting production costs would be lost in higher school taxes. The introduction of Mexicans, for whom, in Southern states as in Texas, inferior and separate schools may be maintained, would eliminate this difficulty.

The plantation system and the tenant system have proved the world over to be systems which are economical only in so far as they favor a selected group of owners and rest upon the foundation of a miserable and poorly paid tenantry or serfdom. There is a vicious circle in which the small-town banker has kept just one jump ahead of the large city banker, and the fertilizer and farm implement retailer just ahead of the small-town banker, and the plantation owner just ahead of the fertilizer and farm implement retailer, and the tenant always lost in the middle with no chance to escape. Frequently, all find themselves caught in the scheme; but the tenant is always entrapped. If there could be assurance of adequate remuneration for their investment, few owners would object to a scheme of land redemption by which either white or black tenants could come into possession of the land they operate, but the entire system has little of profit in the long run for owner, tenant, state, or nation.

It is true that the cry of "forty acres and a mule" would have brought horrified protests from many a few years ago, when there was much greater objection to the entry of government into business than there is today. The more than four million Negroes in the South who belong to tenant families do not stand to profit measurably from any of the schemes devised to aid "the farmer" with the help of government money which have been projected within the past few years. It would obviously be to the long-time benefit of the section to help the white and the Negro tenant to break the vicious circle in which these two luckless groups are now ensnared. When this is done, it will be possible to look forward to an ultimate solution of the educational problem of both races in the South. Until that time arrives, the only measures which can be taken will, of necessity, be half measures.

Social Disorganization

In 1932, the Research Division of the National Educational Association issued a special bulletin dealing with "Crime Prevention Through Education." The study was avowedly intended as a defense against "loose and critical talk about the schools" such as was implied in the rhetorical question of a Newark editor:

> Is it possible that the modern school, emphasizing the creative impulses and personality of the pupils, unwittingly fosters in them a reckless, anarchistic spirit that breeds law-breaking? . . . How does it happen that criminal tendencies are gaining so rapidly at a time when the nation is spending staggering sums on education? [4]

A generation ago, the same questions were being asked by men throughout America with reference to the education of Negroes, although they differed from their modern fellow-critics by indulging in no veiled suggestions. Men as different in region and traditions as Charles Dudley Warner, of New England; Henry Grady, of Georgia; Senators Morrill, of Maine, Ingalls, of Kansas, and Morgan, of Alabama; William Vardaman, of Mississippi; and "Pitchfork Ben" Tillman, of South Carolina, were all agreed that the education of the Negro had been a costly mistake because it had made him a criminal. Speaking in Philadelphia in 1895, Warner blamed Negro crime on the growth of colleges for Negroes in the South.

Booker T. Washington pointed with pride to the fact that no graduate of Tuskegee Institute had ever been convicted of crime. President Merrill, of Fisk University, was obliged regretfully to disclose the presence of one "black sheep" in the four hundred graduates of his school, but this he held to be the exception that proved the rule.

---

[4] *Crime Prevention Through Education*, p. 138.

Throughout the South, and in the North, newspapers editorialized on the growth of Negro crime, and in all cases too much education or faulty methods were blamed for the result. Other forms of social disorganization apparent among Negroes were given wide publicity and again education was blamed.[5]

The reasons for this agitation are not hard to find. The missionaries who had first brought education to Negroes in the South had come with the New England and, indeed, the American tradition that the public school was the universal panacea. Only give the freedmen schools, they said, and all of his problems will be solved. Educate him, and you will make him a good citizen and eliminate pauperism and criminality from the race.

Southerners were still impatient with these advocates, who had come to their section with New England ideas of treating Negroes which they had believed from the first were foredoomed to failure. The growth of Negro crime coincided neatly with the need of the white schools for money and the growing thought that a portion of it could come from funds spent on Negroes.

Governor Vardaman, of Mississippi, officially stated that the South had expended three hundred million dollars on the education of the Negro, and that "we have succeeded only in making a criminal of him and impairing his usefulness and efficiency as a laborer." He pointed to the number of Negroes in the state penitentiary, which had risen steadily since the Civil War. In the North, he said, where Negroes had been much better educated than in the South, the rate of Negroes serving sentences in prisons was higher even than in Mississippi.

Paul Barringer, of the University of Virginia, writing in the *Educational Review* of March, 1901, said:

---

[5] W. E. B. DuBois, *Some Notes on Negro Crime*, Atlanta University Publications No. 9, Atlanta University Press, Atlanta, 1904.

. . . In the next generation (after freedom), the Negro
received from the two sections two hundred millions in education, and he still stands a beggar at the door of the South,
now a criminal beggar. What are we to do with him?

He has grown in criminality and physical depravity since
receiving what he has of education; that kind of education is
surely a failure.

The belief that education makes Negroes criminals is not
a dead issue in the South. In 1931, the writer heard a
school superintendent in Louisiana warn a Negro teachers'
institute that they must teach their charges not to commit
crimes. After much labor, he continued, he had prevailed
upon the local board of education to establish a high school
for Negroes. That year, two graduates of the high school
had been arrested for petty larceny, and, the superintendent
added, there was serious doubt as to whether the members of
the board would feel justified in continuing the high school
if it produced dishonest persons.

The matter warrants examination in greater detail.
Thorsten Sellin [6] has pointed out the fact that all of our
crime data

. . . picture only the *apparent* and not the *real* criminality of the Negro. The latter falls in the category of the
unknowable, for it is the sum total of all crimes committed.
This sum can only be guessed at, since many a crime remains unreported to the authorities, either because the criminal is the only one who knows of its perpetration, or because the desire to avoid all contact with criminal justice
makes the victim of the offense suppress all information
concerning it.

Criminal statistics involving race are open to criticism as
to their actual reflection of *real* criminality. The data
given in official reports are frequently highly inaccurate.
Minneapolis reported the number of Negroes arrested in

---

[6] "The Negro Criminal, a Statistical Note," *The Annals of the American
Academy of Political and Social Science*, 1928, p. 53.

1923, 1924, and 1925 as 470, 930, and 890, respectively. Miss Maurine Boie checked the police records and found that the true totals for these years were 517, 389, and 478.

In both Northern and Southern cities, Negroes are liable to arrest more frequently than are white persons. Not altogether due to race prejudice, this discrimination is sometimes owing to the fact that Negroes are recognized by the police as persons without "pull," whose detention even on the most trivial causes will result in no "comeback." In Alabama, a decision of the Attorney General in 1924 disclosed the fact that individuals were being arrested and taken to the jail for entry on records there in order to allow sheriffs to collect fees for food bills. The prisoners were freed as soon as their names were recorded as having been arrested.[7]

Southern prison records also show a sharp decline in jail confinements during periods of labor shortage. The reason is self-evident. The assumption made by the older controversialists that the number of Negroes and whites in penitentiaries reflected the real criminality of the two races did not take into account the fact that the pardoning power is exercised unevenly where the two races are concerned. At the time when Vardaman was pointing to Negroes in Southern penitentiaries as an index of Negro crime, Frances A. Kellor pointed out that in Virginia one out of $3\frac{1}{2}$ white felons received pardons, in contrast to one out of 14 Negroes; while in Louisiana, a pardon was granted to one out of every $4\frac{1}{2}$ white prisoners but to only one out of every 49 Negroes.

Negroes receive heavier sentences than white convicts in both Northern and Southern states, even in cases where they have been indicted for similar offenses. Steiner and Brown, in a classic study of the North Carolina chain gang system, said:

---

[7] *1925–1926 Report of the State Prison Inspector,* pp. 255–258.

. . . the fact that the chances of receiving a sentence to
the roads of three years or longer are two to one against the
Negro as compared to the white man suggests that justice
is not blind to the color of a man's skin.

Negroes are convicted more frequently than white persons
on indictment.   Sellin [8] cites an editorial from the Jackson,
Mississippi, *Daily News*:

. . . We allow petty officers of the law to harass and op-
press our Negro labor, mulcting them of their wages, assessing stiff fines on trivial charges, and often they are convicted
on charges which if preferred against a white man would
result in prompt acquittal.

The Rise of White Crime in the South

In spite of all of these qualifications as to the nature of
crime statistics, the most confusing fact to the person who
claims that Negro crime is due to education should be the
records of the past few years, in all Southern states, with
reference to the rapid rise of the indices upon which the
former connection between Negro crime and education were
based.   In Mississippi, the number of Negro convicts has
increased from 1,108 to 1,604, or 44 per cent, between 1902
and 1926.   The number of white convicts, however, increased from 101 to 371, an increase of 267 per cent, in
the same period.   In Alabama, the number of Negro males
in jail decreased 2.5 per cent—from 18,047 to 17,579—between 1915 and 1930.   Negro females in jail increased from
2,450 in 1915 to 3,001 in 1930, an increase of 22.4 per cent.
During the same period, the number of white males confined
in Alabama jails increased from 6,162 in 1915 to 17,353 in
1930, or 181.4 per cent.   White females confined showed
the phenomenal increase of 322.7 per cent in the same period, from 383 in 1915 to 1,619 in 1930.

---

[8] *Op. cit.,* p. 55.

The number of Negro convicts in Alabama prisons increased from 1,400 in 1900 to 2,600 in 1930, or 67 per cent. The number of white convicts, however, increased 834.1 per cent in the same period. White convicts were only 9.5 per cent of the prison population in 1900, but in 1930 they were 36.1 per cent of the total, still far below Negro convicts in percentage in the population but gaining rapidly upon them. From 1914 to 1918, 796 white persons were sentenced to the state penitentiary as compared to 2,552 Negroes. From 1926 to 1930, the number of Negroes sentenced to the state penitentiary had increased to 3,855, a gain of 50 per cent. The number of white persons sentenced to the state penitentiary, however, increased to 3,294, a gain of 319 per cent, in the quadrennium 1926–1930.

The same phenomenon is apparent in other states. In the *Negro Year Book*, Mr. Monroe Work, of Tuskegee Institute, cites the statement of a South Carolina judge reported in the *Greenville Piedmont*:

> It used to be that almost every person brought into court was a Negro. Now, it is just the other way around, the whites in court are more numerous and the Negroes are scarce. The Negro race is trying to better itself. Around every little cabin in the country flowers are planted and the place is cleaned up. I wonder sometimes that the colored people are not ashamed to appear in the same court with so many low down white persons.[9]

Mr. Work also reports the following statement from the columns of an Augusta, Georgia, newspaper:

> Strange as it may seem, records disclose the startling information that the number of white convicts in South Carolina and Georgia exceeds the number of Negroes. During the past four years, the records show an increase of 30 per cent of white people to a decrease of 17 per cent of the Negroes in the prisons of these States.[10]

---

[9] *Negro Year Book, 1931–1932*, p. 284.
[10] *Ibid.*

It is apparent that there has been an exaggerated growth in the criminality of white persons in the South, as measured by arrests, jail confinements, and prison populations. In Alabama, the rate of jail confinements for the white male population, reckoned on the basis of 10,000 of the same population, increased from 1925 to 1930 in every county in the state with but one exception—Randolph County. The rate for Negro males decreased in forty-three out of sixty-seven counties. Now, are we to conclude from these data that the rapid growth of the *apparent* criminality, which has coincided with unprecedented development of public schools for the white population, has been due to education? But Negro schools, too, have improved; and yet there is apparent a diminution of criminality among Negroes.

The writer has correlated the rate of jail confinements per 10,000 of the population for the race for whites and Negroes in the 67 counties of the State of Alabama with certain other data. The coefficients of correlation resulting are as follows:

> White rate of jail confinements with Negro rate.................... .727

Apparently, the same forces which elevate the Negro crime rate as measured by jail confinements work in the same direction upon the white population.

> White crime with white literacy .... .13

Apparently, there is little connection between the rate at which white persons are confined in jail and the literacy of the population in the county where they reside.

> Negro crime and Negro literacy .... .34

Apparently, there is a slight positive relationship between Negro literacy and Negro jail confinements.

> White crime and percentage of white population that is
> urban .... .47

Apparently, those counties with a large urban white population have more white jail confinements than counties in
which the urban white population is small.

Negro crime and percentage of Negro population that is
   urban .... .79

Apparently, those counties with a high Negro jail con-
finement rate are those with a high percentage of the Negro
population which is urban.

The counties which show the lowest rates of jail confinements for both Negroes and whites in Alabama are the
"black" counties, where the population is entirely rural, and
where the schools for Negroes are the poorest in the state
and those for whites are among the best. The counties
showing the highest rate for whites of both sexes as well as
for Negroes are the highly urban counties, where school opportunities are best for Negroes but not necessarily best for
whites. Madison County in 1930 showed a rate of arrests
per 10,000 male whites of 556, compared to a Negro rate of
578. The city of Huntsville is located in this county, and
in recent years, a large number of white country people
from the surrounding foothills have been attracted to the
city to work in mills, factories, and other industrial and
manufacturing establishments.

The writer would *suggest* that these data do not show
anything definite with regard to the effect of education upon
either the white or the black population of Alabama. The
opinion is hazarded that education, instead of being a deterrent in crime, may actually be a stimulating factor in that it
may hasten the destruction of old patterns of action and
stimulate the urban movement. The writer is of the opinion
that the growing rate of *apparent* criminality among white
persons in the South is to some degree chargeable to improved educational conditions. The school has without
doubt aided in the migration of country folk to the city, and

in the breaking up of old patterns preliminary to the establishment of new ones. In so far as improved schools have broken the crust of the old order, they have contributed to crime.

Appositely, if Negro crime in the South is decreasing, it means that the great wave of growing Negro crime in the last generation was symptomatic of a fundamental social change. In this break-up of the order, the school played its part. In the diminution of the apparent rate of crime among Negroes in the South today, the writer would see the secondary activity of the school. The violent transition from an agrarian to an urban civilization which white people in the South today are making is reflected in their growing crime rates. The equally violent parturition which Negroes began to make seventy years ago from slavery to freedom was reflected in then-current crime rates. The writer would further suggest the hypothesis that Negroes in the last two decades have reached an adjustment to the life they now live in the South. The adjustment of white people to a new social order is still in process.

For both races, the school has functioned to make the tempo of adjustment more rapid and thus to foreshorten the process. Without the school, generations and not decades would have witnessed an acceleration in the apparent crime rate before the curve began to decline.

Health and Education

The situation. The death rate of Negroes in all sections of the country with few exceptions is higher than the death rate of white persons. According to Dr. Louis I. Dublin, of the Metropolitan Life Insurance Company,

> Colored infants of both sexes suffer from death rates approximately two-thirds above that of the whites. In early childhood, the margin is even larger. From five years of

age up to adolescence, the margin is 57 per cent excess for males and 72 per cent for females. The most pronounced differences, however, are found between 15 and 25 years, where the death rate for colored boys and young men runs to nearly two and a half times that for the whites, and where the mortality among colored girls is more than two and three-quarters times as high as for young white women. From early adult life to "middle age" (25–44 years) the comparison remains extremely unfavorable to the colored; while between 45 and 64 years, the adverse margins for the colored are not so large as with all earlier age groups. The death rate for colored women is still 60 per cent above that for white women. In old age, that is, 65 years and over, the excess mortality for colored males and females is much reduced, being only 11 and 18 per cent respectively.[11]

In spite of this excess of Negro over white deaths, there has been a consistent decrease in Negro mortality during the last several decades. The decrease has been particularly notable in Northern cities, until recently the seat of the gravest problems of Negro health. The cities of the South, such as Birmingham, Atlanta, Charleston, Savannah, and New Orleans, are, just now, the most dangerous places in the United States for Negroes to live, so far as health is concerned. In this respect, they have taken the place held a decade ago by Chicago, Philadelphia, New York, and Baltimore. The rural Negro in the South has the lowest death rate from all causes of any sector of the Negro population.

The relation of the school to Negro health. Negroes may suffer from disease and death more frequently than white persons (1) because of inherited weaknesses in their constitution, moral as well as physical. The high rate of venereal diseases among Negroes is frequently given a moral-instinctive setting by critics of the race. The death rate from tuberculosis, frequently from two to four times as high among Negroes as whites, is held by others to be due to (a)

---

[11] "The Health of the Negro," *The Annals of the American Academy*, 1928, p. 78.

an inherited lack of resistance toward this disease, (*b*) an inherited physical structure more open to its ravages, or (*c*) inherited habits of uncleanliness, carelessness, and unsanitary practices which lead to ready infection and death in the face of the disease.

(2) Negroes may show a high incidence of mortality and morbidity because they belong, for the most part, to a low-income group.   For this reason, (*a*) they have few opportunities to avail themselves of the best medical attention and care; (*b*) they are obliged by poverty to live in the most unsanitary and overcrowded conditions, making infection highly probable and recovery difficult; and (*c*) they can ill afford the expense for necessary clothing, food, fuel, and recreation.

(3) Negroes fall sick, and die, more frequently than white persons because they are more ignorant of the laws of health and sanitation.   There are many white people, for example, who still believe that "night air" is dangerous and will cause a person to fall sick; and there are yet many white children who wear assafœtida bags around their necks as a preventive against infection.   However, a higher level of literacy and education among white persons makes them as a comparable group less susceptible to these and to less innocent superstitions.

The school can do little about instinctive racial weaknesses, if, indeed, they actually exist, which is doubted by many persons who see in other factors ample grounds for explaining the higher mortality among Negroes taken as a group.   With economic difficulties, the school can deal only by indirection.   It cannot as yet build better houses for men and women; but it can teach children to appreciate the need for cleanliness, privacy, and comfort.   It cannot obtain better jobs for its graduates; but it can develop higher standards of living, and to some degree train children so that they will combine an active dissatisfaction with poor

ways of living with an active desire and ability to better
them.

The school can move directly toward the improvement of
health by direct instruction and the establishment of health
habits in the homes from which children come.   It can also
transform itself into a community center for the education
of adults as well as of children in health matters.   A consideration of the more important causes of excessive mortality among Negroes in their relationship to the school will
show that schools for Negroes have not been discharging
their duty so long as they have taught formalized courses
in physiology and hygiene with little transfer to specific
problems.

Tuberculosis.   The writer has never seen, among more
than a thousand Negro public schools he has visited, the
slightest attempt made to teach Negro children anything
about the tuberculosis problem, with the exception of a
health project recently instituted in Davidson County, Tennessee.   Not ten per cent of the children will ever reach the
seventh or eighth grade, where a course in physiology or
hygiene may be taught by a teacher who requires the children to make extensive drawings of the respiratory system
or the alimentary tract, but makes very little application to
the conditions of life under which these Negro children are
living that are so conducive to tuberculosis and its ravages.
This lack of instruction persists in spite of the fact that
in such a state as Tennessee, ten times as many Negro as
white children between the ages of five and fifteen will die
of tuberculosis.[12]

A coöperative experiment recently instituted with the
help of the Julius Rosenwald Fund, the General Education
Board, the Tennessee State Department of Health, the

------

[12] Sibley, Eldridge, *Differential Mortality in Tennessee*, Fisk University
Press, Nashville, 1929.

Davidson County, Tennessee, Public School Health Department, Meharry Medical College, the Tennessee A. & I. State College, and Fisk University, proposes to establish several rural schools as demonstration centers for pupil-education in health matters, and a prime interest will be tuberculosis. Teachers in training in the colleges are to benefit from the methods worked out in the experiment.   Even in localities where such agencies cannot assist, the initiative of a single teacher could assure the coöperation of local medical societies, public health agencies, and school officials in working out a similar program for the benefit of Negro school children.   At the Phipps Institute, in Philadelphia, an institution specifically interested in tuberculosis and located in a Negro settlement, the number of Negro patients coming for diagnosis and treatment to the Institute averaged only 51 per year from 1904 to 1913.   An educational campaign employing a Negro nurse and conducted through Negro churches, schools, and fraternal orders resulted in the following work of the Institute for Negroes in 1927: 1,040 new cases, 6,017 dispensary visits, and 6,760 home visits by nurses.[13]

Venereal diseases. Dr. Louis I. Dublin says, ". . . syphilis and its sequelæ account very largely for the great excess of the Negro death rate today over that for the whites." Schools have hesitated to consider this subject either because of prudery or on account of ignorance. There is a vast amount of misinformation among all populations regarding venereal infections, and, unfortunately, the superstitions engendered by this ignorance are not always confined to the uneducated classes. While teaching a course in social hygiene at a Negro college summer school, the writer found among his students a graduate of an accredited Negro college, himself a college teacher, who insisted heat-

---

[13] Landis, Dr. H. M. R., "Tuberculosis and the Negro," *The Annals of the American Academy*, 1928, p. 88.

edly that gonorrhea was caused by "strain" and was not a germ disease. A principal of a large county training school enrolled in the same class was convinced that he had discovered an herb that would cure this infection, and stated that he had frequently compounded a lotion from this herb which he retailed to the young men of his community at $1.00 per pint. A young man about to graduate from a two-year teacher's course blithely repeated that most vicious of all legends, *i.e.*, that it was possible to effect the cure of a "bad case" of either syphilis or gonorrhea by having sexual intercourse with a young maiden.

The American Social Hygiene Association has demonstrated that it is possible to instruct large numbers of Negro teachers in the fundamental knowledge which all educated people should have regarding sex and the family. In Alabama, a course of study was developed for introduction into the Negro elementary and high schools dealing with the fundamental social and biological facts involved. The problem calls for an approach different from that represented by the popular books of an older period or the "sex lectures" occasionally given in Negro and white schools by itinerant lecturers. Indeed, on one such occasion, the writer heard the president of a Negro college tell his male students that sexual intercourse at monthly periods was essential to the normal functioning of the youthful mind and body.

The schools can and should create a greater intelligence among children and adults as to facts of causation, prophylaxis, and treatment. Along with emphasis upon the matter of health should rightly go the development of attitudes and knowledges regarding the institution of the family and the care and nurture of infants.

The happy delusion has persisted in our romantic literature and in our thinking that the city is the location of all that is vile and vicious, while the country, especially the

Southern plantation, is the idyllic spot where men are very, very happy and contented. It may well be that the peasant is happier than the denizen of our modern cities; but as we learn more and more about rural life, the romantic illusion tends to disappear. The Julius Rosenwald Fund has recently pursued researches into the frequency and treatment of syphilis in certain Southern rural communities. The data disclose a high correlation between economic and cultural factors and the incidence of the disease. Here, again, we have the old story: no thorough-going improvement of any aspect of the welfare of a population can be hoped for until the fundamental problems of its life are sought for and solved.

The data in Table LVI with reference to the educational status of Negroes and whites in the counties surveyed for syphilis are enlightening. Data for all comparisons were not available for Bolivar County, Mississippi.

TABLE LVI [14]

PER CAPITA PAYMENTS FOR WHITE AND NEGRO EDUCABLE AGED 5–19
COMPARED WITH PER CENT OF ILLITERACY FOR BOTH RACES AND
INCIDENCE OF SYPHILIS FOR NEGROES IN TERMS OF RATE PER 1000

County	Per Capita Expenditures for Teachers' Salaries		Ratio of Adult Illiteracy to 1000 of the Population		Ratio of Syphilis Infection for Negroes in Terms of Rate Per 1000 of the Population
	White	Negro	White	Negro	
Macon, Alabama	$34.21	$3.10	23	227	398
Glynn, Georgia	21.35	8.21	25	176	261
Tipton, Tennessee	20.59	4.69	105	227	255
Bolivar, Mississippi	....	......	28	271	235
Pitt, North Carolina	23.26	5.98	45	258	125
Albemarle, Virginia	31.99	20.48	84	220	89

[14] Syphilis data from *The Control of Syphilis in Southern Rural Communities*, Julius Rosenwald Fund, Chicago, 1932; educational data from school reports.

The expenditure ratio for Glynn County, Georgia, includes the city of Brunswick, while that for Albemarle County, Virginia, includes the city of Charlottesville. Considering the fact that all of the syphilis cases studied were from rural areas, the relationship, whether coincidental or causal, between educational expenditures and the incidence of syphilis is patent.

Infant mortality. The high rate of Negro infant mortality finds an analogue in rates for the lower economic levels among white persons. Contributing factors to the differential mortality shown in this as in other aspects of the health of the Negro are poverty and ignorance. The departments of home economics in Negro high schools have not usually taken full advantage of the opportunities presented for creating a greater amount of intelligence among their students with regard to the duties and skills of motherhood. The small percentage of children who reach the high-school years should be remembered in planning curricular adaptations to meet this situation. The lower grades must be depended upon, if the mass of Negro children is to be reached.

Summary

The school affects the social setting of the individual and of the community, and in turn is affected by these social settings. Careful educational interpretation demands caution, whether in assessing the possibilities of the school as an instrument of public policy or in allocating responsibility for progress or lack of progress. There are limits within which the school can affect society. Educational forces work slowly. Social forces gravitate in various directions as though without conscious or intelligible determination. It is the function of the new school to accelerate social change, but also to coördinate its activities with apparent social shifts.

One of the most fundamental of all factors in interpreting the past and present status of education for Negroes is that of land tenure. The easy slogan of an older day can be of doubtful value to the farmer today, when thrift, honesty, and intelligence avail little in maintaining high standards of living in the face of international competition and the complications of world markets. The school may in time create intelligence sufficient to solve the problem of land tenure; but it is caught up in a vicious circle which dulls the efficiency of the school until the more fundamental economic questions are adjusted. The operation of farms by owners will solve our school problem in the South. The school may lead to complete farm ownership if it is effective, but it cannot be effective so long as it exists for a tenant population.

It does not appear that education in itself is either a cure for or a cause of crime and social disorganization. As a part of the general social process, the school certainly plays its part. Urban Negroes are not more or less criminal than rural Negroes because they are more literate any more than this can be said of white persons. There are some factors causative of criminality that are more fundamental than the institution of the school. These factors are in ceaseless operation. It is indeed probable that the school is a valuable bulwark against crime in that it furnishes the individual with the resources necessary to sustain stresses and strains unknown to older generations.

In the sphere of health, the school meets one of the few fields where its direct influence can be made to function with the least hindrance or assistance from other fields. Modern sanitation, which is responsible for the greatest measure of our improved health, is a matter of intelligence and good habits. The laws of infectious diseases can be taught directly and with great immediate success in our classrooms. A literate population, brought into contact with higher standards of living, can be expected to seek those higher

standards.   It was a favorite saying of Booker T. Washington that the American Negro "needed some more wants."
In aiding the community agencies for health and in performing its functions of direct and indirect teaching, schools
for Negro children can contribute most heavily to the continued survival of the race in this country.

CHAPTER XXI

Educational Planning

"PROGRESS," said John Morley, "is not automatic. . . . The world only grows better, even in the moderate degree in which it does grow better, because people wish that it should, and take the right steps to make it better." We live in an age that is distressed and uncertain, and there are many who are doubtful that the world "does grow better" even in the "moderate degree" granted by the distinguished Englishman.

But in spite of the pessimism with which the whole world is at present beclouded, the idea of a planned society whereby men might affect their own destinies directly gives encouragement to men and women and entire nations throughout the world. We have gone far from the time when men resented medical science as an interference with the Divine Will, or when religious assemblies condemned railroads on the grounds that if God had ever intended men to travel so fast, he would have created steam engines at the beginning of human existence. On every side, we come face to face with man's interference with the natural process: filtration plants to eliminate typhoid fever, innoculations to prevent various germ infections, vast irrigation projects to eliminate man's dependence upon rain, and tin cans for preserving food. In India, the typical child at birth has an expectancy of less than thirty years of life; in this country, the typical white child may expect at birth to live more than fifty-five years, and the Negro infant, more than forty-five years.

Where considerations of public health are concerned, we do not allow nature to take its course.

As with many another social problem, the education of Negroes in this country has followed more a "natural process" than a planned one. But the prospect of this course is dreary, not altogether because it is so slow, but because it is subject to so many vagaries and involves so much human misery for the generations which are to be born and must die before the anticipated era of equalitarianism really dawns. Nor should it be forgotten that the problem of equalizing educational opportunity in the South involves not only Negro children, but white as well; and that the present situation should be intolerable for those states in which, because of existing discriminations practiced against Negro children, certain sections furnish magnificent facilities for their white children while other sections give the most meager education to their majority white school population.

It is true that plans must possess an extreme flexibility. We cannot know what will happen within the next decade, and much less, within the next half-century; for war, pestilence, internal discord, and bitter racial antagonisms are still possible. But if the entire fabric of our civilization does not disintegrate, any plan sensible to modifications from time to time is feasible and, indeed, is necessary to an intelligent approach to our problems. In the following paragraphs, an attempt has been made to suggest some elements of a plan which may be suggestive of the things that need to be done.

The Ideal

Federal participation in the support of education in the states. On the basis of a minimum educational program to be worked out by an advisory committee of school finance experts, the Federal Government should appropriate money to the states to aid in the equalization of educational opportunity for all children. When the Blair Bill, providing for the appropriation of money to the states on the basis of illiteracy, was being debated in the Senate in the 1880's, the chief argument against the measure was that it was an unwarranted extension of the Federal power. The proponents of the measure argued that there was ample justification under the "General Welfare Clause" of the Constitution for such expenditures. Governmental regulation of business, and appropriations of all sorts for purposes other than educational, such as we have witnessed in the last several years, can leave but little doubt that the question of "right" is primarily one of congressional willingness to appropriate funds.

Federal appropriations should be made contingent upon (1) guarantees of equal expenditures in separate school systems. In the Blair Bill debate, Senators Plumb, Harrison, Ingalls, Sherman, and other Northern Senators insisted that if there were no such guarantee, with penalties attached, the Federal appropriations would be spent principally on white children. Even those Southern Senators, like Senator Morgan, of Alabama, who opposed the bill hotly insisted that the inclusion of such guarantees in the bill would be an insult to the South, and that no such discrimination then existed or ever would exist in the distribution even of state funds. Despite the imagined outrage to their honor in the mere suggestion of the possibility, we now know that the Southern representatives reckoned without the true tendencies within their states.

Without adequate penalties and guarantees, the appropriation of Federal monies to Southern states would enable those states to provide opportunities for their white children, with no considerable local effort, far superior to those provided in Northern states. The "Black Belt" counties now provide schools for their white children far superior to those

for white children in "white" counties principally through
the appropriation of state funds for Negroes to the white
school system.   There is no reason to believe that the disposition of Federal funds without guarantees would be made
otherwise.

The Majority Report of the National Advisory Committee on Education accepted the principle of financial grants
to the states but was opposed to any sort of Federal control
over these appropriations.   In the opinion of the majority,

> Complete financial audit gives the publicity that protests
> the Federal Government and is an adequate safeguard
> against state expenditure of federal funds for anything out-
> side the broad educational purposes contemplated. . . .
> Wisdom in state allocation and expenditure of funds given
> by the Federal Government is best guaranteed by full and
> detailed reports to the Federal Government.   The printing
> and wide distribution of the same by the Federal Govern-
> ment will inform public opinion, the only competent check
> upon which popular government may rely in the long run.[1]

The Federal funds for unemployment relief distributed in
the South in almost all cases go farther than those expended
in Northern states, because Negro unemployed are paid in
most localities from fifty to seventy-five cents per day while
the white unemployed are paid from $1.25 to $1.75 per day.
In the North, the relief funds must be spread equally over
populations of the same race, for the most part.   The student interested in such matters may or may not find the
record in the "full and detailed reports to the Federal Government" which may be printed and "widely distributed"
several years hence.   Meanwhile, the Northern community
with ten unemployed, on receiving $100, must spread this
relief to each of the ten in equal amounts.   The Southern
community which receives $100 for relief for ten unem-
ployed, six of whom are Negroes, can, and frequently does,

---

[1] *Federal Relations to Education*, Part I, p. 32.

give $60 to the four unemployed white citizens and $40 to the six unemployed Negro citizens.

Public opinion is a competent check, but our democracy has yielded too many examples of the apathy of citizens and of the futility of fastening the stable door after the horse has escaped. All state equalization funds set up certain reasonable requirements and contain guarantees for fulfillment. There is every reason to believe that the simple stipulation that there should be no discrimination in the expenditure of school funds is both necessary and, at the same time, unobjectionable. This financial supervision need not imply the Federal control of "certain specific educational policies and methods in the states" so strenuously objected to by the majority of the National Advisory Committee.

Federal appropriations should be contingent upon (2) the ability and effort of the several states in the support of education. There are many indices which have already been worked out in detail for communities within states, and the development of such indices for the Nation is a matter of research in detail and not in technique. For this purpose, the minimum educational program should consider the separate Negro schools in communities where they exist from the same standpoint as the white schools, with identical salary schedules for identical levels of training and experience and with no distinction made as to the size of the teaching unit.

(3) State participation in Federal aid should be contingent upon the formulation by the state of a satisfactory equalization program within its borders. There are counties in Georgia, for example, where less than six dollars per capita for teachers' salaries is spent on each white child aged 5–19, while there are other Georgia counties where more than thirty dollars is spent per educable. Jackson County, in Alabama, pays $7.48 for teachers' salaries per capita white child aged 5–19, while Lowndes County, in the

same state, spends $48.15 per capita. These differences are not due to inequalities in the wealth of these counties, for Jackson County actually has a higher per capita assessed valuation than Lowndes County, if all children, black and white, are considered. They are due to the fact that the financing of schools is on a basis of racial discrimination in the expenditure of state funds to the extent of this gross inequality. Certainly the white children within a state, if not the Negro, should be placed on a firm basis of equality before the state is allowed to participate in Federal equalization grants.

(4) The participation of states in Federal aid should be left entirely to the willingness of the state. If the state wishes to meet the requirements for participation, it should be allowed to do so; if it does not, it should not be the recipient of a blanket grant which may tend to perpetuate existing inequalities between different white children and between white and black children. The probable use of unrestricted Federal grants would be to eliminate differences between white children, as recent equalization funds have attempted to do.

In effect, such a stipulation would mean that states like Kentucky, Tennessee, North Carolina, Virginia, Missouri, Oklahoma, and possibly Texas, where the percentage of Negroes in the population is not large and the discrepancies between the expenditures for the two races not too exaggerated, would find it profitable to accept the requirements for equalization between the races and agree to share in Federal aid. In these states, the amount of money receivable from the Federal Government under an equalization scheme would compensate for expending more money on schools for Negro children. It is probable that in Alabama, Mississippi, South Carolina, Louisiana, and Georgia, the expense of bringing Negro schools up to even a reasonable minimum standard would be greater at the present time than a correspondingly reasonable Federal allotment would justify.

The Minority Report of the National Advisory Committee on Education submitted by the Negro members, John W. Davis, Mordecai Johnson, and Robert R. Moton suggested that special grants should be made to states with large Negro populations.[2] The minority report justified its position on the well-founded ground that general grants would not in all probability be expended equably where Negroes were concerned. The report pointed out with great clearness that the obligation for the education of Negroes should rest upon the entire Nation rather than upon separate states. The entire Nation countenanced slavery with its resulting degradation of a large portion of the population. The National Government freed the slave but left the responsibility for elevating the population sunk in misery and ignorance largely through its own acquiescence if not through its own active connivance, upon the Southern states. Emancipation turned out to be a badly bungled job, with the hardest work left incomplete in the hands that were least able to perform the task.

The writer cannot agree, however, with the recommendation of the minority report that special grants be made for educating Negroes. To do so would call for the creation of an entirely new machinery of administration and control, immensely complicating the problems of education in Southern states where separate systems already create difficulties which are almost insuperable. Southern school officials can be trusted to "deal righteously and justly" by Negro children if they are freed from the pressure of local discriminatory demands. Federal guarantees and requirements would free their hands, and if it could be seen that equalization meant not only better schools for Negroes, but better schools

---

[2] *Federal Relations to Education*, Part 1, pp. 105–113.

for white children as well, the weight of local pressure would be much less than it is now.

HYPOTHETICAL WORKING OF FEDERAL EQUALIZATION IN THE
STATES OF RURILINA AND LUSITANIA

	Rurilina	Lusitania
No. of Negro Children	30,000	50,000
No. of White Children	70,000	50,000
Present Per Capita, Negroes	$ 20	$ 10
Present Per Capita, Whites	40	80
Total Expenditures, Negroes	600,000	500,000
Total Expenditures, Whites	2,800,000	4,000,000
Federal Minimum Basis, Per Capita	50	50
Amount Necessary to Bring Negroes to Minimum Basis	900,000	2,000,000
Amount Necessary to Bring White Children to Minimum Basis	700,000	
Amount of Federal Equalization	1,600,000	500,000

An equalization scheme which insisted on an equality of expenditures for the two races if aid was accepted would probably have the same effect as a special grant for the education of Negroes while it would not be open to the same involvements of administration or control. In the hypothetical State of Rurilina, similar in many respects to Virginia, North Carolina, Tennessee, Kentucky, Oklahoma, Arkansas, and Texas, Negroes are regarded as constituting 30 per cent of the school population. The present per capita payment for Negroes is assumed to be $20 and that for white children, $40. The total expenditures for Negro and white children combined is $3,400,000. The minimum program set as the basis for possible Federal equalization is $50 per child, which would mean an expenditure of $5,000,000, in which the Government would share by providing sums in excess of $3,400,000, the amount yielded by a maximum tax schedule. The State of Rurilina would then be granted $1,600,000 for equalization of educational opportunity from the Federal Government. As the Negro schools are much farther below the minimum standard than the white schools, the first necessity is to bring them up to the standard for white children.   Altogether, the schools for Negro children would receive $900,000 in order to bring them up to the minimum standard, while schools for white children would receive $700,000.

The State of Lusitania, however, would probably not wish to share in such an equalization scheme.   Lusitania would receive only $500,000 from the Federal Government, for she now expends $4,500,000 on her schools.   To equalize opportunities for Negro and white children would require the expenditure of $2,000,000, or $1,500,000 more than would be receivable from the Federal Government.

It is probable that no single Southern state, with the possible exception of South Carolina, would be in the position of Lusitania.   The schools for white children in the South, as well as the Negro schools, would fall below a minimum Federal program.   The bulk of monies, of course, would be needed to equalize expenditures for schools where Negro children were enrolled.

State administration.   The ideal plan would make the establishment of separate schools discretionary with local authorities.   It is not improbable that in many communities in such Southern states as Oklahoma, Texas, West Virginia, Missouri, Kentucky, and even Tennessee, school officials would not object to a "mixed school" where only one or two Negro children were affected.   There are numerous districts along the Appalachian foothills where single families of Negroes, living in the midst of a white population, are deprived of all educational opportunity by statute or constitutional limitation against their presence in the white schools.   In Northern states, with appropriate guarantees of equality, the choice should be allowed communities of the luxury of maintaining a separate school system or of the economy of a single system.   In any event, public sentiment can be depended upon to demand a compromise of the matter agreeable both to prejudices and to economic self-interest.

State boards of education in states with large separate systems should have Negro representation on the boards proportionate to the Negro population and appointed or selected in the same manner as are the other members. An assistant superintendent of education, either white or Negro, should have in care the supervision of Negro schools. For the rest, the administration of the Negro system might well follow approved administrative practice.

County boards of education should also permit Negro representation. The staff of the county superintendent in counties with large Negro populations should include at least two members, preferably Negroes, who should have the responsibility for administering and supervising the work of the separate Negro schools. The organization of city administrative and supervisory staffs should be similar to that of state and county systems.

Finance. Either the income tax or sales tax should be substituted for property taxes as the basis for school support. Mississippi has recently inaugurated a sales tax as an important factor in state and school finance. Theoretically, this measure should obviate the objection frequently heard, that Negroes pay no taxes for the schools and, accordingly, do not deserve to share in the benefits of the system. However, the sales tax, in Mississippi, and various similar taxes in other Southern states and communities, do not appear to have brought with them any greater degree of participation by the Negroes in the school funds of those states.

Elections. School elections should be open to all adult citizens with a relaxation of the requirements demanded in other elections. Negroes who support school systems by the purchase of gasoline and other commodities should be allowed to vote upon the selection of officials who are to expend the money thus raised.

Social reforms. Through state and Federal allotments, white and black tenants should be aided to purchase the land they now operate. State laws and municipal ordinances governing corporations should be so modified as to permit the elimination of slums and the construction of modern housing units for persons of low-income groups. In this, the Federal Government should aid through non-profit corporations, the facilitation of condemnation proceedings, and the relaxation of tax levies upon such properties and enterprises.

The public health services should be extended so as to make clinics, both medical and dental, available for low-income groups in city and country. The extension of health and educational services of all sorts should be vigorously promoted.

In planning the social services implied here, the experience of a great private corporation has put to shame anything yet achieved by the activity of the state. In the vicinity of Birmingham, Alabama, the Tennessee Coal and Iron Company maintains an excellent public school system for the Negro workers who are employed in its plants. Employees live in houses located in communities owned and operated by the company. These houses are well-spaced and well-built, and the grounds are kept in a state of remarkable neatness and cleanliness. Ample play space is provided for children and adults. The medical service is thorough and efficient, and a staff of trained workers stimulates and directs recreation among the workers. The maintenance of the villages where the workers live and the supervision over the lives of the workers, amounting almost to regimentation, might be regarded by some as a too extreme paternalism. The Tennessee Coal and Iron Company, however, is no philanthropic organization: it is

devoted primarily to the task of paying dividends to stock-
holders of the enterprise.   It is no credit to the State of
Alabama, or to the United States, that this great private
corporation exhibits more intelligence in the education,
health, and social welfare of its black workers than the public corporations of which they are citizens.

The Fact

So far, we have concerned ourselves in this chapter with
the consideration of what might be done with adequate
financial support, which can be furnished only by assumption
on the part of the Federal Government of the responsibility
for equalizing opportunity in the Nation.   The writer haz-
ards the opinion that all of these things will come to pass,
but not in the ordered way in which they occur to the understanding.   As dangerous as prophecies are, it may be
permissible to suggest that the "natural process" will involve a continuation of inequalities between white and black
children in the South for decades to come.   Some day, the
American Nation will stumble into Federal support of education in the states, if it does not consciously march toward
that goal with planned designs.   When the South realizes
that it cannot give its white children an American education even by diverting school money from black to white
children, the section will be the first to ask for and receive
Federal aid for education.

Meanwhile, the stubborn fact of the present remains with
us.   Here in the present is the poverty of a section coexistent with an open and humanly selfish discrimination in
the expenditure of school funds.   What is to be done about
this disturbing fact?

Beyond the unthinkable prospect of doing nothing at all,
we can make the best of what we have, and we can strive with
all our might to foreshorten what may be the inevitable,

long-time road that leads to the equality of educational opportunity for all children. Various suggestions have been made in the course of this text as to how present difficulties may be minimized as far as possible. Nothing can be done without intelligence, character, and sacrifice, but everything is possible with these qualities. That a white teacher receives one thousand dollars for teaching a class or a subject while the Negro teacher receives four hundred need not always mean that the white children will receive two and a half times as much instruction. It will probably mean that the Negro teacher must accommodate herself to an inferior standard of living, both culturally and materially. It will mean fewer opportunities for personal development. It will mean fewer books, shabbier coats, less professional schooling, and no travel at all.

If these difficulties are remembered, it is neither self-deception nor "other-worldliness" to believe that Negroes and Negro teachers have a spiritual value that can be of incomparable assistance to them in their tasks. That value is the essential righteousness of the cause of the oppressed minority. There is no one of the "eternal verities" more certain than that every child, in all lands and in all times, has an inalienable right to that measure of personal development which his capacities warrant. It is not idle sentiment to say that the Negro teacher can override handicaps of a material sort if she exalts the deep spiritual significance of her task and identifies herself completely with the destinies of the racial group to which she belongs.

Planning for the Fact

It is also possible to plan and work for worthy educational objectives in spite of the present difficulties which beset us. Such a "design for living" in the present and immediate future calls for a high order of courage, sympathy, and intelligence.

The County Unit Plan

The county is generally recognized as the smallest school administrative unit that can be controlled and financed without great waste and inefficiency. Fortunately, the county is the principal unit for Negro schools in the South, for, even in those states where the district system operates where white schools are concerned, the control and financing of schools for Negroes has been left largely to the office of the county superintendent.

Within the last few years, several states have developed staffs for conducting county surveys. The attention paid to Negro schools reflects the attitudes toward the education of the race in those counties in which surveys have been made. In some few cases, special surveys have been made of the separate Negro system where interested school boards or superintendents were favorable to the idea.

The root of the problem, of course, is finance. It has been shown elsewhere in this book that the expenditures for teachers' salaries in 269 out of 521 Southern counties studied was less than $4.50 per Negro child aged 5–19. In Lincoln County, Arkansas, where in the school year 1929–1930 there was an expenditure for all purposes of $5.48 per Negro child aged 5–19, the survey commission reported:

> In making this survey the Negro schools have been taken into consideration only just as they are now. It would be desirable to extend the educational advantages for Negroes in Lincoln County, but this is impossible at the present time. Consequently, where there are now separate Negro districts, they have been left just as they are and have not been figured in at all either for expense or income. In districts having Negro schools it is planned for these schools

to continue to run on the same basis as at present and al-
lowance has been made in the budget to take care of them.[3]

In Lincoln County, Negroes constituted 61 per cent of
the school population. The Negro schools were supported
almost entirely by the state apportionment to the county.
Under the district system, one of two proposed new districts was to receive $16,055 from the state equalization
fund. From this source and from local taxes, Negro schools
were not, apparently, to benefit.

The attitude that nothing can be done to improve schools
for Negroes is unfortunate, for much improvement could
be made even without an increase in expenditures. Superintendents and supervisors need to remember that much
of the money now spent on Negro schools, small as the
amounts may be, is wasted because of faulty administration
and ineffective teaching. A minimum of care and sympathetic attention to the needs of schools for Negroes would
result in a raising of morale that would mean much for the
improvement of the efficiency of the school.

In Jefferson County, Arkansas, a survey was made of
the Negro schools of the county, which includes the city of
Pine Bluff.[4] In 1930, there were 10,577 rural Negro educables aged 5–19 reported in the county by the United
States Census. In 1929–1930, total expenditures of $43,-
000 were reported, all of which went to pay the expenses
of teachers' salaries. The expenditure for each Negro
child was $4.06 in the rural districts.

For this amount of money, the county maintained 33
one-teacher, 31 two-teacher, 3 three-teacher, 4 four-teacher,
2 five-teacher, and 2 six-teacher schools. The length of

---

[3] *Lincoln County School News,* April, 1930, Vol. 3, No. 7.

[4] *A Survey of Negro Education in Jefferson County, Arkansas,* by the
Division of Negro Education of the State Department of Education and
the County Superintendent of Schools of Jefferson County.

term in the one-teacher schools ranged from 60 to 180 days with an average of 106 days. The enrollment per teacher in one-room schools averaged 47; in two-teacher schools, 37; in three-teacher schools, 52; in four-teacher schools, 37; in five-teacher schools, 69.6; in six-teacher schools, 46.

The teachers employed in this system showed the following amounts of training: 1 year high school, 2.1 per cent; two years high school, 24.0 per cent; three years high school, 3.6 per cent; four years high school, 35.0 per cent; one year college, 13.8 per cent; two years college, 13.8 per cent; and four years college, 7.2 per cent.

Fourteen schools were housed in churches and had no equipment of any sort. Four schools represented a value of $75 or less. Two were valued at between $100 and $125, and fourteen were estimated to have a value from $125 to $500.

The average annual salary of the 140 teachers reported was $350. The range of salaries paid was from $40 to $1,500.

Two Jeanes supervisors were employed for Negro schools in the county. Two county training schools were maintained.

This brief description of what the Jefferson County program was with a per capita payment for children aged 5–19 of $4.06 reflects, of course, the need for improvement. It does, however, represent a state of affairs vastly superior to that existing in hundreds of counties in the state where per capita payments for Negro children are less than $2 per child and where there are no supervisors, no county training schools, no teachers with training beyond high school, and where no buildings at all are owned by the state. By a planned budget which adds from twenty-five to fifty cents per capita yearly to the budget for the Negro schools, it should be possible to raise expenditures gradually, with a minimum of opposition, to the level of the schools existing in Jefferson County in 1929–1930.

The program suggested for the reorganization of the Jefferson County system holds a peculiar interest for the student of dual systems in the South.   The recommendations, it is true, were made on the basis of transforming the system of finance and control from a district- to a county-unit organization, whereas in most of the Southern states, the Negro schools are already on a county-wide basis.   The plans apply, however, to any county system where there are large numbers of educables to be reached.

The survey committee was guided by the following principles:

1.   Every child has the right to attend school.
2.   Every child has the right to be taught by a trained teacher.
3.   Every child has the right to attend a school which provides for knowledge of, practice in, and ideals of, all the seven cardinal principles of education—health, command of the fundamental processes, worthy home membership, vocational efficiency, citizenship, sane leisure activities, and ethical character.
4.   Every child has the right to be transported to school at public expense when distance from his home to the school warrants it.
5.   Every child has the right to attend school as many days as any other, and has the right to attend high school. He has the right to attend school in a modern building, adequately equipped.

Teachers' salaries have been set at points commensurate with the cost of training.

Advantages of the Proposed Plan

1.   Under the proposed reorganization, every Negro child in Jefferson County will have an opportunity to attend a standard elementary school for at least eight months.
2.   Every child will have an opportunity to attend a public high school.

3. The larger schools proposed will be able to secure better-trained teachers than are employed at present.

4. Costs of operation and maintenance for the county as a whole will be reduced.

5. The plan makes possible the maximum return for the amount of money expended.[5]

Altogether, the plan of reorganization contemplated the expenditure of approximately $92,000 annually on the Negro rural-school population of Jefferson County, or a per capita payment for all purposes of $8.69 annually compared to the former payment of $4.06, per child aged 5–19.

The plan provided for *teaching needs*: one teacher for grade or junior-high-school work to every 40–45 pupils in average daily attendance. This would provide for 133 teachers for the districts outside of Pine Bluff. Teachers were to meet the requirements of the state equalization board as to training, with all elementary and junior-high-school teachers to have not less than two years of college training, and all high-school teachers to have not less than four years of college training. The survey staff explained that

> . . . it had no intention of displacing the many capable teachers now employed in the county who do not have such training as proposed. However, it is hoped that replacements meet the requirements and that teachers now in service begin systematic effort to meet requirements by college attendance, extension and correspondence courses.[6]

The teachers were to be paid an average annual salary of $601, compared to the previous salary of $350.

Consolidation and transportation. The county was to be divided into three areas. In the Pine Bluff area, twenty

---

[5] *A Survey of Negro Education in Jefferson County, Arkansas*, by the Division of Negro Education of the State Department of Education and the County Superintendent of Schools of Jefferson County, pp. 43–44.

[6] *Jefferson County Survey, op. cit.,* p. 28.

of thirty rural schools were to be abolished or consolidated. There would remain two six-teacher, one five-teacher, one three-teacher, four two-teacher, and two one-teacher schools. The cost of providing thirty-four new classrooms to care for this consolidation was placed at an annual load of $5,950, estimated on the current cost of construction in Arkansas and the retirement of bonds, at $87.50 on each $1,000 of indebtedness. Part of this building cost would be necessary for the expansion of the Pine Bluff system. Transportation costs for this area were estimated at $1,710 annually.

In the Altheimer area, fourteen of forty-four schools were to be abolished. There would remain one eight-teacher, two seven-teacher, three five-teacher, two four-teacher, three three-teacher, eight two-teacher, and eleven one-teacher schools. The cost of building forty-five classrooms and five shop-rooms was estimated to mean an annual charge of $6,388 for retiring bonds for equipment and needed buildings. Transportation costs were estimated to be $602 annually for this area.

In the Watson Chapel-Whitehall area, six out of sixteen Negro schools were to be abolished. There would be under the new plan one six-teacher, one four-teacher, two three-teacher, one two-teacher, and three one-teacher schools. Two other schools were to be utilized as demonstration schools for the State Agricultural and Mechanical College for Negroes located near Pine Bluff, and the teachers for these schools were to be provided in part by the state. The cost of building five rooms was estimated to amount to an annual charge of $612. Transportation was estimated at $200.

It will be recalled that the old budget called for an expenditure per Negro child aged 5–19 of $4.06, all of which was devoted to the payment of teachers' salaries. The new budget would find the new expenditure of $8.69 divided as follows:

Annual cost of retiring bonds for equipment and needed
  buildings, per capita Negro child aged 5–19 .... $1.22
Annual cost of transportation, per capita Negro child aged
  5–19 ....   0.23
Annual salary of teachers, per capita Negro child aged 5–19   7.24

The cost of maintaining a satisfactory school system
would vary, of course, with the density of Negroes and with
other local conditions.   There is every reason to believe,
however, that with appropriate state equalization aid and
with a budget planned, let us say, to add as little as fifty
cents annually to the per capita expenditures for Negro
educables, a plan of this sort, which would provide a school
system eminently satisfactory compared to existing conditions, would be feasible of operation in every Southern
state within a ten-year period.   The expenditure of the
state apportionment alone upon Negro schools, with no
aid from local taxes, would suffice, in a state like Louisiana,
where in 1930–1931 the state apportionment amounted to
$7.84 per educable aged 5–15, to support such a plan of
consolidation and to guarantee salaries high enough to warrant the employment of worthy teachers to work under
favorable conditions.

State Equalization

It has been shown elsewhere that most of the equalization
schemes adopted by Southern states have been designed to
equalize education for white children and not for Negroes.
It is, perhaps, a natural evolution that this should be.   The
problem of financing schools for both races, however, would
be immensely simplified if Southern states could adopt equalization schemes based on true wealth rather than on the
percentage of Negroes in the population.   As the situation now is, "black" counties exert their influence to maintain the *status quo*, while "white" counties strive unceasingly
to redistribute the state school funds so as to take the ap-

portionments away from the minority white populations in the "black" counties and spread them more evenly among the white majorities of the "white" counties. The majority of black children in the "black" counties are helpless victims between these two contending white factions.

There are two ways in which the conflict could be resolved. In the first place, the education of Negro children could be made primarily a matter of state and not of local concern, even if the white schools were left to find their support partially from local sources. It would be difficult to accomplish this end by legislative means, for such separate treatment, in all likelihood, would be unconstitutional. The equalization fund laws have been ingeniously framed to avoid the semblance of sectional favoritism within states. An equalization fund based upon illiteracy is, perhaps, the only device which could focus upon counties with a large Negro population; but the "white" counties are not likely to permit any more state funds to go to "black" counties until present inequalities between white children are eliminated.

The other way in which equalization could function in schools for Negro children would be to make participation mandatory upon all counties, with rigid schedules for requirement and enforcement of minimum standards. It would be necessary, of course, to set these minimal standards in such a way that they would represent a real advance upon the current status of the Negro schools. If they did so, however, they would not be acceptable to "black" counties.

It appears that the problem of the separate Negro school in those counties where there is a large proportion of Negroes must wait upon the development of state control, finance, and administration before it can look forward to expansion beyond the bare essentials of an educational system.

City Systems

The differences between educational facilities for rural and urban Negro children are as great as those between white and Negro children in the South. While the per capita expenditures for white children in rural sections may frequently be from twenty to thirty times as great as for Negroes, the variation in cities rarely exceeds the proportion of four to one and in most cases is even less.

Where differences are smaller, the difficulties of equalization are correspondingly less. If a school board adopted the policy of equalization in expenditures for the Negro schools adjusted over a ten-, fifteen-, or twenty-year period, the transition might be made smoothly and without any friction.

The record of expenditures for teachers' salaries in the city of Nashville, Tennessee, has been referred to above. Assuming that expenditures for white children will advance at a constant ratio measured by the development since 1890, a twenty-year plan of equalization for the city would mean that the payments for white children would be used as an index toward which a positive effort would be made year by year to approximate payments for Negro children. In 1931, it would have cost the city of Nashville $87,786 to equalize instructional services for children of the two races. The abrupt attempt to equalize this variance in a single year would hardly be undertaken with equanimity by any school board or school superintendent. It would involve the immediate raising of the tax levy for the city from $29.80 per thousand to $30.30 per thousand. This increase, however moderate in itself, would certainly be resisted vigorously at a time when all taxes are being subjected to extraordinary scrutiny.

However, if the board of education declared as its policy that educational facilities, as shown by expenditures, should be equal for the two races, it would be possible to work in the direction of equalization with certainty, although very gradually. The plan would call for a gradual approximation of per capita payments for Negroes to those for whites. It may be, of course, that educational expenditures have reached their maximal point for both races; but the principle of using expenditures for white children as an index upon which to base payments for Negroes, until the two are equalized, would not be affected by steadily declining expenditures for white children. Per capita payments for white children now exceed those for Negroes by approximately 60 per cent. A twenty-year program of equalization would mean that school officials would adopt a constant rate by which this variation would be decreased by three per cent annually. The amount of equalization attempted yearly, of course, would depend upon the time-span over which the process was projected. A schedule for such an equalization program is presented below, with the period from 1890 to 1930 taken as the basis for projecting the curve of annual increase into the future.

To equalize expenditures between the races in Nashville, so far as the payments for teachers' salaries are concerned, would have cost the difference between white and Negro per capita expenditures ($27.55 and $17.25), or $10.30 for each Negro child in addition to what is now spent on him, or a total of $87,786.70. The present city levy is .0298 per dollar, $2.98 per hundred, $29.80 per thousand. The assessed valuation of the city is $176,620,151. To raise the additional money for equalizing the salaries of Negro with those of white teachers could be done by adding .0005 to the present .0298 on the dollar, making the new rate:

        .0298 plus .0005 on the dollar equals .0303
        $2.98 plus .05 equals $3.03 on the hundred
        $29.80 plus .50 equals $30.30 on the thousand

Equalization would therefore cost approximately fifty cents additional taxation per thousand of assessed valuation in the city of Nashville.

This need not be done at once. If distributed over a twenty-year period, the change could be effected gradually with no shock to the body politic, adding 2½ cents to the thousand each year, or in accordance with the following provision. The expenditures for white children have averaged a two-per-cent annual increase per child since 1890. If this rate is continued, payments per child will be as shown in Table LVII.

TABLE LVII

A SCHEME FOR EQUALIZING TEACHERS' SALARIES IN NASHVILLE

Year	White Payments As Predicted Per Child	Negro Payments As Predicted— No Plan	Negro Payments As Planned to Equalize
1932–1933	$28.10	$17.61	$18.09
1933–1934	28.66	17.97	18.97
1934–1935	29.23	18.34	19.87
1935–1936	29.81	18.72	20.81
1936–1937	30.40	19.11	21.76
1937–1938	31.31	19.51	22.98
1938–1939	31.93	19.92	24.48
1939–1940	32.56	20.34	25.57
1940–1941	33.21	20.77	26.69
1941–1942	33.87	21.20	27.84
1942–1943	34.55	21.64	29.03
1943–1944	35.24	22.09	29.67
1944–1945	35.94	22.55	30.90
1945–1946	36.65	23.02	32.18
1946–1947	37.38	23.50	33.49
1947–1948	38.12	23.99	34.85
1948–1949	38.89	24.49	36.25
1949–1950	39.67	25.00	37.68
1950–1951	40.46	25.52	39.16
1951–1952	41.27	26.05	40.69
1952–1953	42.09	26.59	42.09

Summary—The Ideal

Careful planning of outlays would do much to improve Negro schools, even in those areas where the sums now expended are ridiculously small. In too many cases, school officials have the attitude that nothing can be done because no more money is available. The setting up of definite objectives would allow present resources to be expended with much greater efficiency and would lead the way to the provision of larger opportunities for Negro children through increased funds. A plan which calls only for more interest and sympathy is better than no plan at all.

The ideal system, planned to support education as an enterprise guaranteeing the equality of educational opportunity for all children, white and black, in the United States, would be based upon the responsibility of the Nation for financing schools for the Nation's citizens. This ideal system would involve a much greater degree of centralization of administration than is now in vogue. Federal appropriations would be based upon the ability of states to support education for all of the children and their effort in the assumption of this responsibility. Such Federal equalization would require an equality of educational opportunity within states maintaining separate systems but would leave the determination of policies and particular techniques to local authorities.

State systems with large Negro populations would have Negroes on policy-determining boards of education. The same provision would be made in smaller units of administration.

Along with educational improvements, there should go far-reaching coördinations between other agencies of social betterment in the extension of these services to the masses of Negroes and whites. Housing, health, wages, and working conditions need to be synchronized with educational reforms as objectives of attack.

The Fact

Since the financing of schools for Negroes is the root of the whole matter, where separate systems are involved, the amount of money spent on Negro children can be used as an index to show what progress is being made or what is possible. In county units, the experience of Jefferson County, Arkansas, furnishes an intelligent example of the manner in which intelligent planning can lay a foundation for a greatly improved system even in those cases where a wide variation in expenditures for white and Negro children is permitted to continue. With no compromise with the lasting conviction that Negro children should, in an ideal situation, share equally with whites in the benefits provided by a public school system, it is possible by intelligent budgeting to make the best of situations as they now exist and to enhance greatly the efficiency of the schools.

State equalization is the logical method by which school facilities both for white and for Negro children can be equalized within states. In setting up these funds, care should be taken (*a*) to provide a minimum which shall actually be in advance of existing state-wide conditions for Negroes, and (*b*) to prevent the misuse of state funds such as has occurred in the past, by which counties with large Negro populations avoid the necessity of local effort by misappropriating state apportionments for Negroes to white children. It might even be feasible to treat schools for Negroes as a state function while leaving schools for white children still a partially local responsibility. Such a plan would be of great help to the schools for white children in "white" counties and to those for Negro children in "black" counties. It would bear heavily upon existing provisions for white children in counties with large Negro populations, now far above the state average, and upon schools for Negro children in areas with small Negro populations where there is now but a slight difference between the provisions made for Negroes and whites.

In a typical city system such as is represented by Nashville, Tennessee, the authorities should carefully plan for improvement with advantages provided for white children as the basis of comparison. School officials in the South have a deep-seated prejudice toward any sort of "comparisons" between advantages for the two races, believing that the schools for white children should be measured unto themselves, and the progress in Negro schools reflected against their past, alone. But this prejudice is both harmful and unintelligent. If our ideal is an equality of educational opportunity for all children, the separate system must constantly engage in comparisons between the two branches. "Progress" in Negro schools means nothing if the degree of equality in the provision of opportunity is actually becoming less and less tangible.

Furthermore, a system by which improvements for Negro schools are planned against a background furnished by the advances in white systems gives order and clear understanding to what might otherwise be a hit-or-miss proceeding. The education of white children is bound to remain the dominant interest in all systems in this country which have separate schools for Negroes. The state constitutions of all Southern states call for inequality in the provision of opportunity. Why, then, not use the white system as the basic index for measuring the advances made, or projected, in Negro schools?

In any event, planning means little more than an attempt to socialize individual convictions. With no more than a modal share of catastrophes and disasters, our generation may expect to usher in the day when communities and nations begin to substitute rational and organic development for the vagaries of social evolution. The equality of opportunity for all children has few enemies today even in dictatorships. The new watchword of economic security sounds the battle-cry on a new frontier. A century ago, Horace Mann raised his slogan of "a free school for a free people" in this country. There are yet occasional sectors where the battle still continues, but the vanguard of the

American people has moved on to assume new positions for the struggle of the present.

Although the shouting and the tumult have found a new focus for the national conscience, the grim realities of the day still find here and there a "lost battalion," detached from the main tide of the current but fighting valiantly on in spite of their isolation. It was Horace Mann who said, also, that the man who kept the light of knowledge from a child was performing "devilish miracles." Those of us who still struggle for the complete realization of the American ideal of equal opportunity for all children are contesting the medieval system by which several million children are deprived of the chance that most individual consciences will grant is theirs. The war for human betterment is being prosecuted on other and wider fronts. The contribution which can be made to ultimate success by the occasional skirmishes of detached companies is inconsequential.

Great causes have a pervasive rhythm, a tonicity like that upon which depends the persistence of organic life in individuals. The phrase so dear to a more religious generation, "in tune with the Infinite," finds justification when applied to the historical perspective of the life cycle of individuals and of societies. In identifying herself with the cause of the Negro child, in seeking to give to this child some measure, however slight, of the opportunity not grudged to other American children, the teacher of Negro children, and likewise the administrator of schools for Negro children, is "in tune with the infinite." The thought is not sentimental; it is the sense of human existence in accord with one of the most fundamental of human verities.

CHAPTER XXII

A 1965 Retrospective Of American Negro Education

Acculturation, Assimilation, and Education

STUDENTS have described what happens when people of varying cultures meet in such terms as: acculturation, trans-culturation, assimilation. By the first term we mean "a process of intercultural borrowing, marked by the continuous transmission of traits and elements between diverse peoples and resulting in new and blended patterns," perhaps best represented by what occurs when a "primitive culture" has "direct and prolonged contact with an advanced society."

We talk less today of "primitive" as compared to "advanced" societies. What happened when the African met European culture in the New World was a case of a great variety of "weak" cultures represented by degraded and powerless slaves, coming into contact with an all-powerful culture that despised and scorned the enslaved carriers of similarly despised cultures, and valued slaves only for the raw labor they could contribute to the community. Only the feeblest efforts were made to subject the slave to systematic and purposeful acculturation; the conversion of the heathen to Christianity was long given as a justification for the institution of chattel slavery, and some effort was made to win them to the religious culture of the master race.

"Assimilation" is a term usually applied to the biological

absorption by a dominant group of a subordinate one. Propinquity of diverse ethnic groups has usually been accompanied by miscegenation, although King Alexander's systematic encouragement of intermarriage between his Greek warriors and Persian noblewomen is perhaps the sole example of a planned program of this kind. While there was no such program in the Americas, miscegenation did begin as soon as the Africans reached the Americas and lived in contact with Europeans and with the indigenous Indian population.

The process of acculturation is accelerated by formal, systematic education. As this book indicated thirty years ago, any efforts to acculturate the African, who became the American Negro, were limited up to the time of emancipation to sporadic and exceptional labors with the small free portions of this population, and to individuals. Meanwhile, the African-in-America was developing a subculture of his own, and it was between this subculture and the dominant white American culture, which likewise became in time less European, that the practice of intercultural borrowings went on, particularly in such areas as music and the dance.

Figure 9, below, attempts to present in schematic form a picture of the acculturation of the American Negro. The first American culture mosaic had three major elements in it. There were three major infusions both of ethnic stock and of "continental" culture; two were "weak" cultures, both because of the numbers of persons represented and because of the lack of power possessed by their carriers: the American Indian and the African. Physical miscegenation began early, as the earliest colonial legislation assessing penalties for intermarriage and cohabitation between black and white testify. Miscegenation involving Africans and Indians was not interdicted by law, and there was an appreciable infusion of American Indian strains into the amal-

gam, especially on the borders between the advancing
European settlement front and the retreating Indian areas.
On such borders, the slaves could run away to the Indians,
and they frequently did; the Indians left stranded by the
westward migration of their peoples were a lower caste along
wtih the Africans, and they mingled freely without social
or legal prohibition.   It will be remembered that the
Seminole Wars in Florida were provoked when white settlers
in South Georgia, seeking to recapture runaway slaves,
seized the Negro wife and children of the warrior Chief
Osceola.   There yet remain as far east as the Atlantic Seaboard isolated mixed communities of White-Indian-Negro
extraction that have maintained their identity for two centuries.   The traditions of American Negro families very
often include reference to dimly remembered Indian forebears, men and women; there is every reason to believe that
these oral traditions are authentic.

But Indian-African miscegenation was not a significant
factor in acculturation.   Both cultures were overpowered
by the omnipotent European culture, and by the American
cultural traits that grew out of European roots.   Miscegenation involving Africans and Europeans were important
culturally as well as biologically.   An ancient belief of
Americans has been faith in the "mulatto hypothesis": that
offspring of blacks and whites are genetically more intelligent than their darker and unmixed brethren because of the
superiority of the white "blood."   This "blood mystique"
neglects the fact that miscegenation was likely to be based
on propinquity.   The Negro women most frequently involved in miscegenatory situations were those who were in
closest physical and cultural contact with the white master
class.   They were likely to be the house servants who had
been selected for their close approximation to the cultural
patterns of the "big house" and had been subjected, after

recruiting as personal retainer, to an informal education in those patterns—in manners, in speech, in dress, and even, on occasion, in letters. Once "born to the manor" the mulatto was the more likely, because of his kinship to the master family, to be favored openly, given preferred and personal attention—again extending frequently to formal and informal education that was prescribed for the field hand—and, in the end, likely to be emancipated and even endowed with a substantial economic stake with which to begin a free existence.

The open and unashamed existence of an extensive system of concubinage on southern plantations was described by the southern diarist Mary Boykin Chesnut—in a passage bowdlerized in the first, 1905, edition, that was originally sponsored by the United Daughters of the Confederacy:

> God forgive us, but ours is a monstrous system, a wrong and an iniquity! Like the patriarchs of old, our men live all in one house with their wives and their concubines; and the mulattoes one sees in every family partly resemble the white children. Any lady is ready to tell you who is the father of all the mulattoe children in everybody's household but her own. These, she seems to think, drop from the clouds.[1]

A Negro folk saying up to contemporary generations was a tribute to the informal education that was a part of the acculturation experienced by Negroes who had close contact with members of the dominant culture. An outstanding member of their group would be characterized by saying, "Man, that is a smart Negro! The white folks must have raised him!"

A study of the autobiographies of many early Negro scholars leads one to believe that the acculturation afforded by close contact with disciplined and cultured whites was

[1] Mary Boykin Chesnut (Ed. by Ben Ames Williams), *A Diary from Dixie*, Houghton Mifflin Company, Boston, 1961, pp. 21-22.

probably a more decisive factor than the mystical "white blood" effect. Carleton S. Putnam explains the excellence of George Washington Carver, the chemist, as being due to his "white blood," which, in turn, is proved by "Carver's blue eyes."[22] It will be remembered, also, that Carver was a foundling who was reared through adolescence by a sturdy German farming couple who must certainly have taught the boy the excellent work habits he showed in his later life.

W. S. Scarborough, who was born a slave in Macon, Georgia, in 1854, was the grandson of a wealthy white planter who kept his daughter in slavery but provided her with a house of her own. She married a free Negro who was a railroad conductor, and, with his good wages and help from her father, she found the money to hire white tutors for her son. Scarborough graduated from Oberlin College and became Professor of Latin and Greek (later President) at Wilberforce University in Ohio and an outstanding philologist who read papers at associations of his craft in the United States and England.[3] In this same city, an Irish planter, Patrick Healy, fathered a large family by a Negro woman. Healey sent the boys north for an education at Holy Cross College. One became Bishop of Portland, Maine; another, a parish priest in Boston; and a third,

[2] Carleton S. Putnam, *Race and Reason, A Yankee View,* Public Affairs Press, Washington, 1961. This author knew Carver personally, and is unable to confirm the supposed truth of the statement about Carver's blue eyes. His attending physician during his last illness, who knew Dr. Carver well, states that Dr. Carver was afflicted by *Arcis senilis,* a defect in the aged, ringing the pupil with a whitish-bluish ring that might give the appearance of blueness to light brownish eyes. Apparently no records exist; the Alabama State Department of Vital Statistics has no registration of Dr. Carver's death certificate, on which the color of his eyes might have been indicated.

[3] Frances P. Weisenburger, *Williams Sanders Scarborough,* pamphlet reprinted in *Ohio History,* Vol. 71, No. 3 (October 1962), and Vol. 72, No. 1 (January 1963).

after winning a Ph.D. at Louvain, President of Georgetown University in Washington.[4]

Other instances could be quoted in profusion. Studies conducted by the author indicate that the great majority of Negroes who have earned academic doctorates are the descendants either of long lines of highly literate free Negroes or of slaves who obtained literacy because they were favored by their white relatives in the families that had owned their forebears.

Although he is more aptly described as a leader than a scholar, Booker T. Washington, it will be recalled, was admitted to Hampton Institute by a Yankee preceptress, Miss Mackie, who set his entrance examinations as the task of cleaning up a classroom. His thoroughness won him admission. He had learned to be thorough by working as a houseboy for another Yankee woman, Mrs. Ruffner, in West Virginia.

Such contacts facilitated acculturation and acquisition of the values and habits and patterns of what we may call the "standard American culture."

But it will also be remembered that a great many slaves were in close contact with the vicious, the amoral (if not immoral), the ignorant, the brutal, and the violent master, in a section where these human qualities were not unusual and the slave system was innately vicious. They, too, learned habits and dispositions of the culture that have been handed down to their descendants through the generations.

Similarly, they lost their own forms of family and kinship affections, loyalties, and securities, and they were introduced to a social order in which promiscuous fornication was prized as a device to encourage the early and sustained production of more chattels for use and sale.

---

[4] Albert S. Foley, S.J., *God's Men of Color,* Farrar, Straus, and Co., New York, 1955, pp. 23-31.

If freed, even in the North they faced an endless cycle of proscriptive legislation: disfranchisement, employment bans except in the most menial occupations, and segregation from the communal life.[5] Elementary education was provided scantily, and then as a charity; secondary, collegiate, and professional education were almost everywhere—South and North—beyond the wildest dreams of the freed man.

Under these circumstances, only a small fragment of the American Negro people were participants in free cultural acculturation by 1863. Few had been assimilated, and only a microscopic moiety had received by the end of the slave period—the sixth generation in the United States—a standard American education.

Figure 9 represents the growth of this population, and the extent of its acculturation, by generations since the first United States Decennial Census in 1790, measuring a generation as including three decades, in a social order where early childbearing was encouraged and stimulated.

The first census in 1790 enumerated 757,208 persons of African descent, of whom 7.9 per cent were designated as "free colored persons." By 1810, the total number had swelled to 1,377,808, of whom 186,446 were "free colored;" the percentage of 13.5 listed as free was the highest proportion of free persons enumerated before emancipation, and doubtless was swelled between 1790 and 1810 by the gradual emancipation of numerous persons in the northeastern states. After 1810 the percentage of free persons declined; by 1860, there were 488,071, or 10 per cent of this population, who were free, out of a total of 4,441,130. We repeat: a study of the family histories of Negro leaders in the professionally and technically trained of the group shows

5 Leon F. Litwack, *North of Slavery: The Negro in the Free States, 1790-1860,* University of Chicago Press, Chicago, 1965.

FIGURE 9. SCHEMATIC PRESENTATION OF STATUS OF THE AMERICAN NEGRO, BY SLAVE OR FREE STATUS, 1790·1860, AND BY SOCIAL CLASS, 1870·1960

I	1640 - 1660
II	1670 - 1690
III	1700 - 1720
IV	1730 - 1750
V	1760 - 1780

GENERATION	YEAR	TOTAL POPULATION	FREE POPULATION NO.	FREE POPULATION %
VI	1790	757.808	59.557	7.9
	1800	1.002.059	108.457	10.8
	1810	1.377.808	186.446	13.0
VII	1820	1.771.656	233.634	13.1
	1830	2.328.642	319.599	13.1
	1840	2.873.648	386.293	13.1
VIII	1850	3.638.808	434.495	11.3
	1860	4.441.130	488.070	10.4

POPULATION BY CLASS

GENERATION	YEAR	TOTAL	PERCENTAGE LOWER	PERCENTAGE MIDDLE	PERCENTAGE UPPER
IX	1870	4.880.009	96.9	3.0	0.1
	1880	6.580.793	95.9	4.0	0.1
	1890	7.488.676	94.8	5.0	0.2
	1900	8.883.994	92.7	7.0	0.3
X	1910	9.827.763	89.5	9.0	1.5
	1920	10.463.131	84.0	14.0	2.0
	1930	11.891.143	79.7	18.0	2.3
XI	1940	12.865.518	77.6	20.0	2.4
	1950	14.894.000	72.5	25.0	2.5
	1960	18.872.000	66.0	30.0	4.0

WHITE CLASS DISTRIBUTION—
1960 PERCENTAGE ESTIMATED: 15.0 70.0 15.0

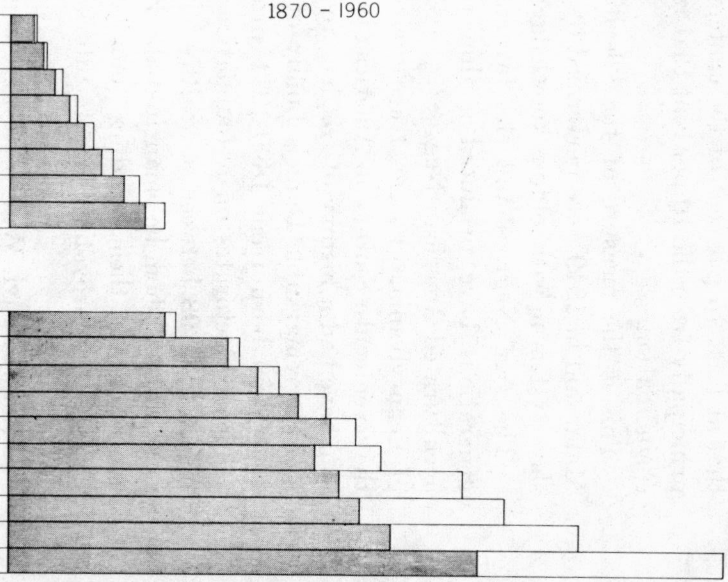

LEGEND

SLAVE, 1790 - 1860; LOWER CLASS, 1870-1960

FREE, 1790 - 1860; MIDDLE AND UPPER CLASS, 1870 - 1960

that at least 75 per cent of the contemporary number come principally from the 10 per cent that was free at the time of emancipation.

This is the measure of the "devilish miracles" Horace Mann said in 1849 were performed by those who upheld the slave system in withholding knowledge from a slave child.

The free Negroes and the favored house servants for generations have produced a thin trickle of thoroughly acculturated American Negroes: the Mossells and Duckerys of Pennsylvania, who can trace their family lines back to the seventeenth century in America; the Colsons of Virginia, who have had a history of freedom and literacy since 1742; and the remarkable Daniels family of Virginia, who in the generation born from 1890-1914 produced six holders of academic doctorates on a foundation that goes back to a liaison in 1798 between a wealthy Virginia planter and a slave woman whom he emancipated. He provided the finest education for them, sending four boys north to Oberlin College, and providing private tutors for the one daughter of the family.

After the Civil War there were a number of new beginnings among the formerly enslaved youth who attended the extraordinary Mission Colleges in the South. In their turn they founded families and begat children upon whom they bestowed the rich blessings of easy literacy, academic discipline, high motivation, and excellent work and study habits.

As seen further in Figure 9, the Civil War marked the end of chattel slavery. For the first time in American history, the Negro entered into a semblance of class-divided society. The direct infusions of African genes and culture ended only with the collapse of the Confederacy, for occasional boatloads of captive Africans were smuggled into the country up to the very end of the conflict. But the agricultural system of the South, where the greatest number of Africans

had lived, was reorganized on a tenant system that in many
areas was scarcely distinguishable from the system operating
in slave times. No effective school system was provided for
the masses. What had been the culture of Africa, and had
become the culture of the American chattel slave, became an
improvised culture of the sharecropper.

The great migration of these folk began fifty years after
emancipation, when the industrial boom in northern industries begun by World War I began to draw labor from
anywhere, to perform the labors the European migrant had
before undertaken. For the next fifty years the migration
continued. The people were segregatd in urban ghettoes
(they call them "zoos"), and the subculture took on new
adaptations to new types of traumatic individual and social
experiences. The subculture became one increasingly difficult to permeate with the ordinary intentions and devices
of formal education as they were applied in the ghetto
schools in the North and the South. To men and women—
and especially the families—the urban ghetto was what the
sociologist E. Franklin Frazier called it: "the City of Destruction."[6] It was of this situation that James Bryant
Conant, on seeing the Negro ghetto for the first time twenty
years after Frazier had described it, said:

> The task with which the school people in the slums must
> struggle is, on the one hand, to prepare a student for getting
> and keeping a job as soon as he leaves school, and on the
> other hand, to encourage those who have academic talent to
> aim at a profession through higher education. The task thus
> stated seems simple. In actual fact the difficulties are
> appalling.[7]

The task in fact is of even more heroic proportions. It is

[6] E. Franklin Frazier, *The Negro Family in the United States,* The University of Chicago Press, Chicago, 1940, pp. 271-392.
[7] *Slums and Suburbs,* McGraw-Hill Book Company, New York, 1961,
p. 2.

to undo what a rigid chattel slave system, followed by a social caste system almost as corrupting, has done to the personality and learning structure of a vast population, and to substitute the attitudes, habits, and knowledge-level of a typically American standard. It is a task beyond the present equipment and powers of the formal school system as presently conceived and functioning.

As Figure 9 shows, there has been a slow growth in the proportion of American Negroes who have attained the habits, understandings, and status of the standard American middle class; perhaps from 2 to 4 per cent have risen above that level. Defining "class" in this instance as the level of comparative mastery of the habits and skills and understandings calculated to be necessary for various occupations in our modern technological culture, the comparable status of American whites and Negroes might be estimated as follows for 1965:

CLASS	High Estimate		Low Estimate	
	White	Negro	White	Negro
Upper Class (Able to pursue successfully prolonged courses of instruction leading to employment as Architects, Engineers, Lawyers, University professors in the Arts and Sciences, high-level employees in the new technology, Civil Service, etc.)	15%	4%	10%	2%
Middle Class (Middle occupations in business, public school teaching, personal service, crafts, technology, manufacturing, industries, transportation, agriculture.)	70%	30%	60%	20%
Lower Class (Laborers, farm day laborers and tenants, lower forms of personal service, unskilled work; the unemployed.)	15%	66%	30%	78%

"Psychological" and Achievement Examinations
as Instruments for Measuring Acculturation

Almost from the beginning of the use of standardized tests in American education, these instruments were regarded as infallible measures of the innate "intelligence" of children and of adults. Only within the last three decades have psychologists, and, later, educators and the general public, begun to see in them marvellously efficient constructions by which the social class and environmental background of the child might be accurately measured, yielding evidence, not as to the innate capacity of the child, but of the degree to which the child approximated standard class performance, or varied from that norm. If our schools operated from the assumption that all men are, indeed, created equal, and that standard tests tell us how far from equality social circumstances have distorted the act of equal creation, we should have laid the foundation for a true scientific theory of education. In this section, the author does espouse the theory that all men *are* created equal; that there are admitted initial defects, due to malformations due to rare genetic imbalances and post-natal and natal accidents, many of which are subject to correction after birth, but which at the most do not affect more than one half of one per cent of children.

This concept is important to the education of American Negro children because since the invention of standardized tests they have been made the particular butt of facile racialistic interpretations of the scores such children make in comparison with other children. The first popularization of the theory that "intelligence tests" give an accurate description of the innate "intelligence" of children by race and national origins was contained in the book *A Study of American Intelligence*, published in 1923 by Carl G. Brigham. The book was a condensation of the larger *Memoir*

XV, sponsored by a committee including the leading American psychologists of the day: R. M. Yerkes, Lewis M. Terman, R. S. Woodworth, E. L. Thorndike, L. L. Thurstone, and others.[8]

The *Memoir* presented evidence purporting to show that Negroes, and whites of southern European racial stock, were inferior to whites of northern European stock. The material of the *Memoir* became a basic "fact" for instruction in American schools of education during the 1920's and 1930's. It was widely used by the Ku Klux Klan and other racialistic and nationalistic organizations to secure the passage of an immigration bill in 1923, in which discriminatory quotas were adopted to limit the number of immigrants admitted from southern and eastern Europe.

Carl C. Brigham recanted before his death in the early 1930's; the great educational psychologists who signed *Memoir XV*, never did. The belief became a part of the folklore of American education that Negroes were innately inferior as proven by "intelligence test" scores. While the great majority of psychologists have, in our generation, abandoned that idea, a vigorous propaganda is yet being pressed, notably by Carleton Putnam and the psychologist Henry E. Garrett, a former professor in Columbia University, now a lecturer in the University of Virginia, and his former student Audrey Shuey, Chairman of the Department of Psychology at the Randolph-Macon College.[9]

[8] R. M. Yerkes, *Psychological Examining in the U. S. Army, Memoir XV*, National Academy of Science, 1921.

[9] See Carleton S. Putnam, *op. cit.;* Audrey M. Shuey, *The Testing of Negro Intelligence*, J. P. Bell and Company, Lynchburg, Virginia, 1958. Their materials are widely circulated by such organizations as Dr. Carl C. McIntire's Twentieth Century Reformation Hour, and the Patrick Henry Group, a "rightish radical" organization with a Richmond, Virginia, post office box. Recently a pamphlet arguing the cause of racial inferiority on test evidence was circulated to a large number of Atlanta public school teachers, including a number of Negro teachers.

The evidence that "intelligence" and other tests are excellent instruments for measuring social class and subcultures of the American culture can be taken in part from the same material used by segregationists to advance their cause. Further analysis of Army Alpha tests than that made initially by Brigham indicated that, in at least four instances, the Negro recruits of World War I from northern states made higher scores than did southern white recruits from four southern states. A neglected body of material has been the scores of individual American colleges as published in the *Educational Record* between 1928 and 1934, in which the scores made by hundreds of colleges in the American Psychological Examination were published. A review of these scores shows that the rigidly segregated white colleges of the South, year by year, tended to make lower scores than the northern and western colleges. In 1929, the scores of 5,716 Freshmen in 21 southern colleges had an average percentile of 29.9. Two Negro colleges reported the attainment of 134 Freshmen—their average percentile was 20.7. However, the better Negro college Fisk University, with a percentile score of 23, had a score superior to several well known, segregated white southern state universities.

No scores for Negro colleges were reported in the 1934 publication of the American Psychological Examination scores. Thirty-nine southern white colleges reported the results of scores in tests given to 11,726 Freshmen. The average median score made by the Freshmen at these 39 colleges was 36.7; the higher relative standing, although still appreciably below national norms, may have been due to the fact that several low-scoring colleges and universities with large enrollments reported in the 1929 results—notably the University of Georgia and the University of North Carolina—had become discouraged either from administering the examination, or from reporting the results for publication.

In Shuey's book, where with commendable industry more than 326 different studies were reviewed, the author reported that in each instance Negro children scored *either* below the white children in the community (where white children were included in the study), or below national norms.   In the 45 studies cited that did report scores for white children in their southern community, the white children in each instance scored below national norms.   Shuey quotes several studies to the effect that ". . . there is no evidence that as the socio-economic status of the Negro increases, racial test-score differences decrease."[10]

This author's argument—that the best hypothesis on which to operate a system of schools for all children should be based on the theory that "all men are created equal"— would readily admit that Negro children, when compared to the white children of the same community—on any level, from elementary to college—will show lower test scores. His explanation for this phenomenon would be that nowhere in the United States can a community including considerable numbers of Negro children be found in which the acculturation of those children has reached the same level as for the white children. He would further state that in very few areas in the South may white children be found who would score—on any level, from elementary to college—at, or above, the norms to be expected of white children in the North and West. And this, he believes, is because the southern white people likewise represent a variant subculture, with a variant degree of acculturation to the standard American culture—and this degree of variation is exposed by differences in test scores.

[10] See Shuey, *Ibid.,* pp. 151-153. A Professor McGurk, in a 1939 study made in Canada of a community of descendants of runaway slaves dating from the 1830's, is the principal reliance for Garrett and Shuey to conclude that even where educational and socio-economic status for Negroes has been equalized for long periods of time, the Negroes still show a test deficiency when compared to whites.

We are just now discovering that test scores have a geography all their own, within cities and within states, regardless of race. Studies of the geographical location of National Merit scholars show that they come principally from suburban and upper-middle-class locations within cities, seldom from the slums. In northern Illinois, for example, they come from the suburban areas in the northwestern and northern sections of Chicago and their adjoining urban upper-class areas; and from an upper-class Jewish neighborhood in southeast Chicago. National Merit winners do not come from the central city. In Kentucky the scholars come from the upper-class suburbs of Louisville, from the suburban Kentucky side of the Ohio river across from Cincinnati, and from the environs of a university community at Lexington; they do not come from the poor mountain counties, where Negroes constitute less than 1 per cent of the population.[11]

Wherever a city-wide testing survey is administered, one knows that the lower-scoring schools are slum schools, white and Negro, and that the high-scoring schools are the schools attended by the children of the upper middle class, and of the upper class.[12] In short: whatever tests do measure, they certainly measure social class—acculturation—with a precision that should make them the principal instruments by which the basic factor accelerating or impeding learning may be measured—after which appropriate steps are in order to attack the causes and the effects.

While test scores have high validity in reflecting the cul-

[11] Horace Mann Bond, "Talents and Toilets," *The Journal of Negro Education*, Vol. XXVIII, No. 1, pp. 3-14.

[12] See Robert J. Havighurst, *The Public Schools of Chicago*, The Board of Education of the City of Chicago, Chicago, 1964 *passim;* California Elementary School Administrators Association, *The Neighborhood and the School, A Study of Socio-Economic Status and School Achievement*, a pamphlet, Burlingame, California, 1962; Educational Testing Service, *Learning and Teaching in Atlanta Public Schools, 1955-1956*, Princeton, New Jersey, 1957.

tural style of the person tested, it must be remembered that they may have doubtful predictive value in gauging the ability of the student to compete with other students in learning materials that are as exotic to the child or adult from the standard culture as to the child from the variant or "deprived" culture. The practice, as in Florida, of adopting, by legislative enactment, an unrealistic "cut-off" score in the National Teachers Examination as the basis for awarding state teaching certificates, or that of some graduate school officials of adopting an arbitrary "cut-off" score in the Graduate Record Examination for admission to, or graduation from, the institution, has dubious validity, especially when applied to students coming from markedly variant subcultures or cultures, either domestic or foreign.

In the 1956 report to medical colleges on the interpretation that should be given to scores made on the Medical Admission Test of that year, the Educational Testing Service stated:

> Scores on these tests for candidates educated outside the United States should be interpreted with considerable caution. While the caution is self-evident in the case of foreign-language-speaking students, it applies also to English-speaking students educated outside the United States.[13]

There is, doubtless, a high correlation generally prevailing between test scores and academic achievement. But every graduate school which does not impose "cut-off" scores will have records of successful students whose high academic achievement is in contrast to unbelievably low test score percentiles.

It is a mechanism that has not been sufficiently studied.

[13] *Medical College Admission Test,* Confidential Report of Scores, Administration of May 5, 1956, prepared for the Association of American Medical Colleges by the Educational Testing Service, Princeton, New Jersey, pp. 1-6. Quoted in Dietrich C. Reitzes, *Negroes in Medicine,* Harvard University Press, Cambridge, 1958, p. 376.

This author believes that the explanation will be found to lie in the fact that such students come from a subculture that varies from the standard American culture.

Steps Toward Equality of Education:
Dismantling the Segregated Culture

The "I.Q."—"intelligence quotient" — of substandard groups in American life might better be called "S.Q."—"segregation quotient." It is an index of the degree to which members of the groups have been segregated from the standard stream of the culture. We have seen, in the last generation, a beginning made toward dismantling the complex of segregated life that is a necessary preface—but only a preface—to attainment of equalization of educational opportunity for all persons in this country.

As were its effects, racial segregation was manifested in every aspect of the individual's life: in transportation, that important aspect determining the free mobility of the individual person; in housing, patterns of which can define areas of residence and schooling and create true ghettoes; in participation in politics, the essential substance of personal and group liberty in a democracy; and in employment.

The landmark case in negative civil rights litigation was that of *Plessy v. Ferguson*, decided by the United States Supreme Court in 1896. This case was brought by a society of members of the old "Free Men of Color" social group in Louisiana. The plaintiffs sought to overturn a Louisiana state law that established segregated facilities in railroad transportation. The Court then ruled that it was constitutional to establish racially segregated transportation facilities, so long as they are equal. The "separate but equal" doctrine thus promulgated became the entrenched attitude of the Court—and of the nation—in regard to school segregation.[14]

The doctrine was not applied in some areas. In the case of *Buchanan v. Warley* (1917), racial zoning housing ordinances were declared to be unreasonable classifications and, under the Fourteenth Amendment to the Constitution, the power of racially restrictive covenants to enforce segregated housing in 1948 and 1953 was denied on the basis of due process. In 1927 the case of *Nixon v. Herndon* resulted in a Supreme Court decision overturning state laws barring Negroes from participation in primary elections. This decision was followed by that of *Nixon v. Condon* (1932), outlawing authorizations by states to political party executives to take such action, and *Smith v. Allwright* (1944), opening the Texas Democratic primary to Negro participation.

Beginning in 1934, the National Association for the Advancement of Colored People began a planned attack against segregation in education, although the direction taken was to sue against the obvious inequality involved, and not against segregation itself as an unconstitutional provision. The strategy involved was to focus attention at first on graduate and professional schools. The case of *Missouri ex rel Gaines v. Canada* (1938) resulted in a decision entitling a Negro applicant to attend the University of Missouri School of Law instead of accepting a scholarship in an out-of-state law school. *Sweatt v. Painter* (1950) upheld the right of a Negro to attend the University of Texas Law School instead of a hastily developed law school established by the State of Texas for Negroes. In *McLaurin v. Oklahoma State Board of Regents* (1950), the Court ruled that a Negro must be admitted to an existing law school even if a segregated law school were being built to care for him and for his class; furthermore, once admitted, the Negro was not to be sub-

[14] For the best survey of the history of civil rights litigation, see Jack Greenberg, *Race Relations and American Law*, Columbia University Press, New York, 1959, *passim*.

jected to internal segregation within the institution.

In 1950, for the first time, the attorneys for the National Association for the Advancement of Colored People made a frontal attack on school segregation as an unconstitutional practice *per se*. Four cases were consolidated in the arguments and in the decision: *Brown v. Board of Education of Topeka, Kansas* (the title case of the decision), *Briggs v. Elliott* (from Clarendon County, South Carolina), *Davis v. County School Board of Prince Edward County, Va.,* and *Gebhart v. Belton* (from Delaware).

The Supreme Court in these cases, in decisions handed down in 1954 and 1955, held "that in the field of public education the doctrine of 'separate but equal' has no place. Separate educational facilities are inherently unequal." The 1955 decision was intended to implement the broad findings of the historic 1954 declaration: ". . . the courts will require that the defendants make a prompt and reasonable start towards full compliance with our May 17, 1954 ruling," and the district courts were directed "to take such proceedings and enter such orders and decrees consistent with (the above) as are necessary and proper to admit to public schools on a racially nondiscriminatory basis *with all deliberate speed* the parties to these cases."

More than a decade has elapsed since the 1954 decision of the United States Supreme Court. The period has been marked by studied delay and evasion, by violent "hard-core" resistance to the Court's orders, and by "token" compliance. The border states, where Negro populations are sparse, have shown a greater readiness to comply, as have sections with few Negroes in other southern states (e.g., Alabama, Tennessee, Texas). In these areas there has been a tendency to consolidate small Negro schools with the larger white school in the district. An irony is that the Negro teachers in the formerly segregated Negro school is likely to be displaced, and not replaced by another Negro.

The Education of the Negro

Elaborate statistics describing the course of desegregation were kept from 1954 to 1963-1964 by the *Southern School News,* now discontinued. From the data given in Table LVIII one can observe the snail-like pace with which the "deliberate speed" enjoined by the Court in 1955 has progressed.

TABLE LVIII

DESEGREGATION OF PUBLIC SCHOOLS IN
THE SOUTHERN STATES, 1954-1955 TO 1965-1966†

State	Negroes in School With Whites					
	1954-1955		1963-1964		1965-1966	
	Number	%	Number	%	Number	%
LOWER SOUTH						
Alabama	0	0.00	21	.007	717	0.25
Arkansas	20	0.02	362	.316	2,343	2.50
Florida	0	0.00	3,650	1.53	17,000	5.90
Georgia	0	0.00	177	.052	4,240	1.30
Louisiana	0	0.00	1,814	.602	1,850	0.68
Mississippi	0	0.00	0	.000	928	0.34
North Carolina	0	0.00	1,865	.537	8,000	2.10
South Carolina	0	0.00	9	.003	3,531	1.50
Tennessee	0	0.00	4,486	2.720	16,422	9.10
Texas	3	0.001	18,000*	5.250	75,340	20.00
Virginia	0	0.00	3,721	1.630	21,045	14.10
TOTAL— LOWER SOUTH	23	0.001	34,105	1.170	151,516	5.23
BORDER STATES						
Delaware	200*	1.91	10,209	56.250	No data	
Dist. of Columbia	No data		98,813	83.800	No data	
Kentucky	0	0.00	29,855	54.400	No data	
Maryland	4,332*	0.12	76,906	47.80	No data	
Missouri	0	0.00	40,000*	42.10	No data	
Oklahoma	0	0.00	12,289*	28.00	No data	
West Virginia	1,100	4.29	13,659*	58.20	No data	
TOTAL—BORDER	5,432*	No data	281,731*	54.80*	No data	

† The data for 1954-1955 and for 1963-1964 are taken from the *Statistical Summaries* published by the *Southern School News,* an independent research and fact-finding publication issued from George Peabody College for Teachers, that was discontinued July, 1965. The data for 1965-1966 are from the estimates of the Southern Regional Council, published in *Special Report,* September, 1965, at 5 Forsyth Street, N. W., Atlanta, Georgia. *Special Report* points out that estimates of the speed of desegregation as given in 1965 by the United States Office of Education are inaccurate and exaggerated.

*Estimated.

The slight acceleration of school desegregation in the states of the Lower South reflected in the statistics for 1965-1966 are doubtless due to the pressures brought by new federal aid-to-education bills accompanied by anti-discrimination requirements imposed by the new legislation and by the Civil Rights Act of 1964.

Dismantling De Facto Segregation

Three decades ago few realized, and no one was permitted to say, that it was an anomalous irony to speak of giving an "American" education to a group designated as "American Negroes." In those thirty years the American people, acting through the executive, judicial, and legislative branches of the government, have begun the serious business of dismantling the marvellously complicated and, educationally speaking, all-important edifice of racial segregation in the United States.

As noted above, political desegregation in the South has been under way during the period here studied; it has been greatly accelerated by the Civil Rights Act of 1964 and the Voting Rights Bill of 1965, as well as by judicial decisions reapportioning state legislatures on a "one-man-one-vote" basis, and so breaking the back of the control of the political machinery by which a white minority oligarchy had preserved and strengthened the caste system in all of its many ramifications. But the fact is that "deliberate speed" in desegregation is yet extremely deliberate.

In the process, we have discovered that the increasingly urban residence of Negroes, North and South, has resulted in a segregation of these people from the main stream of American culture frequently as complete in northern urban centers as in the rural South. In 1910, 73 per cent of Negro people lived in rural areas, as compared to 52 per cent of whites. By 1960, 73 per cent of Negroes lived in cities, while only 70 per cent of white population was urban.[15]

This was a population that principally derived from southern areas that in 1910 were receiving, for their children, per capita annual expenditures of from $0.50 to $2.50, as compared to from $5.00 to $45.00 per child spent on their white contemporaries in the same counties; in short, it was a population that was receiving practically no education from public funds at all. This was the slum population whose educational plight was discovered in 1960 by the former president of Harvard University, and described in the volume, *Slums and Suburbs*.[16] They were living in modern ghettoes, hemmed in, as were the Jews of the Middle Ages, in geographical areas circumscribed by law and by custom and by commercial and social covenants. Unlike the Jewish ghetto of the Middle Ages, however, it was a community with no tradition of highly literate religious leadership; rather, it had a fractured tradition of family life, and no tradition of religious-based literacy.

The urbanization of the Negro and his segregation in the central city ghetto has been accompanied by the increased affluence of sectors of the white population, and the growing "status" aspirations of this portion of the population that has led it to desert the central city and move to the suburbs. An analysis of the enrollment in the schools of Chicago, Baltimore, and Detroit, in 1962-1963, illustrates *de facto* segregation as it increasingly exists:

The schools of Washington, D. C., have now for almost a decade enrolled a majority Negro population in its public schools; such cities as Atlanta, Chicago, and Philadelphia had by 1965 returned in their enrollment a majority Negro

[15] Phillip M. Hauser, "Demographic Factors in the Integration of the Negro," *The Negro American*, in *Daedalus*, Vol. 94, No. 4, pp. 847-877.
[16] Conant, *op. cit.*

TABLE LIX*

EXTENT OF INTEGRATION IN CHICAGO, DETROIT, AND BALTIMORE SCHOOLS

Percent of student body Negro	Detroit 1961		Detroit 1963		Baltimore 1962		Baltimore 1963		Chicago 1963	
	Negro	White	Negro	White	Negro	White	Negro	White	Negro	White
A. Elementary schools										
99+	22.0	.05	36.3	.17	68.0	.10	66.4	.14	63.6	.16
90-99	47.4	1.71	37.0	1.45	15.9	.88	16.0	1.06	22.8	.76
50-89	22.6	7.34	18.0	7.21	9.8	6.4	10.3	6.3	10.1	3.5
10-49	7.4	16.3	7.6	16.6	5.8	17.7	6.6	32.1	3.0	8.0
1-9	.6	10.4	1.0	18.1	.53	17.6	.61	13.7	.46	12.0
0-1	.03	64.2	.09	56.4	.03	57.3	.04	46.8	.06	75.6
Total no. of students	94,000	106,000	101,000	98,000	66,000	45,000	70,000	44,000	200,000	183,000
B. High schools										
99+	0	0	26.6	.13	71.4	0	69.5	0	36.0	0
90-99	50.7	.95	20.7	.32	0	0	0.9	0	24.0	0.8
50-89	21.0	6.24	24.6	9.25	11.5	6.8	13.0	6.3	26.4	3.7
10-49	28.2	47.3	27.4	36.8	14.3	42.3	15.9	57.7	12.2	18.0
1-9	0	0	.5	21.6	2.8	43.2	1.1	26.6	1.5	23.7
0-1	.04	45.5	.12	31.9	0	7.7	0	8.8	0	53.8
Total no. of students	18,000	32,000	21,000	33,000	33,000	36,000	36,000	35,000	38,000	77,000

Note: Baltimore and Detroit have "open attendance." Detroit data are for senior high schools only, Grades 10-12. Junior high schools are omitted. Baltimore data include junior high schools with elementary. Chicago data for 1964 are only slightly different from 1963.

*From Robert J. Havighurst, *The Public Schools of Chicago*, The Board of Education of the City of Chicago, Chicago, 1964, p. 376.

population.   If the considerable white in-migrants from southern Appalachia are included, the socially and economically disadvantaged child is clearly in the majority in a number of the largest cities in the country.   In short, by numbers we are now dealing in large cities with children who have the lowest I.Q.'s (or "S.Q.'s"—segregation quotients), the lowest scores on achievement tests, and the lowest degree of acculturation.

The disadvantages of these children from the standpoint of employment compound the ghetto structure in which their families are snared in the big city slum.   The unemployment rate among Negroes generally in the country has risen from a proportion that was, in the mid-1920's, lower than that among whites, to the point where it is now twice as high for Negroes; in the younger adult age brackets, it is now frequently from three to four times that for whites of the same age.   Despite increased state and federal legal and administrative action concerning employment, up until the passage of the 1964 Civil Rights Act it appeared that the income gap between whites and Negroes still left the Negro at from 65 to 70 per cent of the average annual family income of whites, and, in the South, at less than 60 per cent.   Among the implications of employment and income distribution is that even if housing segregation is outlawed by legislation and judicial action, great masses of Negroes will remain, perforce, in their racial ghetto because they cannot afford to take advantage of better housing in the suburbs.

Compensation: Programs and Prospects

The largest advance in the education of Negroes and of other socially disadvantaged children within the last thirty years rests in the fact that the national conscience has been aroused.   A rising tide of civic, educational, and social legislation has been designed to provide compensation for the disabilities to which the disadvantaged child has been subjected. Special appropriations aimed at improving the level of instruction in schools for the economically deprived, Headstart programs for the very young, work–study programs, equal employment and equal voting laws—all reflect the fact that the nature of the problem has been sensed, and that it is the national will to find a solution.

What is the solution—or solutions—for problems mired in the muck of centuries of a brutalizing economic and social system? If a great multitude of human beings have been excluded from access to the standard American culture for generations, it is not to be expected that the slow growth of generations can be redirected instantaneously. Social advantage, on the one hand, and social disadvantage, on the other, have so early formed the verbal and attitudinal habits of the child that the remediation of variant deficiencies becomes increasingly difficult. We have to deal with a complex of attitudes and habits, substantive knowledge and motivations, that are rooted in encrusted family and community systems.

Effective intervention needs to begin, first, at the level of the social order. If the ghetto child is to be expected to have the aspirations and motivations of children in the standard American culture, it must be clear to him that escape from the ghetto is possible—that he can, indeed, become a full member of the standard way of life. The United States community has far to go before such a condition exists.

The "enrichment" programs that are now being developed need to be strengthened in several directions.

The curriculum. Commendable progress has been made toward the "desegregation" of textbooks and other educational media. There is great need, however, for the rewriting and redesigning of social studies texts and, indeed, other textbooks; these materials need to be brought in line with the findings of modern social anthropology and modern historiography. A realistic treatment of the institution of chattel slavery, for example, is scarcely to be found in an American history textbook; the southern slave plantation is still treated as a happily romantic idyll for black and white, instead of as the brutal instrument for exploiting human beings that it was.

Exposure to the standard culture. Every device that might possibly defeat the effect of residential segregation would seem to be morally and educationally sound. One might ask about one controversial issue: "Why should children not be 'bussed'?" Children are a part of the acculturative process. If the nation, and the community, have accepted the moral obligation to acculturate Negroes and other disadvantaged children, there is every moral reason for asking children of the advantaged classes to share in the task.

Communities, and groups within communities, might explore every opportunity that social ingenuity can devise to expose children from substandard classes to the standard culture. Middle- and upper-class churches, for example, that now subsidize "missions" to the poor, would better serve the desired aim of acculturation by seeking to include the children and adults from slum areas in their own Sunday schools and other church organizations. The same broadening of the base for all child-serving agencies, religious or lay, would serve to facilitate the acculturative process.

The very nature of the school should be altered from its present structure. It should so adapt its physical form that its facilities might truly serve the community, and the families in the community, through all of the child's waking hours. The school should conceive of itself as an agency for educating the whole child, which means the whole child's whole family; the "new school" would be supplied with facilities where entire families could come for instruction and guidance in the art and science of acculturation.

Extension downward of formal educational ages. Operation Headstart recognized the very great importance of an early beginning in learning the habits—verbal, physical, attitudinal, motivational—of the standard culture.

The quality of teaching. Presentation of the standard culture by its best proponents calls for much higher standards for entrance to the teaching profession. To raise the standards would be, of course, an expensive procedure, requiring that the salaries of teachers be made competitive with salaries for similar types of work now offered by business and industry.

Elevating standards of foster homes and stimulating adoption. As we have mentioned above, an analysis of the background of distinguished Negroes is astonishing in revealing the substantial number who, largely by chance, were extracted from their original culture—slave or "free"—and reared in the disciplined regimen of a standard, or above-standard, American cultural family pattern. They include such people as Phyllis Wheatley, the eighteenth century African-born poet reared in a highly literate New England family; James Derham, apprenticed at an early age to a Philadelphia physician and praised by Benjamin Rush for his competence as a successful physician in his own right, in New Orleans; George Washington Carver, reared from infancy by a solid Missouri German farm family; and numerous Negro holders of academic doctorates who had a family background similar to that of the man whose mother worked as a domestic servant for President E. A. Alderman of the University of Virginia. Alderman took the "maid" with his family on trips to Europe, and gave her liberal supplies of books for her children.

In our own day, a substantial extension of the acculturation of Negro and other socially disadvantaged children could come from elevating the standards of foster-home placement—and even from an accelerated and subsidized adoption program, deliberately designed to place lower-class infants and small children in homes affording the stimulation of the standard culture. Admittedly, this would be an expensive procedure, but it is doubtful if the same expenditure on formal educational activities would have as high a yield. Speaking of the high number of National Merit scholars from Chicago suburbs, as compared to their almost total absence from slum areas, Havighurst says: "But there is much doubt that Chicago would increase its output of Merit scholars very greatly even if it spent another $300 or $400 per student."[17]

These suggested devices may be impractical; they are put forward here to suggest the enormity of the task faced by those who wish to see the Negro child and other socially disadvantaged children given their fair chance to become fully participating and equal members of the American community. One difficulty in meeting these needs is the scarcity of persons and of teachers in the nation who truly believe that every child is equal to every other child in his capacity to learn. Another that recurs constantly is the existence of a social structure that teaches the child that he is *not* equal, breeding the certain knowledge in the child that he is hopelessly consigned to an inferior status and future.

In the original edition of this book, when it was published three decades ago, is this tribute to the "Yankee" school teacher:

[17] *Op. cit.*, p. 81.

The missionary teachers who taught these subjects were liberally educated in the current scholarship of the period, and as undergraduates had often been among the best scholars in their colleges. . . . The inspiration of the teachers gave even more than order. The institution of slavery, whatever its more idyllic aspects, was never intended to make men of its chattels. Boys and girls came from the environment of savery and were transported to a place where the students of Mark Hopkins, Theodore Woolseley, Charles Finney, and Henry Fairchild sought to do with Negro students what these men had done with them. They succeeded in an uncommon way.[18]

The added retrospect provided by recent studies of the background of many of these students suggests that the great success of the teachers may have been overstated; for many of the "ex-slaves" who attained academic excellence and mastery under "Yankee" tuition were in fact advantaged "free" Negroes, or the children of favored house-servants, who already had a "headstart" in the process of acculturation.

But there was an alchemy of an uncommon sort for many who had been most degraded. There was alchemy in the devotion and faith and work of the Yankee school marm; there was alchemy in providing, in boarding schools for the most part, a complete new cultural world in which new habits could be developed and new aspirations cultivated.

One of the most inspiring spectacles during the "Negro revolution" of the past decade has been the appearance of thousands of courageous and devoted young white and Negro men and women, who have shown the utmost dedication to the idea of absolute equalitarianism for all men. They do credit to the memory of Horace Mann; they are the spiritual descendants of the Yankee teachers who followed the "war to end slavery" into the South a century ago.

[18] *Supra,* pp. 361-362.

In the sense in which the phrase is used here, these people were—and now are—the most highly cultured persons in the American social order. If the desperate damage to the minds and personalities of the contemporary disadvantaged can now be repaired, it can be done by people such as these —vast numbers of people—working on the job.

The question is: are there enough?

BIBLIOGRAPHY

Bibliography

Note

Monroe Work's *Bibliography of the Negro,* H. W. Wilson, New York, 1928, lists numerous titles in Chapter XXI (pp. 416–430). Successive issues of the *Negro Year Book,* Yearbook Publishing Company, Tuskegee Institute, 1918–1919, 1924–1925, and 1931–1932, contain valuable references. The reports of the United States Commissioner of Education (1870—) are indispensable sources for bibliographical purposes, as are the reports, proceedings, and occasional papers of the philanthropic foundations listed in this bibliography.

Dr. Ambrose Caliver, Senior Specialist in Negro Education, United States Office of Education, is an indefatigable bibliographer. See his *Bibliography on Education of the Negro, Bulletin No. 17,* Washington, Office of Education, 1931. *The Journal of Negro Education,* a quarterly (1932—) published at Howard University, contains excellent bibliographical notices. *The Journal of Negro History,* a quarterly edited by Carter Godwin Woodson, Association for the Study of Negro Life and History, Washington, 1916—, is highly essential for intensive study. Also important are the files of *The Crisis Magazine,* edited by W. E. B. DuBois, The Crisis Publishing Company, 70 Fifth Avenue, New York City, 1910—; *Opportunity, a Journal of Negro Life,* National Urban League, 1133 Broadway, New York, 1923—; *The Southern Workman,* Hampton Institute, Hampton, Virginia, 1871—; *The American Missionary,* formerly the *Congregationalist and Herald of Gospel Liberty,* The American Missionary Association, 14 Beacon Street, Boston, 1850—.

The *Bibliographies of Research Studies in Education,* United States Office of Education, lists numerous theses which may be borrowed for study and inspection through the inter-library loan service of the Library of the Office of Education. These bibliographies also appear in *School Life,* published by the United States Office of Education.

497

A. Books

Armstrong, Samuel Chapman. *Twenty-Two Years' Work of Hampton Institute.* Normal School Press, Hampton, 1893.

Arnett, A. M. *The Populist Movement in Georgia.* The Columbia University Press, New York, 1922.

Bancroft, Frederic. *Slave Trading in the Old South.* J. H. Furst & Company, Baltimore, 1932.

*Brawley, Benjamin. *Dr. Dillard of the Jeanes Fund.* Fleming Revell, New York, 1930.
The life of Doctor Dillard and the work of the great foundations are described in this volume.

Brigham, Carl C. *A Study of American Intelligence.* Princeton University Press, Princeton, 1922.

Brown, Harold Spencer. *The Distribution of Teachers' Salaries by Race in Tennessee.* Unpublished master's thesis, Fisk University, 1933.

Burgess, J. W. *Reconstruction and the Constitution, 1866–1876.* Charles Scribner's Sons, New York, 1902.

Caliver, Ambrose. *A Personnel Study of Negro College Students.* Columbia University, Teachers College Press, New York, 1930.

Charters, W. W. *Curriculum Construction.* The Macmillan Company, New York, 1933.

Chase, Ezra B. *Teachings of Patriots and Statesmen, Or, The Founders of the Republic on Slavery.* J. W. Bradley, Philadelphia, 1860.

*Clark, John B. *Populism in Alabama.* Columbia University Press, New York, 1928.
The rise of the poor white.

Cooke, Dennis Hargrove. *The White Superintendent and the Negro School in North Carolina.* George Peabody College for Teachers, Nashville, 1930.

*Cooley, Rossa Belle. *Homes of the Freed.* New Republic, New York, 1926.
Describes the pioneer mission work of educating Negroes carried on in the Sea Islands by the Penn School.

Cromwell, John Wesley. *The Negro in American History.* The American Negro Academy, Washington, 1914.

*Daniels, W. A. *The Education of Negro Ministers.* George H. Doran, New York, 1925.
An incisive study of one of the most important social problems of Negro communities.

---

* Books in print which are of especial importance for reference are indicated by (*).

Davenport, R. K. *Parental Occupation and School Achievement of Negro Children.* Unpublished master's thesis, Columbia University, Department of Sociology, 1931.

Douglass, Frederick. *Life and Times of Frederick Douglass, written by himself.* DeWolfe, Fiske and Company, Boston, 1892.

Downey, June. *The Will Temperament and its Testing.* World Book Company, Yonkers-on-Hudson, 1923.

Drewry, William S. *Slave Insurrections in Virginia.* Neale Company, Washington, 1900.

*DuBois, W. E. B. *The Common School and the Negro American.* Atlanta University publication, Atlanta, 1910.

*——————— *The Negro Common School.* *Atlanta University Publications, No. 6,* Atlanta University Press, Atlanta, 1901.

——————— *Some Notes on Negro Crime.* *Atlanta University Publications, No. 9,* Atlanta University Press, Atlanta, 1904.

*——————— *The Souls of Black Folk.* A. C. McClurg, Chicago, 1904. Mandatory.

Dunning, William Archibald. *Reconstruction, Political and Economic.* Harper and Brothers, New York and London, 1907. (Vol. 22 of the *American Nation,* ed. by A. B. Hart.)

*Embree, Edwin R. *Brown America, The Story of a New Race.* The Viking Press, New York, 1931.

*Fleming, Walter Lynwood. *Civil War and Reconstruction in Alabama.* Columbia University Press, New York, 1905. Exhaustive treatment.

*Foreman, Clark. *Environmental Factors in Negro Elementary Education.* W. W. Norton, New York, 1932. An extensive study of the achievement of Negro school children. Standard achievement tests were used.

*Frazier, E. Franklin. *The Negro Family in Chicago.* University of Chicago Press, Chicago, 1932. No one can fully understand the social setting of the urban Negro school child without reading this study.

From Servitude to Service, being the Old South lectures on the history and work of Southern institutions for the education of the Negro. American Unitarian Association, Boston, 1905. Contents: Introduction, by R. C. Ogden.—I. Howard University, by K. Miller.—II. Berea College, by W. G. Frost.—

---

* Books in print which are of especial importance for reference are indicated by (*).

III. Tuskegee Institute, by R. C. Bruce.—IV. Hampton Institute, by H. B. Frissell.—V. Atlanta University, by W. E. B. DuBois.—VI. Fisk University, by J. G. Merrill.

Gaines, Francis Pendleton. *The Southern Plantation*. Columbia University Press, New York, 1925.

*Garth, Thomas R. *Race Psychology*. McGraw-Hill Book Company, New York, 1931.

Glasgow, Ellen. *The Deliverance*. Doubleday, Page and Company, New York, 1904.

Harris, Thomas H. *The Story of Education in Louisiana*. Published at Baton Rouge for the author, 1924.

Helper, Hinton Rowland. *The Impending Crisis of the South: How to Meet It*. A. B. Burdick, New York, 1860.

*Johnson, Charles S. *The Negro in American Civilization*. Henry Holt, New York, 1930.
Chapters XVI–XX, inclusive, deal with education. The entire volume is of the utmost value for social factors related to education. Extensive bibliography.

*Knight, Edgar W. *Public Education in the South*. Ginn and Company, Boston, 1922.
Education of Negroes discussed incidentally in Chapters IX, X, XI, and XII.

————— *Public School Education in North Carolina*. Houghton Mifflin Company, Boston, 1916.

*Leavell, Ullin W. *Philanthropy in Negro Education*. George Peabody College for Teachers, Nashville, 1930.
Careful analysis of philanthropic efforts in the field. Especially valuable for tracing work of foundations, and for extensive bibliography.

Lenoir, Zaid D. *Racial Differences in Certain Mental and Educational Abilities*. Unpublished master's thesis, University of Iowa, 1921.

Merriwether, Helen L. *The Per Capita Expenditures by Race for Teacher's Salaries and Racial Population Ratios in the South*. Unpublished master's thesis, Fisk University, 1933.

Moore, George Henry. *Notes on the History of Slavery in Massachusetts*. D. Appleton and Company, New York, 1866.

*Moton, Robert R. *What the Negro Thinks*. Doubleday, Doran, New York, 1929.
Historical, social, and educational data presented with vigor.

Nicolay, John G., and Hay, John. *Abraham Lincoln, A History*. The Century Company, New York, 1904.

---

* Books in print which are of especial importance for reference are indicated by (*).

*Noble, Stuart Grayson. *Forty Years of the Public Schools in Mississippi.* Teachers College, Columbia University, New York, 1918.

*Peabody, Francis Greenwood. *Education for Life, the Story of Hampton Institute.* Doubleday, Page and Company, New York, 1918.
Valuable for treatment of entire period, and for the description of the work of the founder of Hampton Institute, Samuel Chapman Armstrong.

Peterson, Joseph. "A Comparison of the Abilities of White and Colored Children." *Comparative Psychological Monographs,* Vol. I, Series 5. July, 1923.
——————————— and Lanier, Lyle H. "Studies in the Comparative Abilities of Whites and Negroes." *Mental Measurement Monographs,* Serial No. 57. February, 1929.

Phillips, Ulrich Bonnell. *American Negro Slavery.* D. Appleton and Company, New York, 1918.

Pike, Gustavus D. *The Singing Campaign for Ten Thousand Pounds, or The Jubilee Singers in Great Britain.* American Missionary Association, New York, 1875.

Pintner, R. *Educational Psychology.* Henry Holt and Company, New York, 1929.

Reddick, L. D. *Attitudes Toward the Negro in Southern History Textbooks.* Unpublished master's thesis, Fisk University, Nashville, 1933.

*Rhodes, J. F. *History of the United States, 1850–1896.* The Macmillan Company, New York, 1920. See Vols. VI and VII. Important for the Reconstruction Period.

Roberts, H. C. *The Attitude of Congress Toward the Education of Negroes, 1860–1890.* Unpublished master's thesis, Fisk University, Nashville, 1933.

*Scott, Emmett J., and Stowe, Lyman B. *Booker T. Washington, Builder of Civilization.* Garden City, Doubleday, Page and Company, 1916.
The Tuskegee idea oriented with reference to the life of its founder and life in the South.

Sibley, Eldridge. *Differential Mortality in Tennessee.* Fisk University Press, Nashville, 1929.

Simmons, W. J. *Men of Mark.* Geo. M. Revell and Company, Cleveland, 1887.

*Simkins, F. B. *The Tillman Movement in South Carolina.* Duke University Press, Durham, 1926.
The rise of the poor whites.

---

* Books in print which are of especial importance for reference are indicated by (*).

*————————, and Woody, R. H.　*South Carolina during Reconstruction.*　University of North Carolina Press, Chapel Hill, 1932.

One of the best references on the Reconstruction Period.

Smith, J. W.　*Populism in North Carolina.*　Typed Ph.D. thesis, Chicago, 1928.

*Spero, Sterling D., and Harris, Abram.　*The Black Worker.*　Columbia University Press, New York, 1931.

*Stephenson, Gilbert T.　*Race Distinctions in American Law.*　D. Appleton and Company, New York, 1910.

*Stowell, Jay Samuel.　*Methodist Adventures in Negro Education.*　Methodist Book Concern, New York and Cincinnati, 1922.

Review of the work of this denomination in educating Negroes.

Terman, Lewis M., et al.　*Genetic Studies of Genius,* Vol. 1.　Stanford University Press, Palo Alto, 1925.

Twelve Southerners.　*I'll Take My Stand, The South and the Agrarian Tradition,* "The Briar Patch," by Robert Penn Warren.　Harper and Brothers, New York, 1930.

Vance, Rupert B.　*Human Factors in Cotton Culture.*　University of North Carolina Press, Chapel Hill, 1929.

Warmoth, Henry C.　*War, Politics and Reconstruction.*　The Macmillan Company, New York, 1930.

*Washington, Booker T.　*Character Building.*　Doubleday, Page and Company, New York, 1902.

Sunday evening addresses to Tuskegee Institute students which reflect Washington's ideal of "heart, head, and hand" training.

*————————　*My Larger Education; being chapters from my experience.*　Doubleday, Page and Company, Garden City, New York, 1911.

Essays in which race relations and educational and social problems are discussed with characteristic keenness.

*————————　*Up From Slavery, an Autobiography.*　Doubleday, Page and Company, New York, 1900.

This simple story reveals as few other documents could the education of Negroes in the first period after emancipation. Besides its importance for historical purposes, the intensity of the spirit which breathes through the pages of this life history makes it mandatory reading for anyone interested in the education of American boys and girls.

*————————　*Working with the Hands.*　Doubleday, Page and Company, New York, 1904.

A more detailed description of the work at Tuskegee Institute.

---

* Books in print which are of especial importance for reference are indicated by (*).

Wickersham, J. P. *History of Education in Pennsylvania.* Published by the author, Lancaster, 1886.

Williams, George W. *History of the Negro Race in America* (Popular edition). G. P. Putnam's Sons, New York, 1882.

Wilson, Henry. *Anti-Slavery Measures in Congress, 1861–1864.* Walker, Wise and Company, Boston, 1864. See especially Chapter VIII, "Education of Colored Youth in the District of Columbia."

*Woodson, Carter Godwin. *The Education of the Negro Prior to 1861.* Association for the Study of Negro Life and History, Washington, 1919.
The best general source of information for the period.

*———————————— *The Mis-Education of the Negro.* Associated Publishers, Washington, 1933.
Highly critical discussion of higher institutions for Negroes. Extremely stimulating, though very positive in tone.

*———————————— *The Negro in our History.* Associated Publishers, Washington, 1927.
Encyclopædic treatment of the history of the Negro. Invaluable collateral reference for any field in which Negroes figure.

Work, Monroe. *Negro Year Book, 1931–1932.* Tuskegee Institute Printing Company, Tuskegee, 1932.

*Young, Donald. *America's Minority Peoples.* Harper's, New York, 1932.
The educational institutions of minority groups and their problem of adjustments are given attention in this well-balanced treatment.

Young, Kimball. *Social Psychology.* Alfred Knopf, New York, 1930.

B. Periodical References; Occasional Pamphlets

Bache, R. Meade. "Reaction Time with Reference to Race." *Psychological Review,* Vol. 2.

Baldwin, B. T. "The Learning of Delinquent Adolescent Girls as Shown by Substitution Tests." *Journal of Educational Psychology,* Vol. 4.

Bean, R. B. "Some Racial Peculiarities of the Negro Brain." *American Journal of Anatomy,* Vol. 5, September, 1906.

Bond, Horace M. "An Investigation of the Non-Intellectual Traits of a Group of Negro Adults." *Journal of Abnormal Psychology,* Vol. 21, pp. 267–276.

---

* Books in print which are of especial importance for reference are indicated by (*).

——————————— "Shall Federal Funds Be Spent for Adult Negro Relief or the Education of Negro Children?" *School and
Society*, August 13, 1932.

——————————— "The Cash Value of a Negro Child." *School
and Society*, Vol. 37, No. 959, May 13, 1933.

Brown, Andrew W., and Lind, Christine. "School Achievement in
Relation to Mental Age." *Journal of Educational Psychology*,
Vol. 22, pp. 561–576. November, 1931.

Burks, Barbara S. "The Relative Influence of Nature and Nurture
upon Mental Development." *Twenty-Sixth Yearbook, National Society for the Study of Education*, Part I, 1928.

Coon, Charles Lee. "Public Taxation and Schools," a paper read
before the Twelfth Annual Conference for Education in the
South, Atlanta, April, 1909. Committee of Twelve for the
Advancement of the Colored Race, Cheyney, Pa., 1909.
Quoted in DuBois, W. E. B., *The Common School and the Ne-
gro American*, Atlanta University Press, Atlanta, 1911.

Crisis Magazine, The. Published by the Crisis Publishing Company, 70 Fifth Avenue, New York City, 1910–   .
For years the principal forum for Negro writers, *The Crisis*
has evinced a special interest in educational problems. See,
especially, the series of articles in 1926–1927 on the education
of Negroes in the states.

Derrick, S. M. "A Comparative Study of Seventy-five White and
Fifty-two Colored College Students by the Stanford Revision
of the Binet-Simon Scale." *Journal of Applied Psychology*,
Vol. 4.

Dublin, Louis I. "The Health of the Negro." *The Annals of the
American Academy*, November, 1928.

DuBois, W. E. B. "Education for Life." *Journal of Negro Education*, Vol. 1, No. 1, April, 1932.

——————————— "The Field and Function of the Negro College," *Fisk University Herald*, 1933.

Freeman, F. N., *et al.* "The Influence of Environment on the Intelligence, School Achievement, and Conduct of Foster Children,"
Twenty-Sixth Year Book, N. S. S. E., Part I, 1928.

Garth, T. R. "Mental Fatigue during the Continuous Exercise of
a Single Function." *Archives of Psychology*, No. 41, Vol. 26,
No. 2.

Johnson, Guy B. "A Study of the Musical Talent of the American
Negro." Unpublished manuscript, quoted in Garth, *Racial
Psychology*.

Johnson, James Weldon. *The Shining Life*. Pamphlet, printed
for Fisk University, 1933.

Journal of Negro Education, The. Published at Howard University, Washington, D. C.

This quarterly magazine is scholarly, affording for the first time opportunity for the presentation of extended discussions of the problems of educating Negro children. Bibliographies printed occasionally cover the entire field of the education of Negroes. A file is invaluable for class-work reference.

Journal of Negro History, The (Carter G. Woodson, editor). Published quarterly by the Association for the Study of Negro Life and History, Washington, D. C.

Distinguished over a long period of years for both primary and secondary materials; presents all phases of Negro education.

Keith, W. P. "A Job for the County Superintendent." *Education and Race Adjustment,* Inter-racial Commission, Atlanta, 1932.

Koch, Helen Lois, and Simmons, R. "A Study of the Test-Performance of American, Mexican, and Negro Children." *Psychological Monographs,* Vol. 35, No. 5.

Landis, H. M. R. "Tuberculosis and the Negro." *The Annals of the American Academy,* November, 1928.

Lincoln County School News, Lincoln County, Arkansas, April, 1930, Vol. 3, No. 7.

Logan, Rayford W. "Educational Segregation in the North." *The Journal of Negro Education,* Vol. II, No. 1.

Mall, F. P. "On Several Anatomical Characters of the Human Brain Said to Vary according to Race and Sex." *American Journal of Anatomy,* Vol. 9, February, 1909.

Martin, James W. "Industrial Changes and Taxation Problems in the South." *Annals of the American Academy,* Vol. 153, 1931.

Mayo, M. J. "The Mental Capacity of the American Negro." *Archives of Psychology,* Vol. 5.

McAlpin, Alice S. "Changes in the Intelligence Quotients of Negro Children." *Journal of Negro Education,* Vol. 1, No. 1, April, 1932.

Mitchell, Broadus. "Growth of Manufacturing in the South." *Annals of the American Academy,* Vol. 153, 1931.

Montgomery Advertiser, The, January 27, 1869. Newspaper, published at Montgomery, Alabama; files available in Alabama State Department of Archives and History.

Newbold, N. C. "Common Schools for Negroes in the South." *The Annals of the American Academy of Political and Social Science,* Vol. CXXX, November, 1928 *(The American Negro),* the American Academy of Political and Social Science, Philadelphia, 1928.

Opportunity, a Journal of Negro Life. Published by the National Urban League.

Frequent articles on social, economic, and educational problems. Consult index for bibliography.

Payne, George E. "Negroes in the Public Schools of the North." *Annals of the American Academy,* November, 1928.

Pechstein, L. A. "The Problem of Negro Education in Northern and Border Cities." *The Elementary School Journal,* Vol. XXX, No. 3.

Phillips, Frank M. "Educational Ranking of States by Two Methods." *American School Board Journal,* December, 1924.

Pressey, S. L., and Teter, G. P. "A Comparison of Colored and White Children by Means of a Group Scale of Intelligence." *Journal of Applied Psychology,* Vol. 5.

Pyle, William Henry. "The Mentality of the Negro Child Compared with Whites." *Psychological Bulletin,* Vol. 12, January and February, 1915.

Ross, Frank Alexander. "Urbanization and the Negro." Papers on the Social Process, *Publications of the American Sociological Society,* Vol. XXVI, No. 3, August, 1932.

Sellin, Thorsten. "The Negro Criminal, a Statistical Note." *The Annals of the American Academy of Political and Social Science,* November, 1928.

Sewanee Review, October, 1921. Article by Dr. Dillard, quoted in Benjamin Brawley, *Dr. Dillard of the Jeanes Fund.* Fleming H. Revell, New York, 1930.

Southern Workman, The. Published at Hampton Institute, Hampton, Virginia.

The index of this publication gives a valuable bibliography in the field of the education of the Negro. A file is indispensable for reference.

Stephenson, G. T. "Education and Crime among Negroes." *So. Atl. Q.,* Vol. 16, pp. 14–20, January, 1917.

Stetson, B. R. "A Memory Test of Colored and White Children." *Psychological Review,* Vol. 4.

Strong, Alice C. "Three Hundred Fifty White and Colored Children Measured by the Binet-Simon Scale of Intelligence." *Pedagogical Seminar,* Vol. 20.

Thompson, Charles H. "The Educational Achievements of Negro Children." *The Annals of the American Academy of Political and Social Science,* Philadelphia, November, 1928.

Thompson, Holland. "Industrial Changes in the South and Society." *Annals of the American Academy of Political and Social Science,* Philadelphia, 1931.

Thurston, L. L. and T. G.   *Educational Record,* April, 1933.

Tinker, Edward Laroque.   "Les Cenelles—Afri-French Poetry in Louisiana."   *The Colophon,* September, 1930.

Washington, Booker T.   *History of Education for Negroes in Alabama.*   Manuscript, in possession of author; dated at Tuskegee, 1891.

C.   Official Documents, Reports, and Surveys

Acts, General Assembly of the State of Alabama, Session of 1890–1891.   Smith, Allred and Company, Montgomery, 1891.

Agriculture, Reports of the United States Department of.

Alabama, Annual Report of the Superintendent of Education of.   1880.   State Printers, Montgomery, 1881.

Alabama Biennial Reports, State Superintendent, of.   1886, 1891.

Alabama Reports, State Superintendent of Education for.   1875–1891.

Alabama State Journal, The.   May 1, 1869.   Newspaper, published at Montgomery, Alabama; files available in Alabama State Department of Archives and History.

Alabama, State Superintendent of Education, State Reports; file, 1870–1932.

Alvord, J. W.   Semi-Annual Reports on Schools and Finances of Freedmen, 1866–1870; ten reports.   Government Printing Office, Washington, 1866–1870.

Arkansas, A Survey of Negro Education in Jefferson County.   By the Division of Negro Education of the State Department of Education and the County Superintendent of Schools of Jefferson County.   1930.

Statistical and summary accounts of early efforts to educate Negroes and of foundations, and valuable statistical data on present systems.   Refer also to previous issues of the Year Book.

Arkansas, Summary Tables of a Survey of the Public Schools of.   Mimeographed pamphlet, authorized by the State Board of Education of Arkansas, March 12, 1932.

Arlitt, Ada H.   "The Relation of Intelligence to Age in Negro Children."   *Proceedings Thirtieth Annual Meeting, American Psychological Association.*

Auditor's Report, State of Alabama, 1930.

---

* Books in print which are of especial importance for reference are indicated by (*).

Bachman, Frank P. *A Survey of the Public Schools of Nashville, Tennessee.* George Peabody College for Teachers, Nashville, 1931.

*Caliver, Ambrose. *Background Study of Negro College Students.* Bulletin, United States Office of Education, Government Printing Office, 1933.

Census Reports, United States.
The materials available here for the study of literacy, education, and other social factors involving Negroes are far from exhaustion.

Census, United States, "Negro Population, 1790–1915." Government Printing Office, 1918.

Census, United States, "Occupations."

Census, United States, special bulletins on "Illiteracy" and "School Attendance."

"Clanton, James H., Testimony of." *The Joint Select Committee on Affairs in the Late Insurrectionary States, 42nd Congress, 2nd Session, Report No. 22,* Part 8, Alabama. Government Printing Office, Washington, 1872.

Commissioner of Education Reports, United States, 1870.
Statistical data with reference to the education of Negroes are found throughout these volumes. Notable are the volumes issued during the incumbency of A. D. Mayo, Commissioner, 1893–1901, in which the education of Negroes received special attention; and more recent reports (1931—) in which data and bibliographies collected by Dr. Ambrose Caliver, Senior Specialist in Negro Education, Office of Education, appear.

Congressional Globe and The Congressional Record. Printed in Washington, first by private contract, later by the Government Printing Office.
The record of debates on various aspects of national life which concern the Negro is replete with valuable factual information. In addition, sentiments and attitudes expressed in this national forum are of great importance.

Constitutional Convention of 1864, Debates in the Louisiana. Proceedings of May 2nd, 1864. Printed for the convention, New Orleans, 1864.

Constitutional Convention of 1901, McCauley, Pat, *Stenographic Transcript of the Proceedings of the Alabama.* Brown Brothers, Montgomery, 1901.

Constitutional Convention of 1901 for the State of Virginia, Held in the City of Richmond, Debates in the. June 12, 1901, to June 26, 1902. The Hermitage Press, Richmond, 1906.

* Books in print which are of especial importance for reference are indicated by (*).

Constitutional Convention of the State of Mississippi, Journal of the Proceedings of the. E. L. Martin, Jackson, 1890.

Davis, Jefferson. *Remarks on the Bill for the Benefit of the Schools in the District of Columbia. Congressional Globe,* April 12, 1860.

Embree, Edwin R. *Julius Rosenwald Fund, Report for the Year 1931.* The Julius Rosenwald Fund, Chicago, 1932.

Equalization in Alabama, 1929–1930. Bulletin of the State Department of Education, State Printers, Montgomery, 1930.

Favrot, Leo M. *A Study of the County Training Schools for Negroes in the South.* John F. Slater Fund, Charlottesville, 1923.

*Federal Relations to Education, Report of the National Advisory Committee, 1931.

*General Education Board, Publications and Reports of the, 1902–1928.
 Statistical data including report on funds expended on education of Negroes; description of projects and trends which the General Education Board forwarded.

*Jeanes, Anna T., Fund, Report of the President, 1914.
 Statement of expenditures and projects.

Joint Committee, Report of, on Affairs in the Late Insurrectionary States, Alabama, Georgia, Mississippi. Washington, Government Printing Office, *42nd Congress, 2nd Session, Reports.*

Jones, Thomas Jesse. *Education in Africa: A study of West, South, and Equatorial Africa by the African Education Commission.* Phelps-Stokes Fund, New York, 1922.

————————————— *Education in East Africa: A study of East, Central, and South Africa by the second African Education Commission.* Phelps-Stokes Fund, New York, 1925.

*————————————— *Negro Education.* United States Bureau of Education, Bulletin No. 38 (2 vols.), 1916.
 Description of secondary and higher schools for Negroes in the United States.

*Klein, Arthur J. Survey of Negro Colleges and Universities. United States Bureau of Education, Bulletin No. 7 (2 vols.), Government Printing Office, Washington, 1928.
 Detailed analysis of the operation and field of higher education for Negroes.

Louisiana, Report of the State Superintendent of Schools, 1877–1879.

Louisiana, Report, State Superintendent of Education in. 1930.

---

 * Books in print which are of especial importance for reference are indicated by (*).

*McCuistion, Fred. *Financing Schools in the South.* Julius Rosenwald Fund, Chicago, 1930.

*——————— *Higher Education of Negroes.* Southern Association of Colleges and Secondary Schools, Nashville, 1933.

*——————— *The South's Negro Teaching Force.* Julius Rosenwald Fund, Chicago, 1932.

McDavid, (Mrs.) Mary Foster. *Record Files of State Jeanes Agent for Alabama.* Montgomery, Alabama.

Morgan, Senator. Quoted in *Congressional Record,* February 11, 1886. Washington, Government Printing Office, 1886.

Nashville, Tennessee, Reports of Board of Education; file, 1870–1932.

National Educational Association. *Crime Prevention Through Education.* Bulletin of the N. E. A., Washington, 1932.

North Carolina, State Superintendent of Public Instruction State Reports; file, 1870–1930.

Norton, W. W. "The Ability of the States to Support Education." *Bulletin of the Research Division, N. E. A.,* Vol. IV.

O'Shea, M. V. *A State Educational System at Work.* Bernard B. Jones Fund, Washington.

Peabody Education Fund, Proceedings, 1867–1914. (6 vols.) Reports of general agents, of great value as experience of pioneers in adjusting race relations and influencing early school legislation in the South.

Proceedings, Alabama State Board of Education for 1872. J. W. Screws, State Printer, Montgomery, 1873.

Publications and Reports of the Julius Rosenwald Fund. Published at Nashville, Tennessee, 503 Cotton States Building, and Chicago, 4901 Ellis Avenue.

The reports of the Julius Rosenwald Fund for recent years give valuable descriptive material on schools and social condition of Negroes in the South.

The research publications of Fred McCuistion have particular interest for students. They include *Financing Schools in the South,* 1930; *The South's Negro Teaching Force,* 1931; and *Higher Education for Negroes,* 1932. These pamphlets are indispensable for the student of education in the South.

Rosenwald Fund, Julius. *Julius Rosenwald Construction Map, July 1, 1932.* Published by the Fund at Nashville, Tennessee, 1932.

Senate Journal, Session of 1890–1891 of the General Assembly

---

* Books in print which are of especial importance for reference are indicated by (*).

of the State of Alabama. Smith, Allred and Company, Montgomery, 1891.

*Slater Fund, The John F. *Proceedings and Occasional Papers, 1907–1931.*
    The data included in both the *Reports* and the *Occasional Papers* are fundamental in studying separate school systems in the South.

State Prison Inspector, State of Alabama, Reports; file, 1915–1930.

*State Reports of Departments of Health, Agriculture, Vital Statistics, Tax Auditors, and Prison Inspectors.
    Sources of this type yield rich material necessary to the understanding of the complete educational picture.

*State Reports of various state departments of education.
    The building up of files is advisable. Besides the various state archives in which complete files may usually be found, an excellent collection may be found at the Congressional Library, in Washington, and the John C. Crerar Library of Chicago.

*States and the United States, House Journals of.
    Material referring to Negroes has not as yet been thoroughly canvassed in these sources.

Swift, F. H. *Federal Aid to Public Schools.* United States Office of Education, Bulletin 47. Government Printing Office, Washington, 1923.

Syphilis, The Control of, in Southern Rural Communities. Julius Rosenwald Fund, Chicago, 1932.

"Trade Automobile Mechanics." *Special Edition of Course of Study Monographs for the Paul Laurence Dunbar High School of Little Rock, Arkansas.* (Mimeographed.)

Vardaman, James K. "Message of the Governor of Mississippi to the House and Senate of Mississippi, Thursday, January 9, 1909." *Journal of the House.* Brandon Printing Company, Nashville, 1910.

Wilson, Henry. Senator from Massachusetts, in the Senate, as reported in the *Congressional Globe,* April 12, 1860. Wilson cited Stroud, "Sketch of Laws Relating to Slavery."

---

* Books in print which are of especial importance for reference are indicated by (*).

Index

Index

Index

Washington, Booker T., 24, 69, 118,
129, 136, 356, 364, 472, 477
and activity curriculum, 10
and curriculum controversy, 363
and J. L. M. Curry, 133
and Julius Rosenwald, 140
and Samuel C. Armstrong, 117
and the "Tuskegee Idea," 122
and unequal expenditures, 107
as educator, 117
as leader, 121
Atlanta Exposition Speech of, 116,
122
early life of, 116
education of, 116, 130
limitations of program of, 124
objectives of, 119
on crime and education, 418
race relations formula of, 121ff.
Washington, North Carolina, 63
Washington County, Mississippi, 104
Watson, Samuel, 56
Wealth, of Southern states, 210, 227
discrimination adds to potential,
233ff.
growth of, 209, 230
related to education, 213ff.
Webster Parish, Louisiana, 337, 398
West Baton Rouge Parish, Louisiana, 80
West Virginia, 75, 196
equalization in, 256
Negro board of education in, 394
Wetmore, Samuel, 56
White:
crime, rise of, 422ff.
farmers, attitude toward Negro,
19
teachers in Negro schools, 34ff.
"White counties," 79, 88, 96
educational budget of, 246ff.

equalization in, 455
expenditures in Mississippi, 104
political role of, 77
teachers' salaries in Alabama, 109
Whites:
ante-bellum education of, 39
poor, *see* Social classes
Whittier, John G., 127
Wickersham, J. P., 38, 473
Wilberforce University, 371, 380
Wilcox County, Alabama, 80, 337
Wiley, Calvin, 37
Wiley University, 138
Williams, Bert, 263
Williams, D. E., 393
Williams, George, 371, 372, 473
Williams College, 117, 359, 363
Wilmington, North Carolina, 63, 393
Wilson, Henry, 175, 473, 481
Wisconsin, illiteracy in, 180
Woodson, Carter G., 368, 370, 371,
467, 473, 475
Woodworth, R. S., 306
Woodworth Scale, 325
Woody, R. H., 472
Woolseley, Theodore, 361
Work, Monroe, 138, 139, 144, 374,
423, 467, 473

X

Xenia, Ohio, 371

Y

Yale University, 359
Yazoo County, Mississippi, 104
Young, Donald, 473
Young, Kimball, 4, 473
Young Men's Christian Association,
140